Study Guide

to accompany

Uba/Huang

Psychology

Robert J. Pellegrini
San Jose State University

 LONGMAN

An Imprint of Addison Wesley Longman, Inc.

New York • Reading, Massachusetts • Menlo Park, California • Harlow, England

Study Guide
to accompany
Uba/Huang
Psychology

Please visit our website at http://longman.awl.com

ISBN: 0-321-01213-5

2345678910 - CRS - 0100

CONTENTS

ABOUT THIS BOOK

WHY I AGREED TO WRITE IT

I've had the luxury of working for more than thirty years as a psychology instructor and as a student of education in contexts from preschool to post-doctoral programs; from both public and private undergraduate university programs to those conducted in maximum security prisons. I'm still not at all certain as to what constitutes the ideal of instructional effectiveness. I am sure, however, that whatever effectiveness one achieves in teaching the introductory course in psychology, or any other course for that matter, is powerfully influenced by the book one adopts as the required text in that course. Experienced teachers know how crucial is the textbook to the quality of the educational product we're able to offer to our students. So, we tend to take our textbook adoption decisions very seriously, and to be uncompromisingly critical in evaluating the many books from which we have to choose in making those decisions.

The goal for any educational publishing company is to produce a book so good that it will be evaluated and adopted by instructors throughout the country. Most students of introductory psychology don't know just how intense the competition among college and university textbook publishing companies is to win a share of the huge introductory psychology market. Because of this intense competition, not unlike what happens in the production of a new book for the trade market, a new TV show, or a new movie, producing a new introductory psychology textbook is an expensive and risky venture. Tens of thousands of dollars may be invested, with no guarantee whatsoever of market success. Aware as they are of such realities, editors in charge of developing new texts solicit pre-publication draft reviews of one or more chapters from several instructors of the courses to which their books are targeted. Reviewers' comments are then considered by the authors and editors prior to production of the final drafts.

Over the past thirty years or so, I've served as a pre-publication reviewer for dozens of introductory psychology texts, and accepted invitations to write study guides to accompany what I regarded as the very best of those texts. More than a decade ago, after having written in 1985 the last of six study guides for three different publishers, I vowed not to do another one. The enormous amount of work and short time lines associated with such projects, mean that they dominate one's life in painfully memorable ways. Accordingly, I never intended to write another study guide; until I reviewed the Uba/Huang book.

With diversity as its central theme, the Uba/Huang text sets a unique standard in the current marketplace, by organizing its introduction to the content of psychology around what is widely regarded as the major issue and challenge confronting our democratic society in the twenty-first century. Beyond this, its representation of the technical aspects of our discipline is meticulously crafted, its coverage of classical and contemporary methods, theory and research is exquisitely well-balanced, and the engagingly personal style in which it is written shows an uncommon sensitivity to the point of view of the introductory student. In my judgment, it's as good a book as I've ever seen for its intended audience in its time.

Accordingly, I have "put on hold" two research projects and a book of my own, to try to write a study guide worthy of accompanying what I truly believe is the new introductory psychology

1

book of the decade, to help students maximize the productivity of whatever time and energy they may choose to devote to it.

WHAT'S IN THIS STUDY GUIDE, AND WHY SHOULD ANYONE BOTHER TO USE IT?

The introductory section on *Developing Attitudes And Skills Oriented Toward Academic Success*, is designed as a set of guidelines to be consulted before beginning the study assignments of this course. The ideas and techniques given in this first section may also be referred to periodically, as something of an academic survival manual which has relevance to courses throughout the student's educational program. Following this introduction, which is geared to helping students prepare themselves to master the challenges of an academic education efficiently, effectively and productively, there is a chapter in this Study Guide which is designed to help students master efficiently, effectively, and productively the content covered in every corresponding chapter of the Uba/Huang textbook.

This Study Guide thus provides students with a chapter-by-chapter structure for studying their assigned text in the course. That structure incorporates principles which technical studies of learning have shown to be most helpful to students' attempts to master such assignments. Using this Study Guide, of course, is no guarantee that you will achieve an "A" in the course or even that you'll be as successful as you want to be in attaining whatever your academic goal may be in the course. The nature of individual differences and variability in life circumstances makes it just about impossible to make such guarantees when it comes to human behavior and experience. But what we can guarantee, is that you have in this Study Guide a set of tools specially designed to help you learn the content of your textbook and thus the rudiments of psychology as efficiently and enjoyably as possible. In this sense then, the Study Guide doesn't just give you "more work to do" in the course, but a way of helping you to derive the most long-term learning gains and exam performance payoffs for whatever amount of time and energy you invest in the course for which the Uba/Huang book is the assigned text.

SO, WHO NEEDS TO USE THIS STUDY GUIDE ANYWAY?

It is important to note that this Study Guide is not intended as a "remedial" study aide, but as a take-home package designed to give any students who uses it an advantage in the course over all of those who don't use it. In many ways, however, this Study Guide should provide a special opportunity for students whose level of readiness to cope with the demands of a rigorous academic curriculum may be less than optimal, and for any students in the increasing populations we serve for whom English is a second language.

Having taught the introductory psychology class to literally thousands of students over the past thirty years or so, I and most of my other colleagues have noted a very consistent trend toward higher grades for students who use Study Guides such as this one appropriately. For a lot of reasons, that trend isn't very surprising. First, students who use supplementary aids like this Study Guide tend to be more serious about their education and personal development and more intensely motivated to do well academically than are those who don't use such materials for one reason or another. Second, this Study Guide and others of its genre are specifically designed by experienced teachers to help ensure that you're really learning while you're studying. As addressed in the Introduction to this Study Guide, the hard, cold, and ugly reality is that much of the time students spend on what they call "studying" often doesn't produce any long-term, usable knowledge, nor does it contribute very effectively at all to doing well on course exams.

Unfair as it may seem, it's not always the students who work the hardest who get the best grades. Not unlike other aspects of life in the real world, it's much more typically the case that it's those who work the smartest who achieve the most rewarding outcomes. Unfortunately, the only thing that hard work guarantees is fatigue. Sure. It's true that it takes hard work to achieve anything worthy of pride in your own creative effort, whether it be the building of a career, a business, or the foundation for a happy family. But the fact is that it's not just how much or how hard
we work at the things which we find meaningful in life. It's how effectively we work toward our goals.

Insofar as doing well in your first course in psychology is a goal for you, this Study Guide is available as a "work smarter" program for mastering the textbook which has been assigned in that course. By using its component subunits according to the following instructions and adopting the accompanying Suggested Study Strategy, you will contribute substantially to your own long-term, usable knowledge of the material covered in the Uba/Huang text, and to your successful performance on the course exams. Again, there is no guarantee that you'll succeed at what you perceive to be a satisfactory level. But this program does ensure that you've followed a systematic, and proven set of principles to maximize your probability of working effectively toward achieving the level of success you both desire and deserve in this effort.

THE SUBUNITS OF THIS STUDY GUIDE AND HOW TO USE THEM

Learning Objectives

In this first subunit of each chapter in the Study Guide, you'll be given a brief profile of just what it is that you should be "getting out of" the corresponding chapter in the textbook. In other words, this subunit gives you a brief, narrative overview of the kinds of things you should be prepared to learn from your study of that chapter. This subunit can be useful both for anticipating what there is to learn in the chapter before you study it, and later as a check to see how well you've actually mastered the content of the chapter. You might also want to use this subunit as part of your review process in preparing for course exams.

Preview/Review Outline Of Key Terms And Concepts

As suggested in its title, the purpose of this section is to provide a quick overview summary of the key terms and concepts covered in the chapter, and thus an overall perspective on the chapter content. In order to illustrate the relationships between the various concepts, they are listed in an outline format that parallels the organization of the material in the corresponding chapter in the text. This section is also "spiced"' with questions to help keep you oriented to the learning objectives of the chapter, and actively involved in processing the information covered.

You can use this subunit both as a "preview" of the corresponding chapter *before* you read and study it, and as a "review" after reading and studying it and/or in preparing for exams. When using it as a preview, the questions printed in bold, italicized print, will help to give you an idea as to just what kinds of things you should be learning as you study. When using this outline as a review, you might want to try masking off one line of it at a time, trying to recite from memory what you expect to appear on the next line or so. After careful, effective study, just looking at the individual outline entries should trigger meaningful associations that bring to mind larger chunks of information. Also, in your review, try to answer the questions in the bold type.

Another way to use this subunit is to write out a brief definition, description, or notation that explains or describes some or even all of the entries in more detail on separate sheets of paper. You can then use these materials like flash cards, covering up either the description or the outline entry as you try to supply the correct association. As you do this, it is sometimes useful to highlight those items that give you the most trouble.

In the Introduction to this Study Guide, you can read about the difference between "active" and "passive" study techniques. All of the suggestions given here with regard to ways of using this Preview/Review Outline, are designed as active study methods to increase the effectiveness of time you devote to studying each corresponding chapter in your text.

SELF-GENERATED QUESTIONS: What's In This One For Me?

In this subunit, the task is to write down a few questions of your own, about the subject matter of the chapter as it may relate to matters which are of personal concern to you. Write your questions in the spaces provided. After reading and studying the chapter, come back to your questions and see how any of what you have studied and learned in the corresponding chapter may have relevance to the questions you've written out of your own curiosity.

The kind of personal involvement in generating and constructing answers to such questions is directly in line with the philosophy of "active study," and what seems to be an important aspect of memory. Briefly stated, our attention seems to be oriented most directly toward, and we seem to remember best, information which we perceive as meaningfully relevant to our own lives. This subunit is thus intended to help you establish a mind set whereby your attention is oriented to the content of the corresponding chapter in just such a personal way, so as to help you learn and remember that content efficiently.

COMPLETION ITEMS

This subunit is a series of sentences in which you are required to fill in the missing word or words. In each case, the missing information is printed in the margin directly across from the blank. To make the most of the active learning opportunity provided by this task, be sure to cover up the answers in the margin until you've written in your best guess as to what is (are) the missing word(s). Then, uncover the answer in the margin. For each blank that you fill-in correctly, put a plus sign (+) in the parenthesis at the beginning of the blank. For those where you write in an answer other than the one given in the margin, put a minus sign (-) in the parenthesis at the beginning of the blank. This way, you can see at a glance which of the items has given you the most difficulty, and can go back to the text to clarify your understanding accordingly.

This exercise encourages active participation in the learning process in a number of ways because it requires that you do more than just read something. The task here requires that you go through the mental and physical operations involved in completing the incomplete sentence. It also provides immediate feedback as to your mastery of the material in the text. After having written in your answer and then uncovering the answer printed in the margin, your own correct answers are reinforced or rewarded by seeing that you've responded correctly; incorrect answers are corrected immediately when you look at the answer printed in the margin.

Remember, the way to gain the most from these completion subunits is to (1) be sure to actually write in your answer rather than to just think it or say it (although you may do all three as you write); (2) keep the correct answer in the margin covered until you've written in the answer which is your own best guess; (3) write a (+) or a (-) in the parenthesis at the beginning of each blank space to indicate whether your answer is correct (+) or incorrect (-); and (4) go back to the text as soon as possible to clarify those areas where your incorrect responses indicate that you need more study.

SELF-QUIZ

This subunit is made up of a series of multiple-choice and true-false items that, in addition to the Completion Items, are representative of the kinds of questions you may see in your course exams. First, read the item carefully, Then, circle the letter corresponding to the multiple-choice alternative you think is correct. In the True-False section, circle "T" for "true" and "F" if you believe that the statement is false. You may check your answers against the *Answer Key* at the end of this subunit. Again, as with the Completion Items, it's generally a good idea to go back to look again at those areas where your incorrect answers indicate that you're mastery level needs strengthening.

TEACHING-TO-LEARN EXERCISE

As noted in the Introduction to this Study Guide, congruent with the principles of active study, one of the most effective ways of strengthening your mastery of anything is to try to teach it to someone else. For a variety of reasons, the mind set and the kinds of behaviors in which one must engage in efforts to teach, are squarely in line with what it seems to take to learn most efficiently. Ironically, the role of "student," insofar as that role can be enacted passively, is often not nearly as ideally suited to learning as is the role of "teacher." So, the purpose of this exercise is to encourage you to pretend that you were teaching and not just taking the psychology course in which the Uba/Huang text has been assigned. In this regard, your task here will be twofold.

First, note briefly in the space provided under the "Let Me Teach You This" heading, five facts, ideas, concepts, principles, etc., from the corresponding chapter in the textbook that you'd like to teach to someone. Then, after having thus written down your teaching objectives, think about how you'd achieve them by communicating with your student(s). You can go back to the text as required to construct your communication scenario. Ideally, you will have a "real, live" audience for your teaching efforts here, either in the person of another student in the class with whom you study, or someone else in your life who is willing to participate in this activity. Lacking the availability of such "*in vivo*" participants, you may opt to pretend that you are teaching a receptive audience of students as if you were rehearsing for a play. This activity, simulated or actual, is thus totally congruent with the "R" in the SQ3R approach.

Then, as is the case in formal educational settings, it is the teacher's responsibility to develop some kind of procedure for evaluating student's mastery of whatever has been taught. For this part of the process, the task is for you to write under the "Now Answer My Questions" heading, one multiple-choice (M/C) and one true-false (T/F) question for each of the ideas which you covered in the "Let Me Teach You This" section. As you try to construct test items that are clearly written and representative of the content you tried to teach, you'll almost inevitably become personally involved in the material in ways that are also in line with active learning and SQ3R principles.

BRINGING PSYCHOLOGY TO LIFE EXERCISE

My own experience in the teaching of this discipline tends to fit with the impressive body of research data on human learning which indicates quite convincingly that when it comes to acquiring enduring, functional knowledge, there is no substitute for personal involvement in the learning of whatever it is that we're trying to learn. Accordingly, the last subunit of each chapter in this Study Guide is designed to provide students with a series of structured tasks which encourage the <u>using</u> of psychology in a variety of ways.

These subunits deal with some aspect of the content covered in the corresponding chapter in your textbook. Some of the exercises require taking on the role of psychologist as scientist in the conduct of mini-research projects. Other exercises emphasize introspective applications of the relevant concepts and principles to the student's everyday life experience. All are intended to help the student to become more of an active participant in, rather than just a passive recipient of information about contemporary psychology as a social science. Not only does this kind of involvement tend to promote more effective learning, but perhaps more important, it makes the process of learning about this discipline a whole lot more fun.

A SUGGESTED TEN-STEP PROGRAM OF STUDY

Step 1.   Read the Learning Objectives subunit in this Study Guide.
Step 2.   Read the Preview/Review Outline Of Key Terms And Concepts in this Study Guide.
Step 3.   Do the Self-Generated Questions subunit in this Study Guide.
Step 4.   Read and study actively the corresponding chapter in your text.
Step 5.   Repeat Step 2, only this time creating some flash cards based for entries in this subunit, based on your study of the text.
Step 6.   Do the Completion Items subunit in this Study Guide.
Step 7.   Do the Self-Quiz subunit in this Study Guide.
Step 8.   Do the Teaching To Learn subunit in this Study Guide.
Step 9.   Do the Bringing Psychology To Life subunit in this Study Guide.
Step 10.   Repeat Steps 1 & 2 as review, to refresh your memory, and to highlight areas where you feel you still need more study of the chapter to feel a satisfactory sense of familiarity with its content.

ABOUT THE AUTHOR

Bob Pellegrini's formal education includes a B. A. degree from Clark University where he graduated *Phi Beta Kappa* and with High Honors in Psychology. He earned his M. A. and Ph.D. degrees in psychology from the University of Denver, having served as a National Institute For Mental Health Fellow intern in clinical methods at the University of Colorado School Of Medicine. Except for a hiatus as Associate Dean For Research And Sponsored Programs from 1983-1985, and a sabbatical year appointment as a Research Associate at the University of California at Santa Cruz under the mentorship of Dr. T. R. Sarbin, the introductory course has been his primary instructional assignment and commitment since becoming a member of the Psychology Department faculty at San Jose State University in 1967.

Beginning with his pioneering doctoral dissertation research into unobtrusive, non-verbal communicative measures of racial prejudice in social transactions, social cognition and interpersonal evaluative judgments have occupied a central place in his research on human relationships, one applied direction of which is represented by his handbook chapter on job performance assessment of police and correctional officers. The issues of economic inequality, poverty, and interpersonal emotion are among those addressed in a number of projects conducted by Dr. Pellegrini and his students. Professor Pellegrini's current work involves narratologic analyses of attitudes toward education, life in contemporary society, the family, and the development of personal identity.

Dr. Pellegrini has lectured and been a frequent radio and TV talk show guest throughout the United States, and an invited contributor to a number of prestigious professional society presentations including the Lewis M. Terman Conference on Education's master lecture series. In addition to having written the study guides to accompany a number of introductory psychology texts since 1975, as well as an introductory course manual of his own entitled *Bringing Psychology To Life* (Canyon Ridge Press, 1996, 1998), he has authored and co-authored dozens of articles, papers, professional conference presentations and chapters contributed to edited volumes on a variety of basic and applied issues, and been the recipient of a number of distinguished scholar-educator achievement awards including the Outstanding Professor Award from *Psi Chi,* the national honor society for psychology majors, the Austen D. Warburton Award for scholarly excellence, the Western Psychological Association's Distinguished Teacher of the Year Award, and the San Jose State University Disability Resource Center's Outstanding Faculty Award.

Bob has a career-long history of administrative, group instructional and individual mentorship involvement in locally and nationally-funded minority educational outreach efforts, dating from Operation SHARE and Project ABRAZO in Santa Clara County (California) in the early 1970's, to San Jose's East Side Union High School District's Unfinished Journey, and San Jose State University's McNair Scholars and The Minority Access To Research Careers programs in the 1990's. With more than 25 years' experience as a part-time instructor for inmates incarcerated in maximum security prisons, he has been one of the nation's leading advocate-practitioners of correctional education, and his book *Psychology for Correctional Education* (Charles C. Thomas Publishing Co.) is widely-regarded as a standard reference source in the area which it defines. Dr. Pellegrini's work along these lines, and associated advocacy of an epidemiological approach to understanding and managing criminally antisocial conduct, has been directed increasingly in recent years to promoting public policies regarding violent crime and corrections in America, which take into account what he calls the "social contextual realities" of life in our culture. His latest book, co-authored by T. R. Sarbin and entitled *Between Fathers & Sons: Focal Narratives In Men's Lives*, is scheduled for release by Sage Publications in 1999.

INTRODUCTION

DEVELOPING ATTITUDES AND SKILLS ORIENTED TOWARD ACADEMIC SUCCESS: How To Thrive And Not Just Survive In College

ABOUT THIS SECTION

Why It Was Written

Most of us who have built our professional lives around education, tend to feel very keenly the joys of our students' successes and the pains of their failures. From personal experience, I can tell you quite sincerely that even after thirty years or so as an instructor in both undergraduate and graduate courses, there is no grander fulfillment to be derived from the role of "educator" than that of watching one's students make their dreams come true. Along with many of my faculty colleagues here, I delight in sharing proudly with my current students, case history anecdotes about the achievements of our alumni -- especially when the featured person is someone whom I can refer to as a former student in Psychology 1! At some level, I guess, this section is written as part of an overall effort aimed at helping every student reader of this study guide become one of those success stories.

In attempting to help students strengthen the foundation upon which they can build their future, the concept of what I call the ***cumulative spiral of personal development*** is particularly relevant. With specific reference to economic status, this spiral concept is implicit in idiomatic expressions such as: (a) "The rich get richer and the poor get poorer," and (b) "Them that has, gets!" Similarly, people who are enjoying what is perceived by others as a streak of good fortune are said to be "on a roll." Along these same lines with regard to achievement-oriented behaviors, folk wisdom has it that "Nothing succeeds like success." The general sense of this idea then, is that when people start to do well, they seem to do better and better. Conversely, when they start doing badly, they seem to do worse and worse. Above all, this section is written out of the conviction that a solid, well-earned success experience in coping with the demands of a university curriculum, is the psychological equivalent of a boost upward in the educational aspect of a student's personal development spiral.

Its Specific Objectives And Contents

I make no secret about my ambition to have all of my students become winners at the game of doing well in their academic work. But I've served in the role of professional educator long enough and in enough different settings to know that before students can ever win at the game of academic learning, they first have to know how to play that game.

The hard, cold fact of the matter is that college students differ greatly in their readiness to cope effectively with the demands of a quality education. Some are exquisitely talented, have just the right motivational and characterological "stuff," and do supremely well from day one. Others, who may be just as talented, bring a repertoire of self-defeating attitudes and study habits to their college education, that almost certainly predispose them to academic failure. This section is designed to help maximize students' effectiveness in the role of "student." The goal here is to provide students with a set of perspectives and strategies that will prepare them to do their very best work and get the very best grades they can get as they move toward meeting requirements of their college education in general, and their first psychology course in particular. In short, this section is written to help every student get the most out of his/her formal education, regardless of how much time and energy s/he devotes to educational objectives, and regardless of how education fits into his/her overall life plan.

Briefly, this section is organized as follows: (a) the first unit is devoted to helping students understand how a person's attitudes impact on his/her style and effectiveness in coping with academic demands, and some ideas about how "functional" as opposed to "dysfunctional" attitudes develop in people; (b) the second unit provides a set of principles oriented toward enhancing students' skills at note-taking in class, studying productively for course exams, and maximizing their scores and grades on
those exams.

How To Use It

This section is intended to be used before beginning with the formal assignments in the course. As noted above, this section can also be used throughout this and other courses, as something of an "academic survival skills reference guide."

The ideas contained in this mini primer on achieving academic success have been derived from a distillation of dozens of theories and research studies on learning, motivation, memory processes, and decades of formal scientific inquiry by psychologists and educators into what it takes for students to do well in school. Inevitably, this section is also heavily-influenced by your instructor's own experience as a student and as a professional educator. The intent here is to give students a set of guidelines oriented to helping them maximize their satisfaction level with the functional knowledge and the exam scores (and thus grades!) they achieve in this course, and other courses as well. Ultimately, however, it is up to the individual student to choose to assimilate to his/her own academic coping style, some, all, or none of these techniques, concepts and principles.

I cannot guarantee that applying what is given in this section will ensure that you achieve a grade of "A" in this or any other course, or that you will necessarily achieve your life goals as they may depend upon academic effectiveness. But I do guarantee that what is presented here has been constructed to represent the elements of thought, feeling, and action oriented toward the most direct achievement of such objectives.

FUNCTIONAL AND DYSFUNCTIONAL ATTITUDES
TOWARD EDUCATION AND LEARNING

On Academic Success-Failure And Introductory Psychology

The term "dysfunctional" is used a lot these days, by both professionals in human services fields and non-professionals alike. Typically, the word is used to refer to some aspect of a person's life, such as his/her family environment, which is considered to be maladaptive or unhealthy for some reason. In this sense, "dysfunctional" is quite accurately descriptive of the kinds of attitudes and study skills which students often bring with them to the first course (and even advanced courses) in psychology.

The "dysfunctionality" in such cases is due to attitudes and study habits which almost guarantee that the student's experience in the course will be frustrating. Perhaps most unfortunately, the unpleasantness associated with failing to "do well" in any course tends to generalizes to the content of the course or discipline within that course is taught. I don't think I've ever heard anyone say something like, "Yeah, I'm lousy at math and always got low grades in math courses, but I really love to study it." It's difficult indeed to come to enjoy a course, or anything else for that matter, that we perceive as having been unpleasant or even punishing to us. Related to this point, is the fact that living things generally don't approach but seek to escape from and avoid painful situations. It is precisely the latter characteristic of living things, of course, that helps them continue their membership in the class of things still living.

Thus, in the case where a student finds him/herself, for one reason or another, "locked-into" a course or courses where s/he sees failure as inevitable, a not-at-all surprising result is the development of a "Why knock my head against a stone wall?" attitude. Under such circumstances, the student may give up entirely and devote as little energy as possible to the course. To some extent, this kind of response serves as a totally understandable means of psychological escape from an emotionally painful situation in which one feels trapped. Most likely, the whole experience will leave a "bitter aftertaste" attitude of avoidance toward everything one associates with the course -- e.g., the content of the course itself, the discipline within which it was taught, the instructor, and possibly even the college or university where it was taught.

Consulting with your instructor is the first step when such difficulties begin to emerge. Personally, I encourage my students to meet with me as often as we can arrange to chat, even when things are going well for them, but especially when things seem to be going badly for them in the course. As a very last resort when nothing else works, formal withdrawal from the course may be a far preferable alternative to just giving up on it and having to endure the consequences of what is, essentially, a loss by default.

This section has been written *to prevent* the kind of failure experience sequence just described, and to increase the probability that the student will experience success and its "warm afterglows" in this particular course at least, and, hopefully, every other course s/he takes thereafter. The fact that your instructor in this course has adopted the Uba/Huang text, suggests that s/he wants to share with you some of the excitement of discovery in contemporary psychology as a social science, and the ways in which its methods, concepts, principles, and theories of our discipline may be used as the tools for continuing discovery about all aspects of human experience. Some of you may even choose to build your life plan around a career in psychology. But whether or not it enters formally into your academic goal-orientation as a major or minor field of emphasis, my primary motive for involvement in developing the Uba/Huang instructional package is the motive which I brought to my role as a teacher of the introductory course in about thirty-five years ago; namely, to help students come away from the introductory course with lifelong attitude toward psychology as an accessible and useful reference resource for personal issues and/or professional development. The ideas contained in the first section of this Study Guide are intended to promote just such perceptions of this discipline, by helping to make your introduction to it a "user friendly" and rewarding experience.

Education And Quality Of Life

In one way or another, most of you reading this are well aware that life in the modern world is very competitive. The steadily increasing number of people on our planet are frequently in competition with one another for what seems to be a steadily-declining supply of both natural and human-created resources. It is reasonable to assume that most people taking this course wouldn't be here at all if they didn't believe that a college education and the degree which is conferred to acknowledge completion of it, will contribute substantially to their own ability to compete successfully for the kinds of opportunities we tend to identify with "the good life" in our society. Enrollees in this course are often people who have had some experience at a job (or jobs) which they've found to be less than totally fulfilling, and realize that they aren't qualified to secure the kind of place for themselves in the world which would involve doing much of anything that looks truly interesting or personally satisfying to them.

One of the major reasons why many people decide to pursue a college education in the first place, is because they believe that it will advantage them throughout life, by permitting a wider range of options than they would otherwise have in terms of the kind of work they do for a living, the kind of car they drive, where they live as well as the kind of house in which they live, the kinds of things they do for recreation, how and where they take their vacations, and so on. By the time they come to their first college course in psychology, students have these beliefs pretty well-established. And generally speaking, the assumptions underlying such beliefs are quite valid.

You are absolutely correct if you think that in comparison with those whose formal education ends with graduation from high school or even before completion of high school, college graduates tend to: (a) have more choices as to where they work, (b) earn more money throughout the course of their lives, (c) drive better cars, (d) live in better homes, and (e) have more elaborate recreational opportunities and vacation time. There is even some research to suggest that in comparison to people who are what we might refer to as "undereducated" for life in contemporary society, better-educated people tend to live longer, healthier lives, perhaps in part because they feel a greater sense of personal control over what happens to them in life. Generally speaking, although there are exceptional cases where people without a formal education achieve success, even spectacular success, education is still the most reliable means toward a "quality life."

So, whether or not one has a burning passion to become educated purely for the sake of enlightenment and *being* an educated person, or out of altruistic motives inspired by a desire to make a truly meaningful contribution to humankind, there are good, sound, practical, selfish reasons for becoming educated in order to enhance one's chances of living the kind of life most people want to live. Regardless of why one has taken on the role of college student, however, there is another reality that too often stands as a painful and sometimes even a decisively insurmountable obstacle to achieving the goal of a college degree -- namely, grades.

As a fact of life which instructors typically dread as much or more than do their students, academic accreditation standards require formal evaluation of students' mastery of the methods, concepts, and principles covered in the courses they take. From the standpoint of the conventional educational philosophy associated with these standards and practices, it is seen as the instructor's responsibility to devise and implement procedures to measure and thus acknowledge individual differences between students in the extent to which they achieve such mastery. In most college courses, these evaluations typically involve examinations designed to assess how well students have mastered the relevant content. Grades are then assigned on the basis of such tests.

Arguments persist concerning the reliability and validity of grades as criteria of how much one knows and how good a student one really is. In spite of those arguments, granting of college degrees continues to depend upon achievement of some minimal level of overall performance <u>as indexed by grades</u>. At a sort of base level then, one does not graduate from college unless his/her grade point average is high enough to meet this minimum standard.

But the importance of grades extends beyond the question of whether one does or does not <u>graduate</u> from college. Colleges and universities typically distinguish in some formal way among graduating students in terms of how proficiently they have completed their degree requirements. The latter differences are acknowledged in conferral of degrees according to the level of distinction, if any, with which each student has graduated. What is the basis for graduation with varying "honors"? Grades.

Is the attainment of a college degree, with or without honor status, something of which to be enormously proud? You bet it is. Does graduating "with honors" of some sort tend to be advantageous in attempting to compete for jobs or candidacy for graduate education programs that lead to careers in professions such as law, medicine, business, engineering, the arts, the sciences, the social sciences, etc.? I'll let you guess the answer to that one.

To sum up here, whether we like it or not, education is still the most reliable means toward broadening the range of one's "life quality" choices. And grades are the major criterion in terms of which varying levels of success are formally acknowledged in colleges and universities. This section is designed to provide students with attitudinal perspectives and operational techniques oriented toward motivating and maximizing the efficiency of their time and energy expenditures, as they work toward completing the educational elements of their life plans. A much more ambitious, philosophical goal here is to help students succeed in what may be the ultimate achievement in a formal education.   That is, to somehow manage to get good grades without letting the pursuit of "A's" interfere with the process of their development as educated people,

13

for whom the experience of life is enriched by virtue of a more sophisticated appreciation of its complexities.

Avoiding The Linear Fallacy Trap

The Fallacy. It's not unusual for a student who is trying to do well, but performing unsatisfactorily on course exams, to respond to that failure experience by simply doing more of whatever s/he's already doing. This implies acceptance of an idea that is integral to the traditional system of American values -- i.e., that hard work pays-off in success and achievement. A corollary to this idea is what I call a linear fallacy concerning the relationship between work and success-achievement. In other words, it is the not necessarily conscious expectation that the harder I work, the better I'll do at whatever I try to do. If I work twice as hard as I *have been* working at something, I should do twice as well as I *was* doing at it. If I triple my efforts, my rewards from that effort should increase threefold.

The false belief here, lies in the assumption that increases in personal sacrifice and effort expenditure will produce corresponding increments in goal-achievement. The belief is fallacious because there is no guarantee that doubling or even tripling the number of hours one studies or practices something, will result in proportionally greater payoffs.

An Everyday Life Example. Students have no monopoly on dysfunctional work-achievement beliefs and habits. A non-academic illustration of such misguided thought and action, involves my own observations of a severely obese, middle-aged man whom I used to see jogging by my house every day at about 6:00 a.m. Rain. Wind. Cold. Darkness. Nothing seemed to deter this relentless fellow from his daily pavement-pounding. But it wasn't just the consistency his training routine that captured my attention, so much as the palpable pain which he apparently accepted stoically as he endured it.

Day after day, I'd see him dressed in his gray flannel sweat suit, towel around his neck, sweat-soaked, flushed beet-red, and literally gasping for breath between each lumbering, flat-footed step. After watching this scene for several weeks from the window in my study out of which I gaze occasionally as I hack away at my computer in the early morning hours, my curiosity about human motivation got the best of me. One of the really great things about my profession, is that what would have to be characterized for others as invasive snoopiness, I get to justify as anecdotal observation for my work! Thus, indulging my professional curiosity, I walked outside to meet this steadfast jogger as he rounded the curb in front of my house one cold, damp, and dreary Saturday morning.

As he shuffled along in what looked very much like absolute agony, I said, "Excuse me, but I've seen you jogging by here every day for almost three months now, and I've been wondering why you're doing this"? Through his wheezing gasps, I could just barely hear him say, "What do you mean, 'Why am I doing this'? I'm doing it to lose weight; for my health." Invoking one of my favorite reality tracer questions, I asked, "How's this working for you?" "Not too good," he replied. "I've been running about a mile every morning since the first of the year, and I seem to be lighter on Friday night than I was at the beginning of each week. But by Monday morning I'm right back where I started on Monday of the week before." Incurably rational beast that I am, I then asked him if he enjoyed his training. His response: "Hell no. I hate this. And it's just killing my knees. But I'm going to start running two miles a day from now on, so I can <u>really</u> burn this fat."

Relevance To Educational Development In Particular. This case study in dysfunctionality illustrates nicely, I think, a mentality that is almost assuredly self-defeating at anything, whether the objective is to lose weight, learn how to read, or master the requirements of a course in organic chemistry. Our jogger friend here had decided to respond to week after counterproductive week of self-inflicted torture by doing more of what was clearly not working for him as a means of achieving his stated goal. In addition to being ineffectual for its intended purpose, the pattern of action in which he was engaged was probably helping to make him an excellent candidate for a disabling orthopedic injury.

In much the same way, students who are doing poorly in their academic work may decide, by equally erroneous reasoning, to "turn up the intensity" of their accustomed way of dealing with the demands of their school work. Unfortunately, doing more of what you've always done, is almost certain to get you more of what you've always gotten.   That's why coaches so commonly implore their players in athletic contests to stay with a winning game plan or strategy, and to change a losing one.

Relevance To Personal Development In General. The most likely psychological consequences of persistence in, and/or intensification of an inadequate or even counterproductive coping pattern, are frustration, disillusionment, cynicism, and despair over one's own ineptitude. The core of the problem here is that the revered idea that hard work and personal sacrifice lead to success and achievement, requires some qualification to fit the realities of everyday life. But the cognitive, emotional, and motivational aftereffects of dysfunctional responses to failure, may lead the individual to believe that there's no truth at all to the maxim about the relationship between hard work and success-achievement in life. Long and painful histories of wasted human potential often begin with perception of the work ethic as a complete lie, or as a cultural myth devised by "the haves" to encourage continuity of fruitless effort on the part of the "have nots" (e.g., the attitude that "...working people are the suckers of the world"). Rejection of the hard work-achievement value then acts as a systemic toxin, infecting every aspect of the person's consciousness, giving impetus to a downward spiral of personal deterioration which ultimately results in an inability to cope realistically with the demands of everyday life in socially responsible ways.

The Quality Of Effort Factor

Unquestionably, successful goal achievement demands hard work.   But here's the catch. Although increased volume or quantity of effort may be necessary, it is often not a sufficient condition for enhanced performance or improved outcomes <u>at anything</u>. The kicker variable which operates interactively with intensity of effort or energy expenditure, has to do with <u>what</u> we do and <u>how</u> we do it as we work toward achieving our goals. Whether the objective is to learn how to roller blade, play a blues riff on the piano, or get a good grade on our Psychology 1 exam, productive outcomes at most things in life tend to be proportional to <u>both</u> the quality and the quantity of our efforts.

15

Given such realities, as a practical matter, it is generally advisable to try "working smarter" before working harder at things that are important to us. In fact, if "working harder" is taken to mean nothing more than expending a greater amount of time and energy without working more effectively, it may actually interfere with attainment of our goal. When working more hours leads to little or no improvement in our feeling of accomplishment about whatever it is that we're working to achieve, frustration is all that's accelerated for sure. In such circumstances, a "burning out" of our motivational investment in the activity in question is the most likely result of just doing more of what we've <u>been</u> doing without changing the way that we do it. And the foregoing analysis tends to apply as validly to our relationships with the people in our lives, as it does to our work-oriented actions. Here, our focus is on optimizing the productivity of academic goal-oriented actions. If some of the ideas presented here transfer positively to other aspects of life such as interpersonal communication and adjustment, that will be a happy coincidence.

Career Goals And The Motivation To Study

Quite commonly, people who are strongly motivated to learn something develop significantly higher levels of competency in their mastery of it than do people who are not so motivated. One of the most challenging problems in the study of human development, has to do with attempts to discern the reasons why some people are more highly motivated to learn than are others. Relevant to this issue, as discussed below, are individual differences in the personality dimension which psychologists refer to as the "need to achieve." But much of the technical literature on this matter isn't very helpful to the student who says, "You know, to be perfectly honest about it, I'm just not interested enough in any of my courses to put out the kind of energy required to do well in them. I admire people who can discipline themselves to do the kinds of things that you have to do to get good grades, and would love to know just what I can do to get myself motivated to study."

When it comes to working toward an academic degree, there's no simple answer to the question of "how to get motivated." However, having a fairly clear idea as to how the academic requirements for that achievement fit into one 's overall life plan can be extremely helpful in both initiating and sustaining the motivational energy that will be needed for the task.

The pressure which many young (and not so young) people feel to hurry up and decide what to do with their lives, comes from a variety of sources. It is important for the student who feels unduly anxious about and alone in his or her career uncertainties, to understand that many people, and not just students, are burdened by a chronic uneasiness about either not having made a clear choice and commitment as to career direction, or having made the wrong choice along these lines. Some of us, working professionals included, reach the "mature years" of our lives, our 40's, 50's, and sometimes even our 60's and 70's, totally unsure about what we want to be when we "grow up." Worse yet is the specter which haunts many people -- a feeling of intense ambivalence or downright despair about having devoted so much of their life doing work which they regard as trivial or meaningless. Rational decision-making and goal-setting can help to reduce such "after the fact" kinds of regrets and second-guessing about career path choices.

But the crucial point here is that it's not at all unusual to be uncertain about the direction to take for the work aspect of one's life. Such concerns may and often do occur and recur at any stage of life, and there's no law that says you have to make up your mind early and stick forever with

16

whatever decision you've made. In fact, some students of human development have even suggested that a periodic reappraisal and change in one's primary area of work commitment may contribute to both good mental and physical health.

So why the rush to decide? One argument for establishing even a tentative career plan as early in the educational process as possible, is that such long-range planning helps to give a sense of purpose and meaning to the more immediate, separate tasks required along the way. Setting a career objective for oneself, even if it is adopted simply as the most desirable alternative one can identify at the moment, can help students come up with personally satisfying answers to questions such as, "Why should I bother to work as hard as I have to work to get through my college education?" or "What am I really going to be getting for all of this hard work?"

So, a long-range career goal can help to organize and make sense out of one's day-to-day routines. Some people find it helpful to conceptualize each course they take as one more step along a road to where they want to be when they reach a certain age or stage in life, or as rungs on a ladder which they're climbing to reach a higher level or quality of life. But before proceeding further, let's consider how the motivation to achieve operates as a powerful variable which tends to impact very directly on how successful people are in attaining their goals in life.

Individual Differences In Achievement Orientation

People differ widely in just how motivated they are to "do well" at things. Some individuals appear absolutely driven to prove that they're better than everyone else in school work, the arts, athletics, or business, or whatever they do that becomes important to them in some personal way. They are intensely and compulsively competitive against anyone whom they regard as a potential challenger to their need to feel special in those aspects of life which are central to their identity. Accordingly, they mobilize their energies single-mindedly around goals related to these central areas of their lives. Most typically, such people accept the fact that they'll have to make substantial sacrifices in order to achieve what they want to achieve in life. They are rigorously self-disciplined in foregoing immediate gratification and short-term pleasures, as they focus on the sense of fulfillment they expect to enjoy when they finally achieve the goals they set for themselves. For some of these "high need for achievement" people, the process of striving toward their goals becomes motivating in its own right, almost independent of the goal toward which that process is oriented.

In contrast, other people are consistently "mellow" in their attitudes toward goal achievement. Indeed, they may have difficulty even identifying a goal for themselves. Their energies are much more dominated by enjoying life right here and now, or just "kicking back." These differences reflect a dimension of personality that psychologists refer to as "the need for achievement." Why is it that people who have a weak need to achieve give up and stop trying at things in the face of even the slightest adversity, while those who have strong achievement needs persist with seemingly superhuman determination no matter how formidable may be the obstacles they encounter? How do these differences develop in the first place? And how, if at all, can a person change his/her achievement need orientation?

Anyone who promises simple answers to the foregoing questions is either a liar or a fool, especially when it comes to the issue of modifying a long-standing achievement orientation.

With regard to scholastic coping style, for example, there's just no sure-fire way to transform anyone from abject lethargy into an academic equivalent to Sylvester Stallone's "Rocky." The models given below, however, provide descriptive representations of the processes by which competence and achievement motivation develop, and of ways in which such development may be related to self-esteem.

An Accountancy Model Of Work Motivation

As discussed above, competency at things isn't always developed at levels commensurate with the time, money, or energy devoted to them. There may be justice in the world. But the correlation between the amount of hard work a person does and the extent to which s/he achieves his/her goals in life, may not be the very best place to find validation of the assumption that the world is a just place. Some people work diligently to become good golfers, tennis players, or students, but never seem to achieve the kind of success they deserve. In other words, the rewards they reap don't ever seem proportional to the energy they've invested in whatever line of endeavor they've made that investment. With regard to such intuitive observations, the Accountancy Model given in Figure 1 below is designed to describe the cost/reward relationship between work and the motivation to work.

PROFIT (+) -----> Reinvestment
(Material or
Psychological
Gain)

REWARDS ------> minus ---> COSTS =
(Money, Prestige   (Money,
Competence, etc.)   Time, Energy,
etc.)

LOSS (-) -----> No Reinvestment
(Material or
Psychological
Loss)

Figure 1. An Accountancy Model Of Work Motivation [© Pellegrini, 1996]

According to this accountancy model, the inclination to continue to invest time, energy, money, etc., in any activity, is strongly affected by the extent to which one sees the payoffs from such investments as materially or psychologically profitable. Insofar as we perceive our investments to be resulting in rewards (such as money, prestige, or increased competence at something) which we regard as justified relative to the costs incurred in attaining them, the investment is seen as profitable and the probability of reinvestment in the relevant activity is increased. Conversely, the more we consider whatever rewards we may attain as "losing propositions" unworthy of what it cost us to attain them, the greater is the probability that we will discontinue our efforts along such lines. In other words, if we feel that what we're getting out of something isn't worth what we're putting into it, we are inclined to either reduce our commitment to or quit the activity altogether. "Why throw good time, money, energy, etc., after bad?", or "Why should I go on banging my head against a stone wall?"

A Cognitive-Affective Model Of Work Motivation

The Accountancy Model of Figure 1 gives only a simplified introduction to human work motivation. For one thing, hard work, goal-setting, and achievement-oriented conduct don't occur in a social vacuum. Nor does the sense of self which is integrally associated with what we do and how successfully we see ourselves as doing it. All of these evolve in a social context, within the framework of which the component elements of thought, feeling, and action derive their meaning. The Cognitive-Affective Model given in Figure 2 is designed to help articulate some of these complexities, in terms of the psychosocial sequences that tend to be given impetus by the personal experiences of success and failure.

The starting point of each psychological sequence described in Figure 2, is the individual's own experience of success or failure at some activity which is important to him/her. Psychologists tend to refer to such activities as ones which are "ego relevant." A more technically thorough analysis of the alternative sequences outlined here, would require a detailed consideration of factors such as the intensity of the success or failure experience, especially as that level of intensity may be related to the ego-relevance (i.e., importance) of the particular activity in question to the individual, the frequency of such experiences, and so on. The essential point here is that each alternative sequence begins with a personal experience of success or failure.

The second level of this model deals with the way in which personal experiences of success and failure in life tend to be associated with distinctly different forms of both interpersonal feedback and self-perception. It should be noted that there is probably a good deal of reciprocal influence between the latter two elements of any success or failure sequence, but that's an issue for us to explore elsewhere. For now, it's most important to see that the personal experience of success or failure almost inevitably involves associated thoughts and feelings that derive from the responses of other people to our success or failure. When we do well at something, people congratulate us, praise us, express their acceptance of and attraction to us, and offer us encouragement for things we might try to do in the future. By contrast, quite the opposite kinds of reactions tend to be expressed toward us by other people when we fail or do poorly at things. On the self-perception side, success tends to make us feel competent, effective, and worthy of respect from others, while failure induces just the opposite effects.

EXPERIENCES OF SUCCESS/FAILURE

Interpersonal Correlates

Success -----> Praise, Acceptance,

Self-Perceptions

Success -----> Competent, Encouragement
Effective, Worthy Of Respect

Failure -----> Criticism, Rejection
Discouragement

Failure -----> Incompetent,
Ineffective, Unworthy Of Respect

Style Of Response To Future Challenges

Success -----> Poised Assurance,
Self-Confidence, Approach-Attack

Failure -----> Disabling Anxiety,
Self-Doubt, Avoidance-Retreat

Competence Motivation

Success -----> High

Failure -----> Low

Personal Development Consequences

Success	Failure
* Self-Initiated Effort	* Reluctant Effort
* Pride	* Self-Pity
* Mature Independence	* Immature Dependence
* Increased Proficiency	* Frustrated Stagnancy
* Openness To New Experience	* Fearfulness Of New Experience
* Sanguine Appreciativeness	* Bitter Cynicism
* Pro-social Involvement	* Anti-Social Withdrawal

= GROWTH

= DETERIORATION

Figure 2. A Cognitive-Affective Model Of Competence-Motivation And Personal Development [© Pellegrini, 1996]

The power of success and failure to influence our lives, is mediated in large measure by the way in which such experiences impact the way we respond to future challenges, and our sense of "competence motivation," which refers to the desire to do things well. As shown in Figure 2, success tends to lead to attitudes of poised assurance, self-confidence, and approach/attack in meeting new challenges, and a high level of competence motivation. Failure, in contrast, is more likely to engender disabling anxiety, self-doubt, and avoidance/retreat attitudes toward new challenges, and correspondingly low levels of competence motivation. But ultimately, it is the effect of success- and failure-induced attitudes and styles of action on the individual's development as a person which makes the whole matter so critical for our consideration here.

As illustrated in Figure 2, the longer-range effects of success experiences tend to impel (a) self-initiated effort, (b) a sense of pride in personal accomplishments, (c) mature independence, (d) increased proficiency in task performance, (e) openness to new experience, (f) a sanguine (i.e., hopeful) appreciativeness of the beauty in life and of genuinely praiseworthy motives and achievements of others, as well as
(g) pro-social involvement in living as a responsible member of the human community, contributing to the well-being of others.

Also shown in Figure 2, in direct contrast to those described for success, the effects of failure experiences include: (a) a tendency toward reluctant effort in doing even the most routine of life's tasks, (b) self-pity, (c) childlike dependency, long after having presumably outgrown the time in life when such dependency on others is appropriate, (d) a frustrated stagnancy in skill level (e) fearfulness of the kinds or new experiences that tend to expand one's perspectives and enrich one's life, (f) an attitude of bitter cynicism toward life in general, and especially distrustful, disparaging perceptions of the motives and achievements of others, and finally, (g) an angry or even wanton disregard for the well-being of others, accompanied by a withdrawal into preoccupation with self needs and their satisfaction through the most expedient modes of anti-social action.

None of this analysis, of course, takes into consideration the wide range of individual differences in response to success and failure. Nor have we explored the significance of relatively isolated, occasional, or acute as compared to the cumulative effects of recurrent or chronic failure. Certainly, these are relevant issues. But, using the model given here, if we were to characterize the long-range, personal-developmental consequences of success and failure in a single word, the word for success would be "growth." The word for failure would be "deterioration."

A Triangular Model Of Work Motivation

One of the most common explanations which students offer for why they're not working more seriously at their studies, is that they're just not sufficiently interested in what's offered in their courses to expend the kind of energy required to do well in them. The implicit assumption here seems to be that people only work hard at things because they're inspired to do so, and that until one becomes so inspired, presumably by some sort of divine lightning bolt, mediocrity is about all that can be expected of him/her. From the standpoint of a reality orientation to human adjustment, such thinking might be seen as a rationalization for failing to take active responsibility for moving forward with his/her own life.

As inventor Thomas Edison is reputed to have said, "Genius is 99 per cent perspiration and 1 per cent inspiration." Without the benefit of formal education, my Italian immigrant father communicated to us the tough-mindedness of such views in very simple language that emphasized the futility of self-pitying excuses, and the value of lifting oneself off of one's backside and getting to work as the most effective way of dealing with life's challenges. A much more formal alternative to the lightning bolt idea about how people develop interests and the drive to become proficient at things, however, is given in the Triangular Model diagrammed in Figure 3.

Effective Practice   **Competence**

Ego-Enhancement,
Self-Esteem

Figure 3. A Triangular Model Of Work Motivation [© Pellegrini, 1996]

The primary assumption of this Triangular Model is that competent performance of academic or other skills, tends to increase with effective practice. Generally speaking, the more we practice a goal-directed sequence of actions, the better we're able to carry out that sequence. Essentially then, this first assumption affirms the old proverb that "practice makes perfect," with the quality of effort qualifications considered above.

The second premise of the Triangular Model is that the drive for competence itself can be an extremely powerful incentive for growth motivation. One of the classical references for this idea is developmental psychologist Robert White's (1959) conceptualization of the drive for effectiveness in or mastery over the physical environment as a strong, intrinsic motivational basis for early cognitive growth.

Relevant to our attempts to understand such drives for effectance or competence, we know that young children develop their motor skills largely by trying out new actions just to see if they can perform them. Climbing, jumping, pulling, pushing, skipping, running, and so on, are often engaged-in for their own sake. Healthy children often seem to do such things just to do them and not "in order to" anything else. In this sense, these are "intrinsically-motivating" activities. That is, the incentive for their performance is inherent or internal to the activities themselves, apart from any external or extrinsic rewards which might be contingent upon their performance. So, for example, a young child may be given a piece of candy by her proud father when she manages to crawl successfully for the first time across the entire width of the living room. In this case, the feeling of exhilaration aroused within the child, just by the fact of having gotten herself from one side of the room to the other without anyone's help, might be more than enough to motivate the crawling activity quite independent of any sugary reward.

This Triangular Model presupposes that effectance is a generalized form of motivation that operates throughout life. What changes as the person develops, is the range of environmental events and processes to which the motive applies. The young child is preoccupied with exploring and mastering sensory-motor aspects of his/her immediate physical surroundings. As s/he grows, more diversified conceptual forms of exploration and skill-acquisition become important for gaining the kinds of mastery and competence required for effective adjustment to world.

Congruent with its first two elements of practice and competence, this Triangular Model assumes that having attained a sense of mastery from practicing a socially-valued activity, additional investment of personal resources such as time and energy in that activity, is sustained by the good feelings about oneself that derive from doing it. The term "ego enhancement" is used here to refer to the warm afterglow of fulfillment we feel after having performed such activities competently. The competence-induced ego enhancement gives impetus to more practice of the activity, and the cycle continues.

So, in contrast to the popular belief (often expressed by students who are doing poorly in their school work) that people work hard at things only after having become interested in them, the Triangular Model suggests that interest in and motivation to work hard at something may derive from having worked hard at it. The major educational implication of the model is that life is too short to wait, God knows how long, for a magical lightning bolt of insight to inspire in us the interest and motivation we need to sustain us through the hard work required to develop the kinds of knowledge, skills, and abilities that society rewards. Rather than wait for that flash of inspiration to ignite the fires of our ambition, this model suggests that it makes much more sense to begin by working effectively hard at some socially-valued activity.
The motivation for continuing development of proficiency at that activity, is then expected to follow from the increased competence we achieve at it.

It is important to remember, however, that the kind of practice to which the Triangular Model refers is "effective practice." Clearly, achievement and success at anything worthwhile will require hard work. But, as noted above, hard work does not ensure achievement and success or even improved competence. Popular as it may be, the maxim that "practice makes perfect" is much less than perfectly true. The only thing that practice makes for certain is tired. And all that hard work guarantees is fatigue.

To reiterate, effort expenditure is a necessary and not a sufficient condition for goal achievement at anything in life. In order for the sequence described in the Triangular Model to obtain, the effort expended in practice must be effective effort. So it is that the remainder of this section is devoted expressly to the matter of how to use study time most effectively.

From Wanting To Doing

The three models presented above are intended to help students understand the relationships between motivation, effort-expenditure, and success-achievement as these are relevant to making and carrying out life plans. In accord with the rationales and principles of those models, the rest of this section is oriented to the elements of maximizing effectiveness in doing what is required not just to survive, but maybe even to excel in the coursework challenges of a college education, as part of a plan for living a productive and personally fulfilling life.

TIME AND PERSONAL DEVELOPMENT

Individual Differences In Attitudes Toward Time

As is the case with just about every personal characteristic, people differ widely among themselves in their attitudes toward time. Indeed, you can tell a lot about someone, from the way they organize, feel about, and use time. At one extreme of this personality variable, is the person for whom life itself seems to be a condition of rather chronically painful dullness from which s/he persistently seeks to escape in all sorts of ways, and time is thus seen as something to fill or even kill. At the other extreme of the time attitude continuum is the so-called "Type A Personality," who seems almost frantically driven to make every minute count, to be productive, and do something that contributes to advancing his/her progress toward one or another of his/her goals. For the fanatically time urgent person, the clock isn't going around, it's spinning around; s/he is hypersensitively susceptible to frustration-induced anger in situations which s/he perceives as wasteful of his/her time such as having to endure the slow pace of lines at the supermarket or rush hour traffic.

Shaping Realistic Personal Constructs Of Time

Somewhere between the two dysfunctional extremes described above, is a realistic way of thinking about time. Since it is such a critical aspect of how each of us copes with life's challenges, particularly those involved in meeting successfully the demands of a formal education, it might not be a bad idea to add to the standard educational curriculum a required mini-course entitled, "Time: It's Value And How To Use It." I'm quite sure that such a course could provide the basis for some of the most important learning that ever occurs in a formal educational setting. Given the diversity of individual differences in readiness to benefit from the kinds of learning opportunities it would offer, however, I'm not at all sure about just what stage in the educational process would be most appropriate for such a course. Kindergarten might not be too early for some people to assimilate and use the knowledge gained from this learning experience to facilitate their own development throughout the rest of their lives. Others, regardless of how old they get, might never mature to the point where they're ready to benefit from such instruction.

But why should we bother to take the time to study time attitudes, especially as they relate to the role of "student"? As I see it, the need to do so derives from a dubious assumption implicit in the status of benign neglect accorded this issue in our current system of education. That assumption seems to be that people somehow know instinctively, or eventually develop time attitudes that are fit logically with their own life values and goals. After working as a professional educator for more than 30 years in both conventional academic and correctional settings, I don't believe that there's much validity to this view. Moreover, I'm totally convinced that the failure to develop realistic attitudes toward time contributes substantially to dysfunctional life patterns.

It is most unlikely that a person will come to have a strong orientation toward socially-responsible conduct, without first having learned how to use time responsibly and effectively. And responsible, effective use of time presupposes that one has established some kind of life plan, no matter how rudimentary that plan may be, at least for the short-run and maybe even for the long-run of his/her life. Such planning tends to evolve from the individual's priorities as to how important various aspects of life are to him/her, with those priorities framed, consciously or unconsciously in terms of the individual's life values.

Without a sense of one's own values and some knowledge of how to define, clarify, evaluate, and redefine them, it is unlikely that a personally satisfying life plan will be developed; the individual functions like a small boat adrift on the high seas without either rudder or anchor. Under such circumstances, buffeted by the turbulent vagaries of circumstance, one of life's most precious resources is often squandered unproductively or even self-destructively. That resource is time.

Important as the issue of life values clarification may be, it goes beyond the scope of the present purposes and is thus left for the student to deal with in other contexts. For now, let us focus our attention on how to manage and organize <u>whatever</u> amount of time we devote to pursuit of our educational goals.

Time Management And Organizing Your Study Time

Life Plans And Time Budgeting. The first step toward taking control over and personal responsibility for our own lives is to do the kind of thinking necessary to develop a fairly clear and realistic sense of our own values and goals. For those of us who feel that we have neither the skills nor the experience to accomplish this complex task on our own, the help of professionals in the field of counseling psychology may be not only useful but essential in this effort. Assuming, however, that we have at least a reasonably clear albeit tentative foundation in this process of self-definition, we're ready to construct a plan for living a fulfilling life, in accord with our own values (i.e., what's important to us).

No matter what our life plan may be, time is a key resource for achieving personal-developmental goals. Not unlike what is required for the rational use of <u>any</u> valued resource which is in limited supply, such as money, we have to make decisions concerning the expenditure of our time in ways that fit our value priorities. One way to do this is by setting up a schedule in which the hours of every day in the week are designated for certain purposes.

So, once a life plan has been established, the schedule is used to structure the way in which time will be devoted to various aspects of it. A sample format for just such a schedule is given in Figure 4. The amount of blank space corresponding to each day and time, as well as the time units themselves (i.e., hourly, half-hourly, etc.), will vary depending upon the complexity of one's life and just how specific and detailed one chooses to make one's schedule. In any case, drawing up the format for the schedule is the easy part. The challenge here, is in deciding how the various blocks of time within it will be used, so that notations indicating these intended purposes can be written in the corresponding spaces in the schedule.

Setting Up A Weekly Schedule

	Mon	Tues	Wed	Thurs	Fri	Sat	Sun
8:00							
9:00							
10:00							
11:00							
noon							
1:00							
2:00							
3:00							
4:00							
5:00							
6:00							
7:00							
8:00							
9:00							
10:00							
11:00							
12:00							

FIGURE 4. Sample format for setting up a weekly schedule.

After having blocked out those times formally obligated to certain activities (e.g., classes, job, etc.), whatever time remains is "discretionary time." One good reason for establishing a schedule in the first place, is to help us make the most of our discretionary time. Just what "make the most of" means here, depends upon the value judgments which have been made before the scheduling ever begins. For one person, the first priority in life after fulfilling obligatory responsibilities might be to personal fitness and a workout at the health club. For someone else, the most important thing in life after taking care of the things which s/he defines as "necessary" to do, might be to engage in spiritual activities of worship related to his/her religion. In effect then, the schedule implies a set of decisions as to how one's time will be spent, with those decisions reflecting one's own value and associated goal priorities.

Having a schedule helps many people devote their full attention to whatever they're doing at the moment, without being distracted by concerns about anything else that they "could" or "should" be doing. The advantage of a schedule in this regard is that time devoted to the current actions is being expended as planned. There's no need to feel guilty or anxious about what we're not doing, because those other things have a place in the schedule and this is simply not that place.

Assuming that one's personal orientation in life, however it may be structured, includes a commitment to education, some aspect of the weekly schedule has to be reserved for study time. After having determined just how much discretionary time is available each week, decisions have to be made as to just how much of that time will be devoted to studying, and just what days and hours of the week will be so devoted. The amount of time and the particular times allocated for each course to be studied, will depend upon a number of factors such as assignment deadlines, how challenging we find the course assignments, and individual judgments as to how important each course is to the achievement of one's short- and long-term goals.

Making The Schedule "Real." A viable weekly schedule can greatly facilitate the educational component of a personal development plan, and also one's efforts to live as balanced a life as current circumstances permit. A realistic schedule often provides just the kind of structure for a person's day-to-day functioning that is crucial to achieving personal goals and also some measure of overall adjustment to life while working toward such goals. By "realistic" here, I mean a schedule which is both (a) congruent with one's own value priorities and goals, and (b) truly workable in terms of the time one has available to do all that s/he has scheduled for him/herself.

Yes, it takes self-discipline to stay with a schedule that's designed to help us live productive and fulfilling lives. And the tighter the schedule, the more self-discipline will be required to maintain it. But it's important to remember that the schedule is, after all, an artificial structure that *we've* created to help us accomplish our goals and live a fulfilling life. As with the life plan itself, a schedule is only good as long as it works for the person. When it isn't functional, like the total plan which it's designed to facilitate, it's not a good schedule. Even a generally effective schedule, however, may need some (at least) temporary modifications in response to unanticipated changes in life circumstances -- e.g., health, family problems, etc. But it's not O.K. to go ahead and revise one's schedule every time the going gets a bit tough. If I'm not "sticking to" my schedule, in other words, if I'm not actually spending my hours as prescribed in my weekly plan, the schedule isn't working for me. And when a schedule isn't working out for us, a change is in order for the schedule, the plan it's designed to serve, or both.

Setting Specific Study Session Goals. Once the days and times allocated to study have been identified, the next problem to be confronted is that of structuring the study session itself. It's true that every now and then, a great deal can be gained from spontaneous, free-wheeling or exploratory study time, in which one works pretty much "instinctively" on those things that s/he finds to be especially interesting. But too often when we start out with a vague, fuzzy idea as to just what we intend to do during a work period or at the start of a work day, our accomplishments for that period of time tend to be equally vague and fuzzy. As with other aspects of life, when we aim to accomplish nothing in particular, that's often what we accomplish. Nothing. So, it's usually a good idea to begin each study session with a fairly clear definition of our content mastery objective for that session. With the study goal(s) so defined, it's a lot easier to evaluate in some objective way, just how productively our time and energy have been expended. Depending upon the sense of satisfaction we derive from such evaluative feedback, we may then decide to stay with what seems to be working out for us, or modify our study methods and/or goals accordingly.

Study Session Warm-Up And Self-Discipline. Skilled athletes often go through elaborate rituals to prepare themselves for peak performance prior to a contest or event. They stretch, jog about, do breathing exercises, push-ups, shrug a lot while rolling their head around, and so on. In much the same way, students may need to ready themselves before they can begin to do their academic work effectively. Pre-study warm-up time isn't usually devoted to touching one's toes fifty times, or to doing a few dozen abdominal crunches before opening a book -- although either or both of these may work very well for some students. More typically, the pre-study warm-up consists of activities such as pencil-sharpening, paper-shuffling, setting-out reference and note-taking materials, or even watering the plants, playing a few licks on the guitar or grooming the cat.

Even though such preliminary actions may not contribute directly to any substantive progress in study, they may be just as important in the mobilization of a student's mental energy and/or the focusing of his/her attention for sustained concentration, as is leg-stretching before a pole-vaulter's first attempt in a regional track meet. So you needn't feel guilty about engaging in might otherwise be seen as ritualistic avoidance behaviors prior to studying. After all, the process of studying is challenging at best, and not always a whole lot of fun. The fact is that effective study requires us to divert energies away from activities which may be much more intrinsically interesting us. There's no denying that it can be awfully difficult to get into an organic chemistry assignment or to working through a series of algebra problems when what you really want to do is watch the NBA on CBS.

As does holding to a schedule, study requires self-discipline. And what self-discipline means is: (a) foregoing some activity that will bring immediate, short-term pleasure, and (b) investing energy instead in an activity that may not only fail to bring us immediate pleasure, but may be downright arduous. Taking the self-disciplined alternative implies a belief that such efforts are more likely to lead to achievement of goals that will permit us opportunities for enduring self-fulfillment than is the case for immediately self-gratifying choices. So, it's quite O.K. to approach tasks which demand self-discipline with some ambivalence or even outright reluctance. Accordingly, the warm-up ritual may be regarded as one way of coming to terms with the reality of the personal sacrifice one is about to make.

The best way to deal with the study warm-up need, which differs widely from one individual to another, is to acknowledge it and find the pattern that works best for you. It's an entirely natural aspect of "getting down to study." Some people just require longer and somewhat more elaborate pre-study rituals than do others. There's no clear rule as to when such activity becomes maladaptive. Generally speaking though, we're probably doing O.K. unless the ritual becomes so involving that it takes up a significant portion of the study session. In the latter case, some adjustments need to be made. In my own case, for example, I simply accept the fact that I'm going to be eating a few corn chips before I've written even a single line of the new presentation that I'm preparing for a class. When I find, however, that I've gone through a <u>whole bag</u> of Fritos and still haven't written a single line, I know that <u>my</u> pre-work ritual is out of control.

Ultimately, this is one of those instances where it comes down to a personal judgment call. When it feels as though the warm-up is detracting from study effectiveness, as in cases where the study session is more warm-up than study, it's appropriate to ask oneself whether the motivation to do the task is really strong enough to overcome the internal conflicts aroused by (a) our resistance to concentrating on what we've decided to do, (b) uncertainties about our ability to do competently what we've decided to do, and (c) having forsaken more immediately pleasurable alternatives. When the ritual clearly interferes with the doing of the task, then there's reason for concern. Otherwise, such ritual-like preliminary actions may be regarded as an integral part of a productive, well-focused, task-oriented study session.

Distributed Study Sessions vs. "Cramming." Research has shown that shorter, distributed study sessions tend to be more effective than longer, massed practice periods. One explanation for this is that fatigue dissipates during rest intervals, thus helping us to concentrate better and to practice effectively. In competitive athletics, coaches may ask the players whose training they supervise to take breaks during skill-drill sessions, even though the athletes themselves insist that they're not very tired yet. The rationale behind this training strategy, is that sometimes our concentration may begin to decline significantly, even before we begin to <u>feel</u> as though we need to take a break, resulting in the practice of what I call "attention lapse-induced errors." With regard to the learning of conceptual material in particular, another possible reason why shorter sessions are more effective is that incorrect associations are often forgotten more rapidly than the correct ones. So, rest periods can help us to avoid learning erroneous ideas that interfere with our mastery of assigned work.

For the reasons noted here, it's generally advisable to distribute whatever amount of time one may decide to devote to studying, over several shorter sessions, rather than to "cram" in fewer, more extended ones. As with warm-up time, the optimal distribution of practice and rest is largely an individual matter. Again, a personal judgment is required to decide whether: (a) the study session is too long to allow for proper maintenance of good attention, or (b) the rest breaks taken to help dissipate fatigue are so long that the study session is more break than study session. Given these qualifications, however, learning generally occurs most efficiently in relatively short study sessions separated by brief rest periods.

EFFECTIVE STUDY AND ACADEMIC SUCCESS-ACHIEVEMENT

How To Take Notes In Class And What To Do With Them

Listening To Learn. Knowing how to take notes in class can contribute greatly to the knowledge students derive from their formal education, and to their performance on course exams. In order to take class notes effectively, however, not only must we be motivated to listen, but we also need to know how to listen. Given the lifelong experience we've all had as listeners, one might expect that students almost invariably come into the classroom with much-practiced, keenly-honed abilities to process aural communication, with these skills transferring quite directly to efficient note-taking. Unfortunately, this is often more the exception than the rule for students in introductory (and sometimes even advanced) courses at the college and university level.

29

Learning To Listen. The term "listening skills" is perhaps most commonly applied in reference to educational objectives for children in preschool, kindergarten, or the early primary grades. As with other basic skills, however, deficits in listening ability are quite plentiful in the adult population, and often detract significantly from personal effectiveness and development throughout the life cycle. Especially where formal education is concerned, the ability to benefit from aural instruction at any level, requires good listening skills. In this regard, it is important to distinguish between passive and active listening.

Although they may be very difficult to distinguish just by observing what people are doing as they listen, the operational outcomes of these two modes tend to be very different. Thus, two students may attend the same class, one listening passively and the other listening actively, as their teacher presents a lecture about the French revolution, thermodynamics, or the effects of barbiturates on the brain. Both students sit quietly, jotting down notes. Both maintain about the same amount of eye contact with the teacher, and both come away from the class with about the same volume of written material on the lecture. But only the active listener comes away with a useful record of what the instructor covered during that class period.

Both inside and outside of the classroom, much of what passes for "listening" in social encounters, is *passive listening*, which involves little more than remaining silent while someone else is talking. While listening passively in our daily transactions with other people, we quietly wait our turn to talk, giving an "uh-huh" or a head nod now and then to reassure the speaker that we're still tuned-in to him/her, as we mostly plan what *we*'re going to say when it comes our turn to talk or when we interrupt before the other person signals us that s/he's ready to suspend, for a while, his/her own talk so that we may have a chance to say something. Passive listening doesn't require us to do anything much more than to remain silent and *look* as though we're really absorbing what is being said.

In contrast, when *active listening* occurs, information is received, encoded, and stored in one's memory bank. What makes active listening so difficult, is that it often demands a temporary suppression of attention to the kinds of self-interests which dominate our consciousness. In other words, in order to listen actively to what someone is saying, we have to let go of our thoughts and preoccupation with those personal matters which are of immediate concern in our own life, to concentrate our attention on what is being said by someone else. In other words, the more remote the connection we perceive between the content of the other's communication and our own self interests, the more difficult it is to listen actively. Accordingly, effective classroom teaching and textbook writing requires efforts to help students answer the question, "What's in this for me?" Hopefully, such efforts on the part of the authors will be apparent to students using the Uba/Huang book and this Study Guide which accompanies it.

Now, challenging as it may be to listen actively in casual or even intimate social interaction, both formal and informal studies indicate that active listening is especially difficult for students to do in the classroom situation. Experienced educators are well aware of the fact, for example, that even when a lecturer is judged to be very good, the majority of students aren't attending to what s/he's saying at any given moment. One widely-quoted study for which I've never seen a primary source reference, is reputed to have established that the greatest source of distraction for students in a college classroom at any rate, is their own sexual fantasies. Whether or not that observation is validly generalizable to the current student population, is an open question.

30

As with any other skill, active listening takes practice. And one exercise that may prove helpful in developing that skill, involves identifying yourself with the speaker. Figuratively, this means "putting yourself in the speaker's place," as s/he attempts to communicate whatever it is that s/he is expressing. By "taking the role of the other," we are more completely connected to the content of what is communicated as if it were coming from us instead of someone else. From this point of view, personalizing our relationship to what is being communicated brings us "closer to it" in the sense that we begin to perceive that content as our own and not someone else's. Indeed, insofar as this kind of role-reversal helps us to make the content "our own," we have truly "assimilated it" to our own knowledge base.

For a variety of reasons, some people are more adept than others at such role-taking or, what is referred to as empathic identification in the training of human services practitioners. Regardless of your own skills along these lines, you might want to at least experiment with imagining yourself as the lecturer in your classes or as the speaker in interpersonal situations in your everyday life outside of class, as a way of practicing the kind of identification which is often associated with increased strength in one's capacity for active listening. Who knows? You might just become so good at it that you not only get more out of your instructors' class presentations, but decide to pursue a career in clinical psychology, marriage and family counseling, or maybe even teaching!

Being There. Students sometimes ask whether or not there are any penalties for missing classes. My answer is that I don't assess any penalties against students' semester point totals for absences. In fact, the only reason I ever take attendance at all is to get to know my students' names. So there are no formal penalties for absences in my courses. But I qualify this response by suggesting that it's generally a good idea to attend class as regularly as possible. The foregoing recommendation is based on the assumption that the "school game" is one where you have to be present to win. Getting your body to class is just the first step. As in an athletic event, just being there physically while the mind is absent from the scene isn't enough to achieve a productive outcome. You have to be "all there" to play your best game.

A lot of times, even if your mind is on something else so that you're not paying close attention to what's being presented in class, some of the information presented "sinks into" or "registers" in your memory without any intentional effort on your part to process that information. Psychologists refer to this kind of learning as "incidental learning." The glimmer of knowledge gained in this way, could just make the difference between a correct and an incorrect response on an objective test, or a marginal instead of a totally inadequate answer on an essay exam. And don't count on being able to work from the notes of a classmate who attended a class that you missed. Note-taking tends to vary considerably from individual to individual. So, depending upon how closely your own style of information processing and note-taking coincides with that of the person from whom you're borrowing, you may get anything from a relatively clear and reliable to a totally confusing and distorted summary of what was presented.

Being Brief. Students often express the belief that in order to take notes in class effectively, they need to get a verbatim reproduction of everything that is presented in class. By imposing this totally unrealistic expectation upon oneself, the most likely outcome is enormous anxiety, and frantic, almost inevitably frustrating attempts to write a word-for-word record of lectures or other forms of class presentation. This kind of self-imposed pressure tends to be counterproductive in a number of ways. To begin with, a stenographic approach to note-taking may actually interfere with active listening as described above. That is, you may be so busy writing things down that you don't really hear what is being communicated. But an even more dysfunctional side-effect of believing that you have to write down everything presented, is that the whole class experience becomes needlessly unpleasant, sometimes to the point that you end up disliking or even hating a course that you might otherwise have enjoyed.

A much more appropriate objective is to try to write down just enough to help you remember the essential points of a class presentation. One way to decrease verbiage while increasing the informational substance of your notes, is to develop a system of your own "telegraphese," whereby you condense what you actually write by using a set of personal, shorthand-like symbols for common words and phrases.

Being Selective. In order to be brief, one must be selective. And selectivity in note-taking requires on-the-spot judgments about what to write and what not to write. Efficient note-taking in any situation, requires the note-taker to evaluate what is being said in order to summarize the information communicated. In educational situations, instructors usually give at least a few cues as to the points they're trying to emphasize. A major instructional priority in introductory courses such as the one for which this book is written, involves learning the language of the discipline. Thus, definitions of key terms are worthy of notation.

Whenever research studies are reviewed, either in class or in written material, the major points usually involve an understanding of (a) why the study was conducted in the first place, (b) how the researchers collected their data in the study described (that is, the research method that was used), (c) what the researchers actually found in their study (that is, the results of the study or studies covered), and finally, (d) the inferences, judgments or conclusions drawn from the data obtained.

Scientific explanations of the processes or phenomena which are the object of study, are typically offered in the form of theories or "hypotheses." The conventional approach to science requires that no matter how satisfying or exciting such explanations may be, they should still be regarded as tentative. In this case, "tentative" means that we treat these efforts to make sense out of whatever it is that we're studying, as the best that we can do or our best guess, given the limitations of our current state of knowledge. Nonetheless, tentative as they may be, it's usually a good idea to jot down enough words so that we have a working knowledge of the elements of the explanations thus offered when they're presented in class. And generally speaking, it's also a good idea to try to attend closely to and write down any information which your instructor has taken the trouble to present visually in some way -- that is, on the board, overhead transparency, slide, etc.

Reviewing. The best set of class notes imaginable won't do you much good unless you do something with them. How and when you review, depends very much upon your own way of doing such things. Some students find that they get the most out of their class notes when they discuss them with classmates. Others rewrite their notes, or type them out as entries into a separate computer disk file which they keep for each class. Both of the latter approaches are highly recommended as part of what will be described below as "active" study methods, because the process of discussing and/or rewriting and retyping encourages independent thinking about the content presented as you exchange ideas with fellow students, or add some elaborations to your written record of the class which make the material more meaningful to you.

When is the best time to review? Apparently the sooner after class the better. Both formal research and informal observations indicate that even a brief review undertaken immediately after a class is presented, tends to increase dramatically the long-term recall of the material covered in that class.   I recommend that my students also try to review their notes from the previous class a few minutes before each new class session, as a kind of pre-class warm-up exercise to get their attention reoriented to what comes next.

To Tape Or Not To Tape. Audio tape recordings may or may not be more useful to the student than written notes alone. To be sure, the student may benefit from listening over and over again to everything that was presented in class. As will be discussed in more detail below, truly effective study requires "doing something" with the material to be learned. Rewriting and rethinking what was presented can be very useful in this regard.   Whether or not taping is helpful for such purposes, depends upon how each of us learns most efficiently and our own particular circumstances. The value of the tape recording will also vary from class to class and from instructor to instructor. In some cases, listening to the material several times may help tremendously. In other cases, listening to it just once in class may be more than enough.

Some Facts About Studying And Learning

One painful reality of academic life is that time spent studying may or may not result in learning. By "studying" we refer to effort expended in the attempt to learn. By "learning" we mean increased knowledge, skill, or proficiency at something that occurs as a result of study or practice. The fact of the matter is that just because we "study" something doesn't necessarily mean that we're "learning" it very satisfactorily. The ideas and principles given below, are oriented to maximizing the learning gains students derive from their study sessions. In effect, all of what follows is designed to help you really <u>learn</u> while you're studying.

The Importance Of Pace

Competitive athletes know how difficult it is to play a "catch-up-from-behind" game, whether the contest is that of a track meet, a boxing match, or the championship finals on Center Court at Wimbledon. Not unlike what happens in competitive athletic situations, the advantage in academic settings is definitely to those who get a good start. Getting that good start and then staying current with the pace of assignments are often the critical, make-it or break-it factors affecting whether or not a student succeeds or fails in college.

It takes a lot of self-discipline to complete assignments on schedule, and to be prepared consistently for classes and class projects. But once a student begins to fall behind in his/her school work, it becomes easier and easier to fall further and further behind. As is the case with just about everything in life, the further behind we fall, the more formidable and anxiety-provoking is the task of recovery.

A major component of the complex dynamic set in motion by "falling behind," has to do with the cumulative nature of most school learning. Although this cumulative quality is most commonly identified with disciplines such as math, physics, and chemistry, it is characteristic of virtually every form of learning to some extent. Learning is, after all, a process of growth or development, and developmental processes are inherently cumulative. As with any other kind of development, knowledge- and skill-acquisition occurs in progressive stages, with each stage built upon the foundation of the ones which precede it. Failure to fulfill adequately the needs or to accomplish the tasks of an earlier stage, almost inevitably interferes with effectiveness in coping with the challenges of subsequent ones. So, the further behind a student falls in his/her academic assignments, the more remote each subsequent task seems to be (and probably is) from his/her coping resources.

The normative sequence of motor development demands that we sit-up before we crawl, crawl before we stand, stand before we walk, and walk before we run. But cognitive (that is, intellectual) development too, has its sequential stages. And inadequacies in the mastery of earlier stages in a cognitive-developmental process can lead to forms of intellectual paralysis that are just as crippling if not more so than the physical disabilities that can result from restricting a young child's opportunities to engage in the kinds of muscular movement required for normal, healthy development of motor skills. In a parallel sense, falling behind in school assignments is like depriving oneself of the kinds of "exercise" needed to strengthen one's "cognitive muscles" for the intellectual challenges of the next higher level. Insofar as one is late or behind schedule in doing his/her homework assignments, one's formal educational progress toward becoming a more competent, responsible, and fully-functioning person is correspondingly forestalled.

The Importance Of Place

People differ in both the kind of environment in which they feel that they study most effectively, and in the extent to which the study environment actually affects the productivity of their work time. Some students prefer the quiet and solitude of a secluded spot in the library, while others would rather work in a corner of a recreation room with lots of social activity going on all around them. Whatever your preference in this regard, it's important to determine the kinds of conditions under which you study most effectively, and then arrange to study in settings which meet those requirements.

Having to search out a place to study each time you're ready to work, or having to tolerate the frustration of trying to study in an a place that is unsuitable to your attentional style, is both wasteful of time and stressful. It's much easier to carry out a study plan properly if you can count on the availability of a place that fits your own work habit pattern during whatever times you've scheduled for study. Generally speaking, the active study techniques outlined below are best conducted in an environment where external distractions are kept to a minimum. So, time devoted to finding or even creating such a place for oneself, is time well-spent. Trying to meet the demands of a rigorous education without this kind of basic study resource, is like trying to run a marathon with five-pound weights strapped to your feet.

Studying Actively Not Passively

Motivational Differences As A Fundamental Reality. Students differ widely among themselves in their reasons for pursuing a college education. Some are enrolled as part of a plan for achieving a career goal which has been a major aspect of their life ambition for as long as they can remember. Others, who have only a vague sense of their own career direction, are in college because they believe that whatever they do in life, they'll do it with more choices and personal fulfillment if they have a solid educational background.

Another motivational dimension on which students vary quite considerably, has to do with just how much time and energy they devote to their school work, whether or not they've identified a career direction for themselves. To a large extent, differences in this regard are structured by the individual's attitudes toward education. The way in which each of us approaches our education, depends very much upon what our education means to us. Thus, some people choose to study no more than just enough to "get by" or "get through" their courses to fulfill the requirements for a degree, so that they can "get on" with life. For the latter, the educational experience is seen as something of a necessary evil which they must endure, or as an obstacle to be surmounted as a rite of passage to "the good life." Others, in contrast, have a profound commitment to education as a lifelong process to be valued for its own sake, and work diligently at their study assignments not only to achieve a wider range of opportunities in life, but as a means of becoming an educated person. Most students' orientation to their school work, however, is most accurately represented as some combination of the foregoing perceptions and attitudes.

Regardless of one's motives for being in college, the more productively one can use whatever amount of time s/he devotes to study, the more fulfilling the educational experience is likely to be, as it relates to achieving whatever long-range life goals it is intended to serve. In the shorter-run scheme of things, effective study is the key to preparing for course exams. Indeed, achievement of long-range educational objectives typically depends quite directly on these evaluations. And understanding the difference between *active* and *passive* study is an important step toward improving one's effective study skills.

Active vs. Passive Study. Application of a grammatical metaphor may help to clarify the terms used here. In *active* as compared with *passive* study, the student is, respectively, more of a subject than an object in the process. Passive study is exemplified by the student who lies down on a couch, puts a book in front of his/her face, and quietly passes his/her eyes dutifully over every (or almost every) word of a reading assignment. Some people call this "studying." I call it "eyeballing" words until fatigue, boredom, and/or sleep is induced. It is the study strategy commonly relied upon heavily by students who are bewildered at having done poorly on exams after they have "studied" or even "studied hard" for them. More than a few students are so gifted intellectually that they actually do O.K., or even very well using this approach. But for most people, eyeballing is a much-less-than optimal way of trying to learn anything, especially technical material.

Although passive eye-scanning of verbal material may be necessary, it is by no means a sufficient technique for learning. In other words, eyeballing the content of an assignment may be useful as one aspect of your study plan, but it should certainly not be the whole plan. Students often lament having done poorly on a test after reading all of the material twice, three or maybe even more times. The dismal performance in such cases is totally understandable if the study preparation has involved nothing other than the kind of passive processing of involved in eyeballing words on printed pages."

When a person studies actively, s/he is much more than just a passive <u>recipient</u> of information. Instead, s/he does something that produces effects of some sort. The effects may be internal to him/herself such as thoughts or feelings about the meaning of whatever is the object of study. Or, the effects may be tangible products (e.g., 3 x 5 "flashcards," or summary outlines) which the student creates to facilitate his/her learning. In any case, what distinguishes active study is that the learner takes an active role and thus becomes personally involved in the process of knowledge-acquisition. This involvement occurs by *creatively* investing energy in one or more of three ways: (a) *cognitively*, (b) *affectively*, and/or (c) *behaviorally*.

For the sake of clarity here, let's translate the technical terms used in the last sentence of the last paragraph. First of all, when psychologists talk about "cognitive" functions, they're talking about intellectual activity. When they use the term "affect," they're referring to emotions or feelings. To my knowledge, members of this profession still haven't come up with any cryptic way of describing "behavior," so it means here what it means anywhere else -- namely, what people <u>do</u>, which is meant to include what they say.

With the active approach then, the student becomes personally involved in the process of learning something by <u>thinking</u> about it in some critical-analytic or novel way, <u>feeling</u> some sort of emotional response to its implications, and/or engaging in the <u>doing</u> of bodily movements oriented to learning it. Although eyeballing a reading assignment may involve some activity of the visual system and the muscles of the arm and hand which hold the written material in place as we scan it, nothing is produced by the learner. In contrast, the active learner is required to do something to or with the material to be learned, which somehow helps to make that material his/her own. Rather than simply record the thoughts, feelings, and actions of others, the active learner <u>produces</u> thoughts, feelings, and/or actions of his/her own.

There are no simple answers to the question as to why active methods of study tend to be so much more effective than passive ones. An important consideration in this regard, however, is that as we personalize our involvement in learning whatever it is that we're trying to learn, our attention is more adequately focused on the task at hand, and the content of the learning is more readily assimilated to the mass of knowledge which is already a meaningful part of our life. Whatever the dynamics underlying the differences here, the techniques listed below are among those that can be recommended to help "activate" one's study sessions. Since the range of possibilities is by no means exhausted here, students are encouraged to devise their own active study strategies in line with the principles discussed above.

1. Pre-Read. A cursory "pre-reading" of a section to be studied, looking only at major headings, subheadings, the first few words of each paragraph, and the section summary can help to provide a kind of overview-of-the-forest sort of perspective before beginning to try to learn about each individual tree. Having pre-read a whole chapter, for example, a student has at least some idea about what's covered in each of its various sections. In this way, the reader can develop some preliminary familiarity with each section and subsection, before s/he begins to process them in more detail. This can be a very useful first step toward effective study of just about any kind of material, especially when we adopt a mind-set of looking for ideas that somehow relate to our own life experience or something that's already quite important to us.

A major reason why pre-reading is so helpful, is that it helps to reduce our total uncertainty about the content to be learned. As a result, we're more likely to approach each section and subsection with a greater feeling of confidence, and feeling less like a total stranger or novice to it. This simple technique often helps to reduce some of the sense of remoteness of new content from our own life, and the kind of anxiety aroused in us by what may seem to be the forbidding task of having to master ideas or principles which are totally foreign to us.

2. Underline. Selective underlining of key points in a reading assignment makes those points visually salient in a section of text, so that they can be emphasized accordingly in subsequent study and review sessions. But underlining tends to be only as useful as it is selective. If every word on a page is underlined, the purpose of underlining is defeated, and some other technique must be used to make the key points "stand out" from the rest.

Each of us has his/her own way of underlining. Some students prefer to use two or even three different colors of felt-tipped pen, with each color coded to correspond to a different level of importance in what is highlighted. Regardless of the particular style used, almost any approach to selective underlining can prove to be helpful.

Pre-reading can help to provide an overview perspective which makes it easier to decide what to underline. But there is often considerable variability in instructional priorities from course to course, and even from section to section. Especially when it comes to preparing for course exams, it's important for students to know just what those priorities are in each specific situation, so that they can structure their study goals appropriately. If the instructor hasn't articulated those priorities (i.e., as to just what it is that you're expected to get to know), it's a good idea to ask him/her to do so.

3. Outline. If it's done properly, outlining can be a very helpful, active study technique insofar as it requires the kind of critically attentive processing of information out of which major concepts are systematically articulated from subordinate or less major ones. Even abstracting the headings and subheadings in a text can help to give the student reader *personally involving* practice at learning the specific concepts covered, and also in the kind of thinking out of which such organized patterns of content presentation evolves.

4. Write Exam Questions. Virtually everything one has to do to teach effectively constitutes a form of active learning. Perhaps this explains why instructors at just about anything often report feeling, somewhat ironically, that they're learning more about whatever it is that's being taught than are the students who are intended to be the "primary learners" in the situation. One teaching role-derived study method which is quite accessible to students, is to write exam questions on the assigned material. Essentially, all that you have to do here is to pretend that you are the one responsible for making up the quiz or exam that's going to be used to assess students' mastery of material covered in the course.

The items may be written in any format, essay, short-answer, multiple-choice, true-false, fill-in or matching types. Generally speaking, the more different ways in which items are written, the better. I recommend that students set aside the answers to their self-constructed test items, as well as the specific text or lecture note reference page(s) for them, to use for review purposes a few days and possibly even the day or night before the official class exam in which the relevant content will be assessed. This way, you get to prepare for the "real" exam by using a practice mode that's modeled closely on the actual performance mastery evaluation itself. As with all of the other methods suggested here, not every student finds item-writing to be a useful addition to his/her study skill repertoire. But in many cases, it can work to enhance significantly a student's test performance in cases where every other approach has failed.

5. Recite And Rehearse. As noted above, teaching seems to be one of the very best ways to learn. There are a lot of factors that operate to make teaching such a powerfully effective method of learning. But oral recitation is undoubtedly among the key aspects of the instructional role in this regard. Indeed, there's solid research evidence to support the hypothesis that oral recitation dramatically increases learning efficiency, especially when the learner doesn't just read aloud but verbalizes his/her own recollection of the material. In many respects, the latter approach makes just about any kind of learning a lot like what actors and actresses do as they "learn and rehearse" their lines for presentation in theatrical productions. In line with this analogy, studying is the scholastic counterpart to rehearsal and course exams to the opening night performance.

The way I recommend that students use this technique is to pretend that they're teaching and not taking the course for which they're studying. So, for every given section or subsection to be studied, it is the student's task to assimilate and then verbalize the content from memory, as though s/he were teaching it to a group of students. In other words, the material is verbalized as if it were being presented to a large and very attentive audience --- even if nobody is actually attending to this oral presentation but the student-speaker him/herself! Ideally, you might alternate the roles of teacher and listener for different units of the assigned content with one or more classmates in the course, with whom you discuss the material as you alternate in reciting it. Without "live" study partners, the power of this method makes it worth using, even at the risk of raising some disquieting suspicions about one's mental wellness as a person who talks aloud to him/herself "as if s/he were teaching someone."

6. Review. As the word suggests, "review" means to go back over the material to refresh your memory for it. Here is where the selectivity of your underlining will be especially important, and the stage where your self-written exam questions can be used as "practice exams." If you're able to schedule enough time to do so, you can then go back over those areas where your "pre-exam performance" indicates the need for more recitation and rehearsal.

SQ3Ring Your Way Through College And Beyond

The SQ3R is described in virtually every introductory psychology textbook as a model for how to master reading assignments effectively. "SQ3R" stands for *survey, question, read, recite, review.*

The *survey* phase of this overall plan involves looking over headings, subheadings, summaries, etc., to get an idea of what's covered. This preliminary survey can help you get the information into your long-term memory by providing you with an organizational structure which permits you to reduce lots of otherwise seemingly independent facts into a much smaller number of more inclusive categories. It's like looking at a map of an area before you take a trip to it, to see where things are in relationship to one another. From your overview, you get an orientation to the area before actually going there. Reading a map before going on a vacation trip to a place you've never been before helps to reduce your total uncertainty about the geographic elements of it. In much the same way, surveying a chapter gives you a preliminary, overview sense of the conceptual elements in your journey of academic discovery.

The "Q" in SQ3R stands for "question." This phase of the method requires that the student make up his/her own questions about the material to be learned following the survey of it and before getting any more deeply into the study of it. Ideally, the questions are to be written out, with the answers to them written upon more careful reading of the assigned content. According to this plan, the questions may be framed in terms of the student's response to any aspects of the skeletal outline for the section to be studied, as reflected by its headings and subheadings. The questions might also express any genuine curiosity the student may have about the material covered, as generated by his/her survey of it in the first phase. The reason for the self-generated questioning prior to reading for more detail, is to help the student read with a clearer and more personally defined sense of purpose; namely, to answer the questions which the reader her/himself has posed. A more active rather than passive kind of reading is thus encouraged, in that the student brings to his reading a mind set whereby s/he is actively looking for the answers to the questions s/he has posed. Further active involvement in processing the information, is facilitated by the fact that the student then actively writes the best answer s/he can write for each question after reading the material carefully.

Having surveyed and then questioned, you're now ready for the first of the 3 R's of SQ3R. This first R stands for "read." You've surveyed the chapter in order to know where you are, where you're going, and the route by which you'll be getting there. You've formulated your own questions to give you a mind set whereby to read actively and organize your own responses to the content. You're on your way to an effective mastery of the assigned content.

The second R in the SQ3R stands for "recite." What this means, essentially, is for you to somehow express verbally the material you're reading in your own words. You've surveyed, developed questions of our own based on headings and subheadings, and read the sections to answer those questions. Recitation is the next step toward actively processing the information in a personal way. When we articulate information in our own way, movement of that content to our long-term memory is greatly facilitated. The key to this process seems to be that it encourages us to translate otherwise "rote" or "meaningless" material into a form which is meaningful for us. Talking out loud is what this phase of the process is all about. In a lot of ways, it tends to be the case that we listen more intently to ourselves than anyone else. We may be less than completely "tuned in" to others when they speak. But when we talk to ourselves, we often have the most intent listener to what we're saying that we're ever likely to find. Of course, if we have others to serve as audience for our recitation, explanation, and elaboration, as well as to discuss the material with us, all the better. Just be sure that you're comfortable with your understanding of the material before you start to recite it. Because the way you recite it is the way you're probably going to remember it.

The third R in SQ3R stands for "review," and it's the last step in the method. Frequent reviews, even brief reviews can be extremely helpful to solidifying your memory of what you've studied.

A brief review before beginning each new study session is often a very useful way of reestablishing your cognitive momentum to "get back into" studying something. There are many ways of reviewing. One way is to go over the key terms and concepts. Another way is to go over your own questions and answers based on the key content of the assigned reading.

The Suggested Ten-Step Program Of Study given in the "About This Book" section of this Study Guide, incorporates all of the principles of SQ3R. The formal structure provided by the component subunits of this Study Guide, along with the Introduction to it, are oriented totally toward facilitating your mastery of the Uba/Huang book and the course in which it has been adopted. The objective here is for you to come away from the course which introduces you to this discipline with a personal success experience, a sound working understanding of the history, methods, concepts and principles of psychology as a science, and a sense of how that science has important applied implications for everyday life in the world of the twenty-first century.

For some of you, this will be the only course you ever take in psychology. For others, it may be the entry level educational event for a career in which you take your own place as a professional member of this discipline, and contribute to its development in one of the many settings in which psychologists work. Either way, the intent here is for your introduction to psychology to be as rich, fulfilling, and as much fun as it can be. Hopefully, the text and this Study Guide which has been written to accompany it, will provide you with the tools for such an experience. In this regard, there's one more aspect to the process of achieving success in academic settings that can impact very powerfully on such outcomes; namely, test-taking. It is to just that aspect of life in the role of "student" to which we turn next.

HOW TO TAKE A TEST

Test Scores As Payoffs

No matter how hard and skillfully anyone has studied, the extent of his/her success experience as a student is inevitably limited by how effectively s/he can demonstrate his/her mastery of the assigned content on quizzes and exams. It's difficult to overestimate the importance of test-taking abilities in a society which seems to be increasingly oriented to "performance measurement." It is equally difficult to overestimate how profoundly discouraging it can be for a student who seems to have done all the right things in preparing for it, to do poorly on a course exam. Moreover, the intensity of the frustration experienced in such cases, is often proportional to the amount of time and energy devoted to the task. The harder one has worked, the more distressing is the feeling of defeat induced by an unfavorable performance evaluation -- i.e., a bad grade.

But it's not just the student who suffers from unacceptable exam performance. It's difficult to be a professional educator without coming to identify very personally with your students' successes and failures, both inside and outside of the classroom situation. For most of us, there's nothing more exciting and fulfilling than to watch our students grow and succeed. And there's nothing more painful that to see them do poorly. Unequivocally, the responsibility of having to assign grades is the part of my job that I have always liked least. Assigning "A's" is just great. Assigning low and failing grades is agony. I don't know any of my teaching colleagues who would find the latter observation too discrepant from their own experience. So, insofar as the

Introduction to this Study Guide in general, and this particular section on how to take a test helps students to do better on course exams, it also serves the interests of their instructors who will then get to feel better about what they do for a living.

Understanding And Minimizing Test Anxiety

Specific And Generalized Effects. Tests administered in school settings are usually designed to evaluate the extent to which students have mastered a given unit of study. Such performance evaluation often evokes an emotional response in the test-taker that's called "evaluation apprehension," which refers to anxiety about doing well. At the core of this kind of anxiety, which people experience to widely differing degrees and for a lot of different reasons, is a concern about how the test results will reflect on oneself as a person. The problem here, of course, is that this source of anxiety may be so great that it seriously impairs the individual's ability to demonstrate whatever ability or content mastery the test has been constructed to measure. At best, the resulting level of performance depresses one's grade in the specific course in which that test was administered. At worst, doing badly on the test reinforces one's self-doubts about his/her own ability to do anything well.

Awareness and understanding of the idea presented in the foregoing paragraph can have crucial significance for a student's likelihood of success or failure in his/her educational development. The essential point here is that a test may be designed to assess nothing more than how thoroughly an individual has mastered certain fundamentals of algebra. So, objectively speaking, that test focuses only on a specific subset of our abilities. But, despite its limited objectives, the score one achieves on such a test may have a profound impact on his/her attitudes toward him/herself *in general*. Especially on measures of intellectual performance, which is what course exams in academic settings are after all, test scores can contribute powerfully to one's perceptions of his/her own self-worth.

Test anxiety might be less of a problem if scores on measures of achievement or ability were universally regarded as having meaning relevant only to the specific functions which they're intended to evaluate. At some level of consciousness, however, both the test-taker and those who know how s/he performed on the test, are susceptible to having their judgments about that test-taker as a whole person, influenced by their knowledge of the score s/he obtained. The outcomes of such formal assessment may thus have a dramatic effect on one's sense of self, as that dimension of personality develops from the often reciprocal process of our own and others' perceptions of us.

Some Coping Strategies. So what can we do to try to insulate ourselves from the kinds of dysfunctional emotion that we may take with us into our course exams? Well, one approach that may help in this regard, has to do with establishing for ourselves the kind of test-taking attitude or "mind-set" that seems to be associated with productive performance in a variety of contexts, most notably in competitive athletics. Essentially, this technique involves thinking of the test as a game, match, or maybe even a fight, and the process of studying for it as the training or preparation phase. Knowing that we want to perform well on "an event" scheduled for a certain date, we then establish a plan that will enable us to train for it as intensely, skillfully, and consistently as possible. After following-through on that plan, we can then go into the contest secure in the knowledge that we did everything that we could do to get ready for it. In applying

41

such an approach to the psychology course in which the Uba/Huang book has been adopted, you even have the option of taking practice exams based on the Self-Quiz units in your Study Guide, to help desensitize anxieties you may have about the actual test situation.

But there's another element to the test-taking mind-set method recommended here. Along with the knowledge of how solidly we've prepared ourselves, we also take the attitude that we'll now go into the event (a) determined to do the best job we can do with it, and (b) ready to let the chips fall wherever they may fall and accept our outcome on the task for whatever it may be.

Relevant to the latter consideration, it's important to adopt a philosophical view whereby we set our performance goals realistically and define "success" appropriately to the circumstances of the task. Not even the greatest major league baseball player of all times, whomever we might identify as the one most deserving of that honor, connected for a home run or even a base hit on every trip to the plate to face an opposing team pitcher. Mistakes and losing now and then are all part of the game, whether the game is baseball, tennis, fire fighting, international business, neurosurgery, or taking a course in college. Some strikeouts, hits, wins, and some losses are more important than others. But no one time at bat makes a whole game, and no one game makes a whole season. By the same token in a typical educational context, no one item determines the total score on a test, no one test determines the final grade in a course, and no one course grade can make or break our career -- unless we so empower that instance to affect the rest of our life.

Legendary Green Bay Packer Coach Vince Lombardi's name is almost synonymous with commitment to the idea that "Winning isn't everything; it's the only thing." That might be just the kind of thinking required to get somebody into the Pro Football Hall Of Fame. But a healthier outlook, and one that's much more likely to be associated with balanced and longevous fulfillment in life, is to aim to play "the best game we can play" in our attempts to meet each of life's challenges -- which, realistically conceived, is all that any of us can ever demand of ourselves anyway. After having prepared and played as best we are able, it's time to put the last game behind us and move ahead in preparing for the next one.

The ideas discussed here are intended to minimize what is commonly known as "test anxiety." But there are some people whose anxieties are so overwhelming that they require professional clinical help with the problem. If you feel that you are one of those individuals, you are encouraged to make an appointment at the Counseling Center at your college or university, preferably with a staff members there who specializes in the treatment of such problems. Lots of people are challenged by the dysfunctional emotion which exams arouse in them, some to the point of allowing the problem to break their dreams for what they might otherwise achieve. Professional counseling to help overcome the challenge of test anxiety, can thus be an important step toward making the most of formal educational opportunities, as an integral aspect of a life plan.

Taking A Multiple-Choice Test

Tests composed of multiple-choice items are classified by students of psychological and educational measurement as ***objective tests***, which means that they are scored according to whether or not the respondent marks the correct choice from a set of alternative responses on any number of items. This type of test evaluates the respondent's ability to recognize the correct answer when s/he sees it. The recommendations given below can help you to become a much more proficient taker of such tests.

1. Read The Whole Item Carefully. The only way to score points on a multiple-choice test is to identify the correct response alternatives. What makes the task challenging is that good multiple-choice tests are written so that the correct answer has to be chosen from among three or sometimes even four other possible answers, at least one of which "looks very good" but is incorrect. Thus, it's to the student's advantage to read the item carefully and completely before recording his/her final answer. Too often, in their eagerness to get through a test and get it over with, students impulsively select the first alternative that "looks good" or "sounds right" to them, without bothering to even read the others. Unfortunately, if that first "right-sounding" alternative is the seductive but incorrect one, the result is an addition of zero to the student's score on the test.

It's important to remember that the time spent <u>taking</u> the test, is only a small fraction of the total number of hours and minutes you've invested in preparing for it. But taking the test is the aspect of the process on which performance evaluation (i.e., grades) will be based. Experienced teachers can be expected to allow sufficient time for students to do what is required on a test, unless a "speeded" testing procedure is being used for some reason. So, in order to maximize performance evaluation payoffs, you owe it to yourself to use wisely whatever test time is allotted, in order to show clearly just how much you've learned from your study of whatever the test is designed to evaluate.

2. Don't Out-Think Yourself. Students sometimes read into a question, much more than the test-constructor ever intended to put into it, thereby making the item much more difficult than it really is. The only way to avoid this error is to answer the question just as it's written. By looking for hidden meanings, the deeper significance of the question, or relationships between what is stated explicitly and content from another context, the student is often imposing onto the item a level of complexity far beyond anything that's intended to be in it.

Most instructors don't write test items to trick or trap their students. Rather, items are written to ascertain a representative sampling of students' knowledge, skills, and/or abilities. Some items will, inevitably, seem clearer than others. But, so long as the conditions of evaluation are uniform, chances are that the "clear" ones are just about as clear and the "confusing" ones are just about as confusing for everyone else who's taking the test. So, the best way to approach the test is to do the best job you're able to do with it, given the amount of preparation time you've invested in studying for it. Identify the alternative that seems to be the most clearly correct one for whatever item you're attending to. Mark that alternative on your answer form. Then move on to the next item.

3. Deal With One Item At A Time. It's not uncommon for a student to allow what s/he perceives as the difficulty or ambiguity of one item, to upset him/her so much that his/her performance on the rest of the test is seriously disrupted. As is the case with most formal evaluation situations in life, from drivers' license tests to job interviews, good concentration is critical. Generally speaking, no matter what we're doing, performance (i.e., effectiveness) tends to be maximized to the extent that we're able to focus our attention on the subtask with which we're dealing at the moment, without being distracted by our misgivings about what we did on the one(s) before it, and/or our anxieties about how we'll cope with those that come after it.

Indeed, this seems to be the kind of mind-set which characterizes high achievers at just about everything. Whether the activity is that of playing points in a championship tennis match, developing innovative computer software, writing and performing music, working to make pioneering contributions in the field of biotechnology, or taking a midterm exam in Psychology 1, the following strategy can prove to be very helpful:

(a) view each component part of whatever you're doing as a subtask;
(b) take one subtask at a time;
(c) focus your concentration as totally as possible on the subtask of the moment;
(d) deal with the subtask of the moment based on your best judgment;
(e) go on to the next subtask and take your best shot at it, and so on.

Applying this strategy to taking your course exams, try to see every item as a subtask in the total task of the whole exam. Then try to restrict your attention to doing one of those items at a time. After reading the entire item carefully, identify what you judge to be the most clearly correct alternative. Mark your answer accordingly. Then go on to the next item and repeat the procedure. Unless and until you go back over them after finishing the entire exam, items you've answered are history. Those you haven't yet gotten to are future. Your attention is concentrated on the present and the subtask of the moment.

4. When In Doubt, Eliminate Incorrect Alternatives. On a four-choice item, the odds are one in four that you'll pick the right answer by pure guesswork. Eliminate one alternative as clearly incorrect, and you've improved your odds of hitting the correct answer to one in three. Eliminate two alternatives and the odds of getting an answer right just by chance alone jump to 50/50. Of course, the more familiar you are with the target content, the better able you should be to figure out which alternatives to eliminate. But even when you "know your stuff," in cases where two alternatives seem about equally correct, your chances of scoring a point can be improved considerably by eliminating the one that you judge to be the less correct.

5. On The First Read-Through, Skip Those Items Where You "Draw A Blank." Scores on a performance mastery evaluation can be affected tremendously by the test-taker's test-taking strategy. Indeed, this section is devoted to helping students develop the kind of test-taking skills that make for an optimally effective, overall strategy for achieving high scores on all of their college course exams, especially the ones they take in the course for which this Study Guide has been written. And one important element of test-taking strategy has to do with multiple-choice items where you feel as if you just haven't got the foggiest idea as to the answer.

On the first time through the test, it's usually good, basic test-taking strategy to skip those items where you're least confident of the correct alternative. This way, you get to tally credits first for those items about which you're the most confident. To do otherwise is to risk spending so much time puzzling over questions on which your knowledge is shaky, that you don't have enough time left to do well on those where your knowledge is strongest. You might want to put a circle around the number on your answer sheet which corresponds to those items which you've skipped entirely because you hadn't a clue as to how to answer them, and even those for which you marked answers but had serious doubts as to the correctness of your response. This way, you can locate those problem items quite easily when you return to them after finishing the rest of the test.

6. Change Answers Sparingly. After you've gone through the entire test as described above, and assuming that there's still time remaining in the test period, you can go back and answer any questions which you may have skipped because you had little or no idea as to the correct alternative. If there's still time left after doing that, you may also want to go back and take another look at those items where you felt the least confident in your responses. The test-taking strategy outlined here, however, pretty much avoids the need to change answers that you've already marked. Too often, in the last-minute passion to make a final contribution to the test effort, correct answers are impulsively changed to incorrect ones. If you've followed the recommendations given here, you should have already marked your answers based upon your best judgment the first time you answered them. Unless, upon returning to a previously answered question, you've thought of something which you hadn't thought about when you answered it the first time, perhaps inspired by reading and thinking about other items in the test, it's usually advisable to let your first answer stand.

Taking An Essay Test

1. Be Sure You Have A Clear Sense Of The Question Before Writing A Single Word. Reminiscent of the first recommendation listed above with regard to multiple-choice tests, the first step in dealing with an essay-type item is to read the whole item carefully. As in the case of objective test items, there's just no way to answer an essay-type item adequately without understanding the question. If, for some reason, the question isn't clear to you, ask your instructor to clarify it for you.

2. Answer The Question That's Been Asked. Failure to answer the question that's been asked is one of the most common reasons for students' feeling disappointed with their scores and grades based on their responses to essay-type exam items. In such cases, the student is assigned a low score or maybe even no credit at all for what s/he believes to have been a perfectly wonderful essay. The crux of the problem in these instances, is often traceable to the fact that teachers typically adopt some fairly specific response criteria as the guidelines they use to define what constitutes a correct answer to each of the questions on their essay-type exams. No matter how grand your answer may be, it could be worth no points at all if it falls outside these criterion boundaries of relevance. Thus, you may write an absolutely marvelous answer concerning the causes and effects of digestive "gas." But you shouldn't be too surprised to find a red-penciled zero as your score for that answer on your Economics Of Automotive Transportation course exam, where the question asked was actually, "What factors affect <u>the price</u> of gas?"

3. Think And Plan Before You Write. One of the major techniques of Freud's psychoanalytic therapy is known as "free association." In that procedure, the client is asked to simply say anything and everything that comes into his/her mind, no matter how chaotically disorganized, nonsensical, or even vulgar and obscene it may be. This kind of thinking has an important place in the practice of clinical psychology and psychiatry. But it's an abysmally ineffective way of dealing with questions on an essay exam. Unfortunately, students' answers on such exams sometimes sound a lot like free associations in a psychoanalytic therapy session. Apparently, the way such content is produced is by reading hastily through the first item on the test, then writing down as quickly as possible, every idea that gets triggered in one's mind as an association to the words that comprise the question. The rest of the items are treated in the same, frantic manner, until the exam period time runs out or one's wrist and hand become cramped to the point of temporary paralysis.

This free association approach is similar in many respects, to what is known as the "Throw enough mud at the wall and some of it's bound to stick" technique. Valid as it may be for a professional mud-throwing team, it's rarely if ever a sound philosophy for coping with the demands of an essay-type exam. To be sure, there's usually a time limit on essay exams. And there's probably no more distressing feeling that one can experience in an exam situation, than to look up at the clock and find that there's not enough time left to answer adequately the questions that you still haven't answered. To make matters even worse, the one's left to answer may be those which are going to count the most heavily in the total exam score. Yes, it's often difficult to feel O.K. about doing anything other than writing at top speed on an essay test. But the time spent writing is likely to be used much more productively if answers are planned before they're written. Moreover, by planning before you begin to write, you can avoid having to "panic respond" to those items that are weighted most heavily in the scoring and grading criteria.

Especially for students who are more than a little anxious about their essay exam skills, it's a good idea to write a little outline in which the answer to each item is planned and organized. Preferably, your instructor will permit you to write your outline on a separate piece of paper before you begin to write your "official" answer on the test booklet or response form. Ideally, the amount of time spent on any item should be proportional to how heavily that item will count in the total score on the test. If the instructor hasn't specified clearly the relative weighting of each item on the test, it is quite reasonable to ask him/her if s/he could please do so.

O.K. So it's a good idea to outline answers before writing them in full. But how much time should be spent in doing this? As a rule of thumb, I recommend that my students devote about 20% of the time they decide to spend on each item, in planning, organizing, and outlining their answer to it. The total amount of time spent on each item should be proportional to how much it counts in the total score. Thus, if an item counts for 10% of the grade on the test and you've only got about 50 minutes to write the entire exam, that means that you should be spending about 5 minutes on that item, about one minute of which you allocate to thinking about and planning your answer to it. The total volume of your response to each item will be reduced somewhat by having spent time in thinking about what you're going to write. But if the thinking is done effectively, your answer will be accordingly more concisely and aimed directly at the criterion "bulls eye" of the question. As a result, your point total and thus your grade on the exam should be maximized.

4. Emphasize Quality, Not Quantity: Be A Rattler And Not A Boa! Related to the previous recommendation about thinking and planning, students often assume incorrectly that the more they write, the higher the score they'll achieve on an essay-type exam. But more writing isn't always better in such cases. Instructors differ among themselves in the performance criteria they apply in grading essay tests. So it's always a good idea to ask the instructor, well before exam day, just what kinds of answers are going to be given the most point credit. In general, however, instructors tend to be much more impressed by tightly-written essays in which the essential

46

content is covered directly and given the highest priority, while unessential but relevant details are treated as supplementary elaboration, and irrelevant detail is omitted altogether.

To put this in the language suggested by a former student whom I found to be one of the most effective test-takers I've ever known, you can answer essay-type questions in a couple of different ways. One way is to use a lot of words that are only tangentially relevant to what's been asked, hitting the main points almost coincidentally, sort of like a boa constrictor winding itself round and round its victim. Another way is to go straight to the heart of the matter, like a rattlesnake that strikes directly and decisively. Personally, I encourage my students to be as "rattler-like" as possible in their style of essay-exam writing.

KEEPING THINGS IN PERSPECTIVE

A Concluding Comment

There are no hard and fast, universally valid "recipes" for academic success-achievement. Ultimately, when it comes to doing well in college as in anything else, the secret seems to be that there is no secret. No matter how much opportunity we may have to do great things in life, doing things that are prosocially valued in our society requires hard work and plenty of it.

This isn't intended as an encyclopedic cookbook for academic success-achievement. It <u>is</u> designed, however, as a sort of mini-handbook of ideas oriented to minimizing the frustration and enhancing the sense of personal fulfillment that students derive from the time, money, energy, and just plain hard work they invest in their education. If even some of these ideas prove to be useful to you in this regard, the investment <u>I've</u> made here will have been well worthwhile.

CHAPTER 1

Introduction: What Is Psychology ?

A. Learning Objectives

From your effective study of Chapter 1, you should:

1. Know what psychology studies, its goals, and the history of its evolution as a science.

2. Know the terms used to identify, and the distinguishing characteristics of the major alternative perspectives used by modern psychologists to explain why people think, feel, and act as they do.

3. Know the types of work associated with some major career paths pursued by people who earn degrees in psychology.

4. Be able to answer questions about the major types of research methods used as alternative investigative tools in psychology, with special attention to:
    a. How psychology's efforts to understand behavior are conducted within the guidelines of the scientific method;
    b. How psychology has historically relied on critical thinking and evidence;
    c. The fundamentals of <u>experimental</u> research methodology as it allows for examination of relationships between independent and dependent variables, with consideration of the possible influence of so-called "confounding" variables;
    d. How the validity of generalizations to the population(s) of interests, depends upon the procedures used to obtain the test samples in formal research studies;
    e. What is meant by the terms "reliability" and "validity" as applied to evaluating scientific findings, and how such evaluation depends upon operational definitions of the variables studied;
    f. How scientific knowledge is based on an accumulation of data, and how the research on which such knowledge is based can be accessed;
    g. The various types of studies conducted by psychologists, the distinguishing characteristics of these approaches, and the kinds of questions or issues to which each of them is most appropriately applied; and
    h. How multiple theoretical views and methods, as well as cross-cultural, multicultural, and cross-gender studies provide different perspectives on the subject matter of psychology;

5. With regard to the reports of psychological research, you should know:
    a. What kind of knowledge is derived from psychological research, and the limitations on such knowledge;
    b. How the same set of data may be interpreted in more than one way, depending upon the interpreter's point of view; and

c. How to think critically in evaluating <u>for yourself</u> the research and theory you learn about in this course.

B. Preview/Review Outline Of Key Terms And Concepts

<u>Before</u> you read the corresponding chapter in your text, read over the following outline. It is designed to give you an overview of information presented in the chapter, and how the various elements of that information are related to each other. <u>After</u> reading through the whole chapter and/or before course exams, you may use this outline as a quick review guide. In your reviews, mask off one line of the outline at a time , and try to recite from your memory of the chapter, the information that you expect to appear on the next line or so.

In going over this outline as a <u>preview</u> before reading and studying the chapter, the questions posed in bold print will help to keep you focused on the learning objectives here, and keep you actively involved in the process of achieving those objectives. When using this section as a <u>review,</u> try to answer the questions. Refer back to the chapter in the text for a more detailed feedback check on your mastery of the material, and/or to strengthen your knowledge and understanding wherever you feel the need to do so.

<u>ALTERNATIVE PERSPECTIVES -- CAN'T I JUST BE AN "AMERICAN"? (Box 1.1)</u>

A. Considerable controversy over the terms that should be used to refer to various "racial" or ethnic groups.
B. Terms of group reference that will be used here.
1. Aboriginal American
2. Latino/a American
3. Asian American
4. Euro-American
5. African-American

What are the reasons given in your text for adopting each of the terms of group reference used above?

I. <u>PSYCHOLOGY, ITS GOALS AND HISTORY</u>
    A. Psychology as the Study of Behavior Including Mental Processes
    B. The Primary Goals of Psychology?
        1. Description
        2. Explanation
        3. Prediction
        4. Altering or Controlling Behaviors
    C. The Historical Foundations Of Psychology
        1. Wilhelm Wundt's as the first scientific laboratory to study human behavior.
            a. Studies of responses to changes in a stimulus.
            b. Wundt's introspective approach as for forerunner to *structuralism,* focusing on elements of a phenomenon.

2. William James' approach, known as *functionalism*, focused on the reasons and purposes behind people's behavior.

How would you define the meaning of "psychology" to anyone who asked you to tell him/her what the discipline is all about?

What are the four primary goals of psychology as a science?

How did structuralism and functionalism fit into the evolution of psychology as a science?

II. <u>MODERN PSYCHOLOGY: ALTERNATIVE PERSPECTIVES AND USES</u>

    A. Psychological Perspectives -- The seven major approaches in terms of which behavior is explained in modern psychology.
        1. Psychodynamic Perspectives
            a. Sigmund Freud's *psychoanalytic theory*
            b. Known collectively as the *psychodynammic theories*
            c. Freud's emphasis on *unconscious processes* and motivating forces that are *intrapsychic*
        2. Learning Perspectives
            a. *Behaviorism,* the S-R or stimulus-response approach
            b. *Social-Learning*, the S-O-R or stimulus-organism-response approach
        3. Cognitive Perspectives
            a. Emphasize the thinking processes underlying behaviors.
            b. Sometimes referred to as *information-processing* .
        4. Humanistic Perspectives
            a. Emphasize capacity for psychological growth, development of potential and rational decision making.
            b. Focus on personal responsibility for behaviors.
        5. Biopsychological Perspectives
            a. Focus on how body functions determine behaviors.
            b. Neuropsychological approach.
            c. Ethological approach.
            d. Behavior-genetics approach.
         6. Cultural Perspectives
            a. Assumptions about the world, interpretations of behavior, shared, values.
            b. Cross-cultural perspective.
            c. Multicultural perspective.
        7. Gender Perspectives
            a. Learned characteristics of males and females .
            b. Examining how behaviors reflect culture.

What are the seven major perspectives on explaining behavior within the professional discipline of psychology? What is the distinguishing feature of each of these seven perspectives? Which of these seven perspectives do you find to be the most appealing from your own point of view, and why?

      B. Areas of Study in Psychology
          1. Biopsychology.
          2. Developmental Psychology.
          3. Clinical Psychology.
          4. Social Psychology.
          5. Experimental Psychology.
              a. Basic Research
              b. Applied Research

What are the five areas of study in psychology as identified in your text? What is the defining characteristic of each of those areas? What is the difference between basic and applied research?

      C. Careers in Psychology
          1. Sports Psychology.
          2. Forensic Psychology.
          3. Industrial/Organizational Psychology.
          4. Counseling Psychology.
          5. School Psychology.
          6. Teaching Psychology.

Which of the career areas in psychology identified in your text sounds the most interesting to you? Why?

III. <u>RESEARCH METHODS: ALTERNATIVE INVESTIGATIVE TOOLS</u>

      A. The Scientific Method: Combining Analysis And Evidence
          1. Psychological theory, hypotheses, and variables

What is a theory? What are hypotheses and what do they have to do with theories?

          2. Minimizing Contamination
              a. Controlled Observation
              b. Confounding Variables

What is meant by the term "contamination" as it applies to psychological research, and how do psychological researchers attempt to minimize it?

          3. Looking Beyond the Persons Studied
              a. Population
              b. Sample
                  (1) Subjects
                  (2) Participants
                  (3) Respondents

What is the difference between a sample and a population?

      c. Generalizability Of Findings
         (1) Cross-Gender, Cross-Cultural, Multicultural Samples
         (2) Random Sample
         (3) Replicating results
         (4) Reliability
         (5) Validity

What is a random sample, and what does random sampling have to do with the generalizability of findings in psychological research? What is the difference between reliability and validity?

    4. Producing Consistent, Accurate Information
      a. Describing procedure
      b. Operational Definitions

How are operational definitions used by psychological researchers?

    5. Box 1.2: Applications -- Finding The Research
      a. Finding studies in journals
      b. <u>Psychological</u> <u>Abstracts</u>
      c. Computer search methods

What would you do if you wanted to find the original published article in which a particular study in psychology was reported, or other studies dealing with the same topic.

   B. Types of Studies: Alternative Methods Of Gathering Data
     1. Correlation
       a. Positive
       b. Negative
       c. Limitations of correlational studies

Can you think of an example of two variables that are positively correlated? What is the difference between a positive and a negative correlation between two variables?

     2. Surveys
     3. Field Studies, Naturalistic Observation
     4. Case Studies
     5. Experimental Studies
       a. Independent Variable
       b. Dependent Variable
       c. Experimental Group
       d. Control Group
         (1) Placebo
         (2) Minimizing Contamination
       e. Single-Blind Experiment

f. Double-Blind Experiment

g. Random Assignment

h. Matching

Identify the main types of approaches to conducting research studies in psychology. What are the distinguishing characteristics of each of these approaches, and their primary advantages and disadvantages? What is the difference between the independent and dependent variables in an experimental study? What is the difference in the way subjects are treated in the experimental as compared to the control group in an experiment ? What is the difference between a double- as compared with a single-blind experiment? Why are random assignment and matching of subjects important in experimental studies?

C. Ethical Issues in Psychological Research
1. Risk
2. Informed Consent

What is the most important guideline in psychological research?

IV. INTERPRETING PSYCHOLOGICAL RESEARCH: ALTERNATIVE MEANINGS
A. Looking at the Group, Remembering the Individual
1. Focus On Group Differences
2. Statistically Significant Differences

Why are psychological researchers more likely to focus on group differences than on similarities?

B. Remembering the Individual
1. Individual differences within groups
2. Dismissing the validity of psychological research findings which do
not fit with one's own experience
a. "I know someone who isn't like that."
b. Generalizing From Small, Personal Experience Samples

How may the focus on group differences in psychological lead to erroneous impressions about human behavior and experience? How may such erroneous impressions be avoided? Why is one's own experience not necessarily a valid framework in terms of which to evaluate formal psychological research findings?

C. More than One Way to Interpret Data
1. LaPiere's (1934) Study Of Discrimination Against Chinese In U. S.
a. Chinese couple and the Euro-American Man
b. Alternative interpretations of their relationship
2. Blatantly Wrong Interpretations
a. Drapetomania As "Disease" Of Slaves
b. Inferiority Of Women Or Racial Groups

Explain how personal attitudes are reflected in the interpretation of each of the cases described in "C" above.

     E. A Critical Thinking Approach
          1. Rational analysis based on evidence
          2. Assuming that our own cultural values, perspectives, and behaviors are natural
          3. As a creative process

What is "critical thinking" anyway, and how might you apply such an approach as a student of psychology?

C.   Self-Generated Questions: What's In This One For Me?

Most people come to the first course in psychology expecting to learn some things that will help them to better understand themselves, other people in their lives, and/or the nature of life in the world in which they live. Along these same lines, students of psychology often look forward to discovering things about human behavior and experience which may help them to improve their own life by developing their talents, technical skills, knowledge and abilities, and/or the quality of their relationships with other people. On the basis of such self interest, which tends to provide a framework in terms of which new learning becomes personally meaningful and thus easier to remember write down a few questions in the space below about the subject matter covered in this chapter. After reading and studying the chapter, come back to see how any of what you've learned may be useful to you in finding answers to these questions.

D. Completion Items

The words in the margins of this exercise are the ones that correctly complete the sentence on the corresponding line. To get the most out of this exercise, you should try to avoid looking at these words in the margin until after you've filled in the corresponding blanks with the words you think best complete the sentences. So, begin the exercise by covering up all of the margin words with a piece of paper. Then, for each blank, write in the word which you think completes the sentence. Even if you're not sure as to the word, write in your best guess, preferably in pencil so you can erase and re-write any incorrect responses you may make here.

After writing in your "answer," slide the paper covering up the margin words down just far enough to see the word for the blank you just filled-in. For each blank that you fill-in correctly, put a check mark (√) after your answer. If the word you wrote in doesn't match the word corresponding to that blank, mark an (X) next to your response and go on to the next blank. It's probably a good idea to go back to the text and try to strengthen your learning related to topic coverage that corresponds in the textbook chapter to those blanks which you filled-in incorrectly, since those items signal a weak link in your concept mastery chain for this chapter.

1. There has been considerable controversy over the terms that should be used to refer to various "_____" or ethnic groups. In Spanish, "Latino" refers to males and "_____" refers to females. The term "Euro-American" is more inclusive than the term "_____," which actually implies that a person is from the Caucasus Mountain region.
The term "African American" can imply more _____ similarity than actually exists among the people to whom it is applied.

    racial

    Latina

    Caucasian

    cultural

2. Psychology is the study of _____, including mental processes.

    behavior

3. The goals of psychology are to describe behaviors, to _____ why they occur, to predict when and how they tend to occur, and to alter or _____ the occurrence of some behaviors.

    explain

    control

4. Like other sciences, psychology relies on both _____ analysis and sensory information. Wilhelm Wundt established the first scientific _____ dedicated to the study of human behavior. Wundt's introspective approach was psychology's forerunner to the approach known as _____, that focused on distinguishing each element that contributes to the whole of a perceptual or experiential phenomenon. The approach championed by William James and known as _____ focused on the reasons and purposes underlying behaviors.

    rational

    laboratory

    structuralism

    functionalism

5. Each of the seven principal perspectives in psychology offers a different way to _____ behavior. The perspective which the lay public most often equates with psychology is Sigmund Freud's _____ theory. Freud's theory led to the development of a group of theories known collectively as _____ theories, which focus on the life-long effects of experiences in childhood and some internal, psychological conflicts. Freud believed that people behave the way they do because of forces that are _____ , which means within the mind, especially those that are _____, which means outside of the person's conscious awareness.

    interpret

    psychoanalytic

    psychodynamic

    intrapsychic

    unconscious

6. The learning perspective known as _____, and identified as the S-R or stimulus-response approach, restricts its analyses to _____ stimuli and responses. The approach known as

    behaviorism

    observable

the _____ learning perspective, takes into account processes occurring with the organism, such as perceptions, feelings, and interpretations of stimuli, and is thus identified as an _____ approach.

social

S-O-R

7. The _____ perspectives seek to understand behaviors by examining the thought processes which lead to the behaviors in question. Since behaviors are seen as outcomes of the way information is processed, cognitive approaches are sometimes referred to as _____- processing views.

cognitive

information

8. The so-called _____ school of thought in psychology views people as having a capacity to grow psychologically, develop their potential, and make rational choices. From this point of view, each of us must take personal _____ for our behaviors.

humanistic

responsibility

9. _____ perspectives focus on how body functions determine behaviors, and include a variety of approaches such as the _____ approach, which is focused on how the brain, nervous system, and body chemicals affect behavior. Another tradition within this general perspective is the _____ approach, which emphasizes the study of behavior patterns within the natural environment in which a species lives and has evolved. From the standpoint of the behavior _____ approach, attention is focused on the ways in which gene-environment interactions may affect behaviors.

Bio-

neuropsychological

ethological

genetics

10. The term _____ refers primarily to a set of assumptions about the world and ways of interpreting behaviors that lead to a shared set of values, beliefs, etc. Psychologists who take a _____- cultural perspective compare cultural differences and similarities among people in different countries. _____ perspectives focus on the effects of ethnicity, economic status, race, and gender. Even though _____-American males constitute less than 50% of the U. S. population, as a group they are not disadvantaged in power and opportunities, and, therefore, are not considered a _____ group.

culture

cross

Multicultural

Euro

minority

11. Gender refers to those characteristics of females and males that have been _____ in a culture. Thus, a gender perspective broadly involves examining how behaviors reflect differences in _____.

learned

culture

12. _____, or neuropsychology, is the study of biological and physiological bases of behavior. _____ psychology is the area of the discipline which focuses on the study of child development, physical, cognitive, and personality changes that occur as people mature, and the aging process. _____ psychology is the area of the

Biopsychology

Developmental

Social

field which focuses on the study of relationships between people. _____ psychologists often engage in basic research. _____ research deals with matters that are immediately relevant to a specific problem with direct significance for "real life" experience beyond purely scientific contexts.

Experimental
Applied

13. _____ psychologists help athletes to improve their athletic performance. _____ psychologists apply the methods of psychology to problems in the fields of law enforcement and criminal justice. Counseling and _____ psychologists help people who are having difficulty coping with certain kinds of issues or problems in life.

Sports
Forensic

clinical

14. A psychological _____ is an interrelated set of testable assumptions used to explain and predict behaviors. The term "hypothesis" is used to describe the kind of hunch that is used to test how accurately a theory actually _____ the kinds of behaviors it is designed to understand. _____ are characteristics in terms of which people, experiences, situations, etc., tend to differ. A basic assumption of the scientific method is that we should rely more on _____ than on assumptions, beliefs, or claims. A _____ observation is one in which the scientist tries to examine relationships between the variables in which s/he's interested, without the interference of other variables. One way in which scientists try to control for the effects potentially confounding variables is by holding them _____. A subset of the population of interest in a research study is known as a _____. Generalizations from sample data to the population of interest tend to be only as valid as the sample is _____ of that population. A _____ sample is one in which every member of the population has an equal chance of being represented. _____ definitions specify how a variable or construct will be measured.

theory

predicts
Variables

data
controlled

constant
sample

representative
random
Operational

15. The old-fashioned way to do a search of professional literature in psychology which is relevant to a topic one is studying is to go directly to the periodical series known as the *Psychological _____*, which chronicles brief summaries of such work, so that one may consult the original sources as appropriate to one's own project.

Abstracts

16. _____ refers to the consistency with which some result is obtained. A _____ study or measure is one which does what the researcher intends for it to do.

Reliability
valid

17. A _____ correlation exists when high scores on one variable tend to be associated with high scores on another. A negative correlation exists when high scores on one variable or measure tend to be associated with _____ scores on another.

positive

low

58

Correlational studies are limited in that they do not show _____   causal
relationships between the variables measured. A major limitation of the
_____ method of gathering data is that it does not allow   survey
the researcher to know whether different people who report the "same"
attitude, behavior or experience, in fact have the same attitude, behavior, or
experience. Field studies take place outside of laboratory settings, and thus
involve what are referred to as _____ observations of behavior.   naturalistic
The _____ study or history method involves an in-depth   case
examination of a particular individual's past and present experiences,
behaviors, feelings, perceptions, and thoughts. The _____   dependent
 variable in an experiment is the one which is measured to see how it is
affected by variations or manipulations of the _____ variable.   independent
The _____ group in an experiment is the one whose responses   control
are compared as a baseline against those of the experimental group. When
neither the subjects nor the researcher know whether any given subject is
tested under the experimental or control condition, the experimental method
is called _____- blind. After a random sample of subjects has   double
been obtained, differences among subjects may be further controlled by the
methods of random assignment of subjects to conditions or _____   matching
of subjects in the experimental and control groups on variables which the
researcher has reason to believe may affect the results of the study.
One limitation of _____ experiments is that they involve testing   laboratory
subjects under conditions which are more or less artificial or contrived.

18. The most important ethical guideline in psychological research is that
there be minimal physical and psychological _____ to   risk
participants. Prior to becoming involved in the data collection aspect of the
study, each participant must sign an informed _____ statement,   consent
certifying that they have been informed of their rights to confidentiality as to
their responses and to withdrawal from participation in the study at any time
without penalty of any kind.

19. Psychological research most often focuses on _____   group
differences, such as between experimental and control conditions. The
tendency to focus on differences arises, in part, from the fact that studies
that find a difference in behavior are more likely to be _____   published
than studies whose primary finding is no group difference.
A statistically _____ relationship or difference among   significant
 groups is one which the researcher has a mathematical reason for
believing is not due to chance alone. _____ differences   Individual
refer to differences in responses or characteristics among individuals
within groups.

20. One way of interpreting the findings in LaPiere's study of discrimination
against Chinese in the United States is that those who provided services
for the three people in restaurants and motels did so because they saw the
Euro-American member of the trio as the "_____" of the   keeper

Chinese couple. In pre-Civil War days in the United States, the primary "symptom" of what was believed to be the "disease" known as _____ was an uncontrollable desire to seek freedom from being kept as a slave.   drapetomania

E. Self-Quiz

For each of the following multiple-choice items, circle the letter which precedes the correct alternative.

1. Referring to various groups as Americans first with the ethnicity label second, as in "American Mexican," makes the term "American" a(n) _____ and thus makes U. S. nationality the less important aspect of the identity than if ethnicity were stated first.
    a. adjective
    b. adverb
    c. noun
    d. pronoun

2. The term preferred by the authors of your textbook is
    a. Mexican-American
    b. Hispanic
    c. Latino/a
    d. Spanish

3. The term "Caucasian" actually implies that a person is
    a. Asian
    b. Eurasian
    c. Amerasian
    d. from the Caucasus Mountain region

4. The term preferred by the authors of your textbook is
    a. Black American
    b. Black American-African
    c. Black African-American
    d. African-American

5. Wundt's studies focused on how people respond to
    a. emotional crises
    b. unconscious motives
    c. ambiguous interpersonal situations
    d. changes in stimuli

6. Wundt's introspective approach was psychology's forerunner to the approach known as
    a. functionalism
    b. psychoanalysis
    c. structuralism
    d. dianetics

7. Functionalism focused on
    a. an introspective approach to understanding consciousness
    b. multivariate, factor-analytic studies of personality
    c. the neurological foundations of human experience
    d. the reasons and purposes for human behavior

8. Freud's psychoanalytic theory is a _____ approach.
    a. behavioristic
    b. humanistic
    c. social learning
    d. psychodynamic

9. Freud believed that intrapsychic pressures were due to
    a. unconscious processes
    b. learned associations
    c. identification with dysfunctional role models
    d. neurological dysfunctions associated with serotonin imbalances

10. Behaviorism is an _____ approach.
    a. S-R
    b. S-O-R
    c. R-S
    d. R-S-O

11. The social learning perspectives is an _____ approach.
    a. S-R
    b. S-O-R
    c. R-S
    d. R-S-O

12. Cognitive perspectives seek to understand behavior in terms of
    a. unconscious motives
    b. archetypal imagery
    c. thought processes
    d. observable stimuli and responses only

13. Which of the following approaches is most closely identified with a focus on people's capacity to grow psychologically, develop their potential, and make rational choices?
   a. psychoanalysis
   b. behaviorism
   c. humanism
   d. behavior social learning theory

14. Which of the following approaches is most closely identified with studying behavior of species in the natural environment in which its members live and evolve?
   a. ethology
   b. phrenology
   c. epistemology
   d. urology

15. Gender refers to characteristics of females and males that are
   a. biologically given
   b. learned in a cultural context
   c. essentially unmeasurable
   d. impossible to define operationally

16. A confounding variable in an experiment is one which
   a. is actively manipulated by the experimenter to test its effects
   b. is measured to assess how it is affected by some other variable(s)
   c. leads to new hypotheses
   d. is extraneous to the experimental design

17. An experimental sample is said to be random if every member of the population is
   a. known
   b. represented
   c. given an equal chance of being included
   d. systematically excluded from the data collection process

18. Operational definitions specify how variables are
   a. associated
   b. correlated
   c. measured
   d. confounded

19. _____ refers to the consistency of research findings.

   a. Reliability
   b. Validity
   c. Multifactorial determination
   d. Population stratification

20. In instances where increases in one variable are found to be associated with decreases in another, the two variables are said to be
      a. confounded
      b. unreliable
      c. positively correlated
      d. negatively correlated

For each of the following items, circle "T" if the statement is True and "F" if it is false.

21. T F   The survey method is appropriate in cases where the objective is to measure the attitudes of a large sample.

22. T F   Field studies involve naturalistic observations which take place outside of a laboratory setting.

23. T F   Experimental designs do not allow for evaluation of causal relationships between the variables studied.

24. T F   The control group in an experiment is the one to which the independent variable is applied.

25. T F   In a double-blind experimental situation, neither the subject nor the researcher knows whether the subject has been assigned to experimental or control condition.

26. T F   Statistically significant findings in experimental studies are those which are large and psychologically meaningful or important.

27. T F   The classic interpretation of the finding in LaPiere's study of discrimination against Chinese in the United States is that what people do may be different from what they say.

28. T F   The desire to be free from slavery was once labeled as a kind of psychological disorder.

29. T F   Critical thinking involves rational analysis based on evidence.

30. T F   Cultural values have little or no influence on individual differences in the interpretation of behaviors.

F. Teaching-To-Learn Exercise

1. *Let Me Teach You This.*

Write in the space provided below, the five facts, ideas, etc., from this chapter that you'd most like to teach to your own student(s) if you were a teacher. Then, really do try to communicate these facts or ideas to someone in your life; or, pretend to teach this content to a hypothetical or "make-believe" student or class.

2. *Now Answer My Questions.*

Here, write one multiple-choice and one True-False question for each of the facts, ideas, etc., you covered in the "Let Me Teach You This" section of this exercise.

G. Bringing Psychology To Life Exercise

Much of the research which constitutes the very foundation of psychology as a social science involves data gathered by means of the experimental method. So, a working familiarity with the elements of experimental methodology is fundamental to understanding how psychologists seek to extend the existing scientific knowledge in their discipline. The following exercise is thus intended to give the student an opportunity to become familiar with the experimental method in psychological research.

CHAPTER 2

Biopsychology: Biological Bases Of Behavior

A. Learning Objectives

After your effective study of Chapter 2, you should know the following:

1. Why an understanding of how people function psychologically requires an understanding of human biology.

2. How genetics operates in determining biological characteristics of the individual, including:
>   a. What genes are and how they function as the elements of biological heredity;
>   b. How scientists use studies of twins to try to separate out the influence of heredity and environment in the development of individual differences;
>   c. The interactive influence of genes;
>   d. The relationship between genes and environment in determining the expression or manifestation of "inherited" characteristics; and
>   e. The utility of conventionally established criteria for distinguishing among racial groups; and
>   f. The psychological and social realities of (1) race as a cultural idea, and (2) racism.

How the nerves work as the body's communication network, including:
>   a. The basic functions served by the nerves;
>   b. The role of the glial cells in the transmission of nervous impulses;
>   c. The three parts of the nerve cell and their role in nerve function;
>   d. What the sensory and motor neurons do; and
>   e.   What an action potential is and how it occurs.

That the endocrine system is and how it works, including:
>   a. The role of the neurotransmitters in this chemical message system; and
>   b. What hormones are and what they do.

5.   e fundamentals of the nervous system:
>   a. What is meant by the term "peripheral nervous system;"
>   b. The roles of the somatic system and the sympathetic and parasympathetic branches of the autonomic nervous system;
>   c. What the central nervous system is and what it does; and
>   d. The role of the spinal cord in the body's own complex communication system.

6. V   the subcortical brain is, and the functions served by each of its component parts, inclu

>   The brain stem, comprised as it is of the cerebellum, lower part of the reticular
>   mation, the thalamus, hypothalamus and limbic system.
>   The cerebellum;

    c. The reticular activating system;

    d. The thalamus and hypothalamus; and

    e. The limbic system.

7. How complex thinking is controlled by the cerebral cortex, including:

    a. The way sensory information is processed;

    b. Lateralization and sharing of various functions by the two cerebral hemispheres;

    c. The four lobes of the cortex and the functions they control;

    d. The functions controlled by the sensory, motor and association areas of the cortex;

    e. How the brains of different people are similar, but individual differences in all kinds of psychological processes may be due to hemispheric lateralization and sex;

    f. The relationship between handedness and lateralization of the cortex; and

    g. How scientists try to explain differences between the brains of males and females.

B. Preview/Review Outline Of Key Terms And Concepts

Before you read the corresponding chapter in your text, read over the following outline. It is designed to give you an overview of information presented in the chapter, and how the various elements of that information are related to each other. After reading through the whole chapter and/or before course exams, you may use this outline as a quick review guide. In your reviews, mask off one line of the outline at a time , and try to recite from your memory of the chapter, the information that you expect to appear on the next line or so.

In going over this outline as a preview before reading and studying the chapter, the questions posed in bold print will help to keep you focused on the learning objectives here, and keep you actively involved in the process of achieving those objectives. When using this section as a review, try to answer the questions. Refer back to the chapter in the text for a more detailed feedback check on your mastery of the material, and/or to strengthen your knowledge and understanding wherever you feel the need to do so.

I. Genes: The Bases for Biological Characteristics
    A. How We Transmit Genetic Information
        1. Ovum
        2. Sperm
        3. 23 Pairs Of Chromosomes
        4. Dominant And Recessive Genes
    B. Genetic and Environmental Effects
        1. Genes And The Probable Range of a Child's IQ
        2. Studies Of Identical Twins

What are some of the key findings in studies of identical twins raised apart? What do these findings suggest with regard to the role of biological heredity and environment in the development of the person?

    C. Alternative Perspectives On Race (Box 2.1)
        1. Caucasoid, Mongoloid, Negroid

2. Arbitrary Physical Criteria
　　　　a. Blood Type
　　　　b. Proteins
　　　　c. Enzymes
　　　　c. Skull Size
　　　　d. Race As A Cultural Idea
　　　　e. Racism

What facts might you use in arguing against the idea that a person's race is due to genetics and biology?

　　D. Passing Along Psychological Characteristics
　　　　1. Combinations Of Genes
　　　　2. Role Of Environment
　　　　3. Genes And Homosexuality

What research evidence is there to support the controversial proposition that genes may contribute to male homosexuality?

II. Nerves: A Route For Spreading Information and Instructions
　　A. Glial Cells: Support Services
　　B. Neurons: Like Telephone Lines

How is the processing of information by the brain different from the kind of information processing that occurs in a telephone communication system?

　　　　1. Parts Of A Neuron
　　　　　　a. Soma
　　　　　　b. Dendrite
　　　　　　c. Axon
　　　　2. Types Of Neurons
　　　　　　a. Sensory Nerves
　　　　　　b. Motor Nerves
　　　　　　c. Interneurons
　　C. Nerve Impulses: Like Electrical Messages Along A Telephone Line
　　　　1. Communication Along A Neuron
　　　　　　a. Movement Of Positively And Negatively Charged Ions
　　　　　　　　(1) Sodium
　　　　　　　　(2) Potassium
　　　　　　　　(3) Chloride
　　　　　　b. Resting Potential
　　　　　　c. Action Potential
　　　　　　d. Negative Afterpotential
　　　　　　e. Sodium-Potassium Pump
　　　　　　f. All-Or-Nothing Principle
　　　　　　g. Myelin Sheath/Myelinated Axons

What are the symptoms of the condition known as multiple sclerosis, and what causes it?

    2. Communication Between Neurons
       a. Synapse
       b. Terminal Button
          (1) Synaptic Vesicles
          (2) Neurotransmitters
          (3) Presynaptic Membrane
       c. Synaptic Cleft
       d. Receptor Sites And Neurotransmitters

What does the analogy of "keys into locks" have to do with explaining how nervous impulses are transmitted? What happens when one of the "keys" fits one of the "locks" in this analogy?

       e. Reuptake And Degradation

What are the effects on the nervous system of chemicals such as cocaine, nerve gases, and some insecticides? What kinds of symptoms are experienced by the person in whose nervous system such effects occur?

III. Chemical Messages: Another Information Route
    A. Neurotransmitters
       1. Dopamine
          a. Parkinson's Disease
          b. Schizophrenia
       2. Acetylcholine (ACh)

What causes botulism? What happens in the nervous system when this disease is contracted, and what are the health risks associated with it?

       3. Norepinephrine (Noradrenalin)

What are the psychological effects of too much epinephrine?

       4. GABA (Gamma Amino Butyric Acid)

What is the function of GABA in the nervous system? What does the bacterial infection known as "tetanus" do to the release of GABA, and what are the effects on the body of the person afflicted with this condition?

       5. Serotonin
          a. Slowing Of Action Potentials
          b. Calming, Soothing Effect
          c. Disorders Associated With Low Levels
             (1) Treatment By Drugs (e.g., Lithium Carbonate)
             (2) Treatment With Tryptophan

How does the intake of carbohydrates affect amino acid levels in the body and the psychological state of the person?

    B. Hormones
        1. Endocrine system
        2. Endocrine Glands
           (a) Gonads
               (1) Produce Sperm And Egg Cells
               (2) Sex-Linked Physical Characteristics
           (b) Pituitary Gland
               (1)Controls Other Glands
               (2) Regulates Physical Growth, Sex Drive
           (c) Thyroid Gland
               (1)
               (2)
           (d) Adrenal Glands
               (1) Energy Level
               (2) Moods, Reactions To Stress

Why is the pituitary sometimes referred to as "the master gland"? What are some of the basic functions of the thyroid and adrenal glands?

IV. The Nervous System: A Network Of Information Routes
    A. The Peripheral Nervous System (PNS)

What is the function of the system of nerves known as the peripheral nervous system?

        1. The Somatic Nervous System
           a. Information From Sense Organs
           b. Information To Spinal Cord And Brain
        2. The Autonomic Nervous System
           a. Controls Digestive Organs, Glands, Involuntary Muscles
           b. Sympathetic Branch
               (1) Activated By Adrenals
               (2) Prepares Organism For Action
           c. Parasympathetic Branch
               (1) Dominates in Relaxed States
               (2) Conserves and Restores Energy

How does the parasympathetic branch of the autonomic nervous system conserve and restore our energy when we are relaxed?

        3. The Central Nervous System (CNS)
           a. Spinal Cord And Brain
           b. Spinal Cord
               (1) Made Up Of Vertebrae
               (2) Gray Matter Around Center

(3) White Matter Outside Gray
(4) Myelinated Axons
(5) Reflexes

What are reflexes? At what level of the central nervous system are reflexes controlled? How might this level of central nervous system control of reflexes have survival value for the individual?

V. The Subcortical Brain: Basic Biological Functions Of Life

Why is the subcortical brain referred to as the "more primitive" part of the brain?

    A. The Brain Stem
        1. Responsible For Autonomic Functions Like Reflexes, Breathing
        2. Lowest Part Is Hindbrain
            a. Oldest Part Of Brain
            b. Medulla Located Here
                (1) Breathing
                (2) Heart Rate
            c. Pons
                (1) Above Medulla
                (2) Relays Messages To/From Spinal Cord And Cortex
            d. Midbrain
                (1) Upper Part Of Brain Stem
                (2) Connects Hindbrain To Cortical Areas
    B. The Cerebellum
        1. Upright Posture, Balance
        2. Muscle Tone, Coordinated Movements, Skill Memory
        3. Functions Impaired By Alcohol Consumption
    C. The Reticular Formation (Reticular Activating System)
        1. Selectivity Of Attention
        2. Controls Level Of Arousal, Sleep-Wakefulness
    D. The Thalamus
        1. Relays Information From Sense Organs To Cortex
        2. Part Of The Forebrain
    E. The Hypothalamus
        1. Regulates Fear, Aggression, Appetite, Thirst, Sexual Behavior
        2. Neural-Anatomical Differences And Homosexuality
    F. The Limbic System
        1. Experience And Expression Of Emotion
        2. Hippocampus
        3. Amygdala

What seems to be the primary function of the hippocampus? What psychological processes are among those in control of which the amygdala seems to be involved?

VI. The Cerebral Cortex: The Site Of Complex Thinking

Where is the cerebral cortex located?

    A. Cerebral Hemispheres/Left And Right
        1. Information From & Control Of Movement On Opposite Side Of Body
        2. Shared Functions
        3. Lateralization
            a. Left Hemisphere
                (1) Logical Analysis
                (2) Understanding And Memory Of Words
            b. Right Hemisphere
                (1) Art Appreciation, Perception Of Melodies, Spatial Tasks
                (2) Impulsivity, Perception of Part-Whole Relationships,
                    (a) Expression Of Emotion
                    (b) Voice Recognition
            c. Potential For Conflicting Attitudes
            d. Normally Cooperative Functioning

On the basis of your reading in the corresponding chapter in your text, how might you expect someone who is described as a "right-brained person" to differ from one who is described as "left-brained"?

    B. Lobes
        1. Occipital Lobe
            a. Located In Back Of Head
            b. Processing of Visual Messages

        2. Parietal Lobe
            a. Pain, Touch, Pressure, Temperature
            b. Control Over Awareness Of Body Parts

What is it that seems to determine just how much of the parietal lobe corresponds to a given body area?

        3. Temporal Lobe
            a. Processing Of Sounds And Smells
            b. Balance, Emotional Control, Abstract Thinking, Speech
        4. Frontal Lobe
            a. Responsible For Much Of What We Call "Personality,"
                (1) Abstract Thinking, Learning, Memory, Planning,
                (2) Problem Solving
            b. Damage Can Cause Anosognosia, Or Capgras Syndrome
            c. Case Of Phineas Gage As Example Of Role In Personality

What are the symptoms of the clinical conditions known as anosognosia and Capgras syndrome? How does the case of Phineas Gage illustrate the role of the frontal lobe in the determination of one's personality?

C. Functional Divisions Of The Cerebral Cortex
    1. Sensory Cortex
        a. Information From Sense Organs
        b. Visual Cortex In Occipital Lobe
        c. Auditory Cortex In Temporal Lobe
        d. Somatosensory Cortex Along Front Of Parietal Lobe

What kinds of sensory information are processed by the somatosensory cortex?

    2. Motor Cortex

What kinds of functions are controlled by the motor cortex? What seems to be a primary characteristic of those body parts to which the greatest amount of area corresponds in the motor cortex?

    3. Association Areas
        a. Combine Sensory And Motor Information
        b. Broca's Area In Frontal Lobe Of Left Hemisphere
        c. Wernicke's Area

What kind of symptoms would you expect to be associated with damage to Broca's area, as compared to losses in function experienced by a person with damage to Wernicke's area?

    4. Biological Bases Of Learning
        a. Effects of Repetition
        b. Growth Of Dendrites In Association Areas
    5. The Brain's Plasticity
        a. Case Studies Of Accident Or Stroke Patients
        b. In Rehabilitation

How might you explain the idea of "brain plasticity" to someone who has had no formal education whatsoever?

    6. Split Brain
        a. Cerebral Hemispheres Disconnected
        b. Corpus Callosum And Anterior Commissure Are Cut
        c. Treatment Of Severe Epilepsy
        d. Hemispheres Cannot Communicate With Each Other
D. Human Variations In The Brain
    1. The Left Handed And The Right Handed
        a. Lateralization, Handedness And Sex Hormones in the Womb
        b. Individual Differences In Hemispheric Dominance
        c. Dominant Hand On Opposite Side Of Body
    2. Sexual Perspectives On The Brain
        a. Females Better At Tasks Requiring Fluent Speech, Dexterity
        b. Males Better At Finding Hidden Figures In Pictures,

Mental Rotation Of Figures
  c. Differences May Be Due To Genes Or Cultural Factors
  d. More Similarities Than Differences Across Genders

How might you use your knowledge about handedness and sex differences in abilities to answer the question as to whether or not brain organization is related to differences in human behavior and experience?

C. Self-Generated Questions: What's In This One For Me?

Most people come to the first course in psychology expecting to learn some things which will help them to better understand themselves, other people in their lives, and/or the nature of life in the world in which they live. Along these same lines, students of psychology often look forward to discovering things about human behavior and experience which may help them to improve their own life by developing their talents, technical skills, knowledge and abilities, and/or the quality of their relationships with other people. On the basis of such self interest, which tends to provide a framework in terms of which new learning becomes personally meaningful and thus easier to remember, write down a few questions in the space below about the subject matter covered in this chapter. After reading and studying the chapter, come back to see how any of what you've learned may be useful to you in finding answers to these questions.

D. Completion Items

The words in the margins of this exercise are the ones that correctly complete the sentence on the corresponding line. To get the most out of this exercise, you should try to avoid looking at these words in the margin until after you've filled in the corresponding blanks with the words you think best complete the sentences. So, begin the exercise by covering up all of the margin words with a piece of paper. Then, for each blank, write in the word which you think completes the sentence. Even if you're not sure as to the word, write in your best guess, preferably in pencil so you can erase and re-write any incorrect responses you may make here.

After writing in your "answer," slide the paper covering up the margin words down just far enough to see the word for the blank you just filled-in. For each blank that you fill-in correctly, put a check mark (√) after your answer. If the word you wrote in doesn't match the word corresponding to that blank, mark an (X) next to your response and go on to the next blank. It's probably a good idea to go back to the text and try to strengthen your learning related to topic coverage that corresponds in the textbook chapter to those blanks which you filled-in incorrectly, since those items signal a weak link in your concept mastery chain for this chapter.

1. _____ are segments or groupings of DNA that carry hereditary information. At conception, when a woman's ovum is fertilized by a man's sperm, the new cell formed has 23 pairs of _____. A child will have blue eyes only if both parents have contributed a _____ gene for blue eyes.

Genes

chromosomes
recessive

2. _____ twins are siblings who develop from the same fertilized egg, and thus have exactly the same biological heredity.

Identical

3. In contradiction to popular belief, there are not many biologically or hereditarily determined differences across _____ or ethnic groups. Indeed, the physical criteria used to define race are largely _____, and quite different "racial" groups would be identified if different criteria were applied. _____ is reflected in the belief that members of one or another racial group is superior to others. Psychological differences are not due directly to genetics, but rather to the way in which people identified with various racial or ethnic groups are _____ in society.

racial

arbitrary
Racism

treated

3. Research evidence suggests that most psychological characteristics are the result of a _____ of genes, rather than just a single pair. Homosexual males are more likely to have homosexual relatives on their _____ side of the family than would be expected by chance alone.

combination

mother's

4. _____ cells are those which nourish and help to repair damage to nerve cells, and also get rid of dead nerve cells.

Glial

5. The _____ of the neuron is the body of the neuron, which manufactures what the neuron needs to survive and grow. The _____ are the branching surfaces of neurons which receive information from other neurons. The _____ is the part of the neuron from which information is sent to other neurons. _____ nerves are those which carry information from the muscles, internal organs, and sense organs. _____ nerves carry information from the spinal cord and brain out to the muscles. _____ carry information among the different parts of the brain and spinal cord.

soma

dendrites
axon

Sensory
Motor

Interneurons

6. Neurons communicate by means of nerve _____, which are electrical charges that transmit information. Such electrical charges move along a neuron through the electrochemical action of three types of ions. Positively-charged _____ ions outside the nerve

impulses

sodium

78

membrane are attracted to negatively-charged _____ ions inside the axon. Transmission of a nervous impulse occurs by changes in the _____ potential of the nerve. A nerve impulse triggers an action _____, which is a brief period when the electrical charge inside the axon membrane is more positive than the charge outside it. Once a neuron has fired and a nerve impulse passes by, there is a _____ afterpotential, which is a time when the potassium is still outside the axon and the sodium is inside. A sodium-potassium _____ pushes the sodium out and pushes the potassium into the axon so that the normal resting potential is restored. Neuronal action potentials occur according to the all-or-_____ principle, which refers to the fact that a neuron either fires or it doesn't. Action potentials move more quickly down axons that are covered with a thick layer of fat cells forming the _____ sheath, which is destroyed by the body's own immune system in people afflicted with multiple _____.

chloride

resting
potential

negative

pump

nothing

myelin
sclerosis

7. The transfer of a message from the axon of one neuron to the dendrite of another occurs at a junction called the _____. The chemicals by which messages are carried through the nervous system are called _____, and are stored in the synaptic vesicles of the terminal _____ or knobs which are the enlarged ending of axons. When neurotransmitters fit into receptor sites built into the postsynaptic membranes like _____ in a lock, the neurotransmitter can either excite or _____ a response by the particular neuron or muscle involved. _____ is the process in which neurotransmitters are sent back to the presynaptic vesicles. Sometimes, after a neuron has been stimulated, neurotransmitters are broken down by enzymes in a process called _____. Exposure to certain kinds of chemicals such as cocaine, nerve gases and some insecticides, can prevent such de-activation, resulting in overstimulation that may lead to _____, inhibition of movements such as swallowing, and even death.

synapse

neurotransmitters
buttons

keys
inhibit

Reuptake

degradation

convulsions

8. Low levels of the neurotransmitter _____ are characteristic of people with Parkinson's disease, in which the afflicted individual shows inability to control his/her muscle movements. _____ is the neurotransmitter which causes muscles to contract when it stimulates the firing of neurons. Too much of the neurotransmitter _____ (also known as noradrenalin) is associated with the psychiatric condition known as mania, which is characterized by an uncontrollably excited mood. _____ is the neurotransmitter which inhibits behaviors such as eating and aggression. The neurotransmitter _____ slows or prevents action potentials, and thus has a calming, soothing effect that helps

dopamine

Acetylcholine

norepinephrine

GABA
serotonin

us fall asleep. Eating foods high in carbohydrates results in increased levels of the amino acid _____ in the brain, which increases production of serotonin and the calming effects it induces.

tryptophan

9. _____ are chemical messengers released into the blood by glands of the endocrine system. The _____ are the glands which release hormones responsible for development of sex-linked physical characteristics. The release of hormones by other glands is controlled by the brain's _____ gland. The hormones that regulate metabolism and growth are secreted by the _____ gland. Energy level, moods, and long-term reactions to stress are released from the _____ glands.

Hormones
gonads

pituitary

thyroid
adrenal

10. Information is carried from the brain and spinal cord to the rest of the body by way of the nerves in the _____ nervous system (or PNS). Information is sent from the sense organs, skeletal muscles, and joints to the spinal cord and brain by the _____ division of the PNS. Activity of the digestive organs, glands, and involuntary muscles such as the heart is controlled by the _____ division of the PNS; the _____ branch of the latter system prepares us for action when we're aroused or under stress; the _____ branch of it dominates when we are relaxed.

peripheral

somatic

autonomic
sympathetic
parasympathetic

11. The _____ nervous system (or CNS) is composed of the brain and spinal cord. The spinal cord is made up of vertically stacked bones called _____. Unlearned, automatic responses to stimuli are called _____.

central

vertebrae
reflexes

12. The _____ part of the brain, beneath the brain's cortex, is responsible for many of the basic brain functions necessary for maintaining life. The _____ part of this area is responsible for fundamental, primarily autonomic functions required for life, such as breathing and the rhythmical beating of the heart. The lowest part of the brain stem includes the _____, which is the oldest part of the brain, and includes the _____, which controls breathing and heart rate, and above which is located the _____ which relays messages from the spinal cord and face up to cortical areas of the brain. The _____ is a fist-sized structure at the base of the skull that enables us to maintain upright posture, balance, and to make coordinated movements. The selectivity of attention, level of arousal, and sleep-wakefulness are controlled by the _____ formation. The structure which is responsible for relaying information from sensory organs to appropriate places in the cortex where sensory input is interpreted is the _____. The structure that regulates fear, aggression, appetite, thirst, sexual behavior, internal body temperature, heart rate, and blood pressure, is the _____. One structure in the limbic system is the _____, which plays a role in our emotions, ability to remember, and ability to compare sensory input

subcortical

brain stem

hindbrain
medulla

pons
cerebellum

reticular

thalamus

hypothalamus
hippocampus

to expectations; another limbic system structure is the _____,   amygdala
which influences motivation, learning fear responses, memory, control over
emotions, and recognition of nonverbal expressions of emotion.

13. Each hemisphere of the cerebral cortex processes sensory information
from and controls movement of the _____ side of the body.   opposite
The _____ hemisphere is usually the one which is quicker   left
and more efficient in logically analyzing, understanding, and memorizing
words, numbers, and sequences of events or letters.
The _____ hemisphere is usually the one more involved in   right
performance of spatial tasks such as reading maps, drawing, and recognizing
shapes and faces. The _____ lobe is the place in the   occipital
cerebral cortex where visual messages from the eyes are sent and processed.
The _____ lobe is the part of the brain where messages about   parietal
pain, touch, pressure, and temperature are sent and processed. The
_____ lobe is where sounds and smells are processed. The   temporal
cortex area which is apparently responsible for much of what we describe as
human "personality" is the _____ lobe, damage to which   frontal
commonly results in difficulties in the expression of emotion.

14. The _____ cortex along the front of the parietal lobe   somatosensory
processes information about temperature, body position, and touch. The
_____ cortex initiates and directs voluntary movement in the   motor
muscles of the body. The rest of the cerebral cortex is made up of
_____ areas, which combine information from different senses,   association
and enable us to think, remember, learn, use language, and make plans.
_____ area is that part of the frontal lobe in the left hemisphere,   Broca's
which enables us to put our ideas into words. _____ area is   Wernicke's
that part of the temporal lobe which enables us to understand what others
say and to speak to them in an understandable way. When we learn new
things, cells in the association areas of the brain grow
_____ which form links to other neurons which result in new   dendrites
connections among thoughts. The term "_____" is often   plasticity
used to refer to the kind of flexibility in the functioning of the brain,
reflected by the fact that tasks normally handled by one hemisphere may
be handled by the other. Rehabilitation makes use of such flexibility
through _____ movements which are intended to help   repeated
establish new neural pathways or connections among healthy neurons.
Split brain surgery, in which the cerebral hemispheres are disconnected
from each other, involves cutting of the corpus _____ and   callosum
the anterior commissure.

15. Left-handed people tend to have cerebral hemispheres that are not
as _____ as are those of right-handed people. Sex   lateralized
differences in the brain may reflect genetic or inborn differences in
brain structure, or be due to _____ differences in the types   cultural
of tasks with which females and males are most frequently confronted.

81

E. Self-Quiz

For each of the following items, circle the letter which precedes the correct alternative.

1. With the exception of ovum and sperm cells, every other cell in the human body has _____ pairs of chromosomes.
    a. 9
    b. 13
    c. 23
    d. 46

2. Which of the following is not among the functions served by glial cells?
    a. conducting neural impulses
    b. nourishing of nerve cells
    c. getting rid of dead nerve cells
    d. providing a protective covering for nerve cells

3. The body of a neuron, which manufactures what the neuron needs to survive and grow, is the
    a. axon
    b. dendrite
    c. soma
    d. synaptic cleft

4. Which of the following is not among the functions of interneurons?
    a. carry information to and from different parts of the brain and spinal cord
    b. relay sensory information to other interneurons
    c. transmit information from sensory to motor neurons
    d. provide nourishment to neurons and rid the system of dead ones
    e. store memories

5. Which of the following describes the resting potential of a nerve cell?
    a. most of the potassium ions outside the axon
    b. most of the sodium ions outside the axon
    c. most of the chloride ions outside the axon
    d. all of the positively charged ions inside the axon
    e. all of the negatively charged ions outside the axon

6. The "all-or-none principle" of neural transmission refers to the fact that
    a. the more intense a stimulus, the greater the intensity of neural firing
    b. negative afterpotentials occur after each neural firing
    c. negative afterpotentials occur only after the firing of an intense stimulus
    d. a neuron either fires or it doesn't

7. Multiple sclerosis is a disorder in which the body's immune system destroys
    a. the sodium-potassium pump mechanism in neurons
    b. the sodium gate mechanism in neurons
    c. myelin
    d. chlorine ions outside of the neuron

8. _____ is (are) contained within the terminal buttons of synaptic vesicles.
    a. The sodium-potassium pump mechanism in neurons
    b. The sodium gate mechanism in neurons
    c. The myelin sheath
    d. Neurotransmitters

9. Chemicals such as cocaine, nerve gases and some insecticides may have potentially lethal effects on the body due to the fact that they
    a. destroy myelinated neurons
    b. prevent the reuptake that usually occurs after a neuron has been stimulated
    c. cause neurons to become deactivated after they have fired
    d. cause a hardening of the presynaptic membranes and thus a closing of the potasium gates

10. A shortage of which of the following hormones is most closely associated with the symptoms of Parkinson's disease?
    a. dopamine
    b. histamine
    c. acetylchonine
    d. norepinephrine
    e. phencylidine

11. The blocking of the neurotransmitter _____ caused by botulism, which comes from eating spoiled food or exposure to weapons of biological warfare, may induce paralysis and death by suffocation.
    a. dopamine
    b. acetylcholine
    c. norepinephrine
    d. GABA

12. Mania is most likely to be caused by excessive amounts of
    a. dopamine
    b. acetylcholine
    c. norepinephrine
    d. GABA

13. People with low levels of which of the following neurotransmitters are most likely to be treated using drugs such as lithium carbonate.
    a. dopamine
    b. acetylcholine
    c. GABA
    d. serotonin
    e. norepinephrine

14. Eating carbohydrates tends to increase the amount of _____ that reaches the brain.
    a. tryptophan
    b. acetylcholine
    c. norepinephrine
    d. noradrenalin
    e. formalin

15. This is the gland which controls the release of hormones by the other endocrine glands.
    a. thyroid
    b. adrenal
    c. liver
    d. kidney
    e. pituitary

16. The brain and spinal cord comprise what is known as the _____ nervous system.
    a. peripheral
    b. sympathetic
    c. parasympathetic
    d. central

17. Breathing and heart rate are controlled by the
    a. medulla
    b. pons
    c. reticular formation
    d. thalamus

18. The _____ is the structure in the brain that regulates fear, aggression, appetite, thirst, sexual behavior, and internal body temperature, heart rate and blood pressure.
    a. medulla
    b. pons
    c. hippocampus
    d. hypothalamus
    e. thalamus

19. Visual messages are processed in the
   a. parietal lobe
   b. commissural fissure
   c. temporal lobe
   d. occipital lobe
   e. frontal lobe

20. The _____ is that part of the brain where messages about pain, touch, pressure, and temperature are sent and processed.
   a. parietal lobe
   b. temporal lobe
   c. occipital lobe
   d. frontal lobe
   e. reticular formation

For each of the following items, circle "T" if the statement is True, and "F" if the statement is False.

21. T F   A child will have blue eyes only if both of his/her parents have contributed a recessive gene for blue eyes to the child.

22. T F   Identical twins have exactly the same genes.

23. T F   There is a substantial body of literature indicating the validity of significant genetic differences among racial and ethnic groups.

24. T F   Race is a cultural idea used to emphasize a particular set of physically minor differences that exist among people.

25. T F   Motor nerves carry information from the muscles, internal organs and sense organs to the spinal cord.

26. T F   Throughout our lives, new neurons are being created continually in our brain.

27. T F   Messages do not travel as fast along myelinated neurons as they do on non-myelinated ones.

28. T F   The parasympathetic branch of the autonomic nervous system dominates when we are relaxed.

29. T F   The right cerebral hemisphere tends to be dominant in most right-handed people.

30. T F   Females tend to be better than males at tasks requiring the ability to see a figure that is hidden in a picture and on tasks requiring mental rotation of figures.

F. Teaching-To-Learn Exercise

1. *Let Me Teach You This.*

Write in the space provided below, the five facts, ideas, etc., from this chapter that you'd most like to teach to your own student(s) if you were a teacher. Then, really do try to communicate these facts or ideas to someone in your life; or, pretend to teach this content to a hypothetical or "make-believe" student or class.

2. *Now Answer My Questions.*

Here, write one multiple-choice and one True-False question for each of the facts, ideas, etc., you covered in the "Let Me Teach You This" section of this exercise.

G. Bringing Psychology To Life Exercise

Imagine that you are a contestant on a new TV quiz show called "Know It All," where student representatives from colleges and universities throughout the country are chosen at random to compete for outrageous prizes in a game that tests their knowledge about all sorts of things. In the first challenge round, you are matched against a graduating senior honor student from **We're Better Than You Are University**. Your task is to come up with the best argument you can construct to support the proposition that a thorough understanding of human behavior and experience requires study of human biology, because human beings are, essentially, biological creatures. The contestant whose argument is rated highest by the show's impartial panel of expert judges, wins a cash award of $50,000 for him/herself, and a contribution in the same amount for his/her school's scholarship fund. The losers get their choice of a six-pack of Odor Eaters for their running shoes, a compact disc recording of a new album entitled "Friday the 13th part 87: Jason Sings The Best Of Elvis," or an appendectomy for two performed by the Haitian Witch Doctor of their choice.

Drawing upon content presented in Chapter 2 of your text, write your response to the foregoing challenge in the spaces provided below.   Remember, the better organized your essay, and the more convincing the examples you include in it, the higher the score you're likely to receive from the judges and the greater your chances of winning some big bucks for yourself and for the scholarship fund at your own college or university.

ON BIOLOGICAL CONSIDERATIONS
IN UNDERSTANDING HUMAN PSYCHOLOGY

A. <u>Facts Based On The Study Of Genetics</u>

B. <u>Facts Based On The Study of Neural Impulse Transmission</u>

C. Facts Based On The Study Of Neurotransmitters And Hormones

D. Facts Based On The Study Of The Peripheral And Central Nervous System

E. Facts Based On The Study Of The Subcortical Brain

F. Facts Based On Study Of The Cerebral Cortex

Answer Key To Self-Quiz

1. c
2. a
3. c
4. d
5. b
6. d
7. c
8. d
9. b
10. a
11. b
12. c
13. d
14. a
15. e
16. d
17. a
18. d
19. d
20. a
21. T
22. T
23. F
24. T
25. F
26. F
27. F
28. T
29. F
30. F

CHAPTER 3

Sensation & Perception

A. Learning Objectives

After careful study of Chapter 3, you should have a working understanding of how we come to know about the world in which we live. This chapter provides you with an opportunity to learn:

1. About mechanisms of sensation, that is, the ways in which information about our external and internal environment is detected by our sensory systems, with special attention to:
> a. What is meant by transduction, and why it is the process fundamental to every sensory event;
> b. The route of a light wave as it is processed by the visual system;
> c. What causes visual dysfunctions such as near- and far-sightedness;
> d. The different types of cells involved in the processing of light by the visual system, and the kinds of energy to which they are sensitive;
> e. The distinguishing characteristics of the two major theories of color recognition (i.e., the trichromatic and opponent-process theories);
> f. The route of a sound wave as it is processed by the auditory system;
> g. The two major theories as to how we are able to distinguish pitch differences among sounds;
> h. The two major types of deafness and their causes;
> i. How we taste things, the difference between taste and flavor, and how we might account for age differences in taste likes and dislikes ;
> j. The mechanism involved in the detection of smells;
> k. The skin senses, how they operate, and what accounts for differences in sensitivity of different skin areas;
> l. The predominant theory of pain, and how it utilizes a "gate" metaphor;
> m. How factors other than physical stimuli can affect both the interpretation of and reactions to pain; and
> n. The structures, processes, and functions served by the kinesthetic and vestibular senses.

2. About the intriguing psychological processes of perception, by which sensations are interpreted and thus become meaningful to us, including:
> a. How our perceptions are influenced by factors both internal and external to the perceiver;
> b. The kinds of methods used by psychologists to study perception scientifically;
> c. Cues to depth and distance which we get from each eye individually, and those which are the result of integrated information from both eyes;
> d. How perception may be seen as an active process by which reality is constructed rather than just responded to passively by the perceiver;
> e. The various perceptual tendencies that operate to make perception an active construction process; and
> f. What is meant by "bottom-up" and "top-down" processing of information.

3. How one's own personal experience within a social and cultural context influences the processes of perception, with special attention to:

    a. How studies of people born blind who gain sight are relevant to the issue of whether perception is innate or learned;

    b. The relevance of cross-cultural research to understanding the way perception works within any culture; and

    c. How the unique psychological make-up of each individual operates as a complex source of influence on how each of us ultimately interprets the sensory events in our lives.

B. Preview/Review Outline Of Key Terms And Concepts

Before you read the corresponding chapter in your text, read over the following outline. It is designed to give you an overview of information presented in the chapter, and how the various elements of that information are related to each other. After reading through the whole chapter and/or before course exams, you may use this outline as a quick review guide. In your reviews, mask off one line of the outline at a time , and try to recite from your memory of the chapter, the information that you expect to appear on the next line or so.

In going over this outline as a preview before reading and studying the chapter, the questions posed in bold print will help to keep you focused on the learning objectives here, and keep you actively involved in the process of achieving those objectives. When using this section as a review, try to answer the questions. Refer back to the chapter in the text for a more detailed feedback check on your mastery of the material, and/or to strengthen your knowledge and understanding wherever you feel the need to do so.

I. Sensation: Detecting Our Surroundings
    A. Sensation

What is the role of the sense organs in sensation?

        1. Transduction

What happens to physical energy in the process of transduction?

        2. Absolute Threshold
        3. Difference Threshold

Give a real life example to illustrate what psychologists mean by the concept of a "just noticeable difference" or "j.n.d."

        4. Sensory Adaptation

Give an everyday life example to illustrate what psychologists mean by "dark adaptation."

        5. Sensory Deprivation

What has been found to happen to psychological research volunteers placed in a sensory deprivation chamber?

    B. Seeing: How The Eye Behold
        1. Light Waves
            a. Amplitude/Brightness
            b. Wavelength/Color
            c. Visible Spectrum

How would a light wave of very high amplitude be experienced if a person's eye were exposed to it? What does the concept of the visible spectrum imply about the range of human sensitivity to light?

        1. The Parts Of The Eye
            a. Sclera
            b. Cornea
            c. Iris
            d. Pupil
            e. Lens
                (1) Accommodation
                (2) Myopia/Near-Sightedness
                (3) Presbyopia/Far-Sightedness

What causes the conditions of near- and far-sightedness?

        2. Turning Light Into Information For The Brain
            (a) Retina
                (1) Ganglion Cells
                (2) Bipolar Cells
                (3) Photoreceptor Cells

Where on the retina are the rods located in relationship to cones? What are the functional differences between these two types of cells?

            (b) Visual Field

What is the fovea?

        3. From The Eye To The Brain
            (a) Optic Disc
            (b) Optic Nerve

What causes the blind spot in the eye?

            (c) Optic Chiasm
            (d) Feature Detectors

Can you give an example of feature detector cells that respond to different types of lines?

    4. Variations In Color
       (a) Hue
       (b) Saturation

In color vision, how is "saturation" affected by the combination of light waves reflected by a given object?

    5. Alternative Perspectives On Seeing Color
       (a) Trichromatic Theory
       (b) Opponent-Process Theory

What are the essential differences between the trichromatic and opponent-process theories of color vision?

  C. Hearing: What A Sound Signifies
    1. Sound Waves
       a. Loudness/Intensity
       b. Pitch/Frequency
    2. The Parts Of The Ear
       a. Pinna
       b. External Auditory Canal
       c. Eardrum
       d. Middle Ear/Ossicles
          (1) Hammer
          (2) Anvil
          (3) Stirrup
       e. Inner Ear
          (1) Oval Window
          (2) Cochlea
       f. Auditory Nerve

What is the path of a sound wave from outside the ear, to each of the anatomical structures by which it is processed on its way to the brain?

    3. Alternative Perspectives On Distinguishing Among Pitches
       a. Place Theory
       b. Frequency Theory

What is the essential difference between the two major theories as to what determines the pitch of a sound wave?

    4. Hearing Impairments
       a. Conduction Deafness
       b. Nerve Deafness

What is the essential difference between the two major types of hearing impairments?

    D. Other Senses: Taste, Smell, Touch, And Position
        1. Taste
            a. Papillae
            b. Gustatory Cells
                (1) Sweetness
                (2) Sourness
                (3) Bitterness
                (4) Saltiness

What are the four basic taste sensations, and what is the chemical process by which they are activated?

            c. Flavor

Why is age a factor in individual differences in taste sensitivity?

        2. Smell
            a. Olfaction
                (1) Olfactory Epithelium
                (2) Olfactory Nerves
            b. Anosmia

How is the case study observation as to Helen Keller's keen olfactory sensitivity relevant to the idea of the brain's plasticity?

        3. Skin Sensation
            a. Cutaneous Sense
            b. Pain
                (1) Sharp And Quick
                (2) Dull
                (3) Gate Control Theory
                (4) Acupuncture

How might the treatment of pain by the methods of acupuncture be explained in terms of the gate control theory of pain?

        4. Position Senses
            Kinesthetic Sense
            Vestibular Sense

II. Perception: Interpreting Our Sensations
    A. Gestalt Psychology
        1. Perceptual Construction Of Reality
        2. Whole Greater Than Sum Of Its Parts

What is the difference between sensation and perception?

    B. Depth Perception: Judging Distances
        1. Perceiving Depth With One Eye/Monocular Cues
            a. Relative Size
            b. Linear Perspective
            c. Elevation
            d. Texture And Clarity
            e. Overlap
            f. Shading
            g. Motion Parallax
        2. Perceiving Depth With Two Eyes/Binocular Cues
            a. Binocular Disparity
            b. Convergence

How does the psychology of depth perception support your answer to the previous question concerning the difference between sensation and perception?

    C. Perceptual Tendencies: Organizing Our Interpretations

What does the concept of "schema" have to do with the psychology of perception, and how do response differences to the rabbit/duck stimulus illustrate the operation of schemata in perception?

        1. The Familiar, Simple, And Normal

What is meant by "the tendency to assimilate" as that expression in used in the psychology of perception?

        2. Tendency To Perceive Constancy
            a. Color Constancy
            b. Shape Constancy
            c. Size Constancy
        3. Important Figures And Unimportant Background
            a. Figures
            b. Ground
            c. Auditory Figure-Ground Distinctions
        4. Exaggerating Differences Among Stimuli

How does the tendency to perceive contrast illustrate the difference between sensation and perception?

        5. Stimuli As Part Of A Group
            a. Spatial Proximity
            b. Temporal Proximity
            c. Similarity

        d. Common Fate
        e. Good Form
        f. Closure
        g. Phi Phenomenon
  6. Context Affects Perception
  7. Box. 3.1 Applications Of Perceptual Tendencies In Everyday Life
      a. Contrast
          (1) And The Perception Of People
          (2) In The Packaging Of Meat
      (b) Phi Phenomenon And Movies
      (c) Expectations, Schemata And Eyewitness Testimony

How do the examples noted in Box 3.1 illustrate the difference between sensation and perception?

  8. Bottom-Up And Top-Down Processing
     Bottom-Up Processing
         Processing Information From Feature Detectors Or
         Bits Of Sensory Information Until Pattern Is Perceived

     Top-Down Processing
         Concepts And Expectations Affect How Stimuli
         Are Noticed And Organized

How would you explain the difference between bottom-up and top-down processing to someone who has never studied psychology? What illustrations could you use to help clarify the difference between these two modes of perception?

III. Psychosocial Influences On Perception: Perceiving Based On Personal Background

How are case studies of people born blind who later gained sight relevant to the issue as to whether or not perception is innate?

  A. Experiences Affect Perception
     1. Studies Of Kittens Raised In Environment With Only Horizontal Lines
     2. Studies Of Kittens Raised In Cylinder Of Vertical Stripes
  B. Cultural Perspectives On Perception
     1. Studying Responses To Illusions
     2. Muller-Lyer Illusion
        a. Carpentered World Theory Of Cross-Cultural Differences
        b. Response Of Zulu, Rural Africans, And Phillippinos
        c. Response Of African Americans

What do the cross-cultural studies of response to the Muller-Lyer illusion indicate about the nature of perception?

  C. Personal Characteristics Affect Perception

How would you explain the concept of "set" to someone who has never studied psychology? What examples might you use to help clarify this concept?

        1. Selective Perception

What is habituation, and how is it relevant to the selectivity of perception?

        2. Expectations And Beliefs Affect Perception
               a. Selectivity Of Perception And Influence On Schemata
               b. Believing Is Seeing
                    (1) And Belief In ESP
                    (2) Memory Biases

How does the psychology of perception provide us with insights into why people often persist in beliefs for which there is little or no objective supporting evidence?

C. Self-Generated Questions: What's In This One For Me?

Most people come to the first course in psychology expecting to learn some things that will help them to better understand themselves, other people in their lives, and/or the nature of life in the world in which they live. Along these same lines, students of psychology often look forward to discovering things about human behavior and experience which may help them to improve their own life by developing their talents, technical skills, knowledge and abilities, and/or the quality of their relationships with other people. On the basis of such self interest, which tends to provide a framework in terms of which new learning becomes personally meaningful and thus easier to remember, write down a few questions in the space below about the subject matter covered in this chapter. After reading and studying the chapter, come back to see how any of what you've learned may be useful to you in finding answers to these questions.

D. Completion Items

The words in the margins of this exercise are the ones that correctly complete the sentence on the corresponding line. To get the most out of this exercise, you should try to avoid looking at these words in the margin until after you've filled in the corresponding blanks with the words you think best complete the sentences. So, begin the exercise by covering up all of the margin words with a piece of paper. Then, for each blank, write in the word which you think completes the sentence. Even if you're not sure as to the word, write in your best guess, preferably in pencil so you can erase and re-write any incorrect responses you may make here.

After writing in your "answer," slide the paper covering up the margin words down just far enough to see the word for the blank you just filled-in. For each blank that you fill-in correctly, put a check mark (√) after your answer. If the word you wrote in doesn't match the word corresponding to that blank, mark an (X) next to your response and go on to the next blank. It's probably a good idea to go back to the text and try to strengthen your learning related to topic coverage that corresponds in the textbook chapter to those blanks which you filled-in incorrectly, since those items signal a weak link in your concept mastery chain for this chapter.

1. _____ is the detection of information about external and internal environments and the transmission of that information to the brain. _____ is the process by which physical energy is transformed into nervous impulses. The minimum level of stimulus intensity required for a sense receptor to respond to a stimulus is the _____ threshold. The difference threshold or just _____ difference is the smallest difference between stimuli that can be detected 50% of the time. Sensory _____ refers to a reduction in sensitivity and responsiveness to a stimulus of unchanging intensity. Volunteers placed in a sensory _____ chamber become irritable and develop hallucinations such as seeing and hearing things that are not present.

Sensation

Transduction

absolute

noticeable

adaptation

deprivation

2. _____ is the technical term used to refer to the height of a light wave, which determines the apparent brightness of that light wave. The apparent _____ of an object is determined by the length of the lightwaves which it reflects to the eye. Human eyes respond only to lightwaves in what is known as the visible

_____.

Amplitude

color

spectrum

3. The _____ is the white of the eye which protects it and helps maintain its shape. The _____ is the transparent, protective, outer part of the eye through which light enters the eye. The _____ is the colored part of the eye, which is made up of muscles which control the size of the opening in the eye known as the _____, thus controlling the amount of light which enters the eye. The _____ is the transparent structure which changes shape or "accommodates" to allow for sharp focusing of images cast upon the eye from varying distances. _____ is the technical term for what is commonly known as near-sightedness. _____ is the technical term for what is commonly known as far-sightedness. _____ is the technical term for the kind of far-sightedness which is due to old age.

sclera
cornea

iris

pupil
lens

Myopia

Hyperopia
Presbyopia.

4. The _____ is the structure at the back of the eye,   retina
which contains two types of photoreceptor cells:
the _____, which are located toward the periphery or   rods
outer edge and which permit us to see at night or in dim light; and the
_____, which are located mostly in the center and   cones
enable us to see details and color. The visual _____   field
is whatever one sees at any given moment, and the point of clearest
vision within it is known as the _____.   fovea

5. The optic disc is the point at the back of the eye where the optic
_____ exits the eye and goes to the brain. Since there   nerve
are no light receptors at this optic disc, we have a _____   blind
spot in our field of vision of which we are usually unaware. At the
optic _____, most of the optic nerve fibers cross over   chiasm
to the opposite cerebral hemisphere of the brain. The nerve cells in
the visual cortex which are sensitive to different characteristics of stimuli,
are known as _____ detectors.   feature

6. When we refer to a color, such as blue, we are referring to what is
known technically as _____. The fewer the number of   hue
light waves that are combined, the more pure or _____
        saturated
the color. Researchers have found that people in different cultures
differ in the number of _____ they use to describe colors.   words

7. According to the _____ theory, rods enable us to   trichromatic
see black and white, while the ability to see all other colors arises from
combinations of blue-, green-, and _____ -sensitive   red
cones and the speed with which nerve impulses are fired. The
_____-process theory holds that when input to the visual   opponent
system is classified as blue, neurons that detect _____ are   yellow
turned off, and vice versa, with red and green processed in a similar way.

8. The higher the _____ of a sound wave, the louder the   amplitude
sound we hear. The _____ of a sound is measured by   pitch
the frequency with which its wave crests per second; the higher the
frequency, the higher the _____ that sound makes on the   note
musical scale.

9. The _____ is the outermost, fleshy part of the outer ear,   pinna
which connects to the external auditory _____, which is a   canal
passageway into the skull by which sound waves are sent to the
third part of the outer ear, the _____, which connects to the   eardrum
three small bones or _____ of the middle ear. As sound   ossicles
waves vibrations from the eardrum cause movement at the inner-most
middle ear bone known as the _____, that movement   stirrup
causes vibration of the oval _____ of the inner ear,   window

100

which transmits sound waves to a snail-shaped, fluid-filled inner ear structure known as the _____, in which are located receptor cells called auditory _____ cells which fire and synapse with neurons in the auditory _____, along which actions potentials move to the _____ lobes of the cortex.

cochlea
hair
nerve
temporal

10. According to the _____ theory, the pitch of a sound wave determines the place along the cochlea that vibrates the most; an alternative perspective to the foregoing theory is the view that the _____ of a sound wave causes auditory hair cells to vibrate at a matching rate.

place

frequency

11. In the type of hearing impairment known as _____ deafness, there is damage to part of the eardrum or middle ear which prevents sound from being transmitted to the inner ear. In _____ deafness, auditory hair cells have been destroyed or there has been damage to the auditory nerve.

conduction

nerve

12. Many taste buds are contained on the small bumps known as _____ on the surface of the tongue; the receptor cells for taste are the _____ cells contained within the taste buds. Our enjoyment of flavors is due in part to _____, which is the sense of smell, the sensory input from which is processed in the _____ lobes of the cerebral cortex. The complete loss of the sense of smell is known as _____.

papillae
gustatory
olfaction

temporal
anosmia

13. The _____ is the largest sense organ in the body. Sharp pain is transmitted quickly along bundles of _____ sensory nerves. _____ pain is transmitted along small nerves that carry their sensory messages more slowly. The predominant theory of the transmission of pain is the _____ control theory. _____ is the ancient Chinese technique designed to lessen pain by sticking needles into different parts of the body.

skin
large
Dull

gate
Acupuncture

14. The _____ sense provides feedback about our posture, balance, movement, and position of various parts of our body. The receptors for this sense are contained in receptor cells located in _____, joint, skin, and tendon cells. Information about the position of our body is also provided by the _____ sense, the receptors for which are located in the _____ hair cells.

kinesthetic

muscle

vestibular
auditory

15. _____ is the process by which sensory information is organized, integrated, and given meaning. It involves the _____ of stimuli. _____ psychology is an approach to the study of human experience focused on how perception operates as the mechanism by which people construct their understanding of reality.

Perception
interpretation
Gestalt

16. _____ perception is the perception of objects as three-dimensional and at varying distances. _____ cues to such perception are those which are provided by each eye alone, one of which is that of _____ size, by which objects that are small are seen as farther away than larger objects; another of these is _____ perspective, whereby the apparent meeting of lines we believe to be parallel is perceived as meaning increased distance. Motion _____ is the monocular depth cue by which distant objects are seen as moving by us more slowly than do nearby objects. Binocular _____ is the depth cue arising from the fact that our two eyes are a small distance apart, so that each of them gives us a somewhat different sensory input on the visual field. _____ is the binocular depth cue arising from the fact that our eyes are aimed differently when we look at objects which are close as compared to those which are far from us.

Depth
Monocular

relative
linear

parallax

disparity

Convergence

17. The concept of _____ refers to a particular way of interpreting sensory information. The tendency to _____ is the tendency to minimize small differences in stimuli and to interpret stimuli in terms of existing schemata. _____ constancy is the tendency to perceive a familiar figure as the same color, regardless of the actual wavelengths reflected from it. Size _____ is the tendency to perceive an object as maintaining its size, even though it may project a changing image on our retinae.

schema
assimilate

Color

constancy

18. The fact that figure and ground can be _____ means that figure-ground articulation depends upon our perception rather than just the physical characteristics of stimuli.

reversed

19. The tendency to perceive differences larger than those that actually exist, is known as _____ . The tendency to perceive stimuli that occur close together in time as a group or as belonging together, is known as temporal _____.
The tendency for people to perceive stimuli that appear to move in the same direction at the same speed as belonging together or grouped is known as common _____.
One aspect of the tendency to perceive objects in such a way that they appear to have "good form," is that of _____, which means that the figure is seen as closed and complete.

contrast

proximity

fate

closure

20. _____ processing involves processing of information from different feature detectors or bits of separate pieces of sensory information and then building upon those or integrating them in such a way that a meaningful pattern is perceived. _____ processing refers to the kind of perceptions that result from attending to, organizing, and thus interpreting sense impressions according to

Bottom-up

Top-down

established concepts, images and/or expectations in the brain.

21. People born blind but who later gain sight tend not to have completely
_____ perceptual abilities. Kittens raised in an environment   normal
in which they saw only horizontal lines, displayed behaviors which
researchers interpreted as supporting the inference that these animals'
_____ feature detectors, left unused, did not develop   vertical
normally.   Such findings suggest that normal perceptual development
depends partly on _____.   learning

22. The carpentered world theory has been used to explain cross-
_____ differences in perception. Zulu who live in round   cultural
huts with round doors in rolling hills areas of Southeast Africa, are not
as susceptible to the Muller-Lyer _____ as are Americans.   illusion

23. Our expectations or needs may establish a _____,   set
which is the term used to refer to a readiness to respond to stimuli in a
particular way. _____ of perception refers to the fact that   Selectivity
we tend to notice some stimuli and not others. The phenomenon of
_____ refers to the tendency toward a reduction in   habituation
cognitive responsiveness to unchanging or repeated stimuli.
What people _____ often affects what they perceive.   believe
James Randi showed that the feats which Uri Geller claimed he could
perform by ESP, could be replicated and thus explained as
_____ tricks.   magic

24. The adornment of red meat with green parsley in a supermarket
may be seen as an exploitation of the perceptual tendency toward
_____ for commercial purposes. "Motion pictures"   contrast
represent an application of what students of perception refer to as
the _____ phenomenon. Results of the informal   phi
study by an NBC television station in New York in which a 12-second
film depicting a scene in which a young woman was accosted as she
walked down a hallway, validate the fact that perception is influenced
by expectations and schemata as well as information from the sense
organs, and also indicate the fallibility of _____ testimony.   eyewitness

E. Self-Quiz
For each of the following items, circle the letter which precedes the correct alternative.

1. The difference threshold is the smallest difference between stimuli that people
can detect _____ of the time.
      a. 25%
      b. 50%
      c. 75%
      d. 100%

2. Sensory adaptation involves a(n) _____ to a stimulus or stimuli.
    a. reduction in sensitivity and responsiveness
    b. reduction in absolute threshold response
    c. reduction in difference threshold response
    d. increased rate of neural transmission in response

3. The _____ is the transparent structure of the eye which changes shape to bring objects in the visual field into sharper focus.
    a. sclera
    b. cornea
    c. iris
    d. pupil
    e. lens

4. Presbyopia is
    a. near-sightedness due to retinal damage
    b. near-sightedness due to age
    c. far-sightedness due to retinal damage
    d. far-sightedness due to age

5. Which of the following is not true about the photoreceptor cells known as "cones"?
    a. operate best in bright light
    b. enable us to see details and color
    b. more sensitive to red lights than are rods
    c. located mostly toward the periphery of the retina
    d. the only photoreceptors in the fovea

6. Which of the following is not one of the three colors to which cones in the retina are assumed to be sensitive according to the trichromatic theory?
    a. red
    b. yellow
    c. green
    d. blue

7. Which of the following is not one of the three categories in terms of which neuronal response to color is classified according to the opponent-process theory?
    a. blue-yellow
    b. red-green
    c. black-white
    d. red-blue

8. Which of the following is not one of the three small bones or ossicles of the middle ear?
   a. hammer
   b. nail
   c. anvil
   d. stirrup

9. Input from the auditory nerve is processed in the _____ lobes of the cerebral cortex.
   a. occipital
   b. frontal
   c. hemispheric
   d. parietal
   e. temporal

10. According to the frequency theory, the perceived pitch of a sound wave is due primarily to the
   a. vibration rate of auditory hair cells
   b. place along the cochlea that vibrates the most
   c. intensity of that sound wave
   d. amplitude of that sound wave

11. Which of the following is not true about conduction deafness?
   a. causes high absolute thresholds for sounds
   b. caused by damage to part of the eardrum or middle ear
   c. caused by destruction of auditory hair cells or damage to auditory nerve
   d. hearing aids that amplify sounds are helpful for people afflicted with it

12. The strength of an odor is due to the
   a. place in the olfactory epithelium that is stimulated
   b. the number of olfactory receptors activated
   c. the frequency of the olfactory air wave stimulus
   d. the amplitude of the olfactory air wave stimulus

13. Helen Keller's unusual sensory abilities are explained in your text as most likely attributable to
   a. the brain's ability to compensate for sensory loss
   b. the fact that she did not lose her vision until she was almost 15 years old
   c. the phenomenon known as "traumatic learning and memory"
   d. her early training in art and music

14. The gate control theory was developed to try to explain the perception of
   a. light waves
   b. sound waves
   c. pain
   d. tastes
   e. odors

15. Which of the following is not among the parts of the body containing kinesthetic sense receptors?
    a. auditory hair cells
    b. muscles
    c. joints
    d. the skin
    e. tendons

16. Which of the following is not among the monocular cues involved in the perception of depth?
    a. relative size
    b. linear perspective
    c. convergence
    d. texture
    e. overlap

17. _____ is the perceptual grouping tendency whereby we tend to perceive stimuli that occur close together in time as belonging together.
    a. Spatial proximity
    b. Temporal proximity
    c. Similarity
    d. Common fate
    e. Closure

18. The phi phenomenon refers to the perception of apparent
    a. closeness
    b. similarity
    c. difference
    d. movement
    e. closure

19. Which of the following expressions is used by psychologists to refer to the tendency for sensory information to be attended to, organized, and interpreted in terms of concepts and expectations in the brain?
    a. bottom-up processing
    b. top-down processing
    c. upside-down processing
    d. inside-out processing

20. Which of the following has been used to explain cross-cultural differences in perception, such as in susceptibility to the Muller-Lyer illusion?
    a. the matriarchal society model
    b. the patriarchal society model
    c. the carpentered world theory
    d. the carpeted-world theory
    e. the free-market society model

For each of the following items, circle "T" if the statement is True, and "F" if the statement is False.

21. T F   The absolute threshold is the smallest difference between two stimuli that can be detected or "just noticed."

22. T F   Sensory adaptation involves an increase in the sensitivity and responsiveness to a stimulus or stimuli.

23. T F   Hyperopia is a condition of far-sightedness due to a dysfunction whereby the afflicted person's lenses don't become flat enough to bring nearby objects into focus.

24. T F   When dark adaptation occurs, there is a change from reliance on cones to rods.

25. T F   There is a blind spot in the eye where the optic nerve connects the eye to the brain.

26. T F   The greater the number of light waves that are combined, the greater the saturation or purity of a color.

27. T F   According to the opponent-process theory, neurons that detect yellow are turned-off when visual input is classified as blue, and vice versa.

28. T F   Age differences in taste sensitivity are apparently due to the fact that older people have more taste buds that detect bitterness than do youngsters.

29. T F   Ethnic and gender groups differ in their interpretations of and responses to pain.

30. T F   Euro-Americans and white South Africans have been found to be less susceptible to the Muller-Lyer illusion than are people from Southeast African Zulu culture, or those raised in rural areas of the Phillipines.

F. Teaching-To-Learn Exercise

1. *Let Me Teach You This.*

Write in the space provided below, the five facts, ideas, etc., from this chapter that you'd most like to teach to your own student(s) if you were a teacher. Then, really do try to communicate these facts or ideas to someone in your life; or, pretend to teach this content to a hypothetical or "make-believe" student or class.

2. *Now Answer My Questions.*

Here, write one multiple-choice and one True-False question for each of the facts, ideas, etc., you covered in the "Let Me Teach You This" section of this exercise.

G. Bringing Psychology To Life Exercise

The Gestalt tradition in psychology emphasizes the idea that human experience is best understood by considering the individual's entire framework of thought, feeling, and action. From this Gestalt point of view, the meaning of everything that we see, hear, taste, smell, or feel, is assumed to depend in large part upon the whole context within which the sensory event occurs. In order to conduct a test of the validity of this assumption with regard to the perception of relatively simple stimuli, cut out Stimulus Configurations A and B given in the Stimulus Materials section of this exercise.

Once you've gotten your stimulus materials separated, show Stimulus Configuration A to a total of eight individuals, 4 men and 4 women, each of whom you test individually. Just show them the pattern of lines in Stimulus Configuration A and ask each of them to indicate whether the adjective "Short," "Medium," or "Long" is most accurately descriptive of Line 4. Keep a careful record of what each respondent says in response to your test question regarding Line 4, and the Stimulus Configuration (A or B) to which s/he responded.

Remember, test each of your subjects in this mini-experiment individually with either Stimulus Configuration A or B, but not both. To make your test procedure just a bit more "scientific," you might want to alternate testing first a subject with the A configuration and then one with B, or sort of randomly test subjects with one or another of the two configurations. For the purposes of this experiment, we'll refer to the people whom you test with Stimulus Configuration A as "Group A," and the people to whom you present Stimulus Configuration B as "Group B."

After you've collected the data for this mini-project according to the instructions given above, tally the responses to your test question as follows. For every person who described Line 4 as "Short," score a 1. For every person who saw Line 4 as "Medium," score a 2. And for each subject who described Line 4 as "Long," score a 3.

The next step is to get the arithmetic mean score for each group on the test question. The formula for the mean is:

$$\bar{X} = \sum X/n$$

The term "$\sum X$" means "the sum of all the scores." The "n" here refers to the number of scores. So, in order to get the arithmetic mean of the line length estimation scores for each of your two groups, add up the scores for all of the subjects in each group, and then divide the total by the number of people in that group. Enter these numbers in the appropriate spaces below.

GROUP A

$\sum X =$ $n =$ $\bar{X} =$

GROUP B

$\sum X =$ $n =$ $\bar{X} =$

Given the fact that Line 4 is exactly the same length in Stimulus Configurations A and B, check one of the following to indicate whether you think the results of your mini-experiment here support or fail to support the Gestalt assumption concerning the importance of contextual factors in perception. Then, give an explanation for your answer. In that explanation, draw out any implications you may see in these data for understanding the difference between "subjective" and "objective" aspects of human experience and the "construction of reality."

_____ Yes. These results support the Gestalt assumption.

_____ No. These results do not support the Gestalt assumption.

Explanation:

STIMULUS MATERIALS

Photocopy this page and then cut along the dotted lines to separate the two stimulus configurations shown below.

....

Stimulus Configuration A

      Line 1
      Line 2
      Line 3
      Line 4
      Line 5
      Line 6
      Line 7

....

Stimulus Configuration B

      Line 1
      Line 2
      Line 3
      Line 4
      Line 5
      Line 6
      Line 7

....

Cut out these stimulus configurations along the dotted lines.

Answer Key To Self-Quiz

1. b
2. a
3. e
4. d
5. c
6. b
7. d
8. b
9. e
10. a
11. c
12. b
13. a
14. c
15. a
16. c
17. b
18. d
19. b
20. c
21. F
22. F
23. F
24. T
25. T
26. F
27. T
28. F
29. T
30. F

CHAPTER 4

Consciousness

A. Learning Objectives

After careful, effective study of Chapter 4, you should know:

1. Why psychologists are interested in the study of consciousness.

2. About the multiple bases and levels that define the nature of consciousness, with special attention to:
    a. The possibility of several, simultaneous consciousness;
    b. The way in which the hormone melatonin, the limbic system neural connections, and the processing of information in the cerebral cortex may all simultaneously have effects on consciousness;
    c. The content of consciousness, namely, thoughts, motives, and even feelings of which we are unaware and would much rather not acknowledge to anyone, even ourselves; and
    d. How the content of consciousness may be expanded by experience, with the resulting expansion allowing for new experiences that could not otherwise have been achieved.

3. About what psychologists refer to as "altered states of consciousness, including:
    a. The kinds of physiological and psychological changes that occur in altered states of consciousness;
    b. Some of the reasons why people try to expand or alter their consciousness, such as insights that lead to greater understanding of oneself, variety in sensory experience, and access to otherwise unconscious memories;
    c. Cultural differences in ideas about what types of consciousness are desirable and/or achievable;
    d. Meditation as a means of achieving altered states of consciousness, and what people who meditate believe happens to them when they meditate;
    e. Hypnosis as an altered state of consciousness, how its effects may be understood in terms of brain function, and some of the major ways in which it is used to achieve various sorts of clinical psychological objectives;
    f. The four types of psychoactive drugs, with special attention to:
        (1) the specific drugs in each of these four categories and the physiological as well as psychological effects associated with each of them;
        (2) how addictions to psychoactive drugs may develop, the signs of such dependency; and
        (3) the differences in use of psychoactive drugs both within and across cultures;
    g. Sleep, with special attention to:
        (1) The four major theories which have been proposed to explain the various phenomena of sleep and dreams;
        (2) The four stages of sleep;
        (3) REM sleep as dream sleep, and why it is sometimes referred to as a

"paradoxical" state of consciousness;

(4) The typical sleep cycle and how REM or dream sleep is associated with transitions through the various stages of sleep in that cycle;

(5) The major types of sleep disorders and how they are treated;

(6) The major perspectives on why we dream, and how each of these theoretical views is supported by scientific research on dreams; and

(7) Some of the factors that can influence the manifest content of dreams, and the fundamental assumption of Freudian theory about dreams as a means of understanding the dreamer's unconscious thoughts, feelings, and conflicting motives.

B. Preview/Review Outline Of Key Terms And Concepts

Before you read the corresponding chapter in your text, read over the following outline. It is designed to give you an overview of information presented in the chapter, and how the various elements of that information are related to each other. After reading through the whole chapter and/or before course exams, you may use this outline as a quick review guide. In your reviews, mask off one line of the outline at a time, and try to recite from your memory of the chapter, the information that you expect to appear on the next line or so.

In going over this outline as a preview before reading and studying the chapter, the questions posed in bold print will help to keep you focused on the learning objectives here, and keep you actively involved in the process of achieving those objectives. When using this section as a review, try to answer the questions. Refer back to the chapter in the text for a more detailed feedback check on your mastery of the material, and/or to strengthen your knowledge and understanding wherever you feel the need to do so.

I. Boswell: A Case Study Of Prosopagnosia

What is prosopagnosia, and what does the case study of Boswell suggest about the nature of consciousness?

II. Alternative Perspectives On The Consciousness Of The Researcher And The Participant (Box 4.1)

What method of study has been adopted in the discipline of psychology as a science, and what is the basic assumption underlying the adoption of this method? How and why is the latter assumption questioned by a number of psychologists?

    A. The View Of Physicists Einstein And Bohr And Some Psychologists
    B. Interpretation Of Data And The Researcher's Consciousness
    C. Individual Consciousness And Personal Experience

How does the study of females' responses to "I am" statements illustrate the relevance of personal experience and cultural context to understanding the development of individual differences in consciousness?

114

D. The Focus On Participants' Perspectives On Their Own Behavior

What are some of the ways in which the treatment of people as "participants" rather than "subjects" in psychological research studies are reflected in the methods used in such studies?

III. The Nature of Consciousness: Multiple Bases and Levels

What is meant by a "state" of consciousness? What are the "contents" of consciousness?

    A. The Biological Roots Of Consciousness
        1. Hormones and Daily Biological Rhythms
            a. Circadian Rhythm
            b. Early Birds And Night Owls
            c. Circumstances Of Mismatch With Social Demands
            d. Effects Of Odd Or Highly Variable Work Schedules
            e. And The Hormone Melatonin
            f. Jet Lag And Seasonal Affective Disorder

What is there about the biology of consciousness that might help to explain why people differ in the time of day or night when they seem to feel and function best? What does the hormone melatonin have to do with such differences?

        2. Neural Connections And Consciousness
            a. Studies Of Phantom Limb Pain
            b. Studies Of Brain Surgery Patients
            c. The Construction Of Consciousness
                 Influenced By Experiences Within A Cultural Context

How do the studies of phantom limb pain and brain surgery patients support the idea that nerve connections are the basis for the content of consciousness? Can you give at least one example of the way experience may affect the way an individual's consciousness is "constructed"?

    B. Multiple Levels of Consciousness

What does the idea of "layers" or "levels" of consciousness suggest about differences in how accessible are the various contents of our consciousness?

        1. How Do We Know About The Levels Of Consciousness?
        Remembering A Name After You've Stopped Trying To Remember It
            a. Lucid Dreaming
            b. Subliminal Messages
            c. Clinical Observations (e.g., Surgical Patients Under
                 Anesthesia)

Have you ever had a lucid dream? What do you remember about that experience? What do such experiences suggest about the nature of consciousness?

2. A Hidden And Powerful Unconscious?
    a. Unconscious Knowledge
    b. *Deja Vu*
    c. Intuition
    d. Stereotypes
    e. Psychodynamic Theory
        (1) Freud's View Of The Unconscious
        (2) Unconscious Motivation

Have you ever had a deja vu experience? What do you remember about that experience? How might such experiences be explained in terms of "unconscious knowledge"? According to Freud's view, what is contained in the unconscious and why is it there?

C. Expanding Consciousness: Gaining Alternative Perspectives

What is a recent experience in your own life, of the way in which education can serve as a means toward expanding our consciousness?

1. Expanding the Content of One's Consciousness
    a. Heightening Appreciation For Beauty: Looking At A Blue Vase
        (1) Abandoning Western Impulses
        (2) Changed Perceptions Of Vase
    b. Observations Of Scuba Divers As They Learn To Dive Deeper

In the blue vase experiment, what were participants instructed to try to do, and how were their perceptions of the vase changed by this?

2. Ki, a Cross-cultural Perspective On Consciousness
    Asian Belief In Life Force
        a. Chi in Chinese, Ki In Japanese
        b. In *Aikido*
        c. Demonstration Of Change In Consciousness Akin to *Ki*
        d. Factors Affecting Expansion Of Consciousness
        e. Changes In Consciousness As Analogous To States Of An Ocean

What is Ki or Chi? What simple demonstration is suggested in your text to illustrate the power of a change in consciousness akin to Ki? How might the concept of Ki be used to explain the perception of "increased heaviness" in this demonstration? How might this same change in perception be explained in terms of more conventional scientific logic?

IV. Altered States Of Consciousness: Multiple Conditions

How can you explain the apparent effectiveness of strenuous exercise as a means of producing a change in consciousness characterized by feeling "high" and/or reduction in pain?

A. Meditation: A Mellow Consciousness

1. Focusing Of Attention
2. Transcendental Meditation
   (a) Attention Focused On *Mantra*
   (b) Focus On Breathing In Zen Buddhist Meditation

What are some of the goals of meditation? What are some of the beliefs underlying the practice of meditation? What are some of the self reported effects of meditation by people who practice it?

    B. Hypnosis: Increased Suggestibility
        1. Mesmer's "Animal Magnetism" Approach
        2. Self-Reported Experience Of Hypnotized People
        3. Hypnotic State As Involving A Dissociation Of Consciousness: The "Hidden Observer"
        4. Hypnosis As A Weakening Of Control Of Some Parts Of Brain Over Others

What was the role of Mesmer's "animal magnetism" approach in the history of hypnosis? What are some of the characteristics of hypnotized people? How is hypnosis explained as a "dissociation of consciousness," and what is the role of the "hidden observer" from this point of view? How is hypnosis explained from the point of view that it involves a change in brain organization?

        1. How One Becomes Hypnotized
           a. Relaxation And Focusing Of Attention
           b. Hypnotist's Statements

What are some of the factors involved in individual differences among people in their susceptibility to hypnosis?

        2. Hypnotic Suggestions

What is a posthypnotic suggestion, and what risks are involved in such suggestions with regard to inducing people to behave in uncharacteristically immoral ways?

        3. Uses of Hypnosis
           a. Helping People To Stop Smoking
           b. Reduction In Blood Loss During Surgery
           c. Relieving Pain, Nausea, Dizziness

What is the physiology involved in the control of migraine headache pain by means of hypnosis?

    C. Drugged States: Chemically Changing Consciousness

What is a psychoactive drug? What are some of the drawbacks in the use of such drugs as a means of altering consciousness? What are the three ways in which psychoactive drugs achieve their effects by influencing functions of the nervous system?

1. Depressants

What is the general effect of depressant drugs on the central nervous system?

    a. Opiates Or Narcotics (e.g., Heroin, Morphine)

What is the flower which is the source of heroin and morphine?

    b. Barbiturates

For what kinds of symptoms might a physician prescribe barbiturates?

    c. Alcohol

How does alcohol affect the brain, and what kinds of psychological changes are associated with such effects?

    (1) Gender Perspectives On Alcohol Consumption
        (a) Metabolism Of Alcohol
        (b) Water Content Of Body
        (c) Social Factors

Who tends to drink more, males or females? What are some of the factors associated with such differences in alcohol consumption?

    (2) Ethnic Perspectives On Alcohol Consumption
        (a) Euro-Americans Drink The Most
        (b) Face Flushing, Aboriginal And Asian-Americans

What physiological factor is associated with the face-flushing response to alcohol?

    (3) Cultural Factors In Alcohol Use
        (a) In Aboriginal American Tribes
        (b) In Irish American Culture
        (c) Large Differences Within Ethnic Groups
        (d) In Latino/a Cultures
        (e) Machismo In Various Cultures

What are the two most interesting insights you gained into cultural factors associated with alcohol use from your study of this chapter?

2. Stimulants

What is the effect of stimulants on the central nervous system, and what kinds of changes in consciousness are associated with such effects?

    a. Caffeine

          b. Nicotine
          c. Amphetamine

What happens to the amphetamine user when an amphetamine-based euphoria "wears off"? For what kinds of clinical conditions are amphetamines legally prescribed as medical treatment?

          d. Cocaine
               (1) Retards Uptake Of Both Dopamine And Norepinephrine
               (2) Known as "Crack" In Crystalline Form
     3. Hallucinogens

Why are hallucinogenic drugs so named?

          a. Psychedelic, Mind-Expanding Drugs
          b. PCP (Phencyclidine), Angel Dust
          c. LSD
          d. Marijuana
          e. Inhalants
     4. Drug Tolerance and Addiction
          a. Habituation And Tolerance
          b. Psychological Dependency
          c. Addiction
          d. Withdrawal

What is an addiction? What kinds of symptoms occur when an addicted person stops taking the drug to which s/he is addicted?

     5. Cultural Perspectives on Drug Use
          a. Drugs Taken In Their Natural As Compared To Synthetic Forms
          b. Psychological Escape As Compared To Ritual Use

What is the physiological difference between the use of drugs in their natural as compared to manufactured forms? What psychological differences tend to be associated with this physiological difference? What example is given in your text, of the natural as compared to the synthetic use of a stimulant?

     6. Therapeutic Uses of Drugs
          a. Nembutal And Seconal, Prescription Barbiturates
          b. Prozac
          c. Valium

How does Prozac affect the nervous system, and what psychological effects are thereby produced?

V. Sleep: Multiple States and Multiple Contents

What are the essential elements that distinguish the repair theory, from the synaptic connection maintenance and ecological or adaptive theories concerning the need to sleep?

    A. The Stages of Sleep: The Sequence of Our Sleeping Consciousness

What research method has been used to identify the various stages of sleep

        1. Stages 1 Through 4

What is hypnagogic imagery, and during what stage of sleep does it tend to occur?

        2. REM Sleep

What words are represented by the acronym "REM"? Why is REM sleep sometimes referred to as "paradoxical sleep"?

        3. Sleep Cycles

What is a typical sleep cycle with regard to changes in the various stages of sleep? Also, about how much time tends to elapse between REM periods, and how long do the REM periods tend to last?

            a. Individual Differences In Sleep Patterns
            b. Age Differences And Melatonin
    B. Sleep Disorders: Problems of Our Sleeping State
        1. Insomnia
            a. Pseudoinsomnia (Subjective Insomnia)
            b. Use Of Sedatives

What risks or disadvantages are involved in the use of sedatives as a means of treating insomnia? What are some of the "natural" or "drug free" alternatives to the use of sedatives for such purposes?

        2. Narcolepsy
            a. Immediate REM Sleep
            b. Treatment By Stimulant And Antidepressant Drugs
        3. NREM Sleep Disorders
            a. Somnambulism
            b. Bed Wetting
            c. Sleep Apnea
                (1) Incidence In Premature Infants And Adults Who Snore
                (2) And Sudden Infant Death Syndrome
            d. Nightmares And Night Terrors

What are the symptoms of sleep apnea? How does a night terror differ from a nightmare?

    C. Dreams: The Content of Our Sleeping Consciousness

1. A Neural Perspective on Why We Dream
    a. Activation-Synthesis Theory
    b. Computer Model

What is the essential difference between the activation-synthesis and computer model perspectives on dreaming? What kind of research evidence is there to support the one of these two theories which seems to make the most sense to you?

2. A Sensory Perspective On What We Dream
    a. Manifest Content And Recent Waking Experience
    b. Dreams Of People Who Lose Their Sight
    c. Dream Content Counterbalanced To Waking Life Experience
    d. Manifest Content And Sensations Experienced In Sleep

What is the essential idea of the sensory perspective on dream content? In your view, what is the most persuasive research evidence supporting the sensory perspective?

3. A Cognitive Perspective on What We Dream

What is the closest any of your own dreams has come to serving as a way of thinking about or maybe even solving a problem in your life?

4. A Psychodynamic Perspective on What We Dream
    a. Freud's Theory
        (1) Wish-Fulfilling Fantasies
        (2) Latent Content Of Dreams
            (a) Reflection Of Unconscious Conflicts And Motives
            (b) Manifest Content As Symbolic
            (c) Dreams As "Royal Road To Unconscious"
            (d) Dream Analysis
            (e) Condensation Of Dream Characters
            (f) Displacement Of Emotion In Dream
            (g) Some Dreams Simply Trivial Snapshots
    b. Alternative Views As To Why We Forget Our Dreams

From the standpoint of Freud's psychodynamic perspective, how are unconscious images assumed to be represented in our dreams? From your own point of view, what seems to be the most reasonable hypothesis as to why we often tend to forget our dreams?

C. Self-Generated Questions: What's In This One For Me?

Most people come to the first course in psychology expecting to learn some things which will help them to better understand themselves, other people in their lives, and/or the nature of life in the world in which they live. Along these same lines, students of psychology often look forward to discovering things about human behavior and experience which may help them to improve their own life by developing their talents, technical skills, knowledge and abilities, and/or the quality or their relationships with other people. On the basis of such self-interest, which tends to provide a framework in terms of which new learning becomes personally meaningful and thus easier to remember, write down a few questions in the space below, about the subject matter covered in this chapter. After reading and studying the chapter, come back to see how any of what you've learned may be useful to you in finding answers to these questions.

D. Completion Items

The words in the margins of this exercise are the ones that correctly complete the sentence on the corresponding line. To get the most out of this exercise, you should try to avoid looking at these words in the margin until after you've filled in the corresponding blanks with the words you think best complete the sentences. So, begin the exercise by covering up all of the margin words with a piece of paper. Then, for each blank, write in the word which you think completes the sentence. Even if you're not sure as to the word, write in your best guess, preferably in pencil so you can erase and re-write any incorrect responses you may make here.

After writing in your "answer," slide the paper covering up the margin words down just far enough to see the word for the blank you just filled-in. For each blank that you fill-in correctly, put a check mark (√) after your answer. If the word you wrote in doesn't match the word corresponding to that blank, mark an (X) next to your response and go on to the next blank. It's probably a good idea to go back to the text and try to strengthen your learning related to topic coverage that corresponds in the textbook chapter to those blanks which you filled-in incorrectly, since those items signal a weak link in your concept mastery chain for this chapter.

1. _____ is a disorder in which the afflicted person is unable   Prosopagnosia
to recognize faces.

2. Psychologists who question the objectivity of scientific study, argue
that _____ of research data are almost inevitably influenced   interpretations
by the scientist's own consciousness, as determined by his/her personal
experiences, socioeconomic class, race, and gender. The latter view is
supported by studies such as the one in which responses to the word
"_____" were found to differ among female respondents   passive

who differed in their cultural background. An approach to data gathering which is advocated by some psychologists as an alternative which allows for representation of individual differences in participants' consciousness, is the open-ended _____.

interview

3. Psychologists think of two characteristics of consciousness. First, consciousness is a _____, or a temporary condition, such as being asleep. Second, consciousness has _____, which is comprised of the sensations, thoughts, and feelings one is _____ of having when in any particular temporary condition.

state
content

aware

4. Our bodies function according to a _____ rhythm, a 24-hour cycle of biological changes. Levels of the hormone _____ seem to play a role in determining these rhythms.

circadian

melatonin

5. Evidence for the fact that nerve connections are the basis for the _____ of consciousness derives from a variety of sources, such as observations concerning so-called "_____ limb" experiences reported by very recent amputees, and the reports of specific feelings or memories by awake brain surgery patients when particular nerves in their amygdala or _____ are stimulated.

content
phantom

hippocampus

But the nerves do not send information about every stimulus or memory we have. So, ultimately, our consciousness is constructed by the way in which we _____ information about the world. Accordingly, multiple biological influences combine with experience and _____ influences to shape our consciousness.

process

cultural

6. The existence of multiple levels of consciousness is confirmed by the phenomenon of _____ dreaming, wherein the dreamer is simultaneously aware of what is happening in the dream and that s/he is dreaming. A _____ message is one which apparently registers in the mind without conscious awareness of it.

lucid

subliminal

7. _____ is an expression that refers to a subjective feeling that a situation has been experienced before. An _____ is an insight that appears to have been achieved without thought. According to Sigmund Freud, the _____ is the site of socially unacceptable desires and impulses that motivate behaviors and are sometimes revealed in dreams.

Deja vu

intuition
unconscious

8. A _____ is a prejudgment bias in favor of or against a group of people or some characteristic. The result of the exercise in which a researcher had subjects abandon their impulses to mentally

prejudice

grab hold of or analyze a vase, was that the subjects'
_____ of the vase were changed.   perceptions

9. In Asia there is a belief in a "_____" called <u>chi</u> in   life force
Chinese and <u>ki</u> in Japanese. Consciousness of <u>ki</u> is used to increase
strength, improve balance, promote relaxation, or defend oneself as
in the martial art known as _____.   aikido

10. When people are in an _____ state of consciousness,   altered
their arousal levels, moods, and perceptiveness are changed. Fasting,
prayer, and other _____ ceremonies are cultural methods   religious
used to produce a trance or change in consciousness. Strenuous
exercise can also produce such changes, and can also lessen pain
because exercise activates the production of _____,   endorphins
neurohormones which are the body's own, natural pain killers.

11. People who meditate believe that in order to reach a state of peace
and comfort, it is necessary to focus one's _____. Zen   attention
Buddhists do this by focusing on their _____.   breathing

12. Psychologists who believe that a hypnotic state is distinct from other
experiences often think that hypnosis involves a dissociation or
_____ of consciousness into two separate streams of   split
awareness. One part of consciousness is paying attention to what the
hypnotist is saying, while the other part is a hidden _____,   observer
watching what is going on during the hypnosis. Hypnotizable people
tend to have vivid _____ and become engrossed or totally   imaginations
absorbed in their thoughts or activities. The effectiveness of hypnosis in
relieving pain depends, to a great extent, on the pain sufferer's
_____ to hypnosis. As a means of relieving the discomfort   susceptibility
due to _____ headaches, hypnosis works by helping the   migraine
client learn how to reduce the swelling of arteries in his/her head.

13. _____ drugs such as cocaine, primarily affect the   Psychoactive
nervous system by influencing neurotransmitters in the brain. In this
class of drugs, the _____ are those which slow the central   depressants
nervous system, and include opiates which are sometimes referred to
as _____ -- such as heroin and morphine, and   narcotics
barbiturates that are sometimes used in sleeping pills.

14. _____ is the most widely-abused of the depressant drugs.   Alcohol
It is a drug which impairs judgment, coordination, balance, depth perception,
thinking, memory and _____ time -- which is the speed with   reaction
one can respond to stimuli.

15. One reason why females tend to drink less alcohol than do males,
whatever their ethnic group, is that females have smaller amounts

of an enzyme that affects the _____ of alcohol than do males.   metabolism
Also, females have less _____ in their bodies than do males,   water
so that the same amount of alcohol is more heavily concentrated in females
than in males. Asian Americans who exhibit the _____ reaction   flush
to alcohol, report more positive and intense feelings of intoxication than do
those who don't show this response.   Acculturated Latina-Americans, that
is, those who are culturally more similar to _____-Americans,   Euro
tend to be heavier drinkers than less acculturated Latina Americans. In
applying the concept of _____ to try to explain why males   machismo
drink more than do females in Latino/a cultures, it is important to note
that behaviors that appear to be culturally-based are sometimes more
accurately explained in terms of _____ status.   socioeconomic

16. In contrast to depressants, _____, such as caffeine,   stimulants
nicotine, amphetamines, and cocaine, alter the state of consciousness by
increasing or speeding up activity in the central nervous system.
Nicotine increases dopamine secretion and triggers acetylcholine receptor
sites, so smokers often say that it increases their _____.   alertness
But since smoking relieves symptoms smokers start to experience after
not having smoked for, what seems to them, a long time, they often also
say that smoking tends to _____ them. Amphetamines,   relax
informally known as speed, uppers, or pep pills, retard the
reuptake of _____, so that the amount of that neurohormone   norepinephrine
left in synapses continues to stimulate neurons. This is why people who take
such drugs feel aroused, excited, self-confident, alert, and energetic.
Cocaine retards the reuptake of both dopamine and norepinephrine, and
when smoked in its crystalline form, known as _____, gives   crack
the user a rush of energy within seconds; but the rush lasts only about
20 minutes, after which the person "_____," feeling anxious   crashes
depressed, and craving more of the drug.

17. Hallucinogens are _____, meaning mind-expanding,   psychedelic
drugs that produce hallucinations. Just a trace of the hallucinogen
_____ -- short for lysergic acid diethylamide-- can cause   LSD
hallucinogenic experiences, called "trips," that can range from mildly
pleasant to totally terrifying.

18. When some psychoactive drugs are taken repeatedly, a body can
build up a _____, becoming so physically habituated to the   tolerance
drug that increasing amounts of it are needed to produce the desired
effect. An _____ is a physical dependence on a drug,   addiction
wherein discontinuation of its use results in unpleasant feelings
known as _____ symptoms, which may include nausea,   withdrawal
abdominal cramps, headaches, depression, and difficulty sleeping.

19. Studying drug use only from the perspective of U. S. culture gives a _____ picture of human drug use. In many cultures, drugs are taken in their natural forms rather than the _____ or manufactured forms found in the United States. In such natural forms, drugs enter the blood stream more _____ than do the same drugs in their refined forms. Such natural forms of drugs are less _____-forming, produce less intense changes of consciousness, and result in less impairment of the drug user's behavior than do refined drugs.

distorted

synthetic

slowly

habit

20. Nembutal and Seconal are prescription _____ used to treat psychological disorders such as the sleep disorder insomnia. The drug Valium is a _____, which increases the synaptic transmission of GABA, inhibits excitatory neurotransmitters, and is used to treat anxiety, irritability, guilt, and sleep disorders.

barbiturates

tranquilizer

21. The _____ theory argues that we need to sleep so as to replenish ourselves. According to the ecological or _____ theory, we sleep so that we won't harm ourselves and waste energy moving about during the night when we cannot see well.

repair

adaptive

22. The first stage of sleep is a stage of _____ sleep. REM sleep is considered _____ sleep because it is characterized by what seem to be contradictory states. People in this stage of sleep look as though they are about to _____, but waking them is very difficult. Overall, in the first few hours of a full night's sleep, people spend more total time in Stages _____ than in other stages. Generally, dreams are about _____ minutes apart, with the first REM period lasting an average of only about _____ minutes. However, the REM period at the _____ of the night's sleep can last as long as an hour. Age differences in sleep patterns are apparently due, at least in part, to the fact that levels of the neurohormone known as _____ tend to decline after childhood; this decrease may explain why elderly people tend to sleep _____ than do younger people.

light

paradoxical

awaken

3 and 4

90

10

end

malatonin

less

23. _____ is a usually temporary sleep disorder characterized by difficulty falling or staying asleep. The _____ drugs people sometimes take to alleviate this condition are addictive and people can build up a tolerance for them. A safer way to treat this condition is by eating or drinking milk products which induce relaxation naturally as a function of the fact that they contain the amino acid known as

_____.

Insomnia

sedative

tryptophan

_____ is the apparently hereditary sleep disorder in which the person is prone to falling asleep suddenly. The condition known as _____ is more commonly referred to as sleep walking. People

Narcolepsy

somnambulism

with the sleep disorder of sleep _____ do not breathe properly   apnea
when asleep, and may stop breathing, wake up briefly, and then gasp for
breath. A night _____ is a NREM sleep disorder taking place   terror
in Stage 4 sleep, in which the person suddenly wakes up sweating and
breathing heavily.

24. According to the activation-_____ of dreams, dreams   synthesis
have no inherent meaning and are just a manifestation of the brain's
efforts to understand and impose order on otherwise chaotic, random
neural signals that occur in the brain during sleep.

25. From the perspective of the _____ model, dreams serve   computer
as a check-up period during which nerve connections in the brain are
checked and expanded, unimportant thoughts and irrelevant, unneeded
information erased. One line of evidence supporting the latter view, is that
when people are deprived of _____ sleep, their ability to   REM
remember newly-learned information is impaired. This theory is also
supported by research indicating that when animals are in REM sleep
after being exposed to information vital to their _____,   survival
only those neurons triggered when they were learning that material
are reactivated.

26. From the standpoint of the sensory perspective, the
_____ content of dreams -- that is, what we remember   manifest
about the dream's story line, scenes, and situations, usually reflects
a person's beliefs and recent sensory and social experiences while
awake.

27. According to the _____ perspective, dreams are a   cognitive
way of thinking about and solving problems.

28. To explain why we often forget our dreams, Sigmund Freud
argued that while the manifest content of a dream may seem
psychologically meaningless, the _____ content of a   latent
dream reflects a person's unconscious conflicts and motives. From this
_____ perspective, the latent or hidden content of desires,   psychodynamic
fears, conflicts, and impulses are often represented _____,   symbolically
so that characters, behaviors, events, objects, and circumstances in
dreams stand for underlying psychological concerns. Thus, Freud
regarded dreams as the "royal road to the _____,"   unconscious
which could be understood by analyzing their content. Freud also
believed that the meaning of dreams is also hidden by what he called
_____ of characters, so that a single character in a dream   condensation
might actually represent several actual people. Sometimes, Freud
claimed, the meaning of a dream is hidden by _____, in   displacement
which important emotions in the dream are held by unimportant
persons such as bystanders to the main action of the dream, or even by

animals, or objects. Further complicating interpretations of dreams, Freud argued, some dreams are simply trivial snapshots from the day and have no _____ meaning.   hidden

E. Self-Quiz

For each of the following items, circle the letter which precedes the correct alternative.

1. Prosopagnosia is a(n)
   a. motor dysfunction
   b. disorder in which the person expresses emotion inappropriately
   c. inability to recognize faces
   d. language disturbance

2. Melatonin is commonly prescribed as treatment for all of the following except
   a. jet lag
   b. sleeping difficulties
   c. seasonal affective disorder
   d. multiple personality disorder

3. _____ perceptions are those that register in the mind without conscious awareness.
   a. Threshold
   b. Subliminal
   c. Liminal
   d. Gestalt

4. Which of the following is not among the kinds of phenomena invoked by psychologists as reflecting different levels of consciousness?
   a. surgical patients under anesthesia "hearing" what is being said by the medical team during the surgical procedure
   b. deja vu experiences
   c. intuition
   d. body area differences in thresholds for perception of tactile stimuli

5. In the experiment on expansion of consciousness in which the task involved looking at a blue vase, participants were instructed to
   a. concentrate only on the base of the vase
   b. concentrate only on the top of the vase
   c. try not to think analytically or series of thoughts about the vase
   d. think only about how much water or flowers the vase could contain

6. _____ is the "life force" that acupuncturists try to influence by putting needles into their patients.
    a. Aikido
    b. Karma
    c. Mantra
    d. Chi

7. Zen Buddhists meditate by focusing on
    a. their own mortality
    b. their own breathing
    c. memories of their happiest moments in life
    d. their most intense emotions of fear, love, anger, etc.

8. Which of the following is not among the three ways in which psychoactive drugs induce their respective effects?
    a. by increasing the activity of adrenergic osteols in the cerebellum
    b. by increasing the number of neurotransmitters released at a synapse
    c. by decreasing the number of neurotransmitters released at a synapse
    d. by preventing or accelerating the uptake of neurotransmitters

9. Which of the following is most likely to prevent norepinephrine and dopamine from being reabsorbed at the synapse?
    a. heroin
    b. barbiturates
    c. alcohol
    d. cocaine
    e. Rogaine

10. According to research cited in your text, which of the following tends to be associated with more positive and intense feelings of intoxication by alcohol among Asian Americans?
    a. hypertension
    b. low self-esteem
    c. a facial flush reaction
    d. bipolar personality disorder

11. Which of the following is not true about amphetamines?
    a. As "street drugs," they are referred to as "uppers."
    b. They accelerate the reuptake of norepinephrine.
    c. They are legally prescribed by physicians to treat attention deficit disorder.
    d. they are legally prescribed by physicians to treat asthma.

12. Which of the following is not classified technically as an hallucinogenic drug?
    a. marijuana
    b. phencyclidine (PCP, or Angel Dust)
    c. LSD
    d. cocaine

13. Which of the following is not true about drugs in their natural as compared to their synthetic forms?
    a. They enter the bloodstream more slowly.
    b. They produce less intense changes in consciousness.
    c. They are more habit forming.
    d. They result in less impairment of the drug user's behavior.

14. According to the _____ theory, we sleep so that we won't harm ourselves and waste energy moving about at night.
    a. repair
    b. psychodynamic
    c. ecological
    d. cognitive
    e. synaptic connection maintenance

15. Which of the following is most appropriately described as "paradoxical sleep," characterized as it is by what seem to be quite contradictory states of consciousness?
    a. Stage 1 sleep
    b. Stage 2 sleep
    c. Stages 3 and 4 sleep
    d. REM sleep
    e. Non-REM sleep

16. Which of the following is likely to be the most effective way of falling asleep naturally, without the use of drugs?
    a. drinking a glass of milk
    b. doing some vigorous exercise just before bedtime
    c. thinking and planning one's activities for the next day
    d. concentrating on solving the most challenging problems in one's life

17. _____ is the technical term used to describe the condition wherein the person is prone to falling asleep very suddenly.
    a. Reverse insomnia
    b. Narcolepsy
    c. Somnambulism
    d. Apnea

18. The _____ theory argues that dreams result from the brain's attempts to understand and impose order on the otherwise chaotic, random neural signals that occur in the brain during sleep.
    a. Psychodynamic
    b. NREM
    c. Computer model
    d. Activation-synthesis

19. Which of the following theories assumes that the unconscious meaning of dreams is represented symbolically in the manifest content?
    a. psychodynamic theory
    b. activation synthesis theory
    c. the NREM model
    d. cognitive theory

20. The results of a study cited in your text, indicated that women of color were more likely than Euro-American women, to respond to the word "passive" as meaning "_____."
    a. laid-back and easy going
    b. dull and lazy
    c. not saying what I really think
    d. repressed anger

For each of the following items, circle "T" if the statement is True, and "F" if the statement is False.

21. T F   A lucid dream is one which apparently comes true in waking life.

22. T F   Deja vu experiences represent one type of subliminal perception.

23. T F   Endorphins are the body's own natural pain killers.

24. T F   There is still no research evidence to support the view that hypnosis can be used effectively to relieve pain.

25. T F   Alcohol is a stimulant.

26. T F   Research has shown that females have smaller amounts of an enzyme that affects the metabolism of alcohol.

27. T F   Latina Americans who are culturally like Euro-Americans, tend to be heavier drinkers than less acculturated Latina Americans.

28. T F   From the standpoint of Freud's psychodynamic theory, dreams reflect the content of the unconscious.

29. T F   Traditional research methods in psychology ensure objective descriptions and interpretations of the behaviors observed, which are independent of the researcher's own consciousness.

30. T F   Regarding the people whose behaviors constitute the data in a psychological study as "participants" rather than "subjects," is consistent with the goal of acknowledging their own, individual consciousness.

F. Teaching-To-Learn Exercise
1. *Let Me Teach You This.*

Write in the space provided below, the five facts, ideas, etc., from this chapter that you'd most like to teach to your own student(s) if you were a teacher. Then, really do try to communicate these facts or ideas to someone in your life; or, pretend to teach this content to a hypothetical or "make-believe" student or class.

2. *Now Answer My Questions.*

Here, write one multiple-choice and one True-False question for each of the facts, ideas, etc., you covered in the "Let Me Teach You This" section of this exercise.

G. Bringing Psychology To Life Exercise

1. Our bodies function according to the "biological clocks" of what are called circadian rhythms. The fact of the matter, however, is that these "clocks" are set somewhat differently for different people. Thus, some of us are more "lark-like," in that we tend to be "morning people." Others of us are more "owl-like," and tend to dread having to do anything during the early hours of the day besides sleep through them, feeling much more awake and vital in the nighttime hours.

    a. When it comes to circadian rhythm style, are you more "lark" or "owl"?
    b. How long have you felt the kind of circadian rhythm pattern you refer to in "a"?
    c. What is there about the way in which you try to live your life that reflects your own circadian rhythm style?
    d. Give an example of a different circadian rhythm style from your own, based on observations of a person whom you know well.
    e. How do you think that a lack of harmony between two people who are in an intimate relationship with one another (e.g., one is a "lark" and the other is an "owl,") might affect

the quality of that relationship? Give a hypothetical example or two to explain your answer here.

2. The concept of *deja vu* refers to the very common but strange feeling that something is happening to us in exactly the same way that it has happened to us before? Can you describe such an experience in your own life, relating where, when and how it happened, and the people, if any, who were part of the experience?

3. People can and often do seek to experience altered states of consciousness by a variety of means from the use of drugs to exercise to meditation. Can you describe the most memorable such experience in your own life, relating where it occurred, the circumstances which evoked this experience, and the feelings it evoked in you?

4. Psychoactive drugs can be classified as (a) depressants, (b) stimulants, or (c) hallucinogens. Use and even abuse of such drugs is widespread in our society. For the purposes of this exercise, think of a person you know who is using or abusing such a drug or drugs (e.g., barbiturates, alcohol, caffeine, nicotine, amphetamines, cocaine, PCP, or marijuana).

    a. What is (are) the drug or drugs involved here?

    b. What observations could you invoke to support the argument that this person is either using or abusing the drug or drugs you note in "a" above here?

    c. What is your best guess as to how this person started into the pattern of drug use/abuse

        to which you refer here?

    d. How do you feel the kind of drug use/abuse you refer to here is affecting this person's life right now?

    e. How do you think the kind of drug use or abuse you refer to here is likely to affect this person's life in the future?

5. With regard to the various theories of dreaming (i.e., activation-synthesis, computer model, sensory perspective, cognitive theory, or psychodynamic theory):

    a. Which one of these theories seems to make the most sense to you personally? Give an example from your own dream experience which seems to support that theory?

b. Which of the theories noted above seems to make the least sense to you? Give an example from your own dream experience that seems to contradict that theory?

Answer Key To Self-Quiz

1. c
2. d
3. b
4. d
5. c
6. d
7. b
8. a
9. d
10. c
11. b
12. d
13. c
14. c
15. d
16. a
17. b
18. d
19. a
20. c
21. F
22. F
23. T
24. F
25. F
26. T
27. T
28. T
29. F
30. T

CHAPTER 5

Learning

A. Learning Objectives

After careful, effective study of Chapter 5, you should:

1. Have some increased awareness of how the cultural context of people's learning history can help to explain all kinds of psychological differences among them in their characteristic ways of thinking, feeling and acting.

2. Learn what is meant by the idea of "biological readiness" for learning, and how such readiness has been identified in psychological research.

3. Learn about "critical periods" and "sensitive periods" in the capacity for learning, and how these concepts are relevant to understanding individual differences among immigrants in the extent to which they speak with "a foreign accent."

4. Develop some preliminary perspective on how knowledge of the biology of human development provides support for the view that learning is crucial for human survival.

5. Learn about the principles and applications of classical conditioning, including:
    a. The elements of the method by means of which a response evoked naturally and automatically by one stimulus, can be trained to occur to an entirely different stimulus;
    b. Examples of how classical conditioning can help to explain how we learn all kinds of things in the course of our lives, such as emotional responses to the sight of our own blood, and even taste aversions;
    c. "Higher order conditioning," how it operates, and how it helps to explain the complicated ways in which all kinds of stimuli can become cues to which we respond in quite reliable ways;
    d. "Stimulus generalization," and how it helps to explain how a response associated with one stimulus may be evoked by other, similar stimuli;
    e. "Discrimination," and how it helps to explain differentiation in our responses to the many stimuli in our environment; and
    f. How the concept of "extinction" and the method of "counter conditioning" are relevant to the "undoing" or modification of classically-conditioned behaviors.

6. Learn about the principles and applications of operant conditioning, including:
    a. How the methods of operant conditioning presuppose the importance of positive and negative consequences of our behaviors as factors critical in the control and manipulation of those behaviors;
    b. Why the so-called "law of effect" is regarded as the basic principle underlying operant conditioning;
    c. Reinforcement, how it relates to the law of effect, and the difference between positive

and negative reinforcement in their effects on behavior in everyday life situations;

d. The difference between escape and avoidance learning;

e. The technical meaning of "punishment" from the standpoint of the psychology of learning, and cross-cultural differences in the way parents use punishment as a disciplinary technique;

f. The difference between what psychologists refer to as "primary" and "secondary" reinforcers, and how everyday life behavior is affected by them;

g. The so-called "schedules of reinforcement," how they work, and the kinds of everyday life situations in which our behavior is affected by them;

h. What is meant by the term "shaping" of behavior, and how it is implemented in the method of "successive approximations;"

i. How lack of reinforcement may have destructive effects on people's lives, and how it may explain wide ranging instances of apparently dysfunctional behaviors and coping styles;

j. How a condition known as "learned helplessness" can be produced in laboratory animals, and how such research may provide insights into human responses to comparable situations;

k. How the concepts of generalization and discrimination of behaviors acquired by operant conditioning may be applied to understand the way response patterns develop in everyday life;

l. How the process of extinction occurs for a response acquired by operant conditioning, and how it may be implemented in the modification of behaviors;

m. How the concept of "spontaneous recovery" is applied to describe the reappearance of operant conditioned behaviors that seem to have been extinguished;

n. How operant counter conditioning may be implemented to weaken a learned or even over learned response;

o. The fundamental differences between classical and instrumental conditioning, and how conditioning principles may be used to describe and explain the socialization process as people grow up within a particular culture;

p. How the principles of classical and operant conditioning are used in psychotherapeutic situations, as illustrated by application of the behavior modification technique known as "systematic desensitization" in the treatment of anxiety or fear responses; and

q. How operant and classical conditioning principles are being applied to help save the California condor from extinction.

7. About observational learning by what psychologists refer to as "modeling," with special attention to,

a. The "requirements" for such learning to occur according to social learning theory;

b. How emotional responses may be acquired by the combination of observational learning and classical conditioning known as vicarious classical conditioning; and

c. How the acquisition of social behaviors may be influenced by the learning of what psychologists call "scripts," how these scripts develop in a cultural context and may be invoked to explain cultural differences in "customary" behaviors, and the way in which misinterpretations of behavior may arise in instances where the scripts we learn are "unshared" from one cultural context to another.

8. How observational learning without apparent reinforcement may take a "latent" form, so that we're not even aware of what we've learned, and how "insight" learning occurs.

9. Something about ways in which gender, culture, and race may influence what and how we learn, with special attention to:
 a. The way differences in the nature of individuals' experiences are at the root of differences in learning among people of different genders, cultures, and races and what such differences mean for students of the psychology of learning;
 b. Gender differences in learning, especially:
  (1) With regard to learning math; and
  (2) The relevance of social and cultural norms to such differences;
 c. Cultural differences in learning in collectivist as compared to individualist cultural contexts, as illustrated by comparison of the values and norms characteristic of various cultural groups represented in American society; and
 d. Racial differences in learning, especially with regard to an analysis of the kinds of behaviors for which African Americans have been reinforced in America, and how an appreciation of race-relevant realities of life in this society can facilitate understanding of "minority group behaviors."

B. Preview/Review Outline Of Key Terms and Concepts

Before you read the corresponding chapter in your text, read over the following outline. It is designed to give you an overview of information presented in the chapter, and how the various elements of that information are related to each other. After reading through the whole chapter and/or before course exams, you may use this outline as a quick review guide. In your reviews, mask off one line of the outline at a time, and try to recite from your memory of the chapter, the information that you expect to appear on the next line or so.

In going over this outline as a preview before reading and studying the chapter, the questions posed in bold print will help to keep you focused on the learning objectives here, and keep you actively involved in the process of achieving those objectives. When using this section as a review, try to answer the questions. Refer back to the chapter in the text for a more detailed feedback check on your mastery of the material, and/or to strengthen your knowledge and understanding wherever you feel the need to do so.

How is the "C" performance of every student in a classroom of Aboriginal Hawaiian students explained in the anecdote which introduces the content of this chapter? What is "learning" anyway?

I. Humans are Ready to Learn: A Biological Readiness

What kinds of behaviors do the members of various species seem to be particularly "ready" to learn? Can you give at least one example of such "biological readiness"?

 A. Critical and Sensitive Periods for Learning

What is the difference between "critical" and "sensitive" periods? How does the behavior of a duckling following its mother fit the definition of "critical period"? How does language learning seem to fit the definition of a "sensitive period"?

    B. The Importance of Learning for Human Survival
        1. Connected and Unconnected Neurons at Birth
        2. Genetic Foundations of Capacity for Learning

What seems to be the primary ability which has permitted the human species to survive over the ages?

II. Conditioning: Learning by Forming Associations
    A. Classical Conditioning

With regard to Pavlov's studies of salivation and digestion in dogs, what was the (a) Unconditioned Stimulus (UCS), (b) Unconditioned Response (UCR), (c) Conditioned Stimulus, and (d) Conditioned Response? What was the procedure by which the "conditioning" was achieved in these historic studies?

        1. Commonly Classically-Conditioned Behaviors

How may emotional responses such as becoming upset at the sight of blood or taste aversions be explained as the result of classical conditioning?

        2. Higher-Order Conditioning

How might Pavlov have used higher-order conditioning in the training of dogs?

        3. Generalization

How might an emotional response to the sight of anyone's blood be explained as a kind of "generalization" of a classically conditioned response?

        4. Discrimination
            a. In Pavlov's Experimental Situation
            b. In Response to Sight of Blood
        5. Extinction and Counter conditioning
            a. Eliminating CS-UCS Linkage
                (1) In Pavlov's Experimental Situation
                (2) In Response to Sight of Blood
            b. Counter conditioning

How is the original CR weakened in the method known as "counterconditioning"?

    B. Operant Conditioning

What is the law of effect, and what does it have to do with operant conditioning?

    1. Reinforcement
        a. Positive Reinforcement

What is positive reinforcement, and how might it lead to superstitious behaviors?

        b. Negative Reinforcement
            (1) Escape Learning
            (2) Avoidance Learning

What is the fundamental difference between escape and avoidance learning?

    2. Punishment
        a. Negative Consequences
        b. Decreased Probability of Behavior
        c. Negative Effects

What are some of the negative effects associated with the use of physical punishment as a means of disciplining children? How do differences between parents in Japan as compared to parents in the United States in the way they use punishment to discipline their children reflect value differences between the two cultures?

    3. Primary and Secondary Reinforcers

What is the essential difference between primary and secondary reinforcers? Can you give an example of each of these types of reinforcement?

    4. Schedules of Reinforcement
        a. Continuous vs. Intermittent Schedule Of Reinforcement
        b. Fixed Ratio Schedule
        c. Fixed Interval Schedule
        d. Variable Ratio Schedule
        e. Variable Interval Schedule
    5. Shaping

In what sense is the concept of "successive approximations" relevant to the operant conditioning method known as "shaping"?

        a. Teaching A Boy to Read Quietly
        b. Training Pigeons to Help in Coast Guard Rescue Missions
    6. Lack of Reinforcement
        a. Low Sense of Self-Worth
        b. Minority Group Members' Motivation to Do Well in School
        c. Women's Response to Sex Discrimination in the Work Place
        d. Learned Helplessness

(1) In Laboratory Experiments Using Rats as Subjects

(2) Southeast Asian Refugees

What were the experimental conditions under which learned helplessness was observed in laboratory studies using rats as subjects?

       7. Generalization

How might the concept of generalization be used to explain why a person routinely checks coin-return slots in public telephone booths?

       8. Discrimination

           a. Restricts Generalization

           b. The "Niagara Falls" Routine Anecdote

       9. Extinction and Counter conditioning

           a. Removal of Positive Consequences

           b. Spontaneous Recovery

           c. Counter conditioning, The Rewarding Of Competing Responses

Can you given an example of the application of counter conditioning to change behavior in an everyday life situation?

    C. Comparing the Two Types of Conditioning

       a. Classical Conditioning

           (1) Associations Between Stimuli

           (2) Stimulus Occurs Before the Response

           (3) Explains Involuntary, Physiological, Emotional Reactions

       b. Operant Conditioning

           (1) Associations Between Behaviors and Consequences

           (2) Reward or Punishment Occurs After the Behavior

           (3) Explains Socialization

How might you use the concepts of operant conditioning to explain how cultural standards of behavior are transmitted from one generation to another?

    D. Conditioning in Psychotherapy

       1. Behavior Modification

       2. Systematic Desensitization

           a. A Form of Counter conditioning

           b. Relaxation Response is Trained to Compete With Fear

           c. Anxiety Hierarchy

Explain how the method of systematic desensitization might be used to modify a person's irrational fear of going to the dentist?

III. Modeling: Learning by Observing

What was found in Bandura's classical studies in which children watched adults punching and kicking a large Bobo? What is vicarious classical conditioning, and what does it have to do with the study of modeling or observational learning?

      A. Applications--How Learning Principles Are Saving Condors (Box 5.1)
            1. Improving the Survival Rate of Condors Born in Captivity
            2. Planting Fake Power Poles In Zoo's Holding Pen
            3. Teaching Condors to Avoid People
      B. Scripts
            1. Social Knowledge
            2. Cultural Scripts
                  a. *Sympatia* as Example of a Latino/a Script
                  b. Emotional Expressiveness In Italian vs. British Cultures
                  c. Japanese Americans' Response to Offer of Food as Guests
            3. Unshared Scripts

How can unshared scripts result in the misinterpretation of behaviors? Can you give an example of such misinterpretation?

      C. Latent Learning and Insight Learning
            1. Occurs Without Our Awareness
            2. Implies Cognitive Abilities In Learning
            3. Insight Learning

What is the example of insight learning cited in your text, based on Kohler's work with chimps?

IV. Gender, Culture, and Race: Influences on Learning

What is the argument presented in your text, in support of the view that psychologists should study more than just one group of people?

      A. Gender Perspectives on What is Learned
            1. In Learning Math
            2. Differences in Reinforcement and Interest

What are social norms, and what do they have to do with differences in what males and females learn in a given culture?

      B. Cultural Perspectives on What is Learned

Why is culture such an important determinant of what a person learns?

            1. In Collectivist Cultures
            2. Individualist Cultures

What is the fundamental difference between the value orientation of collectivist as compared to individualist cultures?

        3. Positive and Negative Aspects to Each Cultural Pattern
        4. Most Euro-Americans Descendants from Individualist Cultures
        5. Most U. S. Ethnic Minorities Have Collectivist Backgrounds

Give an example of how both types of culture can teach the same value?

        6. Differences as Reflected in "Divide a Pile of Pennies" Task

How is the fundamental difference between collectivist and individualist cultures reflected in the performance of Euro-American as compared to Mexican-American children on the "Divide A Pile Of Pennies" task?

        C. Racial Perspective on What is Learned

According to your text, how can a person's race affect what s/he learns?

        1. Reinforcement History of African Americans and Assertiveness
        2. African Americans' Behavior with Euro- vs. Other African-Americans
        3. Socialization and Learning About Racism
        4. Response to Test Questions and Racial-Experiential History
        5. Understanding Behaviors of Racial Minorities

How may individual differences arise in what is learned by members of any given racial group?

C. Self-Generated Questions: What's In This One For Me?

Most people come to the first course in psychology expecting to learn some things which will help them to better understand themselves, other people in their lives, and/or the nature of life in the world in which they live. Along these same lines, students of psychology often look forward to discovering things about human behavior and experience which may help them to improve their own life by developing their talents, technical skills, knowledge and abilities, and/or the quality or their relationships with other people. On the basis of such self-interest, which tends to provide a framework in terms of which new learning becomes personally meaningful and thus easier to remember, write down a few questions in the space below, about the subject matter covered in this chapter. After reading and studying the chapter, come back to see how any of what you've learned may be useful to you in finding answers to these questions.

D. Completion Items

The words in the margins of this exercise are the ones that correctly complete the sentence on the corresponding line. To get the most out of this exercise, you should try to avoid looking at these words in the margin until after you've filled in the corresponding blanks with the words you think best complete the sentences. So, begin the exercise by covering up all of the margin words with a piece of paper. Then, for each blank, write in the word which you think completes the sentence. Even if you're not sure as to the word, write in your best guess, preferably in pencil so you can erase and re-write any incorrect responses you may make here.

After writing in your "answer," slide the paper covering up the margin words down just far enough to see the word for the blank you just filled-in. For each blank that you fill-in correctly, put a check mark (√) after your answer. If the word you wrote in doesn't match the word corresponding to that blank, mark an (X) next to your response and go on to the next blank. It's probably a good idea to go back to the text and try to strengthen your learning related to topic coverage that corresponds in the textbook chapter to those blanks which you filled-in incorrectly, since those items signal a weak link in your concept mastery chain for this chapter.

1. In Hawaiian culture, people learn to not be _____.   competitive

2. _____ is the process by which experiences lead to   Learning
relatively permanent changes in one's behavior and mental activities.

3. _____ have demonstrated that much of the behavior   Ethologists
of animals and humans is learned. Learning particular behaviors is so
important that each species is _____ to learn the behaviors   prepared
that species needs for its survival.

4. In humans, _____ periods are times when particular   sensitive
behaviors can be learned rather easily. There seems to be such a
period in human development for the learning of _____,   language
and this period seems to be the first six years of a child's life, with the
ability for such learning to occur thoroughly diminishing from age six
to the teenage years. Research has shown that immigrants learning the
language of their new home country when they are teenagers or older,
never lose their "foreign" _____.   accent

5. From a biopsychological perspective, learning takes place when new
_____ are formed and connect with new receptor sites.   dendrites
The fact that such connections are formed after _____,   birth
suggests that rather than being designed to behave only in ways
dictated by our genetics, we are genetically built to _____.   learn

6. In the early 1900's, Russian physiologist Ivan Pavlov was studying
salivation and _____ in dogs. The dogs often   digestion
salivated not only when food was placed in their mouths, but also when
they smelled the food, smelled the person who fed them, or when the

145

light went on in their room _____ feeding time. The kind of   before
learning demonstrated by Pavlov's dogs is known as _____   classical
conditioning.

7. In classical conditioning, a _____ stimulus -- that is, one that   neutral
doesn't naturally evoke any particular response -- is linked to another
stimulus referred to as the _____ stimulus or UCS,   unconditioned
that naturally and automatically triggers a given response. The response
to the UCS is called the unconditioned response or the _____   UC R
for short. The training involved in this method of learning involves linking
or associating the initially neutral stimulus, known as the _____   conditioned
stimulus or CS, with the UCS. When the response originally evoked only
by the UCS is manifested in response to the CS, that behavior is called
a _____ response or CR.   conditioned

8. Feelings of _____ and discomfort in reaction to   fear
various situations, objects or events are often classically conditioned
emotional responses. Thus, for example, for the person who becomes
upset at the sight of his/her blood, the sight of blood is initially a
_____ stimulus. A cut on one's skin is the UCS which   conditioned
automatically triggers discomfort which is the _____ in this   UCR
situation. The feeling of discomfort at the mere sight of one's own blood,
is now evoked as a CR by the sight of blood as the
_____. In much the same way, people may acquire intense   CS
dislikes called _____ for the tastes of certain foods.   aversions

9. _____-order conditioning is a process in which a second,   Higher
neutral stimulus is associated with a CS that produces a CR. The original
CS functions like a _____ for the more remote, second CS.   UCS

10. _____ occurs when a stimulus similar to the original CS   Generalization
produces a CR, or a behavior similar to the CR.

11. People and animals can also learn to _____, that is,   discriminate
to restrict the generalization of their conditioned responses. Such
learning occurs when the generalized CS is no longer associated with
the _____.   UCS

12. The undoing of classical conditioning by what is known as
_____ occurs when the linkage between the CS and UCS   extinction
is eliminated, so that the CS is no longer a signal for the UCS. So, for
example, if someone who was classically conditioned to fear the sight of
blood repeatedly saw blood but didn't feel _____ following   pain
that sight, the sight of blood would, presumably, no longer cause him/her
to feel upset. Another way to undo classical conditioning is by means of
counter conditioning, where the original CS is associated with a new
response that _____ with the established CR, thereby   competes

weakening that response to the original CS.

13. In operant conditioning, the probability that a behavior will be
repeated is determined by the _____ of that behavior.   consequences
The law of _____ is the basic principle underlying   effect
operant conditioning. According to this law, when behaviors are followed by
_____ consequences, those behaviors are more likely to   positive
occur again than if there were no such outcomes. The law further states
that when behaviors are followed by _____ outcomes, the   negative
behaviors are less likely to occur again than if there were no such outcomes.

14. Positive _____ is any behavior or event that follows a   reinforcement
behavior and increases the probability that the behavior will occur again.
_____ reinforcement occurs when an unpleasant stimulus   Negative
is withdrawn, and also increases the probability that a behavior will occur.
_____ learning involves the acquisition of behaviors that Escape
terminate an unpleasant stimulus that has already begun. In contrast,
_____ learning involves the acquisition of behaviors that avoidance
postpone or prevent the unpleasant experience from occurring.

15. _____ is a negative consequence of a behavior and its   Punishment
effect is to decrease the probability that the behavior will occur again.   It can
have several undesirable associated effects. As a means of disciplining
a child, for example, through classical conditioning, the person who does
the punishing serves as the _____ stimulus and the situation conditioned
wherein the punishment takes place serves as yet another CS, and both of
these stimuli may become intensely disliked by the recipient of the punishment.
Another shortcoming of punishment as a technique of discipline is that it
may only eliminate the unwanted behavior for a rather _____   short
time, and then only while the person who does or did the punishing is
present. The use of punishment as a means of disciplining children can
take different forms in different cultures. In _____, for example, Japan
parents sometimes lock misbehaving children out of the house for a short
time. In the United States, by contrast, parents often punish their
children by "_____" them or withholding privileges. These   grounding
differences in the case of the foregoing example, suggest differences in the
relative importance of cultural values on closeness with the family and individual
_____ of movement and independence.   freedom

16. _____ reinforcers are objects or behavior -- such as food, Primary
water or sex that are satisfying on an innate, biological level. In contrast,
_____ reinforcers are objects, symbols, or feelings -- such as secondary
money and good grades in school -- that have come to be associated with
positive experiences as a result of learning.

17. A _____ of reinforcement refers to the way in which   schedule
reinforcement is delivered. On a _____ schedule,   continuous

147

reinforcement occurs every time a particular behavior occurs. In general, continuous reinforcement results in faster learning than does
_____ reinforcement. In a fixed ratio schedule of reinforcement, a behavior is reinforced after a predetermined
_____ of responses. A schedule in which the desired behavior is reinforced after a certain amount of time has passed, is called a fixed _____ schedule. In a variable ratio schedule, the desired behavior is reinforced on _____ every Nth time it occurs. In a _____ interval schedule, reinforcement is delivered after a varying amount of time has passed.

intermittent

number

interval
average
variable

18. _____ is an operant conditioning procedure in which reinforcement is used to produce behaviors that are closer and closer to the desired behavior. In this method, the person or animal is reinforced for behaviors which are closer and closer or successive _____ of the desired behavior. This technique has been used in a wide range of applied situations, including the training of _____ to help Coast Guard rescue teams find people in need of rescue.

Shaping

approximations

pigeons

19. People who don't receive rewards they have earned in society may be reluctant to adopt society's _____ and behave in accordance with its "rules." When people don't experience _____ from representatives of American society, such as parents, teachers, and the media, they are left to find other sources of self-affirmation such as in street _____. In some situations, a person exposed to non-reinforcement may develop a condition known as learned _____ -- a feeling that nothing one does affects outcomes in his/her life, and a corresponding lack of effort to try to influence what happens to oneself. Such a way of responding or non-responding in this case, was demonstrated in laboratory experiments by rats exposed to _____ electrical shocks. This phenomenon may help to explain and understand the behaviors of people such as Southeast Asian refugees who were exposed to the unspeakably inhuman horrors associated with the war in _____.

values

reinforcement

gangs

helplessness

inescapable

Vietnam

20. In operant conditioning, _____ occurs when we behave in a particular way because (1) the same behavior was reinforced in a similar situation or (2) similar behavior was reinforced. This phenomenon helps to explain why a person who absent-mindedly checks a coin-return slot and finds _____ when s/he didn't really deserve any change, checks the coin-return slots of other kinds of machines almost automatically every time s/he uses one.

generalization

money/change

21. In operant as in classical conditioning, _____ refers to learning to learning to distinguish among and respond differently to stimuli in such a way that _____ is restricted.

discrimination

generalization

22. In operant conditioning, _____ occurs when the positive consequences of a behavior are removed. Spontaneous _____ refers to the reappearance of an extinguished response, even in the continued absence of further reinforcement of it.

extinction

recovery

23. In operant conditioning, counter conditioning refers to the weakening of a learned response due to the reinforcement of responses which _____ with the originally learned behavior.

compete

24. Classical conditioning involves learning an association between stimuli whereas operant conditioning involves learning the association between a behavior and the _____ of that behavior. Another difference between the two types of conditioning is that _____ conditioning is more appropriate in efforts to understand involuntary, physiological reactions, since it is built on a biologically based, automatic, natural, unlearned link between a UCS and a UCR. Operant conditioning is not so limited, and is thus more readily applicable to explaining human processes such as _____, whereby people learn just what modes of thought, feeling, and conduct are socially acceptable within the context of their own _____.

consequences

classical

socialization

culture

25. Behavior _____ is the type of therapy in which the principles of classical and operant conditioning are used to change dysfunctional behaviors such as overeating, smoking, etc. One such technique is that of systematic _____, which is a form of counter conditioning in which a relaxation response is trained to compete with the person's anxiety or fear response. One aspect of the latter technique involves establishing the client's anxiety _____ with regard to whatever the emotion-arousing stimulus or stimulus situation may be. Then, the client is trained to _____ in in response to each of the anxiety-arousing stimuli thus identified, beginning with the _____ threatening of those stimuli and progressing gradually upward on the list to successively more and more intensely threatening ones.

modification

desensitization

hierarchy

relax

least

26. Learning by observing and imitating other people is referred to as observational learning or _____. In one of the most famous studies of observational learning, children were more likely to behave aggressively toward a large _____ toy after having seen adults behave similarly toward it. Subsequent studies found that when the model was _____ for being violent, the children were especially likely to behave violently. _____ classical conditioning involves observing another individual's emotional reaction to a stimulus, and learning to respond to that stimulus in the same way as does the model observed.

modeling

Bobo

rewarded

Vicarious

27. Biologists successfully applied principles of operant conditioning to teach California _____ to stay away from power poles,   condors
and classical conditioning principles to teach them to stay away from
_____ .   people

28. The concept of scripts refers to knowledge of what happens in social
_____ , the usual meaning of behaviors, and customary ways   relationships
of relating to people, which is acquired by observing others.
_____ scripts are those that are shared by members of a   Cultural
given cultural group. One example of such a script, is the traditional
inclination for _____ Americans to refuse a first offer of food   Japanese
so as to be polite when they are guests in someone's home. When
people don't have the same scripts, they tend not to _____   interpret
behaviors in the same way.

29. _____ learning is learning that takes place in the   Latent
absence of apparent reinforcement, and is not manifested until the
circumstance evokes it. Such learning implies that _____   cognitive
abilities, such as the ability to decide when knowledge can be applied,
have a role in learning.

30. There are differences in what people learn that are due to
differences in their _____ . Math teachers tend to give   experiences
more attention to male than to female students. Such differences in
_____ might account for some of the difference   reinforcement
between boys and girls in their interest in math. Females and males
learn how to behave in ways that are consistent with their learning of
social _____ -- that is, the often unstated rules, guidelines,   norms
and standards of behavior in a given sociocultural context. Such
learning may occur through direct instruction, or indirectly through
_____ and operant conditioning.   modeling

31. The nature of one's _____ affects the experiences   culture
one has and thus what one learns. _____ cultures   Collectivist
emphasize the connections among and interdependence of people, and
thus place primary value on learning how to fit in, get along with,
avoid hurting and become sensitive to the needs and feelings of
others. In contrast, _____ cultures emphasize the goals   individualist
and well-being of people as individuals rather than groups, and thus
tend to place primary value on independence and self-reliance. Most
_____ -Americans are descendants of people from   Euro
individualist cultures and have a primarily individualist
cultural background. But members of U. S. ethnic _____   minority
groups often have collectivist cultural backgrounds. In a study of 9 to
12 year old children, Euro-American children were more than twice
as likely as were _____ -American children to divide a   Mexican
pile of pennies in a way that would maximize the number of pennies they

personally received.

32. As an illustration of the way in which racial differences in experience
may affect what people learn and thus how they behave, members of
minority groups often learn to discriminate -- in an _____   operant
conditioning sense -- among the "audiences" in their lives, and behave
accordingly in different ways. The response of the African-American
adolescent to the standard intelligence test question, "What is the thing
to do if you see a train approaching a broken track?", is used in your text
as an example of how _____ determined experiences can   racially
affect what is learned. Considering the behaviors of racial minority group
members from the perspective of _____ America may
        mainstream
lead to the erroneous interpretations of those behaviors, which are
more appropriately considered within the context of _____   racism
and collectivism.

E. Self-Quiz

For each of the following items, circle the letter which precedes the correct alternative.

1. The anecdote concerning the "average" performance of every student in a class of
Aboriginal Hawaiian school children, is used in your text to illustrate the behavioral expression of
        a. racial prejudice
        b. individual differences in learning styles
        c. cultural pluralism
        d. a cultural value

2. A duckling's learning to follow the first moving object it sees after its birth, illustrates the
concept of
        a. visual tracking
        b. critical periods
        c. response generalization
        d. response assimilation

3. Research has shown that immigrants who learn the language of their new home country
_____, never lose their "foreign" accent.
        a. when they are very young children
        b. when they are teenagers or older
        c. from their friends
        d. from TV, radio and movies

4. In classical conditioning, when a behavior that was previously manifested only in response to the UCS is now evoked by the CS, that response is called (a)n
    a. discriminated operant
    b. instrumental response
    c. conditioned response
    d. unconditioned response

5. _____ conditioning refers to the situation where a neutral stimulus is paired with the original CS to which a CR has been trained, and this second CS comes to evoke the same CR as the original CS.
    a. Multifactorial
    b. Multimodal
    c. Higher-order
    d. Serial-Order

6. _____ is illustrated by the situation wherein a dog trained to salivate to the sound of a dinner bell, also salivates the first time the phone rings.
    a. Generalization
    b. Symbiotic learning
    c. Entropy
    d. Sensory heterogeneity
    e. Weber's law

7. Extinction occurs in classical conditioning when the linkage between _____ is broken.
    a. UCS and UCR
    b. UCR and CR
    c. CS and UCS
    d. Discriminated operant and UCR

8. _____ is the principle underlying operant conditioning.
    a. Latent learning
    b. Stimulus discrimination
    c. Weber's Law
    d. The law of effect

9. Spanking a child for disobedient conduct is most accurately described as
    a. punishment
    b. negative reinforcement
    c. negative transference
    d. latent learning

10. Research on differences in the way in which Japanese as compared to American parents punish their children for misbehaving, is interpreted in your text as reflecting differences in cultural
    a. maturity
    b. intelligence
    c. values
    d. patterns of aggression
    e. frustration tolerance

11. "Shaping" of behavior refers to the operant conditioning procedure which involves
    a. reinforcing successive approximations of the desired behavior (s)
    b. punishing all but the desired behavior(s)
    c. classical conditioning of the undesired behavior
    d. presenting many different forms of the original CS, but reinforcing only one of them

12. The application of shaping techniques is exemplified in your textbook by the work in which
    a. Australian Aboriginal children have been trained to "see" illusions which they could previously not see
    b. critical periods for both language and sensorimotor abilities are modified
    c. dogs are conditioned to salivate to a light or the sound of a bell
    d. pigeons are trained to help find people lost at sea

13. According to the results of laboratory research cited in your text, learned helplessness is most likely to occur under which of the following conditions?
    a. escapable shock
    b. inescapable shock
    c. primary reinforcement
    d. secondary reinforcement
    e. tertiary reinforcement

14. _____ occurs when the positive consequences of a behavior are removed.
    a. Stimulus generalization
    b. Stimulus discrimination
    c. Extinction
    d. Spontaneous recovery

15. In the behavior therapy approach known as desensitization, a person's anxiety or fear response is
    a. evoked repeatedly until it is exhausted
    b. associated with intensely pleasurable primary reinforcers
    c. a secondary reinforcer
    d. trained to compete with a relaxation response

16. The results of a research study cited in your text indicated that children who observed an adult model behaving aggressively toward a Bobo doll, were more likely to behave aggressively themselves if the model was
      a. a female
      b. a male
      c. of their same race and gender
      d. rewarded for his/her behavior

17. As described in your text, _____ classical conditioning is a combination of observational learning and classical conditioning.
      a. operant
      b. vicarious
      c. Intrinsic
      d. extrinsic

18. The inclination for traditional Japanese Americans to refuse a first offer of food when they are guests in someone's home, is used in your text to exemplify what social psychologists call cultural
      a. demand characteristics
      b. role reversals
      c. scripts
      d. assimilation

19. As noted in your text, which of the following groups is most accurately characterized as individualistic in their cultural heritage?
      a. Asian-Americans
      b. Aboriginal-Americans
      c. Mexican-Americans
      d. Euro-Americans

20. The example used in your text to illustrate racial perspectives on what is learned, involved a standard intelligence test question as to "What is the thing to do if you see...?"
      a. a train approaching a broken track
      b. an automobile accident
      c. someone shoplifting
      d. a classmate cheating on a test

For each of the following items, circle "T" if the statement is True, and "F" if the statement is False.

21. T F   In humans, the times when particular behaviors can be learned rather easily are called "critical periods."

22. T F   Psychological research has shown that immigrants who learn a language when they are teenagers or older never lose their foreign accent.

23. T F   A person's emotional response to the sight of his/her own blood may be explained as the result of classical conditioning, where the blood is the UCS.

24. T F   In classical conditioning, the term "generalization" refers to the tendency for a CR to be evoked by a stimulus similar to the original CS.

25. T F   The law of effect is the principle underlying operant conditioning.

26. T F   Negative reinforcement is the technical term for what is more commonly known as "punishment."

27. T F   In a fixed ratio schedule of reinforcement, a behavior is reinforced after a predetermined number of responses.

28. T F   The results of research by Seligman and others indicate that learned helplessness occurs in situations where animals are exposed to conditions where their own behavior has no effect on what happens to them.

29. T F   The process of socialization, by which people learn what behaviors are and are not socially acceptable, their attitudes, and values, is best explained as due to classical conditioning.

30. T F   In individualist cultures, the goals and well-being of each individual are more important then those of the group.

F. Teaching-To-Learn Exercise

1. *Let Me Teach You This.*

Write in the space provided below, the five facts, ideas, etc., from this chapter that you'd most like to teach to your own student(s) if you were a teacher. Then, really do try to communicate these facts or ideas to someone in your life; or, pretend to teach this content to a hypothetical or "make-believe" student or class.

2. *Now Answer My Questions.*

Here, write one multiple-choice and one True-False question for each of the facts, ideas, etc., you covered in the "Let Me Teach You This" section of this exercise.

G. Bringing Psychology To Life Exercise

I. The <u>operant conditioning</u> method of <u>successive approximations</u> is one of the best-established techniques for modifying or <u>shaping</u> behavior. Essentially, this approach involves <u>reinforcing</u> (i.e., rewarding) behaviors that more and more closely resemble some behavior which is defined as the criterion or desired goal behavior in the situation. The training is thus viewed as a process in which increasingly closer approximations to the criterion behavior are required for delivery of the reinforcement.

Thus, for example, in applying this step-by-step method to train a pigeon to turn 360 degrees in a clockwise rotation, the trainer might begin by giving the bird a food pellet for just moving its head slightly to the right. Once the pigeon is performing this movement rather consistently, the trainer might then provide it with a pellet reward only for each clockwise movement of at least 45 degrees or more in the clockwise direction. When the 45 degree turn is well established, then only a turn of 90 degrees or more is reinforced, and so on until a full 360 degree rotation is required for delivery of a reward.

How might you apply this method of successive approximations the following situations? In each case, be sure to tell what you would use as the reinforcer, and at least two different levels of successive approximation to the goal or criterion behavior.

> **A.** You're the parent of a sixteen year-old boy who always comes home later than the time that you and he have both agreed on as an acceptable curfew for nights before school days. The absolute amount of time that he's late varies rather substantially from about a half hour on some nights, to as much as two hours or more on other nights. You've reminded and even scolded him several times about his lateness and how worried you are when he's late getting home. But none of this has helped. How might you go about "shaping" his behavior by using the method of successive approximations to get him to come home on time?

> **B.** You have an unemployed neighbor who frequently comes knocking at your door at various times on days when s/he knows that you're at home, asking to borrow all sorts of things. Since you find these intrusions enormously disruptive to your life, you've asked and even insisted that s/he restrict his/her spontaneous visits to the lunch hour (from noon to about 1:00 pm). But such communication has failed. Your neighbor's intrusive solicitation visits continue at all hours throughout the day, and seem to be getting more frequent in the past few days. The problem here is that you really do sort of like this person, and don't want to lose him/her as a friend. But you definitely do want to be able to manage his/her intrusions somewhat. How might you use the method of successive approximations to "shape" his/her visits to the noon hour that you take as a planned break, and which you reserve for socializing?

II. In the foregoing instances in which you suggested ways of applying the technique of successive approximations:

> **A.** What did you assume to be true about what we might refer to as the "motivating value" of whatever you proposed to use as the reinforcer? Explain.

B. To what extent did you assume that you had some kind of control over dispensing and/or withholding that reinforcer from the person? Explain.

C. How effective do you think your efforts at modifying the behavior(s) in question would be in such cases, if you had no control whatsoever over anything that might have what we've referred to here as "motivating value" to the person whose behavior you're trying to shape in these hypothetical situations? Explain.

III. Punishment refers to the application of a stimulus which is intended to be experienced as unpleasant or even painful by the organism to which it is applied, or to the withdrawal of something which that organism apparently finds desirable or pleasurable.

A. How might you have attempted to modify by punishment the behaviors:
    1. In the case of the "tardy teenager."
    2. In the case of the "noisome neighbor."

B. Do you think that such punishment would be more or less effective than the shaping procedure you outlined above in either or both of these cases? Explain.

IV. A good friend tells you that he has a serious problem in his family, and wonders if you've learned anything in your study of psychology that might help him to solve or at least understand this problem. Basically, his problem is this. His fourteen year-old daughter has gotten nothing but "A" and "B" grades throughout her public school education. In an effort to give her some extra incentive to keep on studying hard and getting good grades as she prepares for college, he promised to regard her report card as a paycheck for which he would reward her with $50 for every "A," $25 for every "B," $10 for every "C," and nothing for "D's" and "F's." He also confides in you that he didn't develop this new system in consultation with his daughter. Rather, he just sort of did it, assuming that she'd be delighted to "cash-in" on the good grades she's always gotten anyway.

The problem now, he tells you, is that for the past three semesters since this new incentive system has been in effect, his daughter's grades have decreased consistently. In fact, she hasn't gotten even one "A" or "B" since the first time that he gave her a monetary reward for grades.

Drawing upon ideas covered in the text, class presentations by your instructor in this course, and/or your own experience about human behavior, try to explain how the daughter's performance in school may actually have been impaired by the reward system set up by her apparently well-intentioned father?

Answer Key To Self-Quiz

1. d
2. b
3. b
4. c
5. c
6. a
7. c
8. d
9. a
10. c
11. a
12. d
13. b
14. c
15. d
16. d
17. b
18. c
19. d
20. a
21. F
22. T
23. F
24. T
25. T
26. F
27. T
28. T
29. F
30. T

CHAPTER 6

Memory

A. Learning Objectives

After careful, effective study of Chapter 6, you should:

1. Appreciate the fact that <u>what</u> we remember affects the way we think, feel, and act in all sorts of situations.

2. Have a working familiarity with the information-processing model of memory, including:
   a. An understanding of what is meant by the idea of viewing memory as an active rather than a passive process;
   b. The three basic memory processes of encoding, storing, and retrieving information;
   c. The three basic memory systems of
       (1) Sensory memory, including iconic and eidetic storage of visual images, as well as echoic memory for sounds;
       (2) Short-term memory and how it may be increased by "chunking" and "maintenance rehearsal; and
       (3) Long-term memory and the relevance of the following to understanding how it works:
               (a) the idea of "books in a library;"
               (b) the "tip-of-the-tongue" phenomenon;
               (c) the experience of one memory triggering a whole chain of memories;
               (d) studies of amnesia; and
               (e) the different types of memories known as implicit, procedural, declarative or explicit, episodic, biographical, and semantic.

3. The relevance of the following to alternative views concerning the relationship between short- and long-term memory:
       (a) The serial position effect; and
       (b) the levels-of-processing hypothesis of memory storage.

4. The relevance of the following to understanding how memories are constructed:
       (a) The different types of memories:
               (1) Conscious memory as in recognition, and
               (2) Unconscious memory as measured by relearning;
       (b) Mental mechanisms in remembering, including
               (1) The role of clues
                       (a) Retrieval cues;
                       (b) Internal and External cues;
                       (c) State-dependent cues;
                       (d) Context-dependent cues; and
               (2) The role of personal significance as with "flashbulb memories.

5. The physiology of memory, with special attention to:
    (a) The role of neurons in the processes of memory
        (1) As explored in the pioneering work by neurosurgeons; and
        (2) As evidenced in long-term potentiation;
    (b) The role of brain structures in memory:
        (1) As indicated by studies of people with brain damage;
        (2) As revealed in studies of amnesia, both anterograde and retrograde;
        (3) The effect of damage to the hippocampus on memory, and the mechanisms underlying such effects.

6. The processes of forgetting and reconstructing memories, focusing on:
    a. What a forgetting curve indicates;
    b. Forgetting or losing what's in memory storage, as explained by the following theories
        (1) The decay hypothesis, and
        (2) The interference hypothesis as it applies to attempts to explain how both retroactive and proactive learning may affect memory.
    c. What is meant by deliberate forgetting, and how each of the following is relevant to understanding such losses in memory:
        (1) The concept of motivated forgetting as it relates to the unconscious;
        (2) The difference between suppression and repression of memories;
        (3) Alternative ideas about repressed memories of childhood trauma, considering
            (a) The issue as to establishing the truth or falsity of such memories; and
            (b) How the clinical methods used to evoke such memories, as well as the interpretation of the memories evoked, contribute to the controversy surrounding case studies of such matters.

7. The causes of memory reconstruction, whereby a false or distorted memory is created, considering:
    a. The separation of stored information from its source as may occur during encoding of a memory;
    b. The way inferences or assumptions may lead to distortions in memory; and
    c. How memories which are stored accurately in long-term memory may merge, leading to what is known as the misinformation effect.

8. The relationships between culture, education, and memory as evidenced in:
    a. The development of cultural scripts which provide frameworks into which information is stored selectively;
    b. Our memories about ourselves, as shaped by cultural values and experiences;
    c. The way in which our cultural and educational experiences affect how we process information, the situations or activities in which we use memory, and our goals for using memory; and
    d. The way in which cultural values and experience may affect both short- and long- term memory.

9. How to improve your own memory by using strategies such as the following:
    a. Learning how to organize the material to be remembered in ways that relate ideas to

each other;
   b. Using rehearsal and breaking up our learning with rest periods;
   c. Using mental visual images such as the method of loci; and
   d. Learning how to "process deeply" the information to be remembered.

B. Preview/Review Outline Of Key Terms And Concepts

Before you read the corresponding chapter in your text, read over the following outline. It is designed to give you an overview of information presented in the chapter, and how the various elements of that information are related to each other. After reading through the whole chapter and/or before course exams, you may use this outline as a quick review guide. In your reviews, mask off one line of the outline at a time, and try to recite from your memory of the chapter, the information that you expect to appear on the next line or so.

In going over this outline as a preview before reading and studying the chapter, the questions posed in bold print will help to keep you focused on the learning objectives here, and keep you actively involved in the process of achieving those objectives. When using this section as a review, try to answer the questions. Refer back to the chapter in the text for a more detailed feedback check on your mastery of the material, and/or to strengthen your knowledge and understanding wherever you feel the need to do so.

As you read the story of Robert and Marlene's date, what impressions do you get about the nature of this experience for each of these two people?

I. The Information-Processing Model: Memory Processes and Systems
   A. Three Memory Processes
      1. Encoding

Just what is it that gets encoded or registered in memory, and how is this reflected in the differences in Robert and Marlene's memory of their date?

      2. Storing
      3. Retrieving

How are the processes of memory storage and retrieval similar to what happens in the use of a computer as an information processing system?

   B. Three Memory Systems
      1. Sensory Memory
         a. Iconic Memory
         b. Eidetic Memory
         c. Photographic Memory
         d. Echoic Memory

What is the essential difference between eidetic and photographic memory?

      2. Short-term Memory

      a. Chunking
      b. Maintenance Rehearsal

What are the approximate time and unit limits of short-term memory, and what kinds of strategies may be used to extend these limits?

    3. Long-term Memory
      a. Repetition
      b. Kinesthetic Memory
      c. Hierarchical Clusters
      d. Tip-of-the Tongue Phenomenon
      e. Redintegration
      f. Studies of Individuals With Amnesia
         (1) Implicit /Procedural Memory
         (2) Explicit/Declarative Memory
            (a) Episodic and Autobiographical Memory
            (b) Semantic Memory

How are the vast majority of our experiences encoded in our long-term memory? What happens to the information as it is so stored?

    4. Short- vs. Long-term Memory
      a. Separate or Interrelated
      b. Serial Position Effect
         (a) Primacy Effect
         (b) Recency Effect
      c. Levels-of-Processing Hypothesis

From the standpoint of the levels-of-processing hypothesis, what is "elaborative rehearsal," and what does it have to do with the "depth" with which information is processed?

II. Constructing Memories

How is memory performance studied by researchers?

    A. Different Types of Remembering
      1. Conscious Remembering
         a. Declarative Memory
         b. Recall
         c. Recognition
      2. Unconscious Remembering
         a. Implicit Memory
         b. Relearning
            (1) Ebbinghaus' Research
            (2) Nonsense Syllables as Material To Be Learned

What is the fundamental difference between recall and recognition as methods of measuring memory performance? What kinds of items on exams reflect each of these two types of memory measurement?

    B. Mental Mechanisms in Remembering
        1. The Role of Clues
            a. Degree of Similarity Between Learning and Retrieval Contexts
            b. Retrieval Cues
            c. Internal and External Cues
            d. State-Dependent Cues
            e. Context-Dependent Cues

In which kind of memory performance task, recall or recognition, are context cues likely to be more important? Why? How might you apply any of what you've learned about "the role of clues" in memory, to improving your own performance on exams?

        2. The Role of Personal Significance
            a. Flashbulb Memories
            b. Memory Consolidation

What event in your own experience comes closest to fitting the description of a "flashbulb memory"?

    C. Physiological Mechanisms in Remembering
        1. The Role of Neurons
            a. Storage of Memories
            b. Long-Term Potentiation

What is the current status of knowledge as to just how information is stored at the neural level?

        2. The Role of Brain Structures
            a. Studies of People With Brain Damage
            b. Studies Of Amnesia
                (1) Anterograde Amnesia
                (2) Retrograde Amnesia
                (3) Loss of Conscious, Declarative Memory
            c. Cerebellum
                (1) Motor Behavior, Coordination
                (2) Procedural Memories
            d. Hippocampus
                (1) Declarative Memory
                (2) Unified Memories
                (3) Consolidation of Memory
                (4) Effects of Trauma and Release of Neurotransmitters

What kinds of memory loss seem to be most profound in people with amnesia? How is this kind of memory loss explained in terms of the memory functions controlled by different brain structures?

III. Forgetting and Reconstructing
    A. Forgetting What's in Storage
        1. Decay
            a. Lack of Use or Passage of Time
            b. As Exhibited in Older Adults

What are some of the hypotheses as to why older adults show poorer short-term memory performance than do young people?

        2. Interference
            a. Effects of Being Awake or Asleep
            b. Retroactive Interference
            c. Proactive Interference

What were the results of the classic research in which subjects were either awake or asleep before being tested on how well they remembered a list of nonsense syllables? What did this research have to do with the interference hypothesis concerning memory?

        3. Deliberate Forgetting
            a. Motivated Forgetting
            b. Suppression vs. Repression

What is the essential difference between suppression and repression?

    B. Alternative Perspectives on Repressed Memories of Childhood Trauma (Box 6.1)
        1. Women Abused As Children
        2. The Case of Lynn
        3. Professional Controversy
            a. Rights Of Trauma Victims or Survivors
            b. False Recovered Memories and Accusations
            c. Modification and Distortion of Memories by Hypnosis
            d. Therapist's Interpretations And Suggestions

What is the substance of the professional controversy concerning cases where an adult, in the process of treatment by a psychiatrist or psychologist, reports long repressed memories about having been abused as a child?

    C. Reconstructing What We've Forgotten
        1. The Separation of Information and Its Source
            a. Poor Encoding of Link Between Information and Source
            b. Role of Values and Beliefs
         2. The Use of Inferences or Assumptions
            a. Bartlett's Work on Memory for Faces

b. And Marlene's Memory of Her Date With Robert

What is indicated about the nature of memory, by the results of the study in which respondents read and were given a recall test on a passage about a women whom some of them were informed was Helen Keller?

3. The Merging of Misinformation
    a. The Misinformation Effect
    b. Suggestive Questioning and Witnesses' Memory for Details
    c. Explanation of Marlene's Memory of Her Date With Robert
    d. Parents' Childhood Stories About Their Children

What research evidence could you cite in support of the argument that people's memories for events can be distorted or even completely false?

IV. Culture, Education, and Memory
    A. Cultural Scripts
        1. Interpretations of Behavior, Relating to Others, Behaving
        2. Storyline as Framework for Selective Storing of Information
        3. Selective Focusing of Inferences

How would you describe a "cultural script" and the various ways in which it can influence memory, to someone who has never studied psychology?

    B. Memories about Ourselves
        1. Autobiographical Memory
        2. And Cultural Orientation
            a. In Collectivistic vs. Individualistic Cultures
            b. Research on Conversations Between Korean and Euro-American Mothers and Their Children

What do the stories we tell about ourselves to others have to do with our autobiographical memories? Can you give an example of the way in which the cultural context in which a child grows up can affect his/her memory about him/herself?

    C. Cultural Differences in Memory Strategies and Activities
        1. Culture and Short-Term Memory
            a. Short-Term Memory In Chinese Society as Compared to English Speaking Euro-Americans
            b. Short-Term Memory in Children Who Have vs. Those Who Have Not Attended School

How is schooling related to short-term memory? What seems to be the reason for this relationship?

        2. Culture and Long-Term Memory
            a. People With Astounding Memories

b. Nonliterate Folk Singers
    (1) Thoughtless Memorization?
    (2) The Cultural Value of What They Remember
3. Applications: Strategies for Improving Your Memory (Box 6.2)
    a. Organize the Material
    b. Rehearse Regularly
    c. Overlearn
    d. Use Mental Visual Images
    e. Process Information Deeply

What is the "spacing effect," and how can you take advantage of it in maximizing the effectiveness of whatever amount of time you spend studying? What is the method of loci? How do you go about increasing the "depth" with which you process any information as a means of helping you remember it?

C. Self-Generated Questions: What's In This One For Me?

Most people come to the first course in psychology expecting to learn some things which will help them to better understand themselves, other people in their lives, and/or the nature of life in the world in which they live. Along these same lines, students of psychology often look forward to discovering things about human behavior and experience which may help them to improve their own life by developing their talents, technical skills, knowledge and abilities, and/or the quality or their relationships with other people. On the basis of such self-interest, which tends to provide a framework in terms of which new learning becomes personally meaningful and thus easier to remember, write down a few questions in the space below, about the subject matter covered in this chapter. After reading and studying the chapter, come back to see how any of what you've learned may be useful to you in finding answers to these questions.

D. Completion Items

The words in the margins of this exercise are the ones that correctly complete the sentence on the corresponding line. To get the most out of this exercise, you should try to avoid looking at these words in the margin until after you've filled in the corresponding blanks with the words you think best complete the sentences. So, begin the exercise by covering up all of the margin words with a piece of paper. Then, for each blank, write in the word which you think completes the sentence. Even if you're not sure as to the word, write in your best guess, preferably in pencil so you can erase and re-write any incorrect responses you may make here.

After writing in your "answer," slide the paper covering up the margin words down just far enough to see the word for the blank you just filled-in. For each blank that you fill-in correctly, put a check mark (√) after your answer. If the word you wrote in doesn't match the word corresponding to that blank, mark an (X) next to your response and go on to the next blank. It's probably a good idea to go back to the text and try to strengthen your learning related to topic coverage that corresponds in the textbook chapter to those blanks which you filled-in incorrectly, since those items signal a weak link in your concept mastery chain for this chapter.

1. Marlene and Robert had completely different recollections of their
_____. The answer to the question as to how such   date
differences can arise, lie in the nature of _____, a   memory
mental system of encoding, storing, and retrieving information.

2. According to the information-processing approach, people are
_____ participants in the memory process rather than   active
passive containers of information.

3. Our nervous system _____, or registers sensory   encodes
information by transforming it into memory traces or cognitive
representations that our brain can process. We do not record visual
images as our eyes see them, but as we _____ them.   perceive
People differ in what they notice and what they perceive, partly because
they differ in their _____, expectations, and orientations.   values

3. After encoding, we put information in _____, the process   storage
of keeping information for immediate or later use. We access information
through _____, the process by which we locate and then use   retrieval
information in memory.

4. Entry into memory begins with _____ memory, the memory   sensory
system that effortlessly holds vast amounts of current sensory information for
a fleeting moment. _____ memory is fleeting sensory memory   Iconic
for visual images. Some people, most commonly children, have
_____ memory, which is the ability to retain visual images for   eidetic
several seconds, or even minutes, and to "see" the images in the environment
rather than in their "mind's eye." Such images, unlike those in
_____ memory, cannot be retrieved once they have faded.   photographic

167

_____ memory, which is the memory for sounds that one has just heard, can last for a moment or as long as a second.

Echoic

5. Most information in sensory memory disappears before we become consciously _____ of it. Information that we attend to passes into _____ memory, the system that stores information temporarily, but longer than sensory memory. This memory system receives new information from sensory memory, and stored information from _____ memory. It is as if long-term memory is a giant set of _____ shelves storing information that is brought to the short-term memory work space for use. On average, short-term memory has spaces for _____ units of information. _____ information by organizing separate pieces of information into relatively larger, meaningful units, allows us to increase the amount of information stored in short-term memory. The strategy of maintenance _____, whereby one consciously repeats information to oneself, helps to keep information in short-term memory past the usual time limit of about thirty seconds.

aware
short-term

long-term
library

seven
Chunking

rehearsal

6. _____ memory is an unlimited storehouse of our skills, vocabulary, experiences, and knowledge about ourselves and the world around us. _____ memory stores information for body movement as instructions to our muscles. Long-term memory encodes information in terms of its _____ to us, and alters it in the process. Long-term memory appears to index information into topics, then organizes those topics into _____ clusters that are hierarchical linked together. The tip-of-the _____ phenomenon, wherein one knows a word and feels as if on the verge of retrieving it, provides evidence to indicate that long-term memory stores the meanings and the _____ of words separately. Long-term memory also links different words, ideas, and experiences together in a _____ of associations. Because of these links, one can experience _____, a rapid chain of memories triggered by a single memory. Evidence for two long-term memory subsystems comes from studies of people who have _____, a loss of memory caused by brain injury or psychological trauma.

Long-term

Kinesthetic

meaning

tongue

sounds

network
redintegration

amnesia

7. _____ memory is unconscious memory for information, such as conditioned responses and subliminal messages, and also includes _____ memory, which involves behavioral and cognitive procedures. _____ memory, which is also known as explicit memory, is long-term memory for facts and information that one can declare consciously or bring to mind at will. One type of such explicit memory is _____ memory, which is the knowledge of personal experiences that are tied to a particular time and place; some theorists

Implicit

procedural

Declarative

episodic

168

argue that this kind of memory includes _____ memory, or   autobiographical
information about oneself that has personal meaning. Another type of
explicit or declarative memory is _____ memory, our   semantic
knowledge of acts and general information about the world.

8. Those who believe that short- and long-term memory are separate systems,
point to studies that show a _____ position effect, the   serial
tendency for people to remember the first and last but not the middle
items in a series. One component of this effect is the _____   primacy
effect, which is the tendency to remember the first items on a list; the other
component is known as the _____ effect, and is the tendency   recency
to remember the most recently presented items. The _____-   levels
of-processing hypothesis of memory storage is the idea that the depth with
which we think about information has a direct influence on how well we
remember it. Processing at a deep level is elaborative _____,   rehearsal
which refers to conscious analysis of information in order to relate it to our
existing knowledge.

9. We remember information in declarative memory through the conscious
retrieval of information, a process known as _____. Another   recall
form of memory is _____, which involves correctly identifying   recognition
information as is required on multiple choice tests.

10. Both recall and recognition use declarative memory. But they are not
the best way to measure _____, implicit memory, which can be   unconscious
measured by the procedure known as _____, or the amount   relearning
of time saved in a second attempt to learn information that one can no
longer recall or recognize.

11. The context or circumstances in which learning originally occurs,
provides _____ cues, incidental information that we store   retrieval
in connection with the main information of an experience. One's emotional
or physiological state can influence memory performance by acting as a
_____-dependent cue, an internal stimulus that can trigger   state
retrieval of information from long-term memory. Context-
_____ cues, which are features of the physical context in   dependent
which we encode information, can also affect retrieval. Context cues can
enhance recall, but have relatively little effect on _____.   recognition
In a recognition task, retrieval cues make little difference in memory
performance because the _____ themselves serve as   choices
retrieval cues.

12. Flashbulb memories are vivid, elaborate memories of events which have
great _____ meaning in our lives, and are experienced as if a   personal
flashbulb went off when the event occurred. Memory _____   consolidation
is the transfer of information from the hippocampus to areas of the cortex

corresponding to the information to be stored, resulting in an elaborate memory that is easily remembered.

13. Before the information-processing model of memory became established, many people thought that different neurons in the brain stored a _____ memory for every event or stimulus we encountered. Information stored in memory does not reside inside a single neuron, but in the _____ between neurons. Sensory stimulation causes a specific _____ of neurons to fire over and over again. When a neuron, say Neuron A, continually fires on another neuron, Neuron B, physiological and biochemical changes result in alteration to their _____ connection.

complete

communication
pattern

synaptic

14. _____ amnesia involves an inability to learn or remember new experiences occurring after neurological trauma.
_____ amnesia is the loss of memories acquired before
     Retrograde
neurological trauma. Most people with amnesia show profound loss of conscious, _____ memory but relatively less loss of unconscious, implicit memory. Theorists and researchers suggest that the reason for these differences in the kinds of memory lost in amnesia are due to the fact that the _____ is the primary brain structure involved in declarative memory, whereas the skills and information making up implicit memories feature the _____, the brain structure located at the base of the brain. The hippocampus appears to hold unified memories for several weeks, during which time those memories undergo _____, which is a gradual neurological process that can take weeks, months, or even years before the memory becomes firmly established in long-term storage. Events that cause neurological disruption can seriously interfere with or even prevent this process from occurring to completion, with the result that the relevant information is _____.
The _____ lobe of the brain also contributes to declarative memory functions, by directing the storage and retrieval of information by judging stimuli for their meaning and relationship with _____ knowledge.

Anterograde

declarative

hippocampus

cerebellum

consolidation

lost
frontal

existing

15. Sometimes we forget information because the memories _____ from lack of use or the passage of time. Decay from from short-term memory tends to become more noticeable as people _____. This kind of rapid decay might be caused by poor encoding or because of decreased ability to focus one's _____. The decay of declarative memories is variable with age, with _____ memory showing little decline.

decay

age

attention
procedural

16. _____ interference is forgetting that occurs when newly learned information disrupts recall of previously learned information.
_____ interference is forgetting that occurs when previously

Retroactive

Proactive

170

learned information disrupts recall of newly learned information.

17. Through _____ forgetting, we can consciously or   motivated
unconsciously hide memories from conscious awareness. We can use
_____ to consciously rid ourselves of memories. When   suppression
_____ involves unconscious hiding of information from   Repression
conscious awareness.

18. Anywhere from as few as 15 percent to as many as 60 percent of
adult _____ who were abused as children have repressed   women
memories of the abuse. When they remember that abuse, the
challenge they face concerns the _____ of those memories.   accuracy
Instead of the term trauma victims, the term trauma _____   survivors
is used to connote strength and courage rather than weakness and
damage associated with such experiences in the life of the individual.
Skeptics argue that certain techniques used by naive or overeager
psychotherapists can distort memories or even create
_____ memories of abuse. For instance, the techniques   false
of hypnosis can distort memories through an individual's   imagination and a
hypnotist's implicit _____.   suggestions

19. Memory _____ is the process whereby false or distorted   reconstruction
memories are created by piecing together recalled information using the
wrong source, incorrect inferences, or false information. Our
_____ and beliefs may shape the mistaken links that are formed values
when information is separated from its source. Sir Frederick Bartlett was the
first psychologist to demonstrate empirically that people use
_____ when remembering. In one study, he asked respondents inferences
to study several drawings of faces, and then to describe those faces. He found
that people tended to draw an initial _____ when viewing each impression
face, which influenced their subsequent efforts to recall what the person
looked like. As we have an experience, we automatically think of its
theme or meaning and leave out some of the _____. The   details
theme links the new information to our existing knowledge, sometimes
resulting in _____ inference.   false

20. Yet another perspective on memory _____ proposes   distortion
that original memories, stored accurately in long-term memory, can actually
change. New information overwrites or becomes incorporated into an
originally accurate, existing memory in what is known as the
_____ effect. We might mistakenly remember separate   misinformation
events as part of the same event, or unrelated information as related
because the original memory becomes altered by _____   new
information. In everyday life, people incorporate false details into their
memories. For instance, psychologist Elizabeth Loftus has shown that
suggestive _____ can lead witnesses to remember details   questioning
they never actually encountered. There is even some research to show

that completely false memories are possible. In one study along the latter lines, for example, college students "remembered" childhood experiences that never happened to them after repeated _____ with researchers.   interviews

21. Cultural _____ are ways of interpreting behavior,   scripts
relating to other people, and behaving in different situations that are
shared by members of a cultural group. They provide a storyline and a
framework into which we can store information _____.   selectively
They also shape our memory of an event by selectively focusing our
inferences as we _____ a memory.   reconstruct

22. Through conversations with their children, parents indirectly
reward certain autobiographical memories, and teach the social goals
and _____ of their culture. Cultural orientations appear   values
to shape the amount of interest that parents show in response to their
children's _____ memories. Collectivist cultures encourage   autobiographical
individuals to learn to fit in and get along with others, while
_____ cultures encourage their members to develop a   individualistic
feeling of independence and self-reliance. Preliminary research
indicates that children in Korea, a collectivistic culture, discuss their
autobiographical memories _____ often than do children   less
in the United States, a relatively individualistic culture.

23. There is some research to suggest that Chinese people in China
have, on average, better _____ memory skills than do   short-term
English speaking Euro-Americans. This difference may be due to the
fact that Chinese-speakers educated in China develop their
_____ skills. One hypothesis offered to explain the   memorization
finding that short-term memory recall ability is greater in children who
have as compared to those who have not attended school, is that such
memory is strengthened significantly from _____, a   rehearsal
memory strategy that is not commonly used outside of school, because
people generally do not have as much need to remember
_____ information in other aspects of their everyday life.   unrelated
Although there is some research to indicate cultural differences in
short-term memory, when the short-term memory recall task involves
objects presented in a _____ context, a type of task which   meaningful
does not seem to benefit as much from rehearsal, cultural differences
disappear.

24. Examples of people with astounding memories are found in
several cultures. In the mountains of Europe it is not uncommon to
find nonliterate folk singers who can sing epic songs that last an
entire _____. In Africa, griots, the nonliterate oral   night
_____ of the Gola society, remember the history of their   historians
ancestors. In Hebrew communities are Shass Pollacks, people who have

172

memorized the twelve books of the _____ word for word.   Talmud
One way to explain such unusual feats of memory is by taking into account
the fact that both the act of remembering and the content of what is
remembered are very much valued within the _____ of   cultures
the individuals involved.

25. A number of strategies can be used to improve memory. One of these
involves _____ the material to be remembered. It can help to   organizing
remember ideas, when we have a clearly organized framework for
_____ those ideas to each other, as given in the outlines   relating
provided for you in your text and in this study guide. Regular
_____ of the information to be learned also tends to contribute   rehearsal
to memory of that material. _____, studying something until you   Overlearning
think you understand it and then studying it again, is another good memory
enhancing strategy. The term _____ is sometimes used to   mnemonics
refer to aids used to improve memory, one of which, known as the method
of _____, involves relating items to physical locations.   loci
Generally speaking, the more associations any new information has with
information that we already know, the deeper that information is said to be
_____, and the better we're likely to remember that new   processed
information. So, the more we're able to connect what it is that we're learning,
to things we already _____ and care about, the better for our   know
later attempts to remember the new material.

E. Self-Quiz

For each of the following items, circle the letter which precedes the correct alternative.

1. Both Marlene and Robert remembered their date as
    a. exciting
    b. expensive
    c. enjoyable
    d. all of the above
    e. none of the above

2. It is the _____ approach which provides the prevailing model of human memory
processes.
    a. social learning
    b. psychodynamic
    c. information processing
    d. behaviorist
    e. Gestalt or holistic

3. People differ in what they notice and what they perceive, partly because they differ in their
   a. values
   b. expectations
   c. orientations
   d. all of the above
   e. none of the above

4. Which of the following <u>is not</u> one of the three systems of memory as described in your text?
   a. cognitive memory
   b. sensory memory
   c. short-term memory
   d. long-term memory

5. _____ is the term psychologists use to refer to the organization of separate pieces of information into relatively larger, meaningful units of information, thus increasing the amount of information that can be held in short-term memory.
   a. Clumping
   b. Clustering
   c. Chunking
   d. Texturing

6. Which of the following is most directly involved as the basis for the memory strategy of maintenance rehearsal?
   a. repetition
   b. sequencing
   c. patterning
   d. identification

7. _____ memory refers to the storage of information for body movement as instructions to our muscles for various sorts of tasks.
   a. Vestibular
   b. Kinesthetic
   c. Kinescopic
   d. Ambulatory cognitive
   e. Orthopedic

8. Which of the following metaphors is used in your text to describe the way information in long-term memory is organized for efficient retrieval?
   a. traffic signals at a busy intersection
   b. telephone lines in a national communication network
   c. books in a library
   d. the internet

9. Which of the following provides the clearest evidence that the meaning and the sound of a word are stored separately in long-term memory?
    a. the fox-in-the-henhouse effect
    b. chicken and egg dilemma
    c. round-peg-in-square-hole problem
    d. tip-of-the-tongue phenomenon
    e. rat-man illusion

10. Which of the following is not an aspect of implicit memory?
    a. knowledge of one's past experiences
    b. unconscious memory
    c. procedural memory
    d. remembering how to play the piano

11. Which of the following is not an aspect of declarative memory?
    a. explicit memory
    b. memory for the names of composers
    c. episodic memory
    d. remembering how to snap your fingers
    e. semantic memory

12. The serial position effect refers to the tendency for people to remember best the items _____ in a series.
    a. in the middle
    b. in the beginning
    c. at the end
    d. both a and b above
    e. both b and c above

13. According to the levels-of-processing hypothesis, which of the following is most characteristic of information which is "deeply" processed?
    a. perception of a physical stimulus
    b. naming of the stimulus
    c. thinking about the meaning of a stimulus
    d. all of the above
    e. none of the above

14. According to the levels-of-processing hypothesis, which of the following is most likely to lead to "deep processing" of information?
    a. perception of the information as a physical stimulus
    b. elaborative rehearsal of the information
    c. rote memorization
    d. naming the stimulus or stimuli which is (are) the information

15. In order to avoid skewing his results by his own preexisting knowledge, Ebbinghaus used _____ as the material he learned in his classic studies of memory.
    a. nonsense syllables
    b. geometric shapes
    c. notes or sounds made by tuning forks
    d. words he'd never even seen before
    e. names of obscure classical composers with whom he was totally unfamiliar

16. Long-term potentiation refers to
    a. increased sensitivity to excitation in Neuron B, after receiving repeated firing from Neuron A
    b. decreased sensitivity to excitation in Neuron B, after receiving repeated firing from Neuron A
    c. decreased calcium ion permeability of the synapse between two neurons
    d. the situation where Neuron A has to do more firing than usual to get a response from Neuron B
    e. all of the above

17. Which of the following does not seem to be an accurate statement concerning the hippocampus?
    a. a forebrain structure lying inside of the temporal lobe
    b. processes declarative but not procedural memory
    c. controls motor behavior and coordination
    d. retrieves information in storage for comparison with the current stimuli
    e. links the various distinct elements and meanings of a stimulus

18. In a classic study on the role of decay in forgetting, researchers found that students who learned ten nonsense syllables remembered more if they _____ between the original learning and the memory test.
    a. studied other nonsense syllables
    b. studied meaningful material
    c. watched television
    d. had sex
    e. slept

19. Which of the following is not among the causes of memory reconstruction considered in your text?
    a. separation of information and its source
    b. incorrect inferences
    c. the misinformation effect
    d. redintegration of id impulses in the form of false memories

20. Research cited in your text has indicated that in comparison to Korean mothers, Euro-American mothers talk with their children
    a. less often about their children's personal experiences
    b. three times more often about their children's personal experiences
    c. more often about how to behave properly
    d. less often in ways that involved discussion of the children's feelings

For each of the following items, circle "T" if the statement is True, and "F" if the statement is False.

21.　　T　F　Eidetic memory differs from photographic memory in that eidetic images cannot be retrieved once they have faded.

22.　　T　F　Long-term memory has no known limits in capacity or time.

23.　　T　F　Episodic and semantic memory are both types of declarative memory.

24.　　T　F　Retrieval cues are critically important determinants of memory performance in a recognition task.

25.　　T　F　Memory consolidation is the transfer of information from the hippocampus to the cortex.

26.　　T　F　Technological innovations over the past decade have allowed for sophisticated analytical studies indicating quite clearly that the information corresponding to each of our memories is stored inside individual, memory-specific neurons.

27.　　T　F　Retrograde amnesia is the inability to learn or remember new experiences that occurred after some kind of neurological trauma.

28.　　T　F　Damage to the hippocampus appears to impair one's ability to form new and to retrieve old declarative memories.

29.　　T　F　For some reason which has not yet been satisfactorily explained, children who have not attended school seem to have better short-term recall ability than do children who have attended school.

30.　　T　F　The spacing effect refers to the fact that we tend to remember information better when it is learned over a series of sessions broken up by rest periods.

F. Teaching-To-Learn Exercise

1. *Let Me Teach You This.*

Write in the space provided below, the five facts, ideas, etc., from this chapter that you'd most like to teach to your own student(s) if you were a teacher. Then, really do try to communicate these facts or ideas to someone in your life; or, pretend to teach this content to a hypothetical or "make-believe" student or class.

2. *Now Answer My Questions.*

Write in the space provided below, the five facts, ideas, etc., from this chapter that you'd most like to teach to your own student(s) if you were a teacher. Then, really do try to communicate these facts or ideas to someone in your life; or, pretend to teach this content to a hypothetical or "make-believe" student or class.

G. Bringing Psychology To Life Exercise

The so-called *serial position effect* refers to the rather well-established finding that our ability to remember things is often affected very substantially by the order in which we learned them. Research on memory has shown that content learned at the beginning (*primacy effect*) and end (*recency effect*) of a unit of information tends to be remembered better than content in the middle of that unit.

You'll need eight volunteers, preferably four men and four women, to serve as participants in a mini-experiment in which you can test for yourself the generality of such order effects in memory. Tell each participant only that you're conducting an experiment for your psychology class, and that the task in this experiment is to try to remember words that are recited by the experimenter. Tell them also that their participation in the experiment will require about ten minutes. For your laboratory, find a reasonably quiet place where you can test each of participant individually without being interrupted.

Answer Key To Self-Quiz

1. e
2. c
3. d
4. a
5. c
6. a
7. b
8. c
9. d
10. a
11. d
12. e
13. c
14. b
15. a
16. a
17. c
18. e
19. d
20. b
21. T
22. T
23. T
24. F
25. T
26. F
27. F
28. T
29. F
30. T

CHAPTER 7

Cognition And Intelligence

A. Learning Objectives

After your reading and effective study of Chapter 7, you should:

1. Know what the term "cognition" means, and why cognition is important in the study of psychology.

2. Know the following about what psychologists refer to as "concepts:"
    a. The role of concepts in cognition, and what concepts allow humans to do;
    b. The essential idea of the critical features model of concept-formation, and the kind of mental operations which it presumes to occur in the classification of new stimuli;
    c. The essential idea of the prototype model of concept-formation, and the kind of mental operations which it presumes to occur in the classification of new stimuli;
    d. The essential idea of the resembles-an-instance model of concept-formation, and the kind of mental operations which it presumes to occur in the classification of new stimuli; and
    e. What is meant by the term "universal concept," and be able to identify examples of such.

3. Know about the psychological study of information processing strategies and their relevance to the use of concepts in thinking, with attention to the following:
    a. How concept formation is affected by information processing;
    b. The difference between what Piaget referred to as "assimilation" and "accommodation" in the response to new stimuli, as well as the kinds of factors affecting the likelihood of these two response modes;
    c. The difference between "top-down" vs. "bottom-up" modes of information processing, as exemplified in everyday life circumstances with which you are familiar;
    d. The way in which factors such as accessibility, the cognitive structures and schemata within which concepts are embedded, culture, and racially-based experiences help to explain individual differences among people in the concepts they form;
    e. The kinds of factors affecting the accessibility of concepts;
    f. How the use of concepts is associated with individual differences in the cognitive structuring or organization of concepts, and how such structuring may be related to differences in personality and cognitive style variables such as tolerance for ambiguity and openness to complexity;
    g. Cultural differences in concepts as they are associated with factors such as
        (1) The prototypes used to define concepts;
        (2) The kinds of cognitive abilities needed and the values within any culture; as

well as

(3) In-group/out-group schemata and experiences with racism.

h. How cognitive accessibility can affect what we notice and interpret in our world;

i. Some of the many ways in which cognitive structure can have profound effects on our thinking, by influencing all aspects of it from what information we expect, look for, notice, assimilate, remember, and how we interpret that information;

j. About the role of what psychologists refer to as "set" in human thinking, and the kinds of factors that affect both cognitive accessibility and set; and

k. How we use concepts and cognitive strategies to solve problems, being able to identify and define the essential characteristics of the major types of such strategies, including mental imagery, algorithms, and the three types of heuristic approaches.

4. Have a working familiarity with the psychological study of intelligence, including:

a. An ability to give a good, technical definition of intelligence;

b. The first modern intelligence test as developed by Alfred Binet, as well as the way in which problem-solving was emphasized in the definition of intelligence which guided his work;

c. The arguments supporting and contradicting the view of intelligence as either a general cognitive ability or several different cognitive abilities;

d. How most U. S. psychologists tend to favor an operational definition of intelligence, and the difference between group vs. individually-administered tests of intelligence;

e. The Wechsler Intelligence Scales and how they differ from the Stanford-Binet Scale;

f. What an aptitude test is designed to measure and the kinds of factors that tend to influence aptitude test performance;

g. The following about "IQ:"

(1) What an "IQ" is;

(2) The IQ range associated with identification of a person as "gifted," and what psychologists have learned about people so identified;

(3) The IQ range associated with identification of a person as "mentally retarded," and what psychologists have learned about people so identified;

h. How tests themselves are evaluated in terms of their reliability, validity, and standardization;

i. The issue of bias in intelligence tests, considering cultural-specificity of tasks and the use of "culture-fair" tests;

j. How the consistent finding of group differences on traditional tests of intelligence has been the subject of intense controversy regarding racial inferiority and gender differences in cognitive skills; and

k. The role of heredity and environment in the development of intelligence, and the relevance of research on twins and adopted children to identifying just how biology and experience are involved in contributing to individual differences in the nature of human intelligence.

5. The psychological study of creativity, with special attention to:

a. How psychologists define creativity;

b. How creativity happens;

c. The kinds of factors that seem to help us come up with creative ideas;

d. What creativity seems to require in terms of our own assumptions about ideas;

e. How psychologists try to explain the fact that creativity often occurs during what is sometimes referred to as "the incubation period" in development of a creative idea;

f. Some of the ways in which educational situations can be structured so as to nurture the development of creativity in students.

B. Preview/Review Outline Of Key Terms And Concepts

Before you read the corresponding chapter in your text, read over the following outline. It is designed to give you an overview of information presented in the chapter, and how the various elements of that information are related to each other. After reading through the whole chapter and/or before course exams, you may use this outline as a quick review guide. In your reviews, mask off one line of the outline at a time, and try to recite from your memory of the chapter, the information that you expect to appear on the next line or so.

In going over this outline as a preview before reading and studying the chapter, the questions posed in bold print will help to keep you focused on the learning objectives here, and keep you actively involved in the process of achieving those objectives. When using this section as a review, try to answer the questions. Refer back to the chapter in the text for a more detailed feedback check on your mastery of the material, and/or to strengthen your knowledge and understanding wherever you feel the need to do so.

I. Concepts: The Building Blocks of Our Thoughts

How did the improvising by Drs. Wallace and Wong in the British Airways Flight 32 emergency reflect creative thinking?

    A. Forming Concepts to Make Sense of Stimuli

How do people use concepts?

        1. Critical Features Model

What is the major inadequacy of the critical features model?

        2. Prototype Model
            a. Prototypical Example
            b. Family Resemblance To Prototype
        3. Resembles-An-Instance Model
    B. Similarities in Concepts Formed
        1. Universal Human Experiences
        2. Time
        3. Primary And Secondary Colors

II. Information-Processing Strategies: Using Concepts to Think

What is indicated about the nature of human information processing, by psychologists' research into what happens when juries are instructed to disregard testimony immediately after it has been given in a courtroom?

      A. Assimilation vs. Accommodation

How would you describe the dysfunctional effects on a person's thinking, due to habitual imbalance of assimilation and accommodation in the processing of information?

      B. From the Bottom-Up or the Top-Down
          1. Bottom-Up Information-Processing
             a. Collecting And Processing Bits Of Information
             b. Building A Pattern Or Overarching Form Or Concept
          2. Top-Down Information-Processing
             a. Concepts And Expectations
             b. Noticing Stimuli
             c. Organizing And Interpreting Stimuli

How were both bottom-up and top-down information-processing evidenced in the way the physicians Wallace and Wong diagnosed and treated the medical emergency on Flight 32 described in the opening vignette of this chapter?

      C. Differences in Thinking Processes

How might you explain racism and sexism in terms of individual differences in accommodation as a mode of information-processing? What do the differences between people who grow up in Arab cultures as compared to those who grow up in U.S. culture, in the way they think about camels and cars, illustrate about the nature of concept formation?

          1. Differences Due to Concept Accessibility
             a. Experience
                 (1) Recency and Frequency of Use
                 (2) Memorable Experiences More Accessible
             b. Expectations
                 (1) The Representativeness Heuristic
                 (2) Unconscious Defense Against Unpleasant Situations
                 (3) Mood
                 (4) Behavior
             c. And Impressions We Form of Other People
             d. And Perceived Likelihood of Events: The Availability Heuristic

How might you use the idea of the availability heuristic to explain the tendency for people to overestimate their chances of being victims of natural disasters, airplane crashes, or crime?

          2. Differences Due to Cognitive Structure
             a. Exemplified in the Concept of What Is An Intelligent Person

What is reflected by the placement of a concept in a cognitive structure?

      b. The Clustering of Concepts In Thinking
          (1) Schema As Conceptual Framework
              (a) Knowledge and Networks of Concepts
              (b) Beliefs and Expectations
              (c) Individual Differences In Clustering of Concepts
          (2) Effects Of Schema on Information Processing

How does a schema affect the way information is processed ?

          (3) Organization Of Schemata And Personality
              (a) Simple, Rigidly Structured Perceptions of Self and Others
              (b) And Fine Distinctions, Complex Integration of Concepts
   3. Cultural Perspectives on the Concepts We Form
      a. Differences in the Nature of Concepts Formed
      b. Differences in Accessibility and Representativeness of Concepts
      c. Differences in Cognitive Abilities and Schemata Needed
      d. Differences in Schemata and Cultural Values
          (1) In Individualist Cultures
          (2) In Collectivist Cultures
      e. Differences in Euro- and African Americans' Concepts of "Hero"
   4. Racial Perspectives on the Concepts We Form
      a. Different Racial Groups' Perceptions of Each Other
          (1) Differences in Schemata for In-Group and Out-Group Members
          (2) Effects on Schemata of Unusual or Highly-Visible Out-Group Members
      b. Differences in Schemata About Police Officers

How are differences in schemata, accessibility of concepts, and experience used in your text to explain differences between people of color and middle-class, Euro-Americans in their attitudes toward police?

  D. Conceptual Barriers to Problem Solving
      1. Conceptualization and Attitudes
      2. Conceptualization and Problem Solving
      3. Modern Racism and Sexism

As described in your text, how do modern racists and sexists explain the inequalities in the distribution of wealth and power in our society?

      4. Concepts, Set, and Problem Solving
         a. Readiness To Respond
         b. Functional Fixedness

What observations might you invoke to show how functional fixedness was apparently overcome by Dr. Wallace in his treatment of the medical emergency aboard Flight 32?

     E. Using Cognitive Strategies to Solve Problems
          1. Mental Imagery
               a. Forming Pictures in One's Own Mind
               b. Cognitive Maps
          2. Step-by-Step Algorithms

What is the principal "good news" or advantage and "bad news" or disadvantage characteristic of algorithmic approaches to problem solving?

          3. Non-Random Heuristic Strategies
               a. Selectively-Generated Problem-Solving Strategies
               b. Working Backward
               c. Using An Analogy
               d. Means-End Analysis

III. Intelligence: The Ability to Think of Solutions
     A. Different Definitions of Intelligence
          1. Good Judgment
               a. Binet's Definition Of Intelligence As Judgment
                    (1) Facing The Problem and Identifying The Right Solution
                    (2) Monitoring Progress of the Solution
                    (3) Modifying The Solution
               b. Binet's Intelligence Test Comprised of Sub-Tests
          2. General Intelligence
               a. Terman's Concept of Intelligence
                    (1) Single, Measurable Capacity for Abstract Thinking
                    (2) Used In All Activities of Life
               b. Spearman's Work
                    (1) Factor Analysis
                    (2) Different, Correlated Behaviors As Reflecting Single, Underlying Variable
                    (3) The *g factor*
                    (4) Neural Processing Speed

What is factor analysis, and what is it designed to do?

          3. Multiple Intelligence
               a. Several Types of Intelligence
               b. Clusters of Different Types And False Impression of g Factor
               c. Howard Gardner's Proposed Schema
                    (1) Linguistic Intelligence
                    (2) Logical-Mathematical Intelligence

(3) Spatial Intelligence
(4) Interpersonal Intelligence
(5) Intrapersonal Intelligence
(6) Body-Kinesthetic Intelligence
(7) Musical Intelligence
4. Triarchic Theory of Intelligence
    a. Skills in Different Areas of Life
    b. Sternberg's Triarchic Theory
       (1) Academic Intelligence
       (2) Experiential Intelligence
       (3) Practical Intelligence
    c. Academic Intelligence As Fluid Intelligence
    d. Practical Intelligence As Crystallized Intelligence
B. Measuring Intelligence

What is an "operational definition," and how do psychologists define intelligence operationally?

1. Group Intelligence Tests
    a. Paper-and-Pencil Tests
    b. Military Uses
       (1) Army Alpha Test
       (2) Armed Forces Qualification Test

What is "academic tracking"? What arguments might you make both in favor and against such "tracking"? (See Box 7.1. Alternative Perspectives on Uses of Intelligence Tests)

    c. Aptitude Tests

How do aptitude tests differ from intelligence tests?

2. The Stanford-Binet Intelligence Scale
    a. Binet's Test Designed For The French Public School System
    b. Terman's Revision of Binet's Test
    c. Generally Considered A Verbal Test

What are some of the tasks of the Stanford-Binet scale as applied to children? What types of examinees might be at risk for having their cognitive abilities underestimated by their performance on this test?

3. The Wechsler Intelligence Scales
    a. Adult Intelligence Scale, Revised (WAIS-R)
    b. Intelligence Scale for Children, Revised (WISC-R)
    c. Pre-school and Primary Scale of Intelligence (WPPSI)
4. The IQ Score
    a. I.Q. as Shorthand for "Intelligence Quotient"
    b. I.Q. = MA/CA X 100

     (1) MA Refers to "Mental Age"

     (2) CA refers to Chronological Age

     (3) Indicates Ability Relative To Others In One's Age Group

   c. Idea of Mental Age Inappropriate As Applied To Adults

   d. Deviation Scores

   e. Performance and Verbal Sub-Scale Scores on
     Wechsler Scales

 5. Extreme IQ Scores

   a. Mean Of 100

     (1) Score of 130+,"Very Superior"

     (2) Score of 69 or Lower, "Mentally Deficient"

   b. Intellectually Gifted Individuals

     (1) Top Two Or Three Percent of the Population

     (2) The Popular Stereotype

     (3) Terman's Long-Term Study

   c. Mentally Retarded Individuals

     (1) Mild Mental Retardation

     (2) Labeling And Potential For Discrimination

What are some of the findings from formal research studies of gifted individuals, and how do these findings fit the popular stereotype of such people?

 C. Evaluating Intelligence Tests

   1. Reliability

   a. Consistency Of Results

   b. Re-Test Reliability

   2. Validity

   a. Criterion Validity

   b. Content Validity

   c. Intelligence Tests And Academic Performance/Success

   d. Intelligence Tests And Occupational Success

   3. Standardization

   4. Cultural Perspectives on Intelligence Tests

   a. Concerns About Bias Against Children Other Than Middle-Class Euro-
     Americans

   b. Cultural Specificity of Tests

   c. Research On Liberian and U. S. Children Given Sorting Task

     (1) Sorting of Rice Or Geometric Figures

     (2) Task Performance and Familiarity/Unfamiliarity With Items
       To Be Sorted

   d. Cultural Differences in Task Values And Familiarity

   e. Culture-Fair Intelligence Tests

     (1) No Culture Specific Information Or Verbal Skills

     (1) Raven Progressive Matrices

As noted in your text, how effective are intelligence tests in predicting academic achievement?

190

D. Differences in Intelligence
    1. Racial Differences
        a. Criterion Validity Of Intelligence Tests
        b. Interpreting Racial Group Differences
        c. Arthur Jensen's Genetic Inferiority Argument
            (1) Based On Euro-American Population
                Heritability Estimates
            (2) Variation Within A Trait
        d. View Attacked By Most Psychologists As Racist
            (1) Overlooks Impact of Environment
            (2) Racial Differences Disappear With Economic Situation
                and Learning Opportunities Taken Into Account
            (3) Heritability Estimates Apply Only Within
                and Not Between Populations

How did Jensen explain racial differences in intelligence? What seems to be the most serious logical flaw in Jensen's argument?

    2. Gender Differences
        a. Declining Over Second Half of the 1900's
        b. Verbal versus Math and Visual-Spatial Tasks
        c. And Differences in Experiences Such As Play Activities
        d. Biological Perspective: Sex Hormones, Skills, and Abilities
            (1) Prenatal Exposure to Excess Testosterone
            (2) Testosterone Supplementation And Men's Spatial Skills
    3. Differences Due to Heredity
        a. Heredity Provides Possible Range for Our Intelligence
        b. Studies of Twins and Adopted Children

Generally speaking, what do the studies of twins and adopted children indicate about the role of heredity in the development of intelligence?

    4. Differences Due to the Environment
        a. Intellectual Impoverishment In Environment
        b. Schools And Playgrounds in Poor Neighborhoods
        c. Poverty And Emotional Support
        d. Enriched Environments That Provide Intellectual Stimulation
        e. Rise In Intelligence Test Scores During the 1990's

What explanation is offered in your text for the superior math skills of Japanese and Taiwanese children?

II. Creativity: The Ability to Generate Useful, Novel Ideas

How would you define "creativity"? What are the three cognitive characteristics of creativity, and how are each of these three cognitive characteristics measured by the "Alternate Uses Test"?

A. Processes of Creativity
    1. Generating Novel Ideas
        a. Importance of Knowledge and Expertise
        b. Divergent Thinking
        c. Convergent Thinking
        d. Creative Insight

What has "incubation" got to do with the emergence of creative insights?

    2. Evaluating Ideas
        a. Critical Thinking, Rational Analysis, Examining Assumptions
        b. Intelligence And Creativity
B. Developing the Ability to be Creative

In what kinds of environments does creativity tend to emerge? What are some of the environmental characteristics associated with creativity in the classroom?

C. Applying Techniques to Develop Your Own Creative Efforts (Box 7.2)

What are some of the very specific strategies that can be used to help develop one's own creativity?

C. Self-Generated Questions: What's In This One For Me?

Most people come to the first course in psychology expecting to learn some things which will help them to better understand themselves, other people in their lives, and/or the nature of life in the world in which they live. Along these same lines, students of psychology often look forward to discovering things about human behavior and experience which may help them to improve their own life by developing their talents, technical skills, knowledge and abilities, and/or the quality or their relationships with other people. On the basis of such self-interest, which tends to provide a framework in terms of which new learning becomes personally meaningful and thus easier to remember, write down a few questions in the space below, about the subject matter covered in this chapter. After reading and studying the chapter, come back to see how any of what you've learned may be useful to you in finding answers to these questions.

D. Completion Items

The words in the margins of this exercise are the ones that correctly complete the sentence on the corresponding line. To get the most out of this exercise, you should try to avoid looking at these words in the margin until after you've filled in the corresponding blanks with the words you think best complete the sentences. So, begin the exercise by covering up all of the margin words with a piece of paper. Then, for each blank, write in the word which you think completes the sentence. Even if you're not sure as to the word, write in your best guess, preferably in pencil so you can erase and re-write any incorrect responses you may make here.

After writing in your "answer," slide the paper covering up the margin words down just far enough to see the word for the blank you just filled-in. For each blank that you fill-in correctly, put a check mark (√) after your answer. If the word you wrote in doesn't match the word corresponding to that blank, mark an (X) next to your response and go on to the next blank. It's probably a good idea to go back to the text and try to strengthen your learning related to topic coverage that corresponds in the textbook chapter to those blanks which you filled-in incorrectly, since those items signal a weak link in your concept mastery chain for this chapter.

1. In the medical emergency that occurred aboard British Airways Flight 32, the life of passenger Paula Dixon depended on Dr. Wallace's
_____ ability -- that is, his ability to gather, store, and retrieve   cognitive
information. Cognition affects (a) what _____ we notice;   stimuli
(b) how we _____ what we notice; and (c) how we respond.   interpret

2. Concepts are mental _____ or underlying ideas used to   categories
think about and remember situations, ideas, objects, and qualities. Our
concepts determine how we decide whether or not events or ideas are
_____ to each other and how we form impressions of events,   related
people, ideas, qualities, and objects. Our concepts affect what behavior
_____ we think are available to us.   options

3. The critical _____ model states that an object, event,   features
person, quality or idea must have particular characteristics to be included
in a concept. This model doesn't take into consideration _____   variations
in how well an event, object, or person fits the concept.

4. According to the _____ model, each concept has an example   prototype
that is most typical, has most of the characteristics of members of the concept,
or is the most _____ member of the category.   memorable

5. According to the resembles-an- _____ model, a new   instance
stimulus is compared to an instance of the concept that it most closely
resembles. If the new stimulus is similar enough to the instance, that
stimulus is _____ in terms of the concept.   interpreted

6. The concepts of primary and _____ colors are the   secondary

193

same across most cultures. In support of the prototype theory of
concept formation, people also tend to use the same prototypes and
_____ prototypical colors better than unusual ones. In   remember
every language studied, there are terms for both _____   black
and white or dark and colored. When a culture has a third word for color,
the color is always _____.   red

7. Psychologists have found that even when people have been
instructed to ignore _____ and they conscientiously tried   information
to do so, they still process it. When people _____, they   assimilate
interpret new stimuli in terms of concepts that already exist in their minds.
Sometimes people _____ their concepts, which means that   accommodate
they change their concepts to fit new stimuli. Whether people assimilate
or accommodate depends in part on the _____ and their values,   situation
personality, and motives. People who assimilate most of the time form
relatively simplistic concepts and tend to be closed-_____.   minded
If people never assimilated they would have to develop a new
_____ for every new stimulus they   concept
encountered. If people never accommodated, their _____   understanding
of the world would be extremely limited.

8. _____-up information-processing involves collecting and   Bottom
processing bits of information and then building on those bits of information
until a pattern or overarching form or concept is perceived. With top-down
information-processing, an individual starts with a concept and then notices
and _____ stimuli in terms of that concept.   interprets

9. Sometimes people form different concepts because they identify
different _____ features, think of different prototypes, or   critical
have knowledge of different instances of a concept. Another reason why
people differ in their thinking processes is that they vary in whether or not
they _____ or accommodate in response to new stimuli.   assimilate
For example, one way of explaining _____ and sexism is that   racism
when new information is encountered which challenges an existing concept
about the shared characteristics of members of a certain group, rather than
to accommodate the existing concept in recognition of individual differences
among members of the group, the new information is _____   distorted
to fit the existing concept about that group.

10. Some concepts come to mind more easily than do others. A concept
that has been used _____ or frequently is more accessible than   recently
is a concept that has not been so used. When an experience is memorable
it is likely to become cognitively accessible. Expectations can also affect
the accessibility of concepts. The representativeness _____   heuristic
refers to the tendency to expect the prototypical instance of an event or
characteristic to be the most likely to occur. When individuals are in a negative
_____, negative interpretations of behavior become accessible   mood

194

so that negative characteristics are more likely to be "seen" in others. The accessibility of a concept can influence what we notice and how we _____ what we notice. Cognitive accessibility affects the interpret impressions we form of other people. One reason why negative depictions of ethnic and racial minorities in television and movies have been protested, is that these characterizations make negative images cognitively _____. The tendency to think that cognitively accessible events accessible are likely to happen is the _____ heuristic. Thus, for example, availability people tend to _____ the chances of their becoming victims of overestimate natural disasters, airplane crashes, or crime because such events are covered vividly by the media, making them easy to _____. remember

11. Everyone uses the same general methods of forming concepts and neuron connections in the brain. But people differ in their cognitive _____, which means that their concepts are structure organized and connected to other concepts in different ways. The placement of a concept in a cognitive structure reflects the _____ that an individual has assigned to that concept and meaning the behaviors and qualities the individual associates with it. A _____ is a conceptual framework made up of various schema concepts that a person thinks are related to each other. It includes a person's knowledge and networks of concepts, beliefs, and _____ about situations, objects, people, or events. Once expectations a schema is formed, it affects what information is searched for, noticed, assimilated, and _____, and what meaning is attributed to remembered that information. The way in which people organize their concepts into schemata is related to their personality, tolerance of ambiguity, and openness to _____. People who see themselves and others complexity in an unambiguous, simple, rigidly structured way are particularly likely to use _____ when characterizing people. stereotypes

12. One reason for cross-cultural differences in schemata is that different cognitive abilities and schemata are _____ in needed different cultures. Cross-cultural differences in schemata also reflect cultural values. In _____ cultures, people tend to individualist conceive of themselves as independent and they develop rich schemata about their individuality. In collectivist cultures, individuals tend to think of themselves in terms of their interdependence on other people and they develop rich schemata about their _____ relationships with others.

13. Sometimes the way different racial groups see each other reflects a general tendency to see in-groups and _____ differently. out-groups When people belong to a group, all the members of that group are _____ members. All those outside the group are out-group in-group members. People have different _____ for in-group and out- schemata group members. Individuals tend to perceive more variety among in-group

members; out-group members tend to be seen as more _____.   homogeneous

14. Many of the ways we process _____ -- assimilation,   information
accommodation, bottom-up processing and top-down processing -- can
be barriers to problem solving. Concepts affect our _____,   set
our readiness to respond in particular ways. Sometimes a set can interfere
with one's ability to solve problems or see stimuli in _____ ways.   new
One type of set is functional _____, a tendency to perceive and   fixedness
think about objects in the same ways that they have been perceived and
thought of in the past.

15. We also use concepts to solve problems. Sometimes people use
mental _____, forming pictures in their minds to solve   imagery
problems. One type of mental imagery is a _____ map, a   cognitive
concept or mental image of a pathway which enables us to find our way
around the environment.

16. A cognitive strategy that considers all possible solutions to a problem
in a systematic, step- by-step way is an _____. Such   algorithm
strategies always produce a solution to the problem, but not always in the
most _____ way.   efficient

17. _____ are selectively-generated problem-solving   Heuristics
strategies. The strategies selected are often those that previous
_____ or knowledge suggests would be good. These   experience
approaches are short-cuts to problem-solving, but they don't always
lead to a _____. One such strategy involves working   solution
backward to determine how to reach a goal, another is to use an analogy
to the current problem, and yet another is to use a _____-   means
ends analysis, an assessment of a situation and the creation of a plan to
reach a desired goal. The latter involves breaking down a problem into
several small problems or _____.   subgoals

18. Intelligence is the ability to _____ successfully to the   adapt
environment by using cognitive processes to guide behavior. French
psychologist Alfred Binet defined intelligence as _____,   judgment
or "good sense, practical sense, initiative, and the faculty of adapting
one's self to circumstances." Binet strongly opposed the concept of
intelligence as a _____ ability, and did not assume that each   single
person had a stable ability for "good judgment" in all situations.

19. U. S. psychologist Lewis Terman viewed intelligence as a single,
measurable capacity for _____ thinking. Psychologist   abstract
Charles Spearman demonstrated mathematically that intelligence test
sub-test scores were due largely to the common variable of
_____ intelligence. Spearman used a statistical procedure   general
known as _____ analysis to show that different, correlated   factor

behaviors actually reflect a single, underlying variable or factor. The correlations among intelligence test sub-test scores might reflect something other than general intelligence, such as neural _____ speed.

processing

20. Another perspective on intelligence is that there are several types of intelligence that are _____ of each other. Psychologist Howard Gardner is a well-known proponent of multiple intelligence, who does not deny the existence of general intelligence, but questions its usefulness in explaining adaptive behavior outside the _____. Accordingly, Gardner proposes a schema of several types of intelligence, including _____ intelligence, which refers to the ability to use words, and _____ intelligence, which refers to the ability to notice other people's feelings.

independent

classroom

linguistic
interpersonal

21. Psychologist Robert Sternberg proposes a _____ theory of intelligence that includes three types of intelligence: (1) academic intelligence, (2) experiential intelligence, and (3) _____ intelligence. Academic intelligence largely involves fluid intelligence, reasoning and quick thinking. Practical intelligence relies largely on _____ intelligence, or acquired skills and knowledge. Fluid intelligence peaks at the end of formal schooling, then begins to decline around age _____ after a period of stability. Practical intelligence remains stable as people age, and can even increase with age because it involves skills and _____ that add up through the years.

triarchic

practical

crystallized

50

knowledge

22. Most psychologists use an _____ definition of intelligence, an explicit definition of how the variables of a concept are measured. The military uses _____ tests of intelligence, such as the Army Alpha Test and the Armed Forces Qualification Test. Group testing is cheaper and more efficient than _____ testing.

operational

group

individual

23. _____ tests, which are designed to predict your ability to learn a particular set of skills. Unlike aptitude tests, intelligence tests measure a much broader range of skills and are less affected by one's _____ than aptitude test performance.

Aptitude

knowledge

24. Intelligence tests have earned a negative reputation because they have been used for the purpose of academic _____, or the academic segregation of children based solely on test scores. This procedure is intended to match a child's abilities with the proper resources. However, it may _____ against children who are labeled as intellectually delayed or deficient. Children who are assigned to "low" track classrooms may develop low expectations

tracking

discriminate

for themselves and a negative attitude toward _____.   learning
Teachers sometimes direct children who are labeled as
"mentally delayed" toward inappropriately _____ goals.   low

25. At the turn of the nineteenth century, the French government
commissioned French psychologist Alfred Binet to design a test that
would identify students who did not fully benefit from the public
_____ system. American psychologist Lewis Terman   school
changed some of the items in Binet's test and established U. S.
_____ for correct answers, in developing what is called   norms
the _____-Binet Intelligence Scale. The latter test is   Stanford
generally considered by psychologists as a verbal test which tends to
underestimate the cognitive abilities of examinees who have limited
English _____ skills for their age group.   language

26. The _____ Intelligence Scales include a better balance   Wechsler
between verbal and performance tasks than the Stanford-Binet.
Performance tasks require _____ skills, such as arranging   non-verbal
pictures in an order that tells a meaningful story.

27. The Stanford-Binet and Wechsler Scales yield a single intelligence
score referred to as an "I.Q." which is shorthand for intelligence
_____. In the equation for calculation of an IQ, the term "CA"   quotient
refers to the individual's chronological or actual age, and the term "MA"
refers to an individual's _____ age, which is a way of   mental
representing that person's performance relative to the average
performance of a particular age group. The IQ is not an absolute measure
of intelligence, but rather an indication of an individual's ability
_____ to others in his/her age group. the idea of mental age   relative
makes sense for children but not for adults. Hence, both the Stanford-Binet
and the Wechsler scales now provide a _____ score, which   deviation
reflects an examinee's performance in comparison to the average performance
of age-mates.

28. Intellectually gifted individuals have intelligence test scores in the top
_____ percent of the population. Contrary to popular stereotype,   two or three
gifted individuals do not suffer more emotional or _____   social
problems than other people. Mentally retarded individuals are people who
score below _____ points on intelligence tests and often cannot   70
keep up with standard classroom activities without special help. Critics of
intelligence tests argue against the _____ of children as mentally   labeling
retarded because of the potential for discrimination.

29. _____ refers to how consistently a test gives the same results.   Reliability
_____ validity refers to the extent to which test results relate to the   Criterion
behaviors of interest. _____ validity refers to the inclusion of items   Content
that are representative of the concept being tested. Intelligence tests succeed

quite well in predicting _____ success. However, intelligence
test performance has only a modest correlation with _____
success.

academic
occupational

30. Standardization refers to the use of standard procedures for
administration and _____ of tests.

scoring

31. Familiarity with test situations and test materials which is due to cultural
experiences can affect performance even on seemingly culture-
_____ tasks, such as sorting objects. Also, cultural groups
can differ in the types of cognitive tasks that they _____ and
with which they are familiar. The Raven Progressive Matrices test is
considered to be relatively culture-fair because it requires no
_____ skills. However, even on the latter test, performance
can be affected by cultural differences insofar as it requires examinees to
think of a rule or a cognitive _____.

neutral
value

verbal

strategy

32. Psychologist Arthur Jensen argued that African Americans averaged
lower intelligence test scores and poorer academic performance than
Euro-Americans because of _____ inferiority. Most
psychologists disagree with Jensen's argument and regard his view as
a form of _____. Later research has shown that racial
differences in intelligence virtually disappear when a child's
_____ situation and learning opportunities are taken into
account. Jensen's argument is also flawed by the fact that the
heritability estimates he used as the basis for his conclusions apply
only to variation _____ a population, and not to variation
between populations.

genetic

racism

economic

within

33. Females perform slightly better than do males on tasks requiring
_____ production, whereas males have a slight edge on
mathematics and visual-_____ tasks. Gender differences
in experiences, such as _____ activities and social
expectations, might explain these differences. From a biological
perspective, some researchers suggest that sex _____
may play a role in the development of such differences, in that
_____ levels are negatively correlated with spatial ability
for both males and females, whereas males and females exposed to
excess _____ before birth tend to have improved
spatial skills, as do men who receive supplements of this hormone.

verbal
spatial
play

hormones

estrogen

testosterone

34. Research has indicated that _____ twins are more
 alike in intelligence than are fraternal twins, and have very similar but not
identical intelligence test scores whether they grow up together or apart.
But these findings do not prove that _____ causes intelligence,
identical twins share genes and very similar experiences with the
environment. _____ siblings have moderately correlated

identical

heredity

Adoptive

intelligence scores as children, but uncorrelated test scores as adults.
Adopted children have intelligence test scores more similar to those of
their _____ parents than to those of their adoptive parents.   biological

35. Enriched environments that provide intellectual _____   stimulation
and support a child's learning can greatly enhance cognitive development.
An enriched environment is a key reason why children in Japan and Taiwan
have better _____ skills than any other group. The steady   math
rise in intelligence test scores during the 1990's provides other evidence
of the role of _____ in intellectual development.   environment

36. _____ is a way of solving problems with original ideas   Creativity
that are constructive and meaningful. It involves three important cognitive
characteristics: originality, fluency, and _____. Contrary to   flexibility
the stereotype that creativity occurs out-of-the-blue, most creative
solutions emerge thoughtfully. _____ thinking involves   Divergent
exploring many apparently unrelated ideas and alternatives to
a question or problem, and helps people to generate original ideas.
Some people are better able to engage in divergent thinking than others
because their concepts are organized in _____ rather than   flexible
rigid schemas, which makes unusual associations between concepts
more likely to occur. A sudden burst of creative _____ is an   insight
experience often described by math scholars. One reason why an
incubation period may help creativity, is that during such periods the person
may let go of a mental set that was preventing cognitive _____   accessibility
to relevant information.

37. In addition to generating ideas, creativity also requires
_____ thinking, or rationally analyzing, questioning, and   critical
examining one's assumptions about an idea. Intelligent people tend to
perform well on tests of creativity, although creativity and intelligence are
_____ concepts. Exceptionally creative people are not   independent
exceptionally intelligent. Perhaps because creative people tend to think
in _____ images rather than in abstract concepts, they do not   concrete
usually fall in the gifted range of intelligence.

38. Creativity tends to emerge in environments that foster a safe climate
for exploration by being open to new ideas and encouraging
_____ thinking. For instance, classrooms that emphasize   flexible
self-_____ activity, self-evaluation, opportunities to handle   initiated
different materials and open discussions tend to increase creativity in
children. Most approaches to increasing creativity emphasize increasing
the fluidity, originality, and _____ of our thinking. Among the   flexibility
suggestions offered for increasing creativity are the following: (1) When
approaching a problem, absorb yourself in the problem and let go of
the emotional attachment you may have to the final _____   goal
or product; (2) critically evaluate an idea in different contexts and try to

_____ it differently; (3) challenge your assumptions about   perceive
the _____ features of a concept; and (4) keep at it.   critical

E. Self-Quiz

For each of the following items, circle the letter which precedes the correct alternative.

1. People often use concepts in place of
    a. observation
    b. interpretation of stimuli
    c. mental categories
    d. ideas

2. Which of the following is not one of the three prominent perspectives on how concepts are formed or defined?
    a. critical features model
    b. prototype model
    c. behavior social learning model
    d. resembles-an-instance model

3. When a culture has a third word for color after black and white or dark, that third color is always
    a. yellow
    b. green
    c. blue
    d. red

4. the concept of _____ best describes what happens when an individual starts with a concept and then notices and interprets stimuli in terms of that concept.
    a. accommodation
    b. inference
    c. top-down information processing
    d. bottom-up information processing

5. The "accessibility" of a concept refers to
    a. whether it involves top-down or bottom-up processing of information
    b. whether it involves accommodation or assimilation
    c. how easily it comes to mind
    d. how concrete or abstract it is
    e. how well differentiated it is

6. The availability heuristic is exemplified by the tendency to overestimate one's
  chances of being the victim of a
  a. natural disaster
  b. airplane crash
  c. crime
  d. all of the above
  e. none of the above

7. Cognitive _____ refers to the way in which a person's concepts are organized and connected to each other.
  a. assimilation
  b. accommodation
  c. structure
  d. function
  e. mapping

8. Which of the following is not included in a schema?
  a. knowledge
  b. assimilation
  c. beliefs
  d. expectations

9. People who see themselves and others in an unambiguous, simple, rigidly structured way are particularly likely to
  a. use accommodation
  b. be high in creativity
  c. live in collectivist cultures
  d. use stereotypes

10. Which of the following is not among those persons with whom a man is allowed to have sexual relationships in Pawnee culture?
  a. his wife
  b. his maternal uncle
  c. his maternal uncle's wife
  d. his wife's sister

11. Differences in schemata due to real-life experiences of different racial groups is illustrated in your text with regard to Euro-Americans' and African-Americans' attitudes toward which of the following groups?
  a. high-school teachers
  b. college professors
  c. medical and dental professionals
  d. police

12. Which of the following is a type of set which involves a tendency to perceive and think about objects in the same ways that they have been perceived and thought of in the past?
   a. functional fixedness
   b. accommodative inertia
   c. concrete inference
   d. stimulus boundedness
   e. retroactive inhibition

13. A cognitive strategy that considers all possible solutions to a problem in a systematic, step-by-step way that always results in a solution to the problem is a(n)
   a. mental image
   b. cognitive map
   c. algorithm
   d. heuristic

14. Which of the following is not among the primary heuristic strategies?
   a. working forward
   b. working backward
   c. analogy
   d. means-ends analysis

15. French psychologist Alfred Binet defined intelligence as involving all but which one of the following?
   a. judgment
   b. a single underlying ability
   c. initiative
   d. practical sense
   e. the faculty of adapting one's self to circumstances

16. Which of the following is not among the three primary dimensions of intelligence as it is conceptualized within the framework of Sternberg's triarchic theory?
   a. academic intelligence
   b. experiential intelligence
   c. practical intelligence
   d. sensori-motor intelligence

17. Which of the following is not true about "fluid intelligence"?
   a. largely involved in the determination of academic intelligence
   b. refers to acquired skills and knowledge
   c. peaks at the end of formal schooling
   d. begins to decline around age 50

18.   Which of the following provides a numerical way of representing a person's intelligence test performance relative to the average performance of his/her own age group?
    a. fluid intelligence score (FI)
    b. crystallized intelligence score (CI)
    c. deviation score
    d.   triarchic pattern score

19. Criterion validity refers to the extent to which the results of a test
    a. are consistent from one time to another
    b. are based on component measures which are representative of the concept being tested
    c. reflect both fluid and crystallized abilities
    d. relate to and predict the behavior of interest

20. Exposure of both males and females to excess testosterone before birth tends to be associated with
    a. increased likelihood of developing Alzheimer's disease
    b. improved development of spatial skills
    c. improved development of verbal skills
    d. increased probability of body dysmorphic disorder in adolescence

For each of the following items, circle "T" if the statement is True, and "F" if the statement is False.

21. T F   When a person has a concept, that person thinks that members of a particular mental category are all the same.

22. T F   The concepts of primary and secondary colors are the same across most cultures.

23. T F   Piaget's concept of assimilation refers to a person's interpretation of new stimuli in terms of concepts that already exist in that person's mind.

24. T F   Bottom-up information processing involves collecting and processing bits of information and then building on those until a pattern or overarching form or concept is perceived.

25. T F   The availability heuristic refers to the tendency to expect the prototypical instance of an event or characteristic to be most likely to occur.

26. T F   The placement of a concept in a cognitive structure reflects the meaning that an individual has assigned to that concept.

27. T F   Even rather complex schemata have relatively little effect on what information is noticed, assimilated, or remembered.

28. T F   Individuals tend to perceive more homogeneity among in-group than among out-group members.

29. T F Psychologist Charles Spearman interpreted the high correlation among intelligence test sub-tests as mathematical evidence for the idea of general intelligence.

30. T F Psychologists define intelligence operationally in terms of performance on intelligence tests.

F. Teaching-To-Learn Exercise

1. *Let Me Teach You This.*

Write in the space provided below, the five facts, ideas, etc., from this chapter that you'd most like to teach to your own student(s) if you were a teacher. Then, really do try to communicate these facts or ideas to someone in your life; or, pretend to teach this content to a hypothetical or "make-believe" student or class.

2. *Now Answer My Questions.*

Write in the space provided below, the five facts, ideas, etc., from this chapter that you'd most like to teach to your own student(s) if you were a teacher. Then, really do try to communicate these facts or ideas to someone in your life; or, pretend to teach this content to a hypothetical or "make-believe" student or class.

G. Bringing Psychology To Life Exercise

1. As discussed in the corresponding chapter in your textbook, a schema is a conceptual framework that includes a person's knowledge and networks of concepts, beliefs, and expectations about situations, objects, people, or events. People's schemata differ insofar as those schemata are constructed of different concepts and clusters of concepts. The cognitive significance of schemas is that they affect what information is searched for, noticed, assimilated, remembered, and the meaning attributed to that information.

For the purpose of this exercise, write a very brief essay, either completely fictional and hypothetical or based on real life experiences which you've actually observed, about a person who has a prejudicial schema regarding the members of a particular racial or ethnic group. Use this essay to illustrate (a) how a prejudicial schema can create a mind set in the prejudiced person which leads him/her to act prejudicially toward a member or members of the group which is the target of his/her prejudice; and (b) how those prejudicial behaviors can provoke a reaction (i.e., on the part of the person or people toward whom such prejudicial behavior is directed) which reinforces or strengthens the prejudicial schema. In the event that your essay is based on real life events, please do not reveal the true identity of any of the individuals involved.

    a. A Prejudicial Schema Leading To Prejudicial Behavior

    b. Reactions Which Reinforce The Prejudicial Schema

2. On the basis of your study of the corresponding chapter in your textbook, in the designated sections below, write brief arguments concerning (a) the appropriate uses, and (b) potential abuses of intelligence tests. Be sure to relate your arguments here to the material given in your text.

    a. Appropriate Uses Of Intelligence Tests

    b. Potential Abuses Of Intelligence Tests

3. Based on your reading and study of the corresponding chapter in your text, write an argument against Arthur Jensen's view that racial differences in intelligence test scores reflect genetic differences in intellectual inferiority/superiority.

4. Based on your reading and study of the corresponding chapter in your textbook, write brief arguments in the spaces given below for the views that gender differences in intelligence are due to (a) cultural-experiential differences, or (b) biology.

    a. <u>Cultural-Experiential Bases For Gender Differences In Intelligence</u>

    b. <u>Biology And Gender Differences In Intelligence</u>

Answer Key To Self-Quiz

1.	a
2.	c
3.	d
4.	c
5.	c
6.	d
7.	c
8.	b
9.	d
10.	b
11.	d
12.	a
13.	c
14.	a
15.	b
16.	d
17.	b
18.	c
19.	d
20.	b
21.	F
22.	T
23.	T
24.	T
25.	F
26.	T
27.	F
28.	F
29.	T
30.	T

CHAPTER 8

Development From Birth Through Childhood

A. Learning Objectives

After careful, effective study of Chapter 8, you should:

1. Know how and why psychologists characterize the process of human development as involving increasing complexity and integration.

2. Know what a "stage model" of development is, and how such models focus on similarities in the kinds of developmental tasks confronted by people in those various stages.

3.   Have a good understanding of the prenatal period of human development, being able to identify and define:
    a. The events which denote the beginning and end of that period;
    b. The three sub-phases of this period; and
    c. How factors such as exposure to hormones, chemicals, and socioeconomic status may affect prenatal development.

4. Have a working knowledge of infancy and toddlerhood, with special attention to:
    a. The kinds of perceptual abilities which infants possess at birth, the significance of those abilities in terms the child's relationship to his/her parents as crucial to the child's development;
    b. The kinds of reflexes with which children are born;
    c. How the pattern of development tends to unfold with regard to different internal organs, areas of the body, and motor abilities;
    d. How, in spite of cultural differences, children apparently reach the various "milestones" of development at roughly the same age;
    e. How individual differences among children in temperament, modifiable as such differences may be, play an important role in the child's relationships with the other people in his/her young life;
    f. Erikson's psychosocial stage perspective on human development, especially:
        (1) The kinds of "developmental tasks" postulated by this theory, and its assumptions concerning the significance of individual differences in how the challenges of those tasks are met; and
        (2) How other psychologists have focused on aspects of psychosocial development such as attachment and play.
    g. The "attachments" which children form with other people, especially with regard to:
        (1) The similarity among children in the nature of such attachments;
        (2) The significance of physical contact comfort to the formation, maintenance, and emotional function of such attachments; and
        (3) What psychologists have learned about the development of infants who are deprived of the opportunity to form such attachments; and

h. What psychologists have learned about the similarities among children in the nature of their play, and the functional significance of play to the child's development.

5. Know the following about the way mind and identity develop during the period defined as "childhood:"
   a. When "middle childhood" occurs, and the major cognitive and psychosocial developments characteristic of this period;
   b. The four stages of development as postulated by Piaget, and what cross-cultural research has indicated with regard to variation in the timing of these stages;
   c. How psychologists have attempted to study moral development, focusing on,
      (1) The stages in moral development as postulated by Kohlberg, and his "dilemmas" approach to measuring individual differences in moral reasoning; and
      (2) Gilligan's distinction between care and justice orientations in moral reasoning, and how such response orientation may vary with the nature of the dilemma considered;
   d. How the development of self-concept in a child is affected by the attitudes in a society toward members of different gender or ethnic groups and cultural values.
   e. How psychologists have studied the development of gender development, some of the major indications of the research in this area of study, and some of the major conceptual approaches to dealing with issues in this area, focusing on:
      (1) Individual differences in the learning of sex-typed behaviors;
      (2) How the development of gender identity and the learning of sex-typed behavior is conceptualized from the standpoint of cognitive-developmental theory;
      (3) How social learning theory attempts to explain the learning of sex-typed behaviors in terms of the child's observational learning and reinforcement history; and
      (4) How the development of sex-typed behaviors is explained by gender-schema theory in terms of children's observations of differences in the kinds of behaviors displayed by members of each sex.

6. Know something about what social scientists have learned about the perceptions of just what behaviors are and are not appropriate for members of the different gender groups, including:
   a. Differences between males and females in the United States with regard to the range of behaviors which they regard as appropriate for members of the different gender groups; and
   b. Socioeconomic class differences in the kinds of behaviors seen as appropriate for males and females, and in the flexibility of such distinctions.

7. Know about what psychologists have found concerning socioeconomic class differences in parenting style, including:
   a. Differences in the expression of attachment and praise, as well as in the use of reason

when disciplining children; and
    b. The psychsocial impact of such differences on children.

B. Preview/Review Outline Of Key Terms And Concepts

Before you read the corresponding chapter in your text, read over the following outline. It is designed to give you an overview of information presented in the chapter, and how the various elements of that information are related to each other. After reading through the whole chapter and/or before course exams, you may use this outline as a quick review guide. In your reviews, mask off one line of the outline at a time, and try to recite from your memory of the chapter, the information that you expect to appear on the next line or so.

In going over this outline as a preview before reading and studying the chapter, the questions posed in bold print will help to keep you focused on the learning objectives here, and keep you actively involved in the process of achieving those objectives. When using this section as a review, try to answer the questions. Refer back to the chapter in the text for a more detailed feedback check on your mastery of the material, and/or to strengthen your knowledge and understanding wherever you feel the need to do so.

How does "development" differ from "growth" as these concepts are used by developmental psychologists?

To what do the concepts of "differentiation" and "integration" refer within the context of the study of human development?

What are the three broad areas of study within the field of developmental psychology?

I. How We Develop: Similarities and Differences

What is the working assumption of the so-called "stage models" of human development?

II. Prenatal Development: Similar Patterns, Different Influence

What is the prenatal period of human development?

Explain the meaning of the terms "dizygotic" and "monozygotic" as those expressions are used to refer, respectively, to fraternal as compared to identical twins.

    A. Similarities in Prenatal Development
        1. Gestational Period
            a. Germinal Period
            b. Embryonic Period
            c. Maturation During The Prenatal Period
            d. Fetal Period
                (1) Neuronal Growth
                (2) Neural Interconnections

What is the function of the placenta which grows in the uterus during the embryonic period of prenatal development?

In our teenage years, what happens to neural connections which have not been used yet?

      B. Differences in Prenatal Development

What is the meaning of the term "premature" or "pre-term" as it applies to babies?

         1. Hormones
            a. Sex Hormones
            b. Gonads
               (1) Ovaries Produce Estrogen
               (2) Testes Produce Androgens
            c. Studies Of Genetic Females Exposed To Androgens In Womb
            d. Studies Of Females Exposed To Extra Doses Of Progesterone
         2. Chemicals and Infections
            a. Miscarriage
            b. Teratogens
               (1) Aspirin
               (2) Tetracycline
               (3) HIV
               (4) Rubella
               (5) Syphilis
               (6) Cigarette Smoking
               (7) Cocaine
               (8) Alcohol

What causes fetal alcohol syndrome, and how are its effects manifested in the children afflicted with it?

         3. Socioeconomic Perspectives
            a. Prenatal Complications And Problems
            b. Effects of Malnutrition on Babies

III. Infants and Toddlers: New Contacts with the World

What is the developmental time frame for what is commonly known as "infancy" or "babyhood"?

      A. Similarities in Sensation and Perception
         1. The Infant's Vision
            a. Neonates
            b. Near-Sightedness

How has the "visual cliff" been used to test depth perception in young children?

      2. The Infant's Hearing
          a. Prenatal Story-Telling As A Test Of Fetal Response To Sound
          b. Recognition of Familiar Voices
          c. Ability to Localize Sound And Recognize Mother's Voice
      3. The Infant's Sense of Taste and Smell
          a. Sweet, Salty, Bitter Taste Response
          b. Preparation To Recognize Mothers' Smell
  B. Similarities in Physical Development
      1. Congenital Reflexes

Describe at least three reflexes which can be observed in healthy babies. Specifically, what is the Moro reflex?

      2. Physical Development
          a. Begins With Inner Organs Earlier Than Extremities
          b. Control Is Gained Over Large Muscles Before Smaller Ones
          c. Proceeds Fastest In Head And Gradually Moves Down The Body
          d. Young Child's Head More Developed Than Rest Of Body
          e. Relative Head Size In Young Children As Compared To Adults
          f. Ability To Walk As Major Advance In Motor Development

From the standpoint of stage models, what is the significance of games such as "follow-the-leader"?

      3. Cultural Perspectives on Motor Development
          a. Sitting Up And Walking For The First time In Identical Twins
          b. Motor Development in the U. S. And Other Countries
          c. Ethnic Group And Cross-Cultural Differences In Parental Expectations

How might cultural practices help to explain why children in Africa develop some motor skills earlier than do white North-American children?

  C. Temperamental Differences

What is "temperament" anyway, and what are some of the observable behavioral characteristics used as indicators of individual differences among babies' in their temperament?

      1. "Easy" Temperament
      2. "Slow-To-Warm" Temperament
      3. "Difficult" Temperament
  D. Psychosocial Development

From the standpoint of Erikson's theory, what is involved in the "second crisis" of life as it is presumed to occur in infancy, and how is the outcome of that crisis presumed to have a lasting effect on the youngster? What cultural assumption underlies Erikson's analysis of this presumed crisis, and in what kind of cultural context might that assumption be quite invalid?

1. Forming Attachments
   a. Field Studies Of Babies Orphaned After World Wars I and II
   b. Need For Contact Comfort
   c. Harlow's Studies With Baby Monkeys
      (1) Metal "Mother" Monkeys
      (2) Terry Cloth-Covered Metal "Mother" Monkeys
   d. Human Babies Attachment To Their Parents
   e. Is The Person I'm Attached To Leaving Me?
      (1) Stranger Anxiety
      (2) Separation Anxiety
   f. A Two-Way Bond
      (1) Secure Attachments: Ainsworth's Studies
          (a) Mothers Who Pay Close Attention
              To Their Infants
          (b) Semi-Attentive Parents
          (c) Mothers Who Are Not Responsive
              To Their Infants
          (d) When Infants Were One Year Old
              (1) Children of Very Attentive Mothers,
                  Securely Attached
              (2) Children of Semi-Attentive Mothers,
                  Ambivalently Attached
              (3) Children of Mothers Who Were Not
                  Affectionate, Avoidant
      (2) Attachment In Individualist vs. Collectivist Cultures
2. Play
   a. And U. S. Parents' Attachment To Their Children
   b. Children's Self-Esteem And Play With Their Parents
   c. Korean American Parents' Attitudes Toward
      Playing With Their Children
   d. Parallel Play

What are some of the many developmental functions served by children's play?

   E. Alternative Perspectives on Day Care (Box 8.1)
      1. Conflicting Findings
      2. Meta-Analysis Of Findings

IV. Childhood: Developing Mind and Identity
   A. Cognitive Development
      1. Piaget's View of Thinking
         a. Sensorimotor Stage
            (1) Birth To Two Years Of Age
            (2) Object Permanence
         b. Pre-operational Stage
            (1) From 2 to 7 Years Of Age

214

          (2) Inability to Reverse Thinking

          (3) Egocentrism

          (4) Lack of "Conservation" In Thinking

          (5) Animism

     c. Concrete Operational Stage

          (1) From 7 to 11 Years Of Age

          (2) Understanding of Operations, Conservation, Cause-Effect

          (3) Logical Reasoning About Concrete Problems

          (4) Ability To Classify Objects

From the standpoint of Piaget's stage theory of human development, what is the meaning of the term "concrete" as it applies to the thinking of children in the stage of "concrete operations"?

     d. Formal Operations Stage

          (1) From 11 Years Of Age Through Adulthood

          (2) Ability To Talk About Logical Possibilities And Reason By Analogy

          (3) Ability To Reason From General Understanding To Particular Instance and Vice Versa

          (4) Ability To Compare In Terms Of Abstract Qualities

  2. Evaluating Piaget's Model

     a. Research On Object Permanence

     b. Cross-Cultural Research

          (1) Children of the Baolu People In Africa

          (2) Children in Societies That Often Move To New Lands

          (3) Cultures Where People Don't Demonstrate Operational Thinking

          (4) Assumption That Formal Operational Thinking Is Universal

             (a) Western Schooling

             (b) Industrialized vs. Non-Industrialized Cultures

          (5) Stage Models Constructed By People With Western Cultural

How are Western cultural values, assumptions, or biases reflected in the original model of Piaget's stage theory of human development?

  B. The Development of Moral Reasoning

     1. Levels of Moral Reasoning

       a. Kohlberg's Model

          (1) Focused on Reasoning

          (2) Assessment Based on Response to Hypothetical Moral Dilemmas

          (3) Three Levels Of Moral Reasoning Identified

             (a) Preconventional Moral Reasoning

             (b) Conventional Moral Reasoning

          (c) Postconventional Moral Reasoning
      (4) Male-Female Differences In Response To
          Ambiguities in Hypothetical Moral Dilemmas

What is the essential characteristic of the kind of moral reasoning in each of the three levels of moral development as described in Kohlberg's approach?

    2. Weighing of Justice and Care: Gilligan's Approach
       a. Justice Orientation in Males
       b. Care Orientation in Females

What is the essential difference between the justice and care orientations to moral reasoning as described in Gilligan's approach?

    3. Critically Analyzing the Two Models
       a. Failure To Find Male-Female Differences In
          Moral Reasoning Orientations
       b. Position In Society And Moral Reasoning

How might a person's social role or socioeconomic position affect his/her response to hypothetical moral dilemmas such as those used to measure moral reasoning using Kohlberg's approach?

   C. Developing a Self-Concept

How is the influence of cultural factors on the development of self-esteem indicated by research comparing the self-descriptions of Euro-, Chinese- and Japanese-Americans?

How does the research on children's play behavior following their viewing of television programs, indicate the way in which media portrayal of characters may influence children's sense of themselves?

    1. Developing a Gender Identity
       a. Gender Constancy
       b. Sex-Typed Behaviors
       c. U. S. Parents' Tolerance Of Their Children's
          Stereotypic an Non-Stereotypic Sex-Typed Behaviors
       d. Influence Of Culture on Sex-Typed Behaviors
       e. Influence of Genes, Hormones, and Brain Organization

What do the differences between play behaviors of children at one year of age indicate about the development of sex-typed behaviors?

    2. Developing Sex-Typed Behaviors
       a. Cognitive-Developmental Theory
       b. Social-Learning Theory
       c. Gender-Schema Theory

What is the essential assumption which distinguishes each of the three major theories of the way in which children develop sex-typed behaviors?

    D. Socioeconomic Perspectives on Childhood
        1. U. S. Children Living In Families Below the Poverty Line
        2. Socioeconomic Class Differences in Child-Rearing Styles
            a. Expression of Affection For The Child
            b. Attentiveness To Child's Needs
            c. Reinforcement of Child's Positive Behaviors
            d. Use Of Reasoning, Explanations In Disciplining Child
            e. Providing Child With Cognitive Stimulation

What are some of the ways in which the research findings concerning socioeconomic class differences in child-rearing styles indicate the powerful role of environment in human development?

C. Self-Generated Questions: What's In This One For Me?

Most people come to the first course in psychology expecting to learn some things which will help them to better understand themselves, other people in their lives, and/or the nature of life in the world in which they live. Along these same lines, students of psychology often look forward to discovering things about human behavior and experience which may help them to improve their own life by developing their talents, technical skills, knowledge and abilities, and/or the quality or their relationships with other people. On the basis of such self-interest, which tends to provide a framework in terms of which new learning becomes personally meaningful and thus easier to remember, write down a few questions in the space below, about the subject matter covered in this chapter. After reading and studying the chapter, come back to see how any of what you've learned may be useful to you in finding answers to these questions.

D. Completion Items

The words in the margins of this exercise are the ones that correctly complete the sentence on the corresponding line. To get the most out of this exercise, you should try to avoid looking at these words in the margin until after you've filled in the corresponding blanks with the words you think best complete the sentences. So, begin the exercise by covering up all of the margin words with a piece of paper. Then, for each blank, write in the word which you think completes the sentence. Even if you're not sure as to the word, write in your best guess, preferably in pencil so you can erase and re-write any incorrect responses you may make here.

After writing in your "answer," slide the paper covering up the margin words down just far enough to see the word for the blank you just filled-in. For each blank that you fill-in correctly, put a check mark (√) after your answer. If the word you wrote in doesn't match the word corresponding to that blank, mark an (X) next to your response and go on to the next blank. It's probably a good idea to go back to the text and try to strengthen your learning related to topic coverage that corresponds in the textbook chapter to those blanks which you filled-in incorrectly, since those items signal a weak link in your concept mastery chain for this chapter.

1. As people develop, their behaviors, thoughts, and perceptions become increasingly _____ -- increasingly distinct, **differentiated**
precise, and subtle, and also increasingly _____, -- **integrated**
coordinated, and smoothly synchronized.

2. _____ models of human development assume that **Stage**
people in each period of life face similar tasks or challenges.

3. The stage of development before birth is the _____
      prenatal
period. It begins with _____ -- when a sperm cell from **conception**
the father penetrates the ovum, or egg, of the mother. The fertilized egg,
which is called a _____, has half of its chromosomes from the **zygote**
mother and half from the father. _____ or dizygotic twins **fraternal**
result when two eggs are fertilized by different sperm cells.
_____ or monozygotic twins result when one sperm enters **identical**
one egg which splits into two parts.

3. The prenatal period, or _____, lasts 38 to 42 weeks in **gestation**
full-term babies, is divided into three periods. The first is the
_____ period, which lasts only the first two weeks after **germinal**
conception, ends when the zygote attaches itself to the wall of the uterus.
The embryonic phase of the prenatal period is marked by the formation in
the uterus of the _____, an organ that through which oxygen **placenta**
and nutrients are delivered to the embryo and waste is removed from it. The
genetically-determined timing of physical development,
or _____, is roughly the same for everyone during the prenatal **maturation**
period. The third gestational period, the _____ period, extends **fetal**
from approximately two months after conception to birth, during which the
brain grows _____ at the rate of about 250,000 per minute. **neurons**

4. Premature or _____ babies, are those born before 38 weeks **pre-term**
of gestation, are not fully developed at birth and are at more risk of illness than
are full-term babies.

5. The sixth week of gestation is a sensitive period for the development of

218

_____, or sex organs. The XX chromosomes of females produce   gonads
gonads that become ovaries and the hormone _____. The XY   estrogen
chromosomes of males produce gonads that become testes, which produce
_____ which are the masculinizing hormones. Genetic females   androgens
unintentionally exposed to masculinizing hormones in the womb have been
found to _____ in ways more typical of boys than girls. In contrast, play
when females in the womb are exposed to extra doses of _____,   progesterone
a nonandrogen hormone, they tend to show more interest in playing with dolls,
in a physically inactive way, and wearing feminine clothes than do other girls.

6. Genetic abnormalities or exposure to infections and chemicals can result
in a _____, an unintentional, spontaneous abortion. Some fetuses   miscarriage
are exposed in the womb to _____, which are any substances that   teratogens
cause birth defects. Such substances include some types of aspirin, the
antibiotic tetracycline, HIV, and _____, a form of measles which can rubella
cause blindness, deafness, cardiac deformities, and mental retardation in the
fetus. Alcohol is a powerful teratogen, and _____ alcohol   fetal
syndrome (FAS) is a condition that develops in 30% to 50% of the babies
born of alcoholic mothers. FAS children tend to be physically and mentally
_____, often having defects in their hearts and nervous system,   retarded
distorted facial features, and malformed arms and legs.

7. Prenatal complications and problems have worse effects on physical
and psychological development when the family is _____   poor
than when it is middle class. Poor people are less likely than others to
have _____ care because of its cost and their lack of   prenatal
transportation to the doctor's office.

8. Infancy, or babyhood, is roughly the period from birth to the beginning
of the ability to _____, around one year of age .   walk

9. By the time infants are six months old, they apparently do have
_____ perception. Psychologists have based the foregoing   depth
conclusion on studies using a visual _____, a thick, clear sheet   cliff
sheet of glass on top of a two-tiered structure.

10. As indicated by the results of a clever experiment in which pregnant
mothers read aloud from children's _____, fetuses respond   stories
to sound at least two weeks before birth. Newborns can also recognize
familiar voices and, in particular, can distinguish their _____   mother's
voice from the voices of other women.

11. The _____ of a mother's smell seems to be most firmly   memory
established n the neonate's brain if the smell is associated with being touched.
The ability to put together sensory information, such as smell and touch,
means that immediately after birth babies are developing the association

areas of their _____. cortex

12. In addition to the reflexes all humans have, babies have special reflexes which include automatically turning their _____ head
toward anything touching their cheek, making walking movements when their feet are barely touching a surface, or _____ sucki
whatever touches their face.

13. The first rule of physical development in infants is that development begins in the _____ organs earlier than in the extremities. inner
the second rule is that control is gained over _____ muscles large
that control broad, gross body movements before control is gained over smaller muscles used in fine, precise movements. The third rule is that physical development proceeds fastest in the _____ and head
gradually moves down the body. _____ development is the Motor
increased ability to make fine, differentiated movements and smoothly integrate them.

14. Human genes produce the ability to develop physical abilities within a certain _____ frame. One study found that time
identical twins sit up and walk for the first time on almost the _____ day. Differences in parental expectations -- both same
across U. S. ethnic groups and across _____ -- lead to cultures
differences in the time in a child's life when s/he is introduced to certain developmental tasks by his/her parents.

15. Typical _____ reactions, moods, and energy levels emotional
can indicate a baby's temperament, a seemingly inborn tendency or predisposition to behave in a characteristic way. Some psychologists classify temperament into one of four types. About 40% of children are said to have an "_____" temperament, characterized by cheerful and easy
agreeable moods, released and adaptable responses, and predictable patterns of eating, sleeping, and eliminating. Roughly 15% of children have a "slow-to-_____" temperament, demonstrated by somewhat warm
shy behaviors, guarded expressiveness, and slow adaptation to new situations and people. Another 10% have a "_____" temperament, difficult
characterized by intense emotional reactions, easily aroused frustration and anger, unpredictable eating, sleeping, and elimination patterns, and negative reactions to new situations.

16. According to Erikson's theory, the first stage of a child's psychosocial development involves the crisis of learning to _____ or mistrust others, and involves the child's trust
experiences of having or not having his/her needs met. Erikson argued that the second major crisis of psychosocial development occurs during toddlerhood from 1 to 3 years of age, and during which children who are successful in directing their behavior develop a sense of

independence or _____, while those whose attempts to
act independently are blocked learn self-doubt and _____ .

autonomy
shame

17. Researcher Harry Harlow found that when baby monkeys were not
eating, they usually grabbed hold of the "mother" monkey that had a
soft, terry _____-covered "mother." Similar needs for
contact _____ are an important aspect of human infants'
attachment to their parents. Around the age of 7 to 9 months, babies
show _____ anxiety, a kind of distress displayed when
they are left with someone other than parents or primary caregivers.

cloth
comfort

stranger

18. Psychologist Mary Ainsworth spearheaded a large body of research
into relationships between styles of _____ and different
forms of attachment in infants. Her research method involved observing
infants in a _____ environment without their mothers
present, and following their mothers return. She found that infants
raised by very attentive mothers were usually "_____
attached," showing signs of distress when their mothers were absent,
but comfort in exploring new toys and situations when their mother
was _____ . Children whose mothers were semi-
attentive, were found to be "ambivalently attached," showing
distress when their mother left them but also _____
when she returned. Children whose mothers were not affectionate,
were "_____" in their attachment, showing little or no
distress when the mother left them, and ignoring her when she returned.
In individualist cultures, attachment takes place within a context of
encouraging _____ and pursuing one's own goals. In
collectivist cultures, attachment takes place in the context of an emphasis
on _____ dependence.

parenting

strange

securely

present

anger

avoidant

independence

interpersonal

19. The more U. S. parents and children are attached to each other and
the more they play together, the more self-_____ the children
generally have. Even in preschools with other children, toddlers tend to
engage in _____ play, which means that they are next to each
other, playing with the same materials, but not in a coordinated way with
anyone else.

esteem

parallel

20. Meta-_____ involves examination of a combination of
studies on a particular topic. The research consistently indicates that going
to a high-_____ day care center is correlated with positive
outcomes for children. High-quality day care centers have many
_____ for the number of children. Another interpretation
of the latter research is that children who go to high-quality day care centers
come from _____ families than do other children. So, maybe
the children come away from high-quality day care centers with cognitive and
social advantages because of their economically-advantaged
_____ life rather than the nature of the day care centers.

analysis

quality

adults

richer

home

21. Piaget outlined four stages of _____ development. He referred to the first of these stages as the _____ stage, characterizing the thinking of children from birth to two years of age. A major development in this stage is that of object _____, which refers to the understanding that an object or person continues to exist even if the child can't see or hear that object or person. Piaget referred to the next stage in the sequence as the _____ stage, from 2 to 7 years of age. The kind of thinking characteristic of this stage is illustrated first, by _____, or the tendency to perceive situations and people from only one's own perspective and assuming that other people have the same perspective as oneself. Children at this second stage also can't _____, which means that they don't have the ability to understand that quantity stays the same even though it is presented in different arrangements, shapes, or forms. Also in this second stage, thinking is characterized by _____, the belief that inanimate objects have feelings and act intentionally. According to Piaget, children from the ages of 7 to 11 years of age are in the concrete _____ stage, can reason logically about concrete problems. Thinking during the latter period is described as "concrete" because it is based on actual _____ and simple concepts. Finally, Piaget thought that people from about the age of 11 through adulthood have reached the _____ operational stage of thinking, are capable of thinking about logical possibilities and reasoning by using _____.

cognitive
sensorimotor

permanence

pre-operational

egocentrism

conserve

animism

operational

experiences

formal
analogies

22. Cross-_____ research has shown that children differ somewhat in the ages at which they reach the various stages postulated in Piaget's theory. Piaget's assumption that formal operational thinking is universal and the most advanced type of thought, were culturally _____. The development of formal operational thinking is largely based on formal, Western schooling. In a non-_____ society, other forms of thinking may be more useful. One of the problems with _____ models of human development is that they have usually been constructed by Westerners who classified their own behavior as the highest stage. Nonetheless, the general _____ in which mental abilities develop seems to be as Piaget proposed.

cultural

biased
industrialized

stage

sequence

23. Piaget's view was that initially children are all similar in the way the way they think about moral behavior. the decide what is right and what is wrong is based on what produces good or bad _____. Lawrence Kohlberg's model of the development of moral reasoning is based on evaluations of the individual's response to hypothetical moral _____. The first of the three levels of moral reasoning identified in Kohlberg's theory is that of _____ moral reasoning, and is characterized by concern with the practical

results

dilemmas
preconventional

_____ of actions -- particularly whether behavior results in   consequences
the avoidance of punishment or the reaping of rewards. At the second
level, conventional moral reasoning, behavior is considered moral as long
as it _____ to rules established by society and the expectations   conforms
of other people. People at the third level, postconventional moral
reasoning, create their own moral principles based on their
_____, their personal thoughts about underlying principles.   conscience

24. Psychologist Carol Gilligan first noticed that Kohlbereg tended to
highly regard _____, justice and rights. But concerns   fairness
about responsibilities for other people were less valued. Gilligan
originally thought that males tend to have a _____   justice
orientation, seeing morality in terms of rules and each individual's rights,
whereas females tend to use a _____ orientation, seeing   care
morality in terms of regard and responsibility for others.

25. Most studies have found few, if any _____ between males   differences
and females in their use of justice and care orientations. Interpretations of
moral dilemmas are based, in part, on our social _____, or   role
position in society. Thus, in comparison to males, females may be more
concerned about _____ of acts such as stealing, as judged   consequences
from the point of view of people who have limited socioeconomic and
social power. Males, on the other hand, who have an interest in maintaining
a society that puts them in a more powerful position than females, may be
more inclined to regard stealing as potentially disruptive of the
_____, the way society is now.   status quo

26. A major developmental task shared by everyone is constructing a
self-concept, which is a sense of one's own _____.   personality
In one study, Euro-Americans were found to describe themselves in
terms of _____ characteristics, such as "tall" and "strong."   personal
In addition, Chinese- and Japanese-Americans, whose backgrounds are
collectivist as well as individualist, described themselves in terms of their
_____ to other people -- such as "son" and "friend" -- more   relationships
than did those from solely individualistic backgrounds.

27. A major part of our self-concept is our _____ identity,   gender
our sense that we are female or male. Every culture pushes its members
to develop _____ behaviors, which are behaviors, skills,   sex-typed
and interests that the culture considers appropriate for one sex or the
other. U. S. parents tend to be less _____ when sons   tolerant
display female sex-typed behaviors than when daughters display male
sex-typed behaviors. As a result, boys -- as a group -- develop more
_____, exclusive concepts about some activities being   rigid
"for boys" or "for girls" than girls do.

28. According to _____-developmental theory, children   cognitive

223

first develop a gender identity and then think that behaviors associated with their gender are good. _____- learning theory claims that sex-typed behaviors are learned just as are other behaviors. Gender-_____ theory maintains that children notice which behaviors are rarely displayed and which are frequently performed by one sex, but not by the other. The latter theory further assumes that having made such observations, children then develop a concept of sex-typed behaviors to which they compare themselves, and alter their attitudes, appearance, behaviors, or personality to _____ to that concept.

Social

schema

conform

29. In the United States, about 22% of children live in families whose economic status falls below the _____ line. Compared to parents from richer socioeconomic classes, poor parents are less likely to: (a) express _____ for their children; (b) be attentive to their needs, (c) reinforce their children for positive behaviors, (d) use reasoning, explanations, and negotiation when disciplining their children, and (d) provide their children with much _____ stimulation. Children who have been raised by poor parents with such parenting styles tend to have low self-esteem, be depressed, lonely, socially withdrawn, aggressive and destructively _____.

poverty

affection

cognitive

antisocial

E. Self-Quiz

For each of the following items, circle the letter which precedes the correct alternative.

1. In studying development, psychologists generally concern themselves with all but which one of the following areas or domains of human development?
    a. physical development
    b. cognitive development
    c. social development
    d. spiritual development

2. The placenta is formed during the _____ period of prenatal development.
    a. neonatal
    b. germinal
    c. embryonic
    d. fetal

3. The _____ chromosomes of females produce gonads that become ovaries and produce the hormone estrogen, while the _____ chromosomes of males produce gonads that become testes which produce androgens.
    a. XX, XY
    b. XY, XX
    c. YX, YY
    d. YY, XX

4. Research cited in your text has shown that genetic females unintentionally exposed to androgens in the womb tend to
   a. play in ways more typical of boys than girls
   b. identify themselves as tomboys
   c. remain more masculine than other females throughout their lives
   d. all of the above
   e. none of the above

5. Femalein the womb exposed to extra doses of progesterone, tend to show less interest in
   a. playing with dolls
   b. playing in a physically inactive way
   c. wearing feminine clothes than do other girls
   d. all of the above
   e. none of the above

6. The visual cliff apparatus has been used to study the development of _____ in children in the first year of life.
   a. depth perception
   b. emotional attachment
   c. motor coordination
   d. object permanence

7. Which of the following is not characteristic of physical development in infants and toddlers?
   a. development begins in the inner organs earlier than the extremities
   b. control is gained over large muscles earlier than smaller ones
   c. development proceeds fastest in the head and moves down the body
   d. compared to adults, young children have heads that are proportionately
      small for the size of their bodies

8. As noted in your text, which of the following is not one of the categories in terms of which developmental psychologists classify types of temperament differences among children?
   a. easy
   b. maternally overdependent
   c. slow-to-warm
   d. difficult

9. According to Eriksons psychosocial theory, the developmental crisis which confronts the individual in his/her elementary school years is that of
   a. trust vs. mistrust
   b. autonomy vs. shame and doubt
   c. initiative vs. guilt
   d. industry vs. inferiority
   e. identity vs. role confusion

10. The culturally biased underlying assumption of Erikson's psychosocial theory of development which is noted in your text, concerns the idea that _____ is good and _____ is (are) bad.
   a. trust, mistrust
   b. autonomy, shame and doubt
   c. initiative, guilt
   d. industry, inferiority
   e. identity, role confusion

11. Harlow's research with baby monkeys indicated the importance of _____ in the formation of attachments.
   a. prenatal hormones
   b. visual perception
   c. pheremones and smell
   d. contact comfort
   e. sex differences

12. Mary Ainsworth's research indicated that children who were raised by very attentive mothers tended to be
   a. securely attached
   b. ambivalently attached
   c. avoidant in their attachment
   d. all of the above
   e. none of the above

13. The term "_____ play" refers to what happens when children are next to each other, playing with the same materials, but not in a coordinated way.
   a. sequential
   b. serial
   c. sensorimotor
   d. parallel
   e. decentric

14. According to Piaget's theory, object permanence develops in the
   a. sensorimotor stage
   b. preoperational stage
   c. concrete operational stage
   d. formal operational stage
   e. Wells Fargo stage

15. In the study of cognitive development, _____ refers to the ability to understand that quantity stays the same even though it is presented in different arrangements, shapes, or forms.
  a. object permanence
  b. object constancy
  c. conservation
  d. defibrillation
  e. visual homogeneity

16. According to Piaget's theory of cognitive development, at the formal operational stage, people can
  a. think about logical possibilities
  b. reason by analogies
  c. reason from a general understanding to a particular instance and vice versa
  d. all of the above
  e. none of the above

17. As noted in your text, cultural bias is reflected in the Piaget's assumption that
  a. animistic perception occurs only in children who grow up in underdeveloped countries
  b. children such as those of the Baolu people in Africa, tend not to develop conservation until their adolescent years
  c. measures of object permanence can only be used validly with children who grow up in Western cultures
  d. the ideas of children in the period of concrete operations are set in stone
  e. formal operational thinking is universal and the highest level of cognitive development

18. According to Kohlberg's theory, moral reasoning at the postconventional level is characterized by a tendency
  a. for the individual to create his/her own moral principles based on a sense of personal conscience
  b. to be predominantly concerned with the practical consequences of actions
  c. to regard behavior as moral as long as it conforms to rules established by society and the expectations of others
  d. for males and females to display significantly different priorities in their moral thinking with regard to fairness, justice, and personal rights
  e. all of the above

19. In the study by Triandis (1994) cited in your text, Chinese- and Japanese-Americans were found to be more likely than Euro-Americans to describe themselves in terms of their
  a. personal characteristics
  b. relationships to other people
  c. role as citizens of the United States
  d. political ideology
  e. none of the above

20. Compared to parents from richer socioeconomic classes, poor parents are more likely than parents from richer classes to
   a. express affection for their children
   b. be attentive to their children's needs
   c. reinforce their children for positive behaviors
   d. use reasoning, explanations, and negotiation when disciplining their children
   e. none of the above

For each of the following items, circle "T" if the statement is True and "F" if the statement is false.

21. T F   Identical twins develop from the same zygote.

22. T F   Most connections among brain neurons are established before birth.

23. T F   Alcohol is a teratogen.

24. T F   Although a mother's use of cocaine can cause her baby to be born with permanent brain damage, a fathers' use of cocaine tends to have no ill effects on the fetus of the son or daughter he conceives because cocaine does not cling to sperm.

25. T F   The moro reflex is an early indicator of developmental disability due to brain dysfunction in babies.

26. T F   In human development, most growth of the head takes place prenatally and during the first of years of life.

27. T F   The more U. S. parents and children are attached to each other and the more they play together, the less self-esteem the children generally have.

28. T F   The research consistently indicates that going to a high-quality day care center is correlated with positive outcomes for children.

29. T F   Male and female African- and Puerto Rican-Americans acknowledge having fewer of the behaviors associated with the other sex than do Euro-Americans.

30. T F   Cognitive-developmental theory argues that children learn sex-typed behaviors in just the same way as the learn other behaviors, by observational learning and conditioning.

Answer Key To Self-Quiz

1. d
2. c
3. a
4. d
5. e
6. a
7. d
8. b
9. c
10. b
11. d
12. a
13. d
14. a
15. c
16. d
17. e
18. a
19. b
20. e
21. T
22. F
23. T
24. F
25. F
26. T
27. F
28. T
29. F
30. F

CHAPTER 9

Development From Adolescence Through Old Age

A. Learning Objectives

After careful, effective study of Chapter 9, you should:

1. Have a working knowledge of the following aspects of adolescence:
    a. The physical changes associated with the hormonal events of puberty and their effects on the secondary sex characteristics of boys and girls;
    b. The cognitive-developmental characteristics of this period of life, as reflected in adolescent egocentrism, the invention of personal fables and idealism;
    The social-developmental events of adolescence associated with the young person's:
    (1) Increasing independence from parents and intensified connection to peers;
    (2) Emerging sense of identity
        (a) As reflected in the kinds of questions the young person asks and the goals s/he sets for him/herself;
        (b) And the changes in self-concept and self-esteem associated with this period of life, influenced by the cultural and socioeconomic context within which the individual is developing; and
        With special consideration for the way development of ethnic and racial aspects of one's identity is conceptualized from the standpoint of The Minority Identify Development Model as contrasted with Phinney's three-stage model, and some alternative views as to the way white people develop their racial identity.

2. Know the following about the period of life developmental psychologists refer to as "Adulthood:"
    a. What it is that adulthood has in common across various cultures, as well as some of the major differences among cultures in the way adulthood is defined;
    b. The essential difference between the definition of adulthood as expressed in the "successive stages" as compared with the "timing of events" models;
    c. How the social roles of adulthood are conceptualized and studied within the field of developmental psychology, with attention to:
        (1) Erikson's view concerning the importance of "intimacy" during this stage of life;
        (2) The significance of marriage, and a self-administered measure of your own perceptions of marriage;
        (3) Gender perspectives on social roles within the family, the sources and experience of "role strain" and how it is experienced and affected by cultural and socioeconomic factors;
        (4) How caring for one's elderly parents can add to the challenges of this period of life, considering the research indicating diverse issues as they relate to the likelihood that one will care for his/her elderly parents;
        (5) Ethnicity as a factor associated with family structure and roles, what

constitutes the nuclear and extended family, and how fictive kin may play a significant role in people's lives in some cultures;

    (6) The three general types of parenting styles which have been identified by social scientists, how ethnic and socioeconomic, and cultural factors may affect the way people parent their children, how the roles of father and mother are enacted in various cultural situations, and what research has revealed about the incidence and effects of divorce and its effects on children in both cross-sectional and longitudinal studies.

3. Have an understanding of the psychology of "middle age," including
  a. Just when in life this period is presumed to occur, what Erikson means about the importance of "generativity" as the key challenge during mid-life, the kinds of events that can motivate people to reassess their lives at this stage of development, and what is known about the so-called "mid-life crisis;" and
  b. The kinds of physical and cognitive changes that occur during adulthood, including some of the facts and myths about menopause and changes in mental abilities of this period.

4. Gain some important insights into the social status of old people, with special attention to
  a. The significance of the poignant letter written by 84-year-old Anna Mae just before she died in a nursing home, as anecdotal report testimony to a social problem; and
  b. The factors which shape a society's view of old people, how the ageism and technological realities of life in modern, industrialized society impact on the way old people are perceived and treated;
  c. How retirement tends to affect the social status of an old person, and the factors associated with an old person's happiness during the retirement years;
  d. The physical changes that occur in old age:
    (1) With consideration of the important difference between the kinds of changes due to primary as compared to secondary aging;
    (2) The essential premise of the "wear-and-tear theory," especially with regard to role of "genetic errors" in the process of aging;
    (3) The kinds of changes characteristic of "primary aging" and their incidence; and
    (4) The physical changes caused by secondary aging as in cases of Alzheimer's disease.
  e. The cognitive changes of old age, with attention to
    (1) Sensory and memory losses, differences between old people in the incidence of such changes, and explanations of these processes in terms of the neurology of aging; and
    (2) Alzheimer's disease, its symptoms, incidence, and causes.
  f. Some alternative perspectives on old age, focusing on
    (1) The way in which an individual's personal circumstance may play a major role in determining just what old age is like for him/her;
    (2) The "double jeopardy" which confronts elderly women in our society;
    (3) Racial differences in the realities of old age as these are related to the nature of people's socioeconomic situation throughout life; and
    (4) Ethnic differences in old age, as related to characteristics of family

structure in minority group as compared with European-American culture.

5. Become acquainted with fundamentals of the psychology of death and dying as studied by thanatologists, including
    a. What has been learned from studies of people who have had near-death experiences and how such experiences have been explained by thanatologists;
    b. How people respond to and prepare themselves for death;
    c. The kinds of rituals involved in mourning the loss of loved ones, and the psychological function of such rituals;
    d. How social support systems provided by family and friends, and even telling the story of the death of a loved one, can play an important role in bereavement; and
    e. The stages people go through in dealing with the death of a loved one, and the importance of listening as a way of helping a dying person.

B. Preview/Review Outline Of Key Terms And Concepts

Before you read the corresponding chapter in your text, read over the following outline. It is designed to give you an overview of information presented in the chapter, and how the various elements of that information are related to each other. After reading through the whole chapter and/or before course exams, you may use this outline as a quick review guide. In your reviews, mask off one line of the outline at a time, and try to recite from your memory of the chapter, the information that you expect to appear on the next line or so.

In going over this outline as a preview before reading and studying the chapter, the questions posed in bold print will help to keep you focused on the learning objectives here, and keep you actively involved in the process of achieving those objectives. When using this section as a review, try to answer the questions. Refer back to the chapter in the text for a more detailed feedback check on your mastery of the material, and/or to strengthen your knowledge and understanding wherever you feel the need to do so.

In the anecdote which opens this chapter, how can you explain Al 's reaction to the discussion of racial issues in his history class, in terms of the kinds of challenges which confront adolescents?

I. Adolescence: A Period of Transition
    A. Physical Development: Hormonal Changes
        1. Puberty
        2. Female and Male Hormones
            a. Estrogens
            b. Androgens
        3. Secondary Sex Characteristics
        4. Spermarche And Semenarche

Can you give an example of a culture in which adolescents marry and have children shortly after reaching sexual maturity? What explanation is offered in your text for unplanned, adolescent pregnancies?

B. Cognitive Development: New Ways of Thinking in Adolescence

How does egocentrism in adolescents differ from that which is characteristic of young children?

        1. The Personal Fable

How can adolescents' personal fables cause them to engage in risky, and maybe even life-threatening kinds of behaviors?

        2. Idealism

How can an adolescent's unrealistically high expectations for themselves and other be explained in terms of the kind of thinking which is often characteristic of people at this stage of life?

    C. Social Development: An Expanding Social World and Identity

According to Erikson's stage model of development, what is the key goal or crisis of adolescence? What is involved in the achievement of this goal or resolution of the crisis surrounding it?

        1. Forming Identity and Goals
            a. Identity Search Questions
            b. "Trying on" different Identities
            c. Concern About The Future
            d. Career Choice And First Jobs

What kinds of questions do adolescents ask of themselves as they search for their identities?

        2. Influences on Self-Concept And Self Esteem
            a. Cultural Factors
            b. Socioeconomic Factors

How might a person's sense of his/her self be impacted differently by the primary values of an individualistic as compared to a collectivistic culture?

    D. Developing an Ethnic and Racial Identity
        1. In African-, Asian-, and Latino/a-Americans vs. European-Americans
        2. Ethnic Identity As A Source of Division or Self-Esteem
        3. And Exposure to One's Ethnic Culture of Origin

How has the variable of skin tone been found to be related to degree of racial awareness among African-Americans? What explanation is offered for this finding in your text?

        1. Alternative Perspectives on Minority Identity
            a. Minority Identity Development Model

            (1) First State, Conformity
            (2) Second Stage, Dissonance
            (3) Third Stage, Resistance
            (4) Fourth Stage, Introspection
            (5) Fifth Stage, Synergetic Articulation And Awareness
     b. Jean Phinney's Three-Stage Model
            (1) First Stage, No Consideration of Ethnic Identity
            (2) Second Stage, Exploration Of Identity
            (3) Third Stage, Resolution Of Racial and Ethnic Identity

What do the two models of racial and ethnic identity described above have in common? How do they differ?

     2. Alternative Perspectives on White Racial Identity
        a. White Racial Identity Model (WRIM)
            (1) First Stage, Whiteness Not Regarded As Important
            (2) Second Stage, Heightened Consciousness of Whiteness and Sensitivity to Racism
            (3) Third Stage
                (a) Avoidance of Minorities
                (b) Denial of Importance of Racism
                (c) Perception of Minorities as Inferior
            (4) Fourth Stage
                (a) Continuation of White Point of View
                (b) "Helping" Minorities to Assimilate
            (5) Fifth Stage
                (a) Open to Learning From Other Cultures
                (b) Motivated to Eliminate All Forms of Oppression
     3. As A Changing Series of Attitudes
        a. Types of White Racial Consciousness
        b. Changes Stimulated By New Experiences

What is the major shortcoming shared by all of the various models of ethnic and racial identity discussed above?

II. Adulthood: New Tasks and Responsibilities

What is the "timing of events model" of adulthood, and how does it differ from the view of adulthood as a succession of "stages"?

     A. Box 9.1, "Applications -- The Marriage Quiz"

On which items of the "marriage quiz" were your own answers most similar and different in comparison with the percentages given for others of your sex?

     B. Social Roles in Adulthood

According to Erikson's theory of life span development, what is the key challenge or crisis of adulthood?

        1. Gender Perspectives on Family Roles
            a. Social Roles
            b. Role Strain
            c. Gender Roles In Different Racial And Ethnic Groups

How is the tendency for low-SES men to hold gender stereotypes explained in your text?

        2. The Care of Elderly Parents
            a. And Role Strain
            b. As Related To Gender And Ethnicity

What cultural difference is noted in your text with regard to elder care in African-American as compared to English-, German- and Irish-American families?

        3. Ethnic Perspectives on Family Structure and Roles
            a. Family Structure
            b. Nuclear Family
            c. Extended Families
            d. Fictive Kin
    C. Parenting Styles, Roles, Conflicts

What are the essential differences between the three general types of parenting styles identified as authoritarian, permissive, and authoritarian?

        1. Ethnic and Socioeconomic Perspectives on Parenting
            a. Cultural Differences In Skill-Learning Emphasis
                (1) In Puerto-Rican Families
                (2) In European-American Families
            b. Variations Across Ethnic And Racial Groups
            c. And Social Class
        2. Gender Perspectives on Parenting

What conclusion is drawn in your text with regard to the research indicating that single fathers who are raising their children behave more like mothers than like married fathers?

        3. Effects of Divorce
             a. Incidence
            b. Economic Differences Between Divorced Men And Women
            c. Psychological Tasks Confronting Divorced People
            d. Research On Children Of Divorce
                (1) Cross-Sectional Studies
                (2) Longitudinal Studies

What conclusions were drawn from the meta-analysis of several studies of more than 13,000 children of divorce?

    D. Middle-Age Accomplishments and Cognitive Reassessments
        1. Between the Ages of 40 and 65
        2. According to Erikson, "Generativity" Is Primary Concern
        3. Reflection on Personal and Professional Development
        4. Parents' Death
        5. Mid-Life Crisis
    E. Physical and Cognitive Changes in Adulthood
        1. Bodily Decline From Youthful Peak
        2. Menopause
        3. Changes in Cognitive Abilities
            a. Memory Changes
            b. Superiority in Vocabulary And Reasoning Ability In Comparison
                To Young Adults

How has the term "mid-life crisis" often been misinterpreted, and what is one of the common myths or stereotypes concerning menopausal and post-menopausal women?

III. Old Age: Changing Responsibilities and Abilities

What did you find to be the most memorable aspect of the poignant letter written by "Anna Mae," the 84-year-old nursing home resident? What qualifies a person for membership in the so-called "baby boom" generation?

    A. Social Change: A Change of Social Status for the Elderly
        1. Ageism
            a. And The Treatment of Anna Mae by Nursing Home Employees
            b. And Negative Stereotypes About Old People
        2. Before And After the Industrial Revolution
        3. Retirement And Loss Of Social Status

What is the explanation given in your text for the virtual absence of old people from the media, and particularly from commercial advertising? Also, what factors seem to be associated with happiness during the retirement years?

    B. Physical Changes in Old Age

What seems to be true about elderly people's perceptions of themselves as compared with the way they are perceived by others?

        1. Normal Changes of Primary Aging
            a. Wear-and-Tear Theory
                (1) Environmental Damage
                (2) Genetic Errors
                      (a) The Enzyme Helicase

(b) Expulsion of Harmful Substances From The Body
b. Sensory Losses
(1) In Visual Acuity
(2) In Binocular Vision
(3) In Hearing
(4) In Ability to Detect and Identify Odors
c. Changes in Skin, Hair, Bones, Muscles, Etc.
d. Sexuality in Old People

What observation is noted in your text concerning the relationship between regular exercise and the aging process?

2. Disease and Deterioration of Secondary Aging

How can a misunderstanding of the difference between primary and secondary aging result in faulty decisions with regard to the treatment of various sorts of symptomology in old people?

C. Cognitive Changes in Old Age
1. Sensory Losses
2. Wear-And-Tear Theory As It Relates to the Neurology of Aging
3. Memory Loss And Primary Aging
(a) Short-Term Memory
(b) As Related To Formal Education
(c) Disease and Lack of Stimulation
4. Senility
5. Alzheimer's Disease
(a) Symptoms And Course of the Disease
(b) Incidence
(c) Causes

What explanation is offered in your text for the finding that elderly people with little or no formal education are more likely to experience a decline in memory than are those who are better educated?

D. Alternative Perspectives on Old Age
1. Gender Perspectives on Old Age
a. Double Jeopardy Confronting Elderly Women
b. Disadvantage Confronting Elderly Men
2. Racial Perspectives on Old Age

As noted in your text, what is the "double jeopardy" confronting elderly people of color?

3. Ethnic Perspectives on Old Age
a. Family Structure as Advantage for Minority Group Members
b. Social Roles of Elderly African-Americans
c. Satisfaction With Life In Elderly African-Americans

244

What specific factors might you cite in trying to explain the research findings indicating that elderly African-Americans report greater satisfaction with their lives than do elderly European-Americans?

    E. Dying
        1. Thanatology
        2. Studies of Near-Death Experiences
            a. Self-Reported Experiences
            b. Alternative Explanations
        3. Mental Preparation for Death
        4. Death Rituals and Their Functional Significance
        5. Social Support and Bereavement
        6. Relating to the Dying Person

What are the various stages or components of the bereavement experience in dealing with the death of a loved one? What observation is noted in your text concerning such experiences?

C. Self-Generated Questions: What's In This One For Me?

Most people come to the first course in psychology expecting to learn some things which will help them to better understand themselves, other people in their lives, and/or the nature of life in the world in which they live. Along these same lines, students of psychology often look forward to discovering things about human behavior and experience which may help them to improve their own life by developing their talents, technical skills, knowledge and abilities, and/or the quality or their relationships with other people. On the basis of such self-interest, which tends to provide a framework in terms of which new learning becomes personally meaningful and thus easier to remember, write down a few questions in the space below, about the subject matter covered in this chapter. After reading and studying the chapter, come back to see how any of what you've learned may be useful to you in finding answers to these questions.

D. Completion Items

The words in the margins of this exercise are the ones that correctly complete the sentence on the corresponding line. To get the most out of this exercise, you should try to avoid looking at these words in the margin until after you've filled in the corresponding blanks with the words you think best complete the sentences. So, begin the exercise by covering up all of the margin words with a piece of paper. Then, for each blank, write in the word which you think completes the sentence. Even if you're not sure as to the word, write in your best guess, preferably in pencil so you can erase and re-write any incorrect responses you may make here.

After writing in your "answer," slide the paper covering up the margin words down just far enough to see the word for the blank you just filled-in. For each blank that you fill-in correctly, put a check mark (√) after your answer. If the word you wrote in doesn't match the word corresponding to that blank, mark an (X) next to your response and go on to the next blank. It's probably a good idea to go back to the text and try to strengthen your learning related to topic coverage that corresponds in the textbook chapter to those blanks which you filled-in incorrectly, since those items signal a weak link in your concept mastery chain for this chapter.

1. _____ marks the beginning of the physical changes associated with adolescence. Girls begin to produce larger amounts of the feminizing hormones known as _____; while boys produce more of the masculinizing hormones known as _____. The most immediate effect puberty is to prompt the development of _____ sex characteristics, the external features that distinguish men from women. In males, the event known as _____ or semenarche, the first ejaculation, usually takes place during sexual activity or while sleeping, in a so-called "wet dream." Within a few years, women typically reach _____, the beginning of menstruation.

Puberty

estrogens

androgens
secondary

spermarche

menarche

2. Adolescent _____ is not the same as that of a six year old who thinks s/he is the center of the universe. Instead, adolescents often feel as if an imaginary audience is judging them. Under the spell of a personal _____, a teen might believe that no one has ever loved another person as much as s/he does, or grieved as deeply, or felt as bored. Adolescents who recognize that it is theoretically possible to be consistently good or truthful may form unrealistically _____ expectations for themselves and others. Such _____ is based on what is possible, rather than on experience r on realistic concepts of human behavior. Forming a social _____ -- that is, an understanding of what s/he is in relation to other people -- is an important part of every adolescent's development.

egocentrism

fable

high
idealism

identity

3. In the U. S., adolescents become increasingly _____ from their parents. This process is sometimes marked by repeated cycles of conflict and negotiation between adolescents and _____ figures, typically parents and teachers.

independent

authority

4. As adolescents and adults explore and reinvent their identities, their view of themselves, or self-_____, is subject to change as well. Self-_____ -- an aspect of self-concept determined by a person's belief that s/he is essentially good or bad -- also tends to waver during this time. For European-Americans, whose culture emphasizes _____, independence is generally considered to be an important part of a person's character and self-concept is affected accordingly. For people in _____ societies, such as Korea, are likely to judge themselves and others based on the number and quality of their relationships with other people.

concept
esteem

individualism

collectivist

5. African-, Asian-, and Latino/a-American adolescents tend to put more effort than do _____-Americans into exploring their ethnic identity. One reason for this disparity may be that Western society tends

European

to _____ non-whites to their ethnicity. Members of minority   sensitize
groups who have developed an understanding of the personal and social
significance of their ethnicity tend to have _____ self-esteem   higher
than do those who have not done so. The more _____   exposure
people have to their ethnic culture of origin, the more likely they are to
develop a strong sense of ethnic identity. African-Americans with
lighter skin tones tend to be _____ racially conscious than   less
are those with darker skin. Presumably, the latter differences is attributable
to the fact that our society is dominated by light-skinned
_____-Americans.   European

6. The Minority _____ Development Model depicts five   Identity
stages of growth toward an increasingly sophisticated self-concept. The
first stage is that of _____, wherein minority group members   conformity
would prefer to be European-Americans. The second stage involves
_____ produced by learning or experiencing things that cause   dissonance
the individual to doubt their first-stage beliefs and values. The unstable
feeling of the second stage resolve in the third stage of _____   resistance
and immersion, as minority people reject the dominant group and completely
and unquestioningly embrace their own ethnic culture. The fourth stage is
that of _____, wherein minority people are sufficiently secure   introspection
that they can begin to accept the dominant group. The fifth and final stage is
that of _____ articulation and awareness, as the minorities   synergetic
accept and embrace their own ethnic group's values, meanwhile
acknowledging other groups' positive attributes as well. In the first stage of
Jean Phinney's three-stage model describing identity development in
minorities, people do not consider their ethnic identities because they are
too _____ or inexperienced to recognize themselves as   young
members of a minority group. In the second stage of Phinney's model,
people explore their identities, and in the third and final stage there is
a _____ of racial and ethnic identity.   resolution

7. The first stage in the White Racial Identity Model or WRIM, is
characterized by a tendency for _____-Americans   European
not to regard their whiteness as especially important. In the second
stage, they become more conscious of their whiteness and more
sensitive to racism. In the third stage, avoidance of contact with
minority group members continues, and there is either a conscious
or unconscious conclusion that non-whites are disproportionately poor
as a result of inherent character flaws or the lack of an appropriate
_____ ethic. In the fourth stage, there is not only   work
a rejection of _____ ideas, but avoidance of people who   racist
espouse them. In the fifth stage, there is an attempt to learn from
other cultures, and to eliminate all forms of _____   oppression
by any arbitrary criterion. In contrast to the WRIM, identity may be

viewed as a changing series of attitudes or "types of white racial
_____."

consciousness

8. European-Americans tend to consider someone to be an adult
when s/he takes for his/her actions, is _____ self-
sufficient, and lives separately from his/her parents. In
collectivist as opposed to individualist societies, however, adulthood is
less associated with _____ than with increasing responsibility
     independence
to the community. According to the timing-of-_____
model, adults share several important milestones in their lives -- such as
achieving financial independence, living apart from parents, marriage,
etc., -- but the timing of these events varies from person to person.

financially

events

9. Erikson noted that _____ -- the formation of close
relationships-- is a key aspect of adulthood. The concept of role
strain refers to _____ resulting from the difficulty associated
with attempting to fulfill several different roles. Because of the number of
different _____ roles they are expected to fulfill, females
in North America appear to suffer from role strain more often than do
their male counterparts. The tendency for men of low SES or
_____ status to hold gender stereotypes may be due to
their limited education or to dissatisfaction with their social and
financial status.

intimacy

stress

gender

socioeconomic

10. In one study, _____-Americans as a group were
found to take on more care giving duties for disabled parents or
elderly relatives than did European-Americans. In another,
European-Americans rated care giving or parents as more
_____ than did African-Americans.

African

11. Family _____--the composition of a family and
the relationships among its members--can vary tremendously. The
prototypical family consisting of a married couple and their children
is called a _____ family. African- and Latino/a-
Americans tend to think of themselves as belonging to
_____ families-- which include grandparents, uncles
aunts and cousins--rather than nuclear families. Extended African-,
Filipino/a and Latino/a-American families also often include what are
called _____ kin: close friends who are treated as if they
were family members.

structure

nuclear

extended

fictive

12. Parenting styles are often classified into three general types.
_____ parents place firm, uncompromising limits on their
children's behavior and demand total obedience from them.
_____ parents, by contrast, exert little control over

Authoritarian

Permissive

their children and make few rules for their behavior. _____ Authoritative
parents set firm standards for their children's behavior, but also try to
explain why certain behaviors are not permissible.

13. A person's race and _____ strongly influence which   culture
childrearing practices s/he considers to be effective, appropriate, and
acceptable. Most middle-class Americans believe that authoritative parenting
is best. The latter conclusion partly reflects a _____-   European
American cultural perspective. By contrast, the Inuit (aboriginal
_____) prefer a permissive style, in which they do not strictly   Alaskan
limit their children's behavior, believing that their own style of parenting
permits a natural unfolding of each child's _____ and allows   individuality
children to learn without being manipulated.

14. Research indicates that among European-Americans, fathers tend to
be perceived as more _____ than mothers, while mothers are   authoritarian
likely to be perceived as more authoritative than fathers. Research has also
indicated that _____ fathers who are raising their children   single
behave more like mothers than like married fathers.
mothers than like married fathers.

15. About _____ of all marriages in the United States end in   half
divorce. Among the psychological tasks that face divorcing men and women
before they can get on with their new lives are the needs to
_____ the loss of their marriage, resolve their anger, and re-   mourn
examine their former assumptions about marriage. Before they reach the age
of _____ years of age, an estimated 50% to 60% of U. S.
children born in the early 1980's will have spent at least a year living with only
one parent. Most research on the effects of divorce has been conducted
in what are known as cross-_____ studies, wherein a group   sectional
of people is studied at a single time. By contrast, in a _____   longitudinal
research design, the same individuals are studied over several years. Based
on the results of both kinds of studies, psychologists have concluded that
the effects of divorce on children depend partly on the _____   age
of the children at the time of the divorce. As adults, children of divorced
parents are themselves more likely to _____. It also appears that   divorce
parents can reduce the negative effects of divorce on their children by
continuing to _____ them in a consistent way, and by refraining   discipline
from hostility or from forcing children to take sides in the divorce.

16. Middle age occurs roughly between the ages of _____   40
and 65. According to Erikson, this is a period of life during which people
are concerned primarily with _____: being productive and   generativity
and accomplishing life goals. Middle-age marks the first time most people
question why their lives have turned out as they have. Such self-examination
has been labeled a "mid-life _____"- - which is really an internal   crisis

struggle for self-_____; it does not generally provoke an
extreme reaction such as a psychological breakdown, overwhelming anxiety,
or radical life _____.

knowledge

change

17. During their mid-40's and early-50's, most women go through
_____, a period during which declining estrogen triggers
the end of ovulation and menstruation. Contrary to myth and stereotypes,
the vast majority of women during and after this period do not become
_____ or moody. While females' estrogen levels drop
relatively quickly during menopause, males' levels of the corresponding
androgen, _____, decline more gradually with age. Some
cognitive abilities decline after early adulthood, but others _____;
memory for some tasks, such as remembering to call someone, is poorer than in
young adults, but vocabulary and _____ ability are generally
superior to those of young adults.

menopause

depressed

testosterone

improve

reasoning

18. In the letter written by Anna Mae, the 84-year-old nursing home patient,
as she relates the way she is treated by the nursing home staff she asks,
"Have I lost my right to respect and _____."
_____ is the study of the elderly. In the U. S., old age is
generally considered to begin at age _____, the mandatory
retirement age in many businesses, ad also the age when people begin
to receive Social Security benefits. The large baby-boom generation
which includes people born between _____ and 1966,
will start entering old age shortly after the year 2001.

dignity

Gerontology

65

1946

19. One reason why the elderly lose social status is as a result of
_____: prejudice and discrimination against people
because of their relatively advanced age. A second reason that
the elderly lose social status is that they are no longer the people
in our society with the most _____. Before the
_____ revolution, elders were highly respected
    industrial
in most societies, because their many years of experience in
running businesses or farms, gave them valuable knowledge that they
passed on to succeeding generations. But now, in
the computer age, knowledge quickly becomes _____.
Retirement can also lead to a loss of social status for the elderly, if the
retired person is viewed as having lost his/her _____.

ageism

knowledge

obsolete

usefulness

20. Primary aging refers to changes brought about as a natural part of the
aging process, whereas _____ aging describes changes
brought about by disease or deterioration from lack of use. The
predominant theory of primary aging is the _____-and-tear
theory, which states that the body parts wear down in much the same way
as do those of machines, with the physical and mental deterioration of the body
caused by environmental damage or _____ errors. Primary aging

secondary

wear

often causes the senses to become less keen. Visual acuity declines
because, with age, the _____ of the eye loses its flexibility   lens
and less light reaches the retina. By getting regular _____,   exercise
elderly people can not only slow down much of the deterioration associated
with primary aging, but can also improve their mental acuity. People often
mistake secondary aging for primary aging, presuming that all types of
deterioration are just a _____ natural part of old age. One   natural
unfortunate result of such mistaken beliefs, is that underlying
_____ which cause various sorts of decline in the elderly,   diseases
are often left untreated.

21. Elderly people are more likely to lose their _____-term   short
than their long-term memory, and those who have had little or no formal
_____ are more likely to experience a decline in memory than   education
are those who are better educated. It may be that relatively uneducated
people have developed fewer _____ pathways and a less   neural
complex cognitive structure, so that when such pathways begin to
deteriorate, more memory is lost. Elderly peoples' memory abilities can
also fade from _____, as well as from the effects of primary   disuse
aging.   The condition known as _____- - characterized by   senility
unusual forgetfulness and confusion - - is not an inevitable result of
aging. Instead, these cognitive problems are often due to disorder that
restrict _____ flow the brain, such as heart disease or stroke.   blood
Severe cognitive impairment in old age is also sometimes due to
_____ disease, a disorder characterized by a jumbling   Alzheimer's
of the nerves in the brain, and, eventually, its wasting away.

22. Elderly women often face a double _____, since both   jeopardy
their age and gender put them at a disadvantage. Men are particularly
vulnerable to feeling a loss of _____ in old since, compared   authority
with women, they tend to hold positions of greater power during their
working lives.

23. African- and Latino/a-Americans make less money than do
European-Americans and the differences in their income _____   grow
as they become older. Differences in family _____ offer some
        structure
advantages to older members of minority groups. Elderly African-Americans
are more likely to live in a household with _____ family members,   extended
and are thus more likely to receive consistent support than are European-
Americans. Although they tend to be both poorer and less healthy than
elderly European-Americans, elderly African-Americans usually report greater
_____ with their lives.   satisfaction

24. _____ is the study of death and dying. People who have   Thanatolgy
had near-death experiences, frequently report feeling relief from pain, and
seeing a tunnel and/or a _____. One explanation of such   light

experiences, is that they are due to visual hallucinations and a sense of peace caused by _____ which are known to circulate in the   endorphins
brain just before death. One way that people cope with bereavement is to
tell the _____ of the death repeatedly. Various researchers   story
have described the _____ that people go through in dealing   stages
with the death of a loved one. The various aspects of such emotional
events are rarely experienced in a neat or orderly fashion. Shock, confusion
temporary disbelief that the person is dying or dead, depression, and even
_____ at the deceased for leaving and acceptance of the death   anger
are all common reactions.

E. Self-Quiz

For each of the following items, circle the letter which precedes the correct alternative.

1. Which of the following is not true of puberty?
    a. marks the beginning of the physical changes associated with adolescence
    b. begins somewhat earlier in boys than in girls
    c. during this period, boys and girls become sexually mature men and women
    d. the entire process takes approximately four years in both sexes

2. In the anecdote which opens this chapter, Al's personal fable caused him to think that he alone, among his classmates, was
    a. having difficulty controlling his sexual fantasies and spontaneous sexual arousal
    b. confused about his sexual identity
    c. confused about his career choices
    d. confused about racial issues

3. For the most part, adolescent idealism seems to be based on
    a. visions of what is possible
    b. their own experience in life
    c. realistic concepts of human behavior
    d. the belief that inconsistency between a person's words and his/her actions is not really a sign of hypocrisy

4. According to Erikson's stage model of development, the key challenge and crisis of adolescence involves establishing a sense of
    a. one's own identity
    b. basic trust vs. mistrust in the world
    c. integrity
    d. generativity

5. As noted in your text, which of the following groups tends to put the least energy into exploring their ethnic identity?
>   a. African-Americans
>   b. Latino/a-Americans
>   c. European-Americans
>   d. Asian-Americans

6. Which of the following is not characteristic of the first stage in the development of ethnic and racial identity in minorities according to the Minority Identity Development Model as described in your text?
>   a. intense resentment of one's own parents
>   b. preferring to be a European-American rather than a member of one's own ethnic or racial group
>   c. both consciously and unconsciously looking down on one's own group's distinctive features and culture
>   d. adoption of European-American values and patterns of behavior

7. According to the Minority Identity Development Model as described in your text, in which stage of such development does the person accept and embrace his/her own ethnic group's values, while acknowledging other groups' positive attributes?
>   a. conformity
>   b. dissonance
>   c. introspection
>   d. resistance
>   e. synergetic articulation and awareness

8. According to the White Racial Identity Model as described in your text, European-Americans tend to stay in the first stage of such development
>   a. until they reach adolescence
>   b. until they reach young adulthood
>   c. until late adulthood
>   d. because of their personal relationships with members of minority groups
>   e. unless they form personal relationships with members of minority groups

9. According to the White Racial Identity Model as described in your text, which of the following is not among the ways in which European-Americans try to resolve their conflicting feelings about race in the second stage of such development?
>   a. by avoiding further contact with members of minority groups
>   b. by changing their ideas about minorities
>   c. by claiming that race is unimportant to them
>   d. by counter identifying with the white race

10. Which of the following tends to be emphasized less in individualist as compared with collectivist societies in the perception of that person as an adult?
    a. when the person takes responsibility for his/her actions
    b. when the person becomes financially self-sufficient
    c. when the person begins to assume greater responsibility to the community
    d. when the person begins to live separately from his/her parents

11. Which of the following is not among the three general types of parenting styles described in your text?
    a. authoritarian
    b. authoritative
    c. communicative
    d. permissive

12. According to research cited in your text, parenting is more likely to be authoritative which of the following groups?
    a. European-American
    b. African-American
    c. Latino/a-American
    d. Asian-American

13. According to research cited in your text, among European-Americans,
    a. fathers are likely to be perceived as more authoritative than mothers
    b. mothers are likely to be perceived as more authoritative than fathers
    c. mothers tend to be perceived as more authoritarian than fathers
    d. fathers tend to bear greater responsibility for child care than do mothers

14. According to data cited in your text, which of the following percentages most closely approximates the estimated percentage of children born in the United States in the early 1980's who will have spent at least a year living with only one parent?
    a. 10-20%
    b. 30-40%
    c. 50-60%
    d. 70-80%

15. According to research cited in your text, negative effects of divorce on children can be reduced by
    a. allowing the children to witness the conflict and hostility between their mother and father prior to divorce
    b. involving them in the conflict between mother and father following the divorce
    c. continuing to discipline their children in a consistent way
    d. all of the above
    e. none of the above

16. According to Erikson's life span development theory, tends to be concerned primarily with
    a. basic trust in the world
    b. identity
    c. autonomy
    d. generativity
    e. integrity

17. According to your text, the mid-life crisis
    a. is really an internal struggle for self-knowledge
    b. is a psychological breakdown
    c. involves overwhelming anxiety
    d. typically results in radical life change

18. As cells divide over a lifetime, the DNA inside -- which carries the instructions for cellular operations -- is damaged by
    a. toxic chemicals
    b. viruses
    c. radiation
    d. all of the above
    e. none of the above

19. Secondary aging
    a. occurs in all people during old age
    b. is the focus of the "wear-and-tear" theory
    c. results from diseases
    d. is just a natural part of the aging process

20. According to research cited in your text, which of the following variables was found not to contribute significantly to subjective feelings of well-being among elderly African-Americans?
    a. social support
    b. the role they played in the family
    c. participation in church activities
    d. income

For each of the following items, circle "T" if the statement is True, and "F" if the statement is False.

21. T F   Adolescent egocentrism is essentially the same as that f a six year-old who thinks s/he is the center of the universe.

22. T F   Among Mexican-American children, those who know most about their ethnic group tend to have mothers who speak Spanish and enjoy Mexican food.

23. T F   According to the White Racial Identity Model, even in the fifth and highest or final stage of such development, the individual is essentially a racist who actively avoids experiences which will allow him/her to learn from other cultures and endorses policies which lead to oppression of people of color.

24. T F   Males in North America appear to suffer from role strain more often than do their female counterparts.

25. T F   In research cited in your text, European-Americans rated caring for parents as more burdensome than did African-Americans.

26. T F   Uncompromising limits on children's behavior and demanding total obedience of them is characteristic of what is known as the authoritarian style of parenting.

27. T F   According to your text, most middle-class Americans believe that authoritative parenting is best.

28. T F   Research cited in your text indicates that single fathers who are raising their children behave more like married fathers than like mothers.

29. T F   The vast majority of menopausal and post-menopausal women show significant increases in their experience of depression and moodiness.

30. T F   Elderly people are more likely to lose their short-term than long-term memory.

F. Teaching-To-Learn Exercise

1. *Let Me Teach You This.*

Write in the space provided below, the five facts, ideas, etc., from this chapter that you'd most like to teach to your own student(s) if you were a teacher. Then, really do try to communicate these facts or ideas to someone in your life; or, pretend to teach this content to a hypothetical or "make-believe" student or class.

2. *Now Answer My Questions.*

Here, write one multiple-choice and one True-False question for each of the facts, ideas, etc., you covered in the "Let Me Teach You This" section of this exercise.

Answer Key To Self-Quiz

1.	b
2.	d
3.	a
4.	a
5.	c
6.	a
7.	e
8.	e
9.	d
10.	c
11.	c
12.	a
13.	b
14.	c
15.	c
16.	d
17.	a
18.	d
19.	c
20.	d
21.	F
22.	T
23.	F
24.	F
25.	T
26.	T
27.	T
28.	F
29.	F
30.	T

CHAPTER 10

Communication

A. Learning Objectives

After your reading and careful, effective study of Chapter 10, you should:

1. Know about the nature of communication as both a verbal and a nonverbal, person-to-person activity, through which we express ourselves, share information, and establish relationships with other people, with special attention to:
    a. The process or the "how it works" of interpersonal communication including:
    b. the various components of that process;
    c. how problems with any of the components can lead to miscommunication;
    d. the kinds of circumstances in which such miscommunication is most likely to occur;
    e. Understanding what active listening is, and why it is so important to clear, effective communication; and
    f. The facts that communication
        (1) Can have both intended and unintended consequences;
        (2) Is not reversible; and
        (3) Can be affected by the context in which it occurs.

2. Become familiar with the following with regard to the use of language as our verbal communication device:
    a. Just what it is that language allows us to communicate;
    b. What is meant by "the productivity of language," what words do, and the function of grammar in the use of words;
    c. What is meant by "paralanguage," how it may lead to both valid and invalid inferences, and how culture may influence its interpretation;
    d. The facts and issues involved in considering the way in which language may influence our thoughts and emotions, with special attention to:
        (1) The essential premise of the theory of linguistic determinism; and
        (2) How the implications of the foregoing theory are contradicted by observations concerning:
            (a) people who first learned language as adults; and
            (b) the Dani people.
    e. How the learning of more than one language may affect one's thinking skills, as evidenced in comparisons of monolingual and bilingual children;
    f. How negative emotions tend to be expressed by bilingual people; and
    g. The symptoms, causes, and adaptations involved in the major types of the clinical condition known as aphasia.

3. Have a working familiarity with the psychology of language development, focusing on:
    a. The time frame within which language becomes established in children as a universal human behavior, and how the use of vocalizations for the purposes of communication

261

progresses in terms of the kinds of speech sounds emitted;

b. How the use of words progresses in children, from the "overextended" first words, to multiple-word sentences rendered "telegraphically," to complex sentences;

c. The combination of circumstances involved in the process by which children acquire their native languages, including

   (1) Living environment;

   (2) Practice; and

   (3) Biological readiness.

d. The issue concerning theoretical explanations as to just how language is learned, including

   (1) The aspects of language acquisition which are not accounted for very well at all by learning theory; and

   (2) How the idea of an innate Language Acquisition Device has been invoked as a credible alternative to learning theory in this regard.

4. Have a working knowledge of the following fundamentals of the psychology of nonverbal communication:

   a. How nonverbal communication can convey more information, especially about emotions, than do spoken words;

   b. Cross cultural considerations in the decoding and effectiveness of nonverbal communication;

   c. The kinds of meaning communicated by various aspects of "body language;"

   d. The use of gestures and how cultural factors may affect their interpretation;

   e. How emotion is communicated in facial expressions;

   f. The way eye contact operates as a nonverbal communicative device, and how cultural factors may lead to miscommunication with regard to such behaviors;

   g. What is communicated by smiling, and how both culture and context may be important factors in the communicative significance of a smile;

   h. The factors associated with individual differences in the use and communicative significance of "personal space," and how cultural differences may lead to miscommunication in the expression of physical interaction distance behaviors; and

   i. Individualist versus collectivist differences in communication style;

5. Know the following about the nature of communication between men and women in European-American culture:

   a. That there are important differences in the way men and women communicate, especially when it comes to the use of nonverbal cues;

   b. The kinds of emotions that women are most effective at communicating, the kind of emotional communication at which men are apparently most adept, and the developmental "roots" of such differences;

   c. The differences between men and women in the use of eye contact and smiling;

   d. The reality of sex differences in verbal fluency;

   e. Verbal style differences between men and women, and how such stylistic differences may be due to traditional social status differences between men and women and the kinds of reinforcements each derives from various sorts of behaviors; and

   f. Differences between men and women in their expectations in conversations, and in their use of questions and expressions of personal desires.

B. Preview/Review Outline Of Key Terms And Concepts

Before you read the corresponding chapter in your text, read over the following outline. It is designed to give you an overview of information presented in the chapter, and how the various elements of that information are related to each other. After reading through the whole chapter and/or before course exams, you may use this outline as a quick review guide. In your reviews, mask off one line of the outline at a time, and try to recite from your memory of the chapter, the information that you expect to appear on the next line or so.

In going over this outline as a preview before reading and studying the chapter, the questions posed in bold print will help to keep you focused on the learning objectives here, and keep you actively involved in the process of achieving those objectives. When using this section as a review, try to answer the questions. Refer back to the chapter in the text for a more detailed feedback check on your mastery of the material, and/or to strengthen your knowledge and understanding wherever you feel the need to do so.

What is the most memorable aspect of Dr. Martin Luther King, Jr.'s "I Have A Dream" speech? for you?

I. Communication: An Interpersonal Activity

What does it mean to refer to any activity as "interpersonal?"

    A. The Components of Communication
        1. Sender
        2. Message
        3. Physical Channel
        4. Encoding
        5. Receiver
        6. decoding
        7. Feedback

What is an example of at least one aspect of communication which is influenced by social rules or conventions?

        8. Miscommunication

Generally speaking, what is it that causes miscommunication? What is an example of miscommunication that occurs due to a decoding failure?

        9. Active Listening
            a. Working To Discover Meaning
                (1) Decoding Message
                (2) Paying Attention
                (3) Comparing Contents To Existing Knowledge
                (4) Translating Message Into Usable Ideas

      b. Thinking About What We Hear
      c. Considering The Speaker's Perspective
      d. Asking Questions
      e. Paraphrasing Message

From your own experience, what do you think are the two greatest obstacles to "active listening" among people who know each other very well?

   B. The Characteristics of Communication
      1. Consequences
      2. Can Be Conscious Or Unconscious
      3. Can Be Self-Reflective
      4. Not Reversible
      5. Contexts

Can you given an example from your own experience, of the way in which the same message can be interpreted very differently in two different contexts?

II. Verbal Communication: Using Language

What is the game "charades," and what does the playing of it illustrate about the nature of communication?

   A. Producing Unique Expressions

What is meant by the expression "productivity" as it applies to language?

      1. Words Represent Things
         a. Words As Symbols
         b. Denotative Meaning
         c. Connotative Meaning

How may response to the word "family" reflect cultural differences in connotative meaning?

      2. Grammar Organizes the Message
         a. Syntax
         b. Sign Language
         c. Morse Code
         d. Braille
  B. What Your Voice Communicates
      1. Paralanguage
         a. Prosody
         b. Vocal Segregates
         c. Guesses and Assumptions About Spoken Messages
         d. Influence Of Cultural Background
            (1) Pace Of Speech

(2) Length of Pauses

What is an example of the way in which cultural differences in conversational conventions may lead to misunderstanding?

2. Alternative Perspectives: Ebonics, A Language In Its Own Right? (Box 10.1)
   a. Black English
   b. Distinct Features of Grammar and Word Meaning
   c. Can Be Described as an Argot
      (1) Source of Identity and Pride
      (2) Solidarity
      (3) Awareness of Shared Culture and History
      (4) Political Purpose
      (5) Secret" Communication

In what respect does Ebonics fulfill each of the five functions served by an argot for the people who speak it?

C. Language and Thought
   1. Linguistic Determinism
      a. Language, Perception, and Cherokee Words for "We"
      b. Current Status of Issue
      c. Ildefonso
      d. Color Perception in the Dani People of New Guinea
      e. Language Difference and Expression of Thoughts

How do observations concerning the Cherokee language, the Mexican man Ildefonso, and the Dani people in New Guinea all contradict the basic premise of linguistic determinism?

2. The Influence of Language on Thinking
   a. Gender Bias and Use of the Suffix, -Man
   b. Impressions of Story Character Referred to as "Chairman" or "Chairperson"
   c. Use of Male Pronouns
      (1) And Judgments of Appropriate Behavior
      (2) And Perceptions of Female Political Candidates

In the corresponding research studies described in your text: (a) How did participants' impressions of story characters differ when those characters were referred to as "Chairman" or "Chairperson?"; and (b) How did the description of the offices for which they were presumably candidates affect participants' impressions of female political candidates?

3. Expansion of Thinking by Language
   a. Use of Precise or Abstract Terms
   b. Studies of Bilingual People

265

In the study cited in your text, what was found regarding the motivation to learn and learning effectiveness of monolingual as compared with bilingual children?

      D. Language and Emotions
           1. Expression of and Thoughts About Negative Emotion In Bilingual People
           2. Memory Storage Of Emotionally Charged Information in Bilingual People
      E. Applications: The Value of Multilingualism (Box 10.2)
           1. Affirmation of Cultural Identity
           2. Controversy Surrounding "Standard English"
           3. Thinking and Fluency Among Adults Who Learn a Second Language

What is your own view regarding the "Standard English" controversy, and what material covered in this chapter might you use to argue in support of that point of view?

      F. Language and the Brain
           1. Broca's Aphasia
           2. Wernicke's Aphasia
           3. Brain Damage And Recovery Of Language Skills

What are some of the factors associated with likelihood of recovering language skills following various sorts of brain injury?

III. Language Development

In your study of this chapter, what did you learn about cultural similarities and differences in the basic steps of language acquisition, and the use of "motherese" in talking to babies?

      A. Learning to Talk
           1. Cooing and Babbling
               a. Cooing and the Simulation of Conversation
               b. Vowels as First Sounds
               c. Babbling as a Universal Phenomenon

In your study of this chapter, what did you learn that may help to explain why English-speaking babies usually say "dada" before they say "mama?

           2. Phonemes and Accents
               a. All Babies Make the Same Phoneme Sounds
               b. Every Language Has Its Own Set of Phonemes

At approximately what age does a child stop making the phonemes that are not a characteristic of his/her native language? What seems to be the reason for this change in the child's speech sound production?

           3. Morphemes and Meanings
               a. Morphemes Combined to Produce Words
               b. Vocalizations Refined to Increasingly Approximate Words

4. Early Words and Sentences
    a. Overextended Use of Words
    b. Acquisition of Syntax
    c. Description of Simple Actions
    d. Function Words
    e. Multiple-Word Sentences
    f. Telegraphic Speech
    g. Private Speech

According to your text, by what age have most children learned all of the basic words and structures of their native language?

B. How Is Language Acquired?

As noted in your text, what are the three conditions required for children to "readily learn their native language"?

1. Learning Language
    a. Language as an Operant Behavior
    b. Learning Theorists' View of Language Acquisition
    c. Factors Affecting Rate of Language Acquisition
        (1) Richness of Language Environment
        (2) Opportunity To Practice Vocalization
    d. Language Mistakes Made By Children Born Deaf
    e. Acquisition of Grammar Without Reinforcement

What observations are cited in your text which suggest that language acquisition may involve more than just "learning"?

2. An Innate Language Mechanism
    a. Language Acquisition Device (LAD)
    b. LAD as Universal "Blueprint" For Grammar
        (1) Divide Words Into Categories
        (2) Distinguish Individual Words
        (3) Figure Out Correct Noun-Verb Sequence
        (4) Plurality, Ongoing Action, Past Tense
    c. Research Using Picture of Imaginary Creature Called a "Wug"

What did the results of the classic study in which children were shown a picture of the imaginary creature called a "wug" suggest about the nature of how children learn their native language?

IV. Nonverbal Communication

Based on the observation cited in your book, how might cultural differences between individuals in "turn-taking schema" with regard to interpersonal communication, result in miscommunication?

A. Body Movements
    1. Nonverbal Messages And Impressions of a Person's Competence and Attractiveness
    2. And Impressions of Job Applicants
    3. Walking Behaviors and Impressions of the Person

How may cultural differences in standards as to what constitutes "normal walking" result in misunderstandings or false impressions of a person?

B. Gestures
C. Facial Expressions
    1. Eye Contact
        a. Generally Used To Invite or Discourage Communication
        b. To Signal Attention
        c. Valued by Many Euro-Americans As Showing Respect
        d. Avoidance May Be Seen as Signaling Shame or Lack of Respect
        e. Cultural Differences As Indicator of Attention and Respect
        f. As a Signal of Hostility or Sexual Excitement

Based on your reading in the corresponding chapter, give an example of the way cultural differences in the perception and use of eye contact may be a source of miscommunication in an everyday life situation?

    2. Smiling

According to your text, what are three communicative functions served by smiling behavior? What example is given of the way a smile may have different meaning in different cultural contexts?

D. Personal Space
    1. In City Dwellers As Compared With Suburban or Rural Residents
    2. Cultural Differences As An Aspect Of Conversational Etiquette
    3. As Affected by Factors Unrelated to Culture

How might miscommunication occur between two people as a result of differences between them in their culturally acquired differences with regard to the use of personal space?

E. Cultural Perspectives on Nonverbal Communication
    1. Importance of Context
        a. High-Context Communication
            (1) Meanings Implied Rather Than Stated
            (2) *Hanxu* in China
        b. Low-Context Communication
    2. In Collectivistic as Compared With Individualistic Cultures

What are some of the specific ways in which high- or low-context communication is more characteristic of collectivistic as compared with individualistic cultures? How might such differences lead to misunderstandings when collectivists and individualists try to communicate with each other?

V. Communication Between Men and Women in European-American Culture
    A. Nonverbal Communication
        1. And Self-Expression in Men and Women
        2. Differences in Attention to Facial Expressions

As noted in your text, how do men and women differ in their reliance on nonverbal communication as a means of self-expression?

        1. Eye Contact
            a. Differences Between Men And Women as Reflecting Relationship
Status
            b. Gender Differences Do Not Apply To All Cultural Backgrounds
        2. Smiling

What are some of the differences between European-American women and men in their smiling behavior, and how are such differences explained in your text? What similarities are there in the communicative significance of smiling behaviors between men and women?

    B. Verbal Communication
        1. Gender and Verbal Skill

How does the magnitude of gender differences (that is, between boys and girls) in verbal skills compare with the range of variation among members (that is, within groups) of either gender considered individually?

        2. Gender and Verbal Style
            a. Willingness to Verbally Attack Other People And Their Ideas
            b. Loudness and Pitch
            c. Use of Sports Clichés
            d. Amount of Talk and Interrupting Behavior
    C. Gender and Conversational Expectations

As noted in your text, what is one of the major differences between men and women in their use of conversation?

        1. Showing Interest Versus Indicating Agreement

As noted in your text, what is a major difference between men and women in their use of questions in conversations, and how might this difference lead to miscommunication between men and women?

        2. Expressing Desires

a. Gender Differences in Ways of Making Requests and Demands

b. As Related to Differences in Socialization

As noted in your text, how may differences in what gets learned in the play behavior of boys and girls, help to explain differences in the way in which men and women express their desires?

C. Self-Generated Questions: What's In This One For Me?

Most people come to the first course in psychology expecting to learn some things which will help them to better understand themselves, other people in their lives, and/or the nature of life in the world in which they live. Along these same lines, students of psychology often look forward to discovering things about human behavior and experience which may help them to improve their own life by developing their talents, technical skills, knowledge and abilities, and/or the quality or their relationships with other people. On the basis of such self-interest, which tends to provide a framework in terms of which new learning becomes personally meaningful and thus easier to remember, write down a few questions in the space below, about the subject matter covered in this chapter. After reading and studying the chapter, come back to see how any of what you've learned may be useful to you in finding answers to these questions.

D. Completion Items

The words in the margins of this exercise are the ones that correctly complete the sentence on the corresponding line. To get the most out of this exercise, you should try to avoid looking at these words in the margin until after you've filled in the corresponding blanks with the words you think best complete the sentences. So, begin the exercise by covering up all of the margin words with a piece of paper. Then, for each blank, write in the word which you think completes the sentence. Even if you're not sure as to the word, write in your best guess, preferably in pencil so you can erase and re-write any incorrect responses you may make here.

After writing in your "answer," slide the paper covering up the margin words down just far enough to see the word for the blank you just filled-in. For each blank that you fill-in correctly, put a check mark (√) after your answer. If the word you wrote in doesn't match the word corresponding to that blank, mark an (X) next to your response and go on to the next blank. It's probably a good idea to go back to the text and try to strengthen your learning related to topic coverage that corresponds in the textbook chapter to those blanks which you filled-in incorrectly, since those items signal a weak link in your concept mastery chain for this chapter.

1. In August of 1963, before a diverse audience of 250,000 people, Dr. Martin Luther King, Jr.'s "I have a dream speech is considered by many as the high point of the non-violent _____ movement. In simple, moving words, he described the ugliness of _____ and inspired a generation to political action. That speech is an eloquent example of _____ communication, the process by which we exchange meaningful information with other people.

civil rights
racism

interpersonal

2. Communication can be analyzed in terms of its various components. An act of communication begins with a person who sends a _____, which is the thought or feeling s/he wants to convey. The sender must select a physical _____, such as speech, writing or gesturing by which to communicate, and must _____, or translate the idea into a symbol that represents it. Once the message is transmitted, it must be _____ or interpreted by the receiver -- the person who gets it. The receiver's reaction to the message is called _____. Communication is defined by a variety of social rules or conventions which vary considerably among different _____. If any component of a single act of communication fails, _____ is likely to occur.

message
channel

encode
decoded

feedback

cultures
miscommunication

3. True listening is an _____, effortful process whereby a person receives and thinks about a message. The listener must work to discover _____ in all the available information in a message. In order to pay attention to a message, you must keep from thinking about _____ topics, focusing on your own feelings, or forming your own thoughts before fully considering the speaker's message. When we truly listen, we actively _____ about what we hear. Asking _____ is one way to acknowledge that you have truly heard a speaker's message. Another way is to _____ the message as you understand it.

active

meaning

distracting

think
questions

paraphrase

4. A successful act of communication has consequences, which refers to the _____ evoked from its receiver. Also, communications can be self-_____, which refers to the sender's efforts to judge whether or not his/her messages are getting across to the intended receiver(s). The _____ of any communicative act depends to a large extent on the context within which it occurs.

reaction
reflective

meaning

5. _____ is the process by which we encode meanings into words and combine words to express ideas; It allows us to share our knowledge and experiences. The _____ of language refers to its amazing capacity to generate a seemingly infinite number of sentences from a finite number of words and rules. Words act as _____ by representing objects, experiences, and ideas. The _____ meaning of a word is equivalent to its

Language

productivity

symbols

271

definition. The more personal, subjective meaning each listener may give to a word as a result of his/her own unique experience is referred to as the _____ meaning of that word. The set of rules which defines how we build meaningful messages from words and phrases is called the _____ of a language, which also includes _____, which dictates how we organize words into phrases and sentences. _____ language, which is used primarily by people with impaired hearing, employs both symbols and grammar to direct the specific use of gestures and facial expressions, rather than spoken or written words.

connotative

grammar
syntax
Sign

6. _____ refers to the non-word sounds that we make when speaking. It includes _____, the speed and pitch or our voice; vocal _____, such as laughing, crying, or sighing; and vocal _____, such as "uh" and "um." Listeners often attach greater importance to our paralanguage than to our words, especially if our words and paralanguage appear to be _____ contradictory. Our cultural backgrounds influence the _____ we read into other people's paralanguage, and paralanguage is a more integral aspect of communication in some cultures than in others. African-Americans, for example, often use the _____ of words, rather than their exact meanings, to convey messages. Indeed, one definition of Ebonics is the use of the voice as a _____ instrument, rather than a channel for spoken words.

Paralanguage
prosody
qualifiers
segregates

meanings

sound

musical

7. Ebonics, also known as Black English, can be described as an _____, a combination of language and style used exclusively by members of a non-mainstream social group. In this kind It uses words from the mainstream culture's language but gives them new _____ known only to the people who speak it. Such special languages serve several purposes, one of which is that they are a source of identity and _____ pride. Argots can also serve a political purpose, by helping speakers to assert their identity as distinctly _____ from the mainstream society. Furthermore, argots provide group members with a way to communicate "_____" in from of non-members.

argot

meanings

pride

separate

secretly

8. The _____ at which we speak, and especially the length of the pauses we take while speaking, invest our words with additional meaning. Because conversations proceed at different paces in different _____, the importance of pauses varies greatly. For example, European-Americans are typically uncomfortable with long pauses in conversations, and so tend to fill them with _____. When people with different conversational _____ attempt to talk with each other, it is not surprising that misunderstandings sometimes occur. For instance, a prospective employer who interviews a Native American may conclude that the applicant, who takes lengthy

pace

cultures

words
conventions

272

_____ between sentences, isn't intellectually quick   pauses
enough for the job.

9. According to the theory of linguistic _____, the language   determinism
we speak organizes our views of the world. Another way of expressing
the major premise of this approach is that, "As we speak, so we
_____." This theory has been largely rejected by contemporary   think
scholars. One striking example contradicting the theory, is in the fact that
the _____ people in New Guinea who have only two words   Dani
in their language for colors, can distinguish between red, blue, yellow, and
many other colors. The latter example, and many others, indicate that
language differences between cultures affect the ability to _____   express
thoughts, but not to have them.

10. Although language does not determine thinking, it can surely
influence it. One example along these lines, is the way in which the
-man suffix can promote gender-_____ thinking. Some   biased
research even suggests that the use of male _____ can   pronouns
affect our judgments of appropriate behavior by men and women, as
indicated by the results of a study which examined people's perceptions
of female _____ candidates who sought "masculine" offices   political
such as "councilman" or "neutral" offices such as "council person."

11. Research indicates that bilingual children have a greater ability to
form conceptual ideas, more cognitive _____, and enhanced   flexibility
verbal creativity as compared with monolingual children. Another study
found that bilingual children are more _____ to learn and more   motivated
effective learners than are monolingual children.

12. Bilinguals tend to think about and express negative emotions such as
anger, fear, and disgust through their _____ languages.   native

13. For people who no longer live in their native or ancestral countries,
speaking and reading their languages of origin provide a way for them to
affirm their cultural _____. Some residents of the U.S.,   identities
however, consider the use of languages other than English to be
harmful to both foreign-born speakers and to the social
_____ of the whole country. Since we all live in the   cohesiveness
same country, they argue, we should all speak the same
language. According to this "_____ English" point of view,   Standard
languages other than English should be outlawed in the workplace.
Some native speakers of English consider it the only correct way to speak
English, and may consciously or unconsciously dislike, devalue, disapprove of
or _____ other forms of English. Bilingual people typically   misinterpret
continue using their native language to express and think about their
_____.   feelings

14. Damage to the _____ cerebral hemisphere, which is   left
normally dominant for language, can produce several forms of aphasia.
People with _____ Aphasia can understand spoken   Broca's
language, but have difficulty producing grammatical speech. In contrast,
people with _____ Aphasia generally speak clearly and   Wernicke's
grammatically, and at a normal rate, but they do not understand the
precise meaning of words.

15. The use of a lilting voice with a higher than normal pitch and
exaggerated tone -- called _____, seems to have a   motherese
soothing effect on babies and captures their attention. Around two to
three months of age, most children make _____ noises   cooing
in response to adult speech or to express themselves. Most babies
first sounds are _____, such as e and a. After learning to   vowels
make consonant sounds, babies begin _____ by stringing   babbling
consonants and vowels together into multi-syllabic "words" such as
"bababa" and "lala."

16. In their babbling, babies produce consonant-vowel pairs which
constitute what are known as _____, the smallest units of   phonemes
sound in any language. Once babies begin to pay attention to adult
speech, they gradually stop making the phonemes that are not part of
their _____ language. Phonemes combine to create   native
_____, the smallest meaningful units of sound in a   morphemes
language, which are either whole words that cannot be divided or
word elements such as un and ing.

17. Children do not initially use words in the same way as do adults.
At first, children _____ words, using a single word to refer   overextend
to many items, and then use two-word sentences to describe simple
_____, such as "me go." Later, they learn to use   actions
_____ words that specify grammatical relationships, such as   function
the prepositions in, out, and above. Between the ages of two and three,
children typically use _____ speech, which is characterized by   telegraphic
short sentences containing nouns and verbs in the correct order, but lacking
figures of speech such as plurals, possessives, and conjunctions.

18. Language is an operant behavior which is _____ by   reinforced
children's experiences in a language-rich world. _____   Learning
theorists propose that children acquire language if their efforts to speak
are encouraged. But learning theory fails to explain how children learn
words after hearing them only once, and without benefit of reinforcement,
or how they can compose non-_____ sentences. Children   grammatical
seem to develop the ability to speak grammatically whether or not their parents
_____ or praise their efforts. Similarly, hearing-impaired children   reinforce

learn to use grammatical _____ language, whether or not their parents set a good grammatical example using American Sign Language.

sign

19. How do children learn correct grammar if not by _____ their parents? Some psychologists have proposed that babies are born with an _____ ability to acquire language. Noam Chomsky, a renowned linguist, proposes that children are born with a Language _____ Device (LAD) that enables them to discover and master grammar. He believes that babies use the LAD as a sort of "_____" for grammar, which allows them to make sense of the voices around them. According to the LAD theory, as children hear language spoken around them, they automatically attempt to identify the rules of _____ characteristic of that language.

imitating

innate

Acquisition
blueprint

grammar

20. Without accurately decoding a speaker's _____ messages, we cannot claim to understand what s/he intends to say. Typically, people take turns speaking based on a _____ that specifies how long and how often a person can speak without being considered rude. Cultural differences in this schema can lead to _____ and misunderstanding.

nonverbal

schema

miscommunication

21. If we are unaware of _____ influences on the way we encode and decode nonverbal information, we can accidentally misjudge people or their messages. Walking, for example, is one of the most obvious forms of movement to which people give meaning. One might take _____ strides or mincing steps, you may march or sashay along, swinging your hips. Each of these walking styles communicates something about the walker's _____, anatomy, and culture. An outsider's walk may be judged negatively when that judgment is based on one's own cultural _____.

cultural

deliberate

personality

standards

22. Unlike words, the _____ we use in place of speech, such as waving our hands in greeting, or nodding of the head in agreement, do not have universal meaning.

gestures

23. People generally use eye contact either to _____ or to discourage communication. When European-Americans meet another person's gaze, it is a signal that they are paying _____, interested in what the other person is saying, or perhaps that the other person arouses them. High-_____ European-Americans tend to make the same amount of eye contact regardless of whether they are talking or listening. In comparison, low-status people tend to make more eye contact when _____ than when talking. In some cultures, such as in Laos, people signal their _____ for and attention to another person by looking away. Still other cultures view direct eye contact as a signal of hostility or _____ excitement.

invite

attention

status

listening
respect

sexual

24. _____ space is an important aspect of conversational   Personal
etiquette in most cultures, although the accepted distances between people
may vary widely. People from Arab and Eastern European Jewish cultures, for
instance, are often comfortable speaking with each other within less than an
_____ length. In comparison, some European-Americans prefer   arm's
to be a _____ apart, and some Japanese people feel most   yard
comfortable with an even greater distance between themselves during
conversation. As a result of such differing standards, people who feel
comfortable with physical closeness may view those who prefer more
room as emotionally _____ and unapproachable, while those   distant
who prefer space might view the others as _____ and invasive.   pushy

25. Some cultures emphasize high-context communication, in which
meanings are _____ rather than stated in a straightforward   implied
way. Other cultures tend to emphasize low-context communication, in which
information is stated _____. High-context communication is   explicitly
thought to predominate in _____ cultures, where the good of   collectivistic
the community is the primary goal; low-context communication is thought to
predominate in _____ cultures, which emphasize   individualistic
independence and personal fulfillment. Collectivists tend to pay greater
attention to decoding _____ communication than do people   nonverbal
from individualistic cultures. Such differences may lead to
_____ when collectivists and individualists try to communicate   misunderstandings
with each other. Collectivists may feel frustrated when individualists do not
understand their _____ meanings, while individualists an be   implied
frustrated by collectivists' apparent lack of clarity and _____.   forthrightness

26. Women tend to rely heavily on _____ communication   nonverbal
behaviors in expressing themselves. While women may be better than men
at expressing some emotions such as happiness and sadness, men appear
to be better at communicating _____. Social scientists have   anger
suggested that these differences occur because girls are encouraged to
recognize when they are happy or sad and to express how they feel, while
boys are generally taught to _____ feelings other than anger.   control

27. Women generally pay more _____ than do men to a   attention
speaker's facial expressions and tend to be more skillful interpreters of
nonverbal signals.

28. Women tend to make eye contact more frequently, hold eye contact
_____, and reciprocate eye contact more frequently than do   longer
men. One interpretation of such differences, revolves around the assumption
that women tend to be more concerned with social and interpersonal
_____ than are men.   relationships

29. One explanation offered for the tendency for European-American

276

women to smile more than do European-American men, is premised on the view that women -- but not men -- often smile to indicate submission, to signal that no harm is intended, to cover up uneasiness or nervousness, and to indicate _____ or friendliness.

approval

30. Girls appear to acquire verbal skills _____ than do boys, and to outperform boys on tests of verbal fluency. These differences are slight, however, tend to matter only little in everyday life, and are actually _____ than the range of variation of verbal skills among either boys or girls.

earlier

smaller

31. Among the other gender differences in style of communication are the following. First, men tend to pepper their speech with _____ clichés typically not used by women. Also, when talking in a mixed-gender group in a public setting, men tend to talk and to _____ more than do women.

sports

interrupt

32. Women often expect that by talking with their romantic partners -- particularly about their _____ -- the couple's intimacy will grow. Men, on the other hand, often use conversation as a way to demonstrate their _____ by telling their partners what they think. In conversations between men and women, women tend to ask more _____ and to give more signals that they are listening.

feelings

independence

questions

33. Because boys and girls are _____ differently, they learn different ways to make requests and demands. Many girls play in _____, intimate groups that minimize conflict and maximize a sense of togetherness. Through such experiences, girls learn to consider their needs in light of others' _____ and the good of the group. Boys, however, tend to play in large groups that foster _____ and self-promotion. Through such experiences, boys learn to take care of their own _____, and to give commands in order to do so. Gender differences in making _____ often carry over into adulthood. Male doctors, for example, tend to _____ patients, whereas female doctors tend to make proposals such as "Maybe what _____ ought to do is to stay on this dose."

socialized

small

feelings
competition

needs
requests
command

we

E. Self-Quiz

For each of the following items, circle the letter which precedes the correct alternative.

1. Which of the following is not among the components of communication as described in your text?
   a. physical channel
   b. psychological channel
   c. encoding of a message
   d. decoding of message
   e. none of the above are among the necessary components of communication

2. Which of the following is not required of an active listener as the process of active listening is described in your text?
   a. decoding of the message
   b. attention to important aspects of the message
   c. comparison of message contents to listener's existing knowledge
   d. focusing on the listener's own feelings

3. Which of the following is not among the characteristics of all types of communication?
   a. communications are reversible
   b. communications can be conscious or unconscious
   c. communications can be self-reflective
   d. the meaning of a message is largely determined by its context
   e. all of the above are true of all types of communication

4. The grammar of a language includes
   a. prosody
   b. vocal qualifiers
   c. syntax
   d. vocal segregates
   e. all of the above

5. _____ is the term used to refer to a combination of language and style used exclusively by members of a non-mainstream social group.
   a. Ascot
   b. Argot
   c. Marmot
   d. Linguot
   e. Juggernaut

6. Paralanguage includes all of the following except
   a. prosody
   b. vocal qualifiers
   c. vocal segregates
   d. syntax
   e. using the sound of words rather than their exact meanings to convey messages

278

7. The essential premise of the theory of linguistic determinism has been supported by research indicating that
    a. speakers of Cherokee are less sensitive to social groupings than are speakers of English
    b. speakers of English do not perceive social groupings as efficiently as do speakers of Cherokee
    c. people who do not learn to speak until they are adults cannot describe their life experiences that occurred before they learned to speak
    d. the Dani people, who have only two words for colors, cannot distinguish between red blue
    e. none of the above

8. According to the results of research cited in your text, bilingual children have greater _____ than do monolingual children.
    a. ability to form conceptual ideas
    b. cognitive flexibility
    c. verbal creativity
    d. all of the above
    e. none of the above

9. According to research cited in your text, which of the following is (are) among those emotions that bilingual tend to think about and express which in their native language?
    a. anger
    b. fear
    c. disgust
    d. all of the above
    e. none of the above

10. The characterization of children's first words as "overextended" refers to the fact that children at this early stage of language development tend to use
    a. cooing as a means of conversation
    b. babbling as a means of conversation
    c. a single word to refer to many items
    d. primarily phonemes
    e. primarily morphemes

11. The fact(s) that children _____, is (are) not accounted for very well by learning theories.
    a. can learn words after hearing them only once, even without the benefit of reinforcement
    b. compose non-grammatical sentences that they are unlikely to have heard an adult say
    c. born deaf make many of the same language mistakes as do their hearing counterparts
    d. develop their ability to speak grammatically whether or not their parents reinforce or praise their efforts with praise
    e. all of the above

12. The ability to _____ is not among those assumed to be provided as an element of the "universal blueprint" for language acquisition according to the perspective of Chomsky's language acquisition device theory?
    a. divide words into categories
    b. learn correct grammar through social reinforcement
    c. distinguish individual words or meaningful phrases
    d. figure out the correct sequence for nouns and verbs
    e. notice how words are changed to denote plurality, ongoing action, and past tense

13. The results of the classic experiment in which children were shown a picture of an imaginary creature called a "wug," supported the language acquisition device theory of language acquisition, with regard to children's ability to
    a. learn correct grammar through social reinforcement
    b. imitate adult models of correct grammar
    c. figure out the correct sequence for nouns and verbs
    d. identify words as nouns and change them to designate their plurality

14. As noted in your text, in the Middle East, brief eye contact is
    a. often interpreted as impolite disinterest
    b. the rule of polite conversation
    c. regarded as a signal of hostility
    d. perceived as communicating sexual excitement

15. Which of the following was found to have the least influence on personal space, in a study wherein researchers secretly videotaped hundreds of conversations?
    a. type of relationship
    b. conversation topic
    c. emotions
    d. gender
    e. culture

16. Which of the following is not true of high-context communication?
    a. meanings are implied
    b. exemplified by the *hanxu* in Chinese culture
    c. thought to predominate in individualistic cultures
    d. characterized by ambiguity and use of indirect terms

17. Which of the following is not a characteristic of communication among collectivistic individuals?
    a. They tend to focus more on speakers' words than on their nonverbal signals.
    b. They tend to speak in ambiguous terms.
    c. The tend to hint at ideas.
    d. Their communication style is oriented to avoiding direct conflict with others.

18. In comparison to men, women tend to
    a. make eye contact more frequently
    b. hold eye contact longer
    c. reciprocate eye contact more frequently
    d. all of the above
    e. none of the above

19. Which of the following is not characteristic of conversations between men and women?
    a. Women tend to ask more questions.
    b. Women give more signals that they're listening.
    c. Men ask questions primarily to express interest and keep conversation going.
    d. Women tend to do more nodding and smiling.

20. According to the line of reasoning offered in your text, differences between men and women in their style of communication is attributed to which of the following elements of socialization in our society?
    a. parent-child relationships
    b. the media
    c. sex differences in brain physiology and chemistry
    d. children's play behaviors
    e. gender stereotypes that are reinforced in school

For each of the following items, circle "T" if the statement is True, and "F" if the statement is False.

21. T F   Dr. Martin Luther King, Jr.'s "I have a dream speech" was an eloquent call for an end to racial oppression in America.

22. T F   Asking questions and paraphrasing the speaker's message are two of the major obstacles to effective communication which tend to interfere with active listening.

23. T F   The "productivity" of language refers to its capacity to generate a seemingly infinite number of sentences from a finite number of words and rules.

24. T F   The "denotative" meaning of a word is the more personal, subjective meaning each listener gives to that word as a result of his/her own unique experiences.

25. T F   The expression "As we speak, so we think," reflects the essential premise of linguistic determinism.

26. T F   According to the "Standard English" point of view, languages other than English should be outlawed in the workplace.

27. T F   People with Broca's Aphasia can understand spoken language, but have difficulty producing grammatical speech.

28. T F   In contradiction to what might be called the common sense experience of parenting, research has indicated quite clearly that babies are stressed rather than comforted by being spoken to in the lilting voice with higher than normal pitch and exaggerated tone that is sometimes referred to as "motherese."

29. T F   Women generally pay more attention than do men to a speaker's facial expressions and tend to be more skillful interpreters of nonverbal signals.

30. T F   When talking in a mixed-gender group, men tend to talk and interrupt more than do women.

F. Teaching-To-Learn Exercise

1. *Let Me Teach You This.*

Write in the space provided below, the five facts, ideas, etc., from this chapter that you'd most like to teach to your own student(s) if you were a teacher. Then, really do try to communicate these facts or ideas to someone in your life; or, pretend to teach this content to a hypothetical or "make-believe" student or class.

2. *Now Answer My Questions.*

Here, write one multiple-choice and one True-False question for each of the facts, ideas, etc., you covered in the "Let Me Teach You This" section of this exercise.

Answer Key To Self-Quiz

1. b
2. d
3. a
4. c
5. b
6. d
7. e
8. d
9. d
10. c
11. e
12. b
13. d
14. a
15. e
16. c
17. a
18. d
19. c
20. d
21. T
22. F
23. T
24. F
25. F
26. T
27. T
28. F
29. T
30. T

CHAPTER 11

Motivation And Emotion

A. Learning Objectives

After your careful reading and effective study of Chapter 11, you should:

1. Know what the term "motivation" means, and also know the processes that have been proposed as "driving forces" which energize and direct behavior.

2. Develop a working familiarity with the following motivational aspects of the psychological study of eating, aggression, sexual behavior, and achievement:
    a. With regard to hunger,
        (1) How it is controlled by the brain and various types of body signals;
        (2) Why it is regarded as a "primary drive;"
        (3) What the "primary drive" status of hunger has to do with conceptualization of the human body as a homeostatic system, and how that system works in regulating eating behavior;
        (4) How social factors such as incentives and learned food cues affect the motivation to eat, and the nature of individual differences in both the psychological as well as physiological response to food cues.
    b. With regard to aggressive behaviors,
        (1) How such behaviors are defined operationally;
        (2) How instincts, a drive to escape frustration, brain dysfunction, testosterone, thought patterns, and incentive have been studied as factors which may contribute to the expression of aggression, and what such studies have revealed about the nature of aggressive behaviors;
    c. With regard to sexual behavior,
        (1) The four phases of the human sexual response cycle which healthy men and women are able to experience;
        (2) How testosterone, physical pleasure, sexual scripts, and social context contribute to both the arousal and expression of sexual behavior;
        (3) How cultural and gender experiences can influence sexual behavior; and
        (4) The range of individual variation in sexual behavior.
    d. With regard to achievement,
        (1) What is meant by "achievement motivation," as that concept has been defined in the discipline of psychology;
        (2) How the traditional definition of "achievement" and "achievement motivation" presuppose an individualistic point of view;
        (3) How "achievement" and "achievement motivation" might be conceptualized from the standpoint of a collectivistic point of view; and
        (4) How individualistic as compared to collectivistic cultural value orientations may have quite distinctively different kinds of influence on the kinds of goals for which people strive.

3. Develop a working familiarity with the following aspects of the psychological study of emotion:
   a. The components of "emotion" as studied by psychologists;
   b. How emotions have been conceptualized as "primary" and "secondary," as represented graphically by means of an adaptation of the "color wheel;"
   c. The central premise of the opponent-process theory, and its implication concerning the experience of strong emotion;
   d. The role of the sympathetic and parasympathetic nervous systems in the ebb and flow of emotional arousal, and the experiential counterparts to these events;
   e. The relationship between level of arousal, attention, and task difficulty as factors affecting level of performance;
   f. The overlap as well as subtle differences observed in the patterns of autonomic arousal characteristic of the primary emotions of anger, fear, sadness, happiness, surprise, as such observations also raise considerations with regard to:
      (1) What may be viewed as the biologically unique package of coordinated responses associated with each of those emotions; or
      (2) The universal similarities in human experiences with the environment.
   g. The cognitive appraisal of emotion and
      (1) How it can affect our goal-directed behavior as well as the particular emotion we experience in a given situation;
      (2) How cultural factors can affect the dimensions of an experience on which we focus our attention in the appraisal process;
      (3) How it has stimulated debate among psychologists as to whether or not cognition is a necessary component of emotion.

4. The research indicating universality in recognition of facial expressions associated with the primary emotions, and the related indications that culture plays a significant role in both
   a. the subjective experience of emotion, and
   b. providing the display rules regulating emotional expression.

5. The major theories of emotion, including:
   a. The James-Lange theory, focusing on the importance of inferences of emotion aroused by internal bodily changes;
   b. The Cannon-Bard theory, focusing on the role of the hypothalamus;
   c. The facial feedback hypothesis, with its emphasis on the idea that emotion derives from the effects of brain response to what the facial muscles do;
   d. The two-factor theory, with its assumption about the way in which emotion arises out of the individual's cognitive appraisal or attribution of his/her own physiological arousal; and
   e. The different points of view regarding the relationship between emotions and motivation.

B. Preview/Review Outline Of Key Terms And Concepts

Before you read the corresponding chapter in your text, read over the following outline. It is designed to give you an overview of information presented in the chapter, and how the various elements of that information are related to each other. After reading through the whole chapter and/or before course exams, you may use this outline as a quick review guide. In your reviews, mask off one line of the outline at a time, and try to recite from your memory of the chapter, the information that you expect to appear on the next line or so.

In going over this outline as a preview before reading and studying the chapter, the questions posed in bold print will help to keep you focused on the learning objectives here, and keep you actively involved in the process of achieving those objectives. When using this section as a review, try to answer the questions. Refer back to the chapter in the text for a more detailed feedback check on your mastery of the material, and/or to strengthen your knowledge and understanding wherever you feel the need to do so.

What is the anecdote about Kerri Strug's achievement, and what does it have to do with the study of motivation?

I. Motivation: The Driving Forces Behind Behavior

Based on your reading in Chapter 11, define "motivation" and explain briefly the relationship between motivation and goals.

What does goal-oriented behavior have to do with "well- being?"

How has the traditionally individualistic perspective of research in psychology influenced the focus of attention in the study of motivation by psychologists?

    A. An Instinct for Action

What are the three defining characteristics of an instinct?

        1. Freud's Idea Of "Death Instinct"
        2. Two-Fold Problem With Instinct Perspective
            a. Naming Instinct Does Not Explain Behavior
            b. Fails To Explain Complexity And Unpredictability Of Behavior
    B. A Drive to Fulfill Needs
        1. Drive Reduction Theory
            a. Bodily Need Results In Drive
            b. As Related to Bodily Homeostasis
            c. Humanistic Psychologist Maslow's Hierarchy Of Needs Theory
                (1) Physiological Needs
                (2) Safety And Security Needs
                (3) Belonging Needs
                (4) Esteem Needs
                (5) Self-Actualization

What is the essential idea of the "hierarchy" of needs proposed by Maslow?

How does Maslow's idea of "self-actualization" reflect an individualistic cultural orientation?

As noted in your text, what has the research on human motivation indicated about the validity of Maslow's hierarchical theory of needs?

    C. A Search for Stimulation
        1. Stimulus Motivation
        2. The Behaviors Of Sensation-Seekers
    D. An Attempt to Reap Rewards
        1. Incentives
            a. Intrinsic Motivation
            b. Extrinsic Motivation
        2. Replacing Intrinsic With Extrinsic Motivation
    E. A Response to Beliefs and Expectations

From the standpoint of the cognitive perspective, how are beliefs and expectations assumed to contribute to motivation?

II. Motivated Behaviors
    A. Eating

What is the essential difference between primary drives and social motives?

        1. A Response to Bodily Needs
            a. Food For Energy
            b. The Role Of Insulin
            c. Body As Homeostatic System
                (1) Hunger As Response To Available Energy
                (2) Stomach Pangs Or Contractions
                (3) Sensory And Neurochemical Cues From Many
                        Parts Of Body
                        (a) Role Of Hormones Such As Cholecystokinin
                        (b) Information From Liver And Intestines
            d. Role Of the Hypothalamus
                (1) Lateral Hypothalamus As "Feeding Center"
                (2) Ventromedial Hypothalamus As "Stop Eating" Center
            e. Set Point For Body Weight
                (1) And Dieting To Achieve Weight Loss
                (2) Stability In Body Weight Despite Temporary Changes
                        In Food Intake

What evidence is there to support the "set point" theory of body weight?

        2. The Rewards of Food
            a. Food Cues As Extrinsic Incentives To Eating
            b. Effect On Physiology As Well As Thinking
    B. Aggression
        1. Instincts and Needs

a. Ethologist Konrad Lorenz's View Of Human Aggression As Innate Instinct That Aided Survival
b. Lack Of Empirical Support For Instinct Theories
c. Evidence For Genetic Contribution To Aggressive Behavior
d. Central Nervous System Dysfunction And Aggression
    (1) Tumors In Temporal Lobe
    (2) Damage To Frontal Lobe
    (3) Abnormalities In Functioning Of Neurotransmitters
e. Role Of Testosterone
    (1) Levels Increased By Aggressive Behavior
    (2) And Attempts To Explain Sex Differences In Aggression
    (3) And Frustration Tolerance

How is aggression explained from the standpoint of the drive reduction perspective on motivation?

2. The Rewards of Aggression
    a. The Social Learning Theory Perspective
    b. Effects Of Watching Televised Aggression On Aggression In Children
        (1) Mighty Morphin Power Rangers Cartoon Study
        (2) Rehearsal Of Aggressive Scripts

How can education be used to counter the negative effects of social learning on aggression?

3. Triggering Thoughts
    a. Aggression And Assumption That People Are Intentionally Hostile
    b. Effects Of Alcohol Myopia
    c. Effects Of Uncomfortably High Temperatures
        (1) Heat-Induced Arousal And Appraisal Of Hostility As Intentional
        (2) Study Of Police Officers' Response To Video Portrayal Of Officer Interacting With A Suspect
        (3) Inconsistent Research Findings
C. Sexual Behavior
  1. An Instinct for Pleasure and a Drive Toward Orgasm
    a. Minimal Level Of Testosterone And Capacity To Engage In Sex
    b. Freud's Idea Of Instinct For Pleasure
    c. Insufficient Testosterone And Diminished Interest In Sex
    d. Masters And Johnson's Research On Volunteers
        (1) View Of Unlearned, Inborn Drive Toward Orgasm
        (2) The Human Sexual Response Cycle
            (a) Excitement
            (b) Plateau
            (c) Orgasm
            (d) Resolution
        (3) Criticism Of Focus On Orgasm

2. The Rewards of Sex
    a. Goals Other Than Orgasm
    b. Masturbation As A Common Sexual Behavior
    c. Physical Or Emotional Pain Due To Sexual Dysfunction
3. Gender Perspectives on Sexual Scripts
    a. Socially Acceptable Forms Of Sexual Arousal And Behavior
    b. Males Have More Permissive Sexual Scripts Than Females
    c. Males Learn That Coitus Enhances Their Status
    d. Girls Receive Mixed Messages Regarding Coitus
    e. Male-Female Differences In The First Coital Experience
    f. And Varying Reactions Of Men And Women To Sexual Activities

Based on the material covered in Chapter 11, what evidence is there for the way in which gender differences in sexual scripts affect the way men and women in our society react to their first coital experience, and the apparent focus in their behaviors with sexual partners?

4. Cultural Perspectives On Sexual Scripts
    a. Religious And Cultural Beliefs Shape Our Sexual Scripts
    b. Male Homosexuality In some Papua New Guinea As Compared To
        Euro-American Cultures
    c. Female Virginity In Traditional Cultures
    d. Struggle With Contradictory Sexual Scripts In Ethnic Minority Cultures
5. Alternative Perspectives: Why People Do Not Bother Using Condoms
    (Box 11.1)
    a. Survey Concerning Incidence Of Sexually Transmitted Diseases (STDs)
    b. Why Don't People At Risk Of STDs Use Condoms?
    c. Reasoned Action Perspective
    d. Social-Cognition Perspective
    e. Beliefs Concerning Costs vs. Benefits Of Using Condoms
    f. Male-Female Socioeconomic Power Differences and Condom Use

Which of the perspectives on condom use represented in Box 11.1 makes the most sense to you? Why?

5. The Influence of the Social Context
    a. Much Research On Sex Rooted In Individualistic Perspective
    b. Sexual Activities Occur In A Social Context
    c. Results Of Survey On Why People Engage In Coitus
    d. National Survey Of Health And Social Living (NSHSL)
        (1) Number Of Self-Reported Sex Partners Over Entire Lifetime
            For Female Respondents
            (a) Indicated Change In Social Context
            (b) Generational Differences
        (2) Effects Of Interpersonal Pressures On Sexual Behavior
            (a) In The First Sexual Experience
            (b) Percentage Of Women Forced To Have Sex

      b. Secondary Emotions
          (1) Blending Of Different Emotions
          (2) Disappointment As Example
      c. Three-Dimensional Color Wheel

What is the "three-dimensional color wheel" used to describe and represent?

    2. Emotional Ups Balance Emotional Downs:
      The Opponent-Process Theory Of Emotion
      a. Brain As Seeking Emotional Homeostasis
      b. Extreme Swing Followed By Swing To Opposite Extreme
      c. Result Is Feeling Of First Emotion Minus The Opposing One
      d. As Applied To Experience Of Winning A Competition
          (1) Joyful High Triggers Disappointment
          (2) Reduction In Intensity Of Joy
          (3) Disappointment Lingers After Joy Wears Off
          (4) End Result Is Feeling "A Little Down"

How can the opponent process theory of emotion be used to explain why some highly successful competitors at virtually anything, may come to respond to their victories or successes with little joy?

  B. Physiological Arousal and Emotion

What are some of the aspects of physiological arousal which occur as a component of emotion? What is the role of the sympathetic branch of the autonomic nervous system in emotional arousal? What is the function of the parasympathetic division of the autonomic nervous system in the regulation of emotion?

    1. General Arousal and Performance
      a. Arousal And Narrowing Of Attention
      b. General Arousal And Performance
          (1) Increased Arousal And Improvement In Performance
          (2) Too Much Arousal Associated With
             Decline In Performance
          (3) Optimal Level Of Arousal And Task Familiarity
             (a) Low Arousal For Unfamiliar Tasks
             (b) Moderately High Arousal For Familiar Tasks

How might you apply the knowledge you derived from studying about the relationship between level of arousal and performance in Chapter 11, to improve your own performance on the exams you take in this and other courses?

    2. Applications: How Do Liars Give Themselves Away? (Box 11.2)
      a. How People Lie About Their Emotions
      b. Using The Polygraph As A "Lie Detector"
          (1) Physiological Measures (e.g., Heart Rate, Blood Pressure,

Perspiration, Respiration)
(2) Establishing Baseline With Neutral Questions
(3) Autonomic Arousal And Emotion
c. No Unique Pattern Of Arousal Associated With Lying
d. Some People Feel No Emotion And Show No Autonomic Arousal When They Lie
e. Unreliability And Invalidity Of "Lie Detector" Method
f. Using Facial Expression To Detect Lying
(1) And Sensitivity To Nonverbal Facial Expressions
(2) Noticing Contradictions Between Words And Nonverbal Expressions Of Emotion

On the basis of what you read in Box 11.2, what observations would you invoke to argue against the idea that "polygraphic interrogation" is an effective technique to use in criminal investigation and prosecution? What alternative to the use of the polygraph might you suggest as potentially more useful in this regard, and why?

3. Specific Patterns of Arousal
a. Each Primary Emotion Has Its Own, Specific Pattern Of Emotion
b. The Subtle Differences Suggest Biological Uniqueness
C. Cognitive Appraisal and Emotion

What does it mean to say that cognitive appraisals of situations may be either conscious or unconscious?

1. Cultural Perspectives on Appraisal
a. Influence Of Cultural Experiences
b. Being The Only One In Class To Earn An "A" On Final Exam
c. Cultural Background And Attention To Specific Dimensions Of Experiences
d. Help To Explain Differences Among People In Their Emotional Reactions To Situation
2. Cognition and Emotion
a. Relationship Between Thoughts And Emotions
b. Experimental Evidence For Emotional Reactions Occurring Apparently Without Thought
c. Traditional Definition Of Cognition
d. Definition Of Cognition As Information Processing Involving The Brain
(1) Processing Of Information In Areas Other Than Cortex
(2) Fear Triggered By Sensory Information Directly To Amygdala

In this section, the authors of your text summarize an experiment in which respondents who did not understand Chinese were presented with slides in which Chinese language symbol characters were preceded by slides of various types of emotion-triggering stimuli. How did the results of that experiment provide evidence to support the view that emotional reactions can occur without cognition?

D. Expression of Emotion
    1. Facial Expressions
        a. Universal Recognition Of Primary Emotions
        b. Anger, Fear, Disgust, Sadness, Happiness
        c. Brain Organization Theory Of Apparent Universality
            (1) Supported By Studies Of Infants
            (2) Expression Of All Primary Emotions In Infants

Why do the findings indicating facial expression of primary emotions by blind infants provide especially convincing support for the view that emotions are at least partly due to universal features of brain organization that have developed throughout the course of evolution?

    2. Cultural Perspectives on Facial Expressions
        a. Some Cultures Value Verbal Expressions Of Emotion, Others Do Not
        b. Cultural Guidelines For Appropriateness Of Nonverbal Expression Of Emotion: Display Rules
            (1) In U. S., Boys Discouraged From Crying In Public
            (2) Similarities In Emotional Expressions Of Japanese And U. S. Students Shown Graphic Surgery Movie
                (a) Japanese Students Smiled More Often
                (b) Alternative Interpretations Of Smiling Differences

Japanese students were found to smile more than their U. S. counterparts in an experiment where respondents viewed movies in which surgery was graphically portrayed. What were the alternative interpretations of this difference offered in your text, with regard to its relevance to culturally acquired display rules regarding the facial expression of emotion?

IV. Behavior and Emotion
    A. Theories of Emotion
        1. The James-Lange and Cannon-Bard Theories
            a. James-Lange Theory
                (1) Emotions Inferred From Bodily Changes
                (2) Feel Sorry Because We Cry, Etc.
            b. Cannon-Bard Theory
                (1) Observation That Animals With Severed Spinal Cord Show Emotional Reactions
                (2) Observation That Physiological Arousal Often Unrelated To Emotion
                (3) Observation That Physiological Reactions May Happen More Slowly Than Emotions
                (4) Conclusion That Emotional Feelings And Autonomic Arousal Occur Simultaneously

How might the following sequence be modified to fit the James-Lange theory of emotion? I see a bear. I feel afraid, and so I run.

2. The Facial Feedback Hypothesis
    a. Facial Muscle Movements Influence Emotion
    b. Information From Muscle Movements Sent To Brain
    c. Experiment On Response To Cartoons By Respondents
        With A Pencil In Their Lips Or Teeth
    d. View That Facial Expressions May Initiate Emotions:
        (1) Experiment With Minangkabau Respondents
        (2) Facial Expression Of Disgust And Corresponding
            Nervous System Changes
    e. Effects Due To Cultural Influence On Cognitive Appraisals
        Of Our Physiological Reactions

How do the differences observed between Minangkabau and Euro-American respondents in the experiment in the experiment described above, indicate the way in which cultural factors may affect the way in which facial feedback is related to emotion?

3. The Schacter-Singer Two Factor theory
    a. Cognitive Appraisal In Labeling Of Autonomic Arousal
    b. Experiment In Which Two Different Groups Of Respondents
        Felt The Same Physical Arousal
        (1) Respondents Had different Needs For Finding A
            Reason For Their Arousal
        (2) No Particular Emotions Reported By Those Who
            Expected The Arousal To Be Produced By Injection
        (3) Same Emotions As Expressed By Confederate
            Reported By Those Who Expected No Physical
            Effects From Injection
    c. Experiment In Which Men Were Interviewed By An Attractive
        Woman On Bridge

How did the results of the experiment in which respondents given injections of epinephrine and then put into a room with a confederate who acted out various sorts of emotion, tend to support the Schacter-Singer theory? How did the differences in men's sexual attraction to the woman they met on either the "scary" or "safe and solid" bridge support this theory?

B. The Motivating Quality of Emotion
    1. Positive Emotions And Motivation To Engage In Behaviors
        a. Maintenance Of Positive State
        b. Maintenance of Intrinsic Motivation
    2. Possibility That Specific Emotions Are Innate And
        Have Specific Motivational Purpose That Aids Survival

How do the results of the study in which respondents were given a small bag of candy and then given the choice between an unpaid task of solving an interesting puzzle or a paid but boring task, support the view that people who are happy prefer to engage in tasks that will keep them happy?

C. Self-Generated Questions: What's In This One For Me?

Most people come to the first course in psychology expecting to learn some things which will help them to better understand themselves, other people in their lives, and/or the nature of life in the world in which they live. Along these same lines, students of psychology often look forward to discovering things about human behavior and experience which may help them to improve their own life by developing their talents, technical skills, knowledge and abilities, and/or the quality or their relationships with other people. On the basis of such self-interest, which tends to provide a framework in terms of which new learning becomes personally meaningful and thus easier to remember, write down a few questions in the space below, about the subject matter covered in this chapter. After reading and studying the chapter, come back to see how any of what you've learned may be useful to you in finding answers to these questions.

D. Completion Items

The words in the margins of this exercise are the ones that correctly complete the sentence on the corresponding line. To get the most out of this exercise, you should try to avoid looking at these words in the margin until after you've filled in the corresponding blanks with the words you think best complete the sentences. So, begin the exercise by covering up all of the margin words with a piece of paper. Then, for each blank, write in the word which you think completes the sentence. Even if you're not sure as to the word, write in your best guess, preferably in pencil so you can erase and re-write any incorrect responses you may make here.

After writing in your "answer," slide the paper covering up the margin words down just far enough to see the word for the blank you just filled-in. For each blank that you fill-in correctly, put a check mark (√) after your answer. If the word you wrote in doesn't match the word corresponding to that blank, mark an (X) next to your response and go on to the next blank. It's probably a good idea to go back to the text and try to strengthen your learning related to topic coverage that corresponds in the textbook chapter to those blanks which you filled-in incorrectly, since those items signal a weak link in your concept mastery chain for this chapter.

1. Kerri Strug's famous vault in the 1996 Olympics reflected her
_____, a term which refers to processes that initiate, direct and   motivation
maintain psychological and physical behavior toward a goal. A goal is a mental
representation of what we _____, and can be specific or general.   want
In studying motivation, we can focus our investigations in one of two ways.
From an _____ perspective, the self is separate and distinct from   individualistic
others, and it is motivated by internal processes such as thoughts and feelings.

300

From a _____ perspective in contrast, the self is fundamentally   collectivistic
interdependent with others, and motivated by the thoughts and feelings of those
with whom the self is interdependent. The majority of research on goal-oriented
behavior has originated from the _____ perspective.   individualistic

2. An _____ is an innate, highly rigid, unlearned, complex pattern   instinct
of behavior. Freud believed that humans had a _____ instinct   death
that motivated them toward self-destructive behavior. The instinct perspective
has a two-fold problem First of all, just _____ an instinct does not   naming
explain the behavior to which it refers. Second, the instinct perspective fails to
account for the full _____ and unpredictability of human behavior.   complexity
As an alternative to instincts, psychologists began to think of _____   needs
as the motivation for goal-directed behavior.

3. To explain the motivating force of needs, scholars have offered the
_____ reduction theory, in terms of which bodily need is thought   drive
to result in a temporary state of tension that motivates behavior intended to
address that need. _____ psychologist Abraham Maslow proposed   Humanistic
that humans are born with five essential needs, which he conceptualized in terms
of a _____ within which a need at any given level can be met only   hierarchy
after the needs below it are met. At the bottom of that hierarchy Maslow placed
the physiological needs, and at the top he placed the need for self-
_____ whereby a person becomes "fully oneself."   actualization

4. One psychological need not included in Maslow's hierarchy is the need for
_____. Stimulus motivation, an unlearned desire to explore, to be   stimulation
curious, and to approach experiences for their _____, motivates   novelty
behavior. Research on stimulus motivation has examined the behaviors of
_____-seekers, people who are high in stimulus motivation.   sensation
Such people actively look for excitement, feel uninhibited in experimenting
with _____ experiences, and are inclined to take risks that other   new
people will not take.

5. Many goal-oriented behaviors are motivated by _____, the   incentives
positive consequences they elicit. _____ motivation is the   Intrinsic
desire to engage in a behavior for the sake of a consequence essential to the
behavior. In contrast, _____ motivation is the desire to engage in   extrinsic
a behavior for the sake of a consequence that is external to the behavior.
Intrinsic incentives are generally more _____ than are extrinsic ones.   enduring

6. The _____ view is that beliefs and expectations contribute to   cognitive
motivation.

7. _____ drives are unlearned motives necessary for survival.   Primary
Social motives in contrast, are those that are _____ by interacting   learned
with others.

8. Food provides the fuel to energize the body. The body uses _____, insulin a hormone produced by the pancreas, to convert food into glucose, a form of stored energy used by body cells. As a _____ system, the human body homeostatic automatically seeks to maintain a certain balance in its use and replacement of energy. As the body uses up its available energy, it sends more and stronger signals of _____ to the brain. Food in the stomach triggers certain hunger hormones, such as _____, or CCK, to inform the brain how much cholecystokinin food has been eaten. The liver sends information about _____ levels glucose and the intestines send information about digestive activity. An animal that has just finished eating will resume eating if its _____ hypothalamus is lateral stimulated, and even a starving animal will not eat if that structure is destroyed. In contrast, when the _____ hypothalamus is stimulated, an animal ventromedial stops eating, and without it, animals with free access to food seem unable to stop eating. The latter two parts of the hypothalamus are thought to regulate eating according to the body's _____ point, a particular weight toward set which a body homeostatically tends. The set point theory is based on the observation that human body weight tends to be quite _____ stable in spite of apparent changes in food intake and energy expenditure. Some eating is motivated by food _____, aspects of a stimulus, such as cues its appearance, flavor, and aroma, that trigger a response, such as salivation or eating.

9. Early theorists viewed aggression as a basic human _____. instinct Ethologist Konrad Lorenz, for example, thought that people had an innate aggression instinct that aided _____. In an analysis of 24 survival studies of adopted children or identical and fraternal _____, twins researchers found a significant correlation between genetic similarity and aggressive behavior. Aside from genes, certain types of central nervous system dysfunction, such as tumors in the temporal lobe and damage to the _____ lobe of the brain are associated with outbursts of frontal inappropriate aggression. Studies show that behaving aggressively increases levels of the hormone _____. testosterone

10. From the drive reduction perspective, aggression arises from the need to rid ourselves of _____. frustration According to social learning theorists, people are not born with aggressive thoughts and behavior tendencies; they learn to associate them with _____. Not only do children imitate television characters incentives with whom they identify, they also mentally _____ the aggressive rehearse scripts that they view. Psychologists suspect that some children behave aggressively because they _____ themselves harming a person imagine who provokes them.

11. Aggressive behavior is associated with a cognitive tendency to assume that other people are _____ hostile. Alcohol contributes to aggression intentionally by causing alcohol _____, whereby some people become overly myopia sensitive to hostile cues and unaware of aggression inhibiting cues. In addition

to alcohol, uncomfortably high _____ in the environment might also   temperatures
distort thought processes that contribute to aggression. Perhaps heat causes
arousal that in turn increases one's tendency to appraise another person's
_____ as intentional.   hostility

12. The earliest empirical study of sexual behavior in the United States was a
_____ of 10,000 U.S. adults conducted by Alfred Kinsey. The   survey
results of that survey were criticized because the sample, although large, was
not _____ of the general population.   representative

13. In some sense, humans have an _____ for sexual behavior.   instinct
Without being taught, all healthy human adults who have a minimal level of the
hormone _____, have the capacity to engage in sex. From the   testosterone
drive perspective, Masters and Johnson thought that sexual behavior arose from
an unlearned, inborn drive toward _____. On the basis of their study orgasm
of thousands of instances of sexual arousal, they described the human sexual
response _____ as a sequence of four stages of sexual arousal.   cycle
The first stage in this cycle is that of excitement, which levels of to a plateau phase,
sometimes followed by orgasm, which is followed by a _____ phase, resolution
characterized by a reduction in arousal and blood flow away from the genitals.
Criticism of Masters and Johnson's focus on orgasm has been based on the fact
that sexual _____ does not always require progression through all   satisfaction
four phases of the sexual response cycle, sometimes including only excitement
or excitement and _____.   plateau

14. Even people who believe that _____ is bad or sinful tend to do it. masturbation
Sex does not reward some people with pleasure. Instead, it causes them
physical or emotional pain because of a sexual _____, a persistent   dysfunction
problem with sexual arousal, desire, or performance.

16. Through socialization, we develop sexual _____, mental plans   scripts
for how to relate to, behave during, and interpret situations that involve sex. U. S.
males have more _____ sexual scripts than do females. Unlike boys, permissive
girls usually feel in _____ with their first sexual partner and want to love
have sex because they feel affection toward their partner. Not surprisingly,
compared to boys, adolescent girls typically experience less _____,   pleasure
and afterwards feel less positive, less satisfied, more guilty, and a greater loss of
self-_____ after their first coital experience.   respect

15. Religious and cultural beliefs also shape our sexual scripts. Some ethnic
minorities who live in the United States struggle with _____ sexual   contradictory
scripts. For instance, some ethnic minority women face the dilemma of whether to
follow the conservative sexual scripts taught by their parents, or to adopt the
relatively more _____ Euro-American scripts expected by their peers. permissive

16. The risk of sexually transmitted _____ (STD) transmission can be disease
significantly reduced through the use of condoms. The _____   reasoned

action perspective hypothesizes that people will use condoms if their attitudes, feelings, and peer influences motivate an intention to use condoms. The social-_____ perspective emphasizes an individual's ability to deal with a situation that requires the use of condoms. Research indicates that women and men who feel comfortable _____ about safer sex and sexual histories are about six times more likely to use condoms than are people who do not feel comfortable about such communication. In heterosexual relationships in which men have more _____ than do women, a woman may feel that she has no choice but to consent to sex without a condom, out of fear of physical harm, emotional rejection, _____ backlash, or accusations that she is infected.

cognition

talking

power

socioeconomic

17. Much of the research on sexual behavior has been rooted in an individualistic perspective that emphasizes the individual's _____ motivation, such as hormones and sex drive. But some of the important findings of the National Survey of Health and Social Living study point out the importance of considering the social and interpersonal _____ when studying sexual behavior. In the 1950's, women were expected to enter into marriage as _____ or to be sexually experienced only with their fiancées. Two generations later, society became relatively more accepting of women experiencing sex with more than one partner and _____ with their husbands-to-be before marrying.

internal

context

virgins

living

18. Achievement motivation is the desire to excel and achieve a difficult _____. Achievement-motivated people want to achieve, set challenging but _____ for themselves, prefer to receive feedback on their performance, and pursue their goals with disciplined effort. Theorists propose three competing factors that influence the achievement goals that people choose: (1) a need to achieve, (2) expectations for success, and (3) fear of _____. Among Euro-Americans, achievement motivation has also been linked with having parents who encourage a sense of personal mastery, _____, and self-reliance.

goal
realistic

failure

independence

19. In the U. S., most of the research on achievement motivation has originated from an individualistic perspective that emphasizes _____ rather than interpersonal goals. As a result of their interdependent self, many collectivistically-oriented people are motivated toward achieving goals that meet with _____ approval. In addition, collectivistic cultures tend to disapprove of _____ success that takes one above the group. Most _____ cultures value achievement goals that collectivistic respect group harmony, personal loyalty, humility, and interdependence, not just personal goals.

personal

social
individual

20. We don't always experience _____ arousal as an emotion. If we did, we would experience the huffing and puffing that results from

physiological

304

climbing a flight of _____ as emotion.   stairs

21. Primary emotions, like primary _____, are the fundamental   colors
or basic emotions. When different emotions blend, they comprise
_____ emotions, such as disappointment which is a combination   secondary
of sadness and surprise. One way of describing the relationship between primary
and secondary emotions is to use a three-dimensional "color _____"   wheel
of emotions.

22. According to the _____-process theory of emotion, our brain   opponent
naturally seeks emotional homeostasis by causing us to experience an opposing
emotion when we experience any strong emotion. According to this view, after
swinging to one emotional extreme we automatically swing in the _____   opposite
emotional direction, with the net result being that we feel the first emotion minus
the opposing one. Perhaps this explains why some highly successful
competitors respond to _____ with little joy.   winning

23. When people encounter emotionally significant stimuli, especially negative ones,
the _____ branch of the autonomic nervous system activates the   sympathetic
adrenal glands. These glands release epinephrine and _____,   norepinephrine
hormones that prepare the body for action by mobilizing stored energy. All of the
latter changes prepare the body for _____. As an emotion and the   action
need for energy fades away, the _____ division of the autonomic   parasympathetic
nervous system calms the body down.

24. A _____ is a machine that measures and records changes in a   polygraph
person's autonomic arousal, such as heart rate, blood pressure, perspiration, and
respiration. When this instrument is used as a lie detector, the interviewer
usually begins by establishing a _____ of autonomic arousal by   baseline
asking a respondent questions that have no relevance to the issue or topic about
which lying is being investigated. The validity of the polygraph as a lie detection
instrument is based on the false assumption that lying is consistently associated
with a _____ pattern of autonomic arousal. In addition, some   particular
people feel no emotion or autonomic _____ whey they lie. As a   arousal
result, a polygraph test would wrongly categorize them as telling the
_____. The latter arousal occurs particularly often among   truth
_____ liars. Although physiological arousal does not consistently   chronic
give liars away to polygraphs, people who are sensitive to nonverbal
_____ expressions of emotion have a much better chance of   facial
identifying a liar than do people who are not. They successfully detect lying
by noticing a _____ between a liar's words and nonverbal   contradiction
expressions of emotion.

25. Performance improves as arousal _____, but then declines   increases
once arousal becomes too high. However, the optimal level of arousal for good
performance depends on one's _____ with the task. We perform   familiarity
best on unfamiliar tasks when arousal is _____, and perform best   low

on familiar tasks when arousal is moderately high.

26. Research suggests that each _____ emotion is characterized
by a specific pattern of arousal, and thus involves a biologically unique package
of coordinated _____.

primary

responses

27. When we encounter a stimulus, we make several cognitive appraisals or
_____ of it, the first of which involves appraisal of its relevance.
Situations that we appraise as beneficial or harmful commonly result in
_____ and negative emotions, respectively.

evaluations

positive

28. Experiences related to our cultural background can guide our
_____ to certain dimensions of a situation. Such differences
provide some explanation for why people have different emotional reactions
to the same stimulus or _____.

attention

situation

29. In support of the view that emotions do not require cognition, researchers
have shown that people have emotional reactions without _____
about a stimulus. A traditional way to define cognition is "the gathering, storing,
and retrieving of information in the brain and how we use _____
about ourselves and our environment. Other theorists define cognition as any
form of _____ processing that involves the brain. By this latter
definition, cognition involves all brain activity, including activity that does not
involve the _____. Some brain areas, such as the amygdala,
process information in a way which helps our body decide whether a stimulus
is emotionally _____ or not.

thinking

knowledge

information

cortex

significant

30. Facial expression of _____ emotions appear to be universally
recognized. In laboratory research studies, men and women of various
_____ usually recognize photographed facial expressions of
anger, fear, disgust, sadness, and happiness. Some psychologists believe that
the universal recognition of emotion may be partly due to universal features of
_____ organization that have developed through evolution.
Studies of _____ expressions of emotion provide further evidence
for this perspective. Even _____ babies who cannot possibly
learn facial expressions from other people show these same facial expressions.

primary

cultures

brain
infant
blind

31. Cultures provide _____ rules, which are guidelines for when,
how, and to what degree people should show their emotions in a given situation.
For instance, boys in the United States are discouraged from _____
in public. In a study in which respondents watched a graphic movie of different
types of surgery, Japanese students _____ more often than did
U. S. students when they watched the film with an interviewer. In a re-interpretation
of this study, it was observed that perhaps the Japanese students smiled to
communicate _____ toward the interviewer, and not to hide their
feelings.

display

crying

smiled

politeness

32. According to the James-Lange theory, people _____ their   infer
emotions by noticing their bodily changes. Walter Cannon, a physiologist
proposed an alternative theory based on findings including those indicating
that animals with no ability to experience physiological arousal because of a
severe _____ cord still showed normal emotional reactions.   spinal
Cannon also pointed out that an immediate emotional response occurs in many
different situations, where people have no time to _____ their   evaluate
physiological state. According to the Cannon-Bard theory, emotion and
autonomic arousal occur at the _____ time.   same

33. The facial _____ hypothesis is that facial muscle movements   feedback
can influence the experience of emotion by sending information to the brain.
Culture may limit such facial muscle effects on emotion by affecting the
cognitive _____ we make of physiological reactions.   appraisals

34. According to the Schacter-Singer two factor theory, emotion results when
people feel autonomic arousal and make cognitive appraisals of their situation
in order to _____ their autonomic arousal as an experience of   label
emotion. These theorists proposed that people make meaning of their
physical sensations by appraising the _____ in which they occur.   context
In a classic experimental test of this theory, respondents who had been misled
to expect no physical effects from an injection of _____, reported epinephrine
feeling the same feelings expressed by an experimental confederate, whether
the emotion enacted was that of silliness and happiness, or irritation and
_____. In another experiment the results of which are invoked   anger
as supporting the two-factor theory, men reported feeling more
_____ attraction to an attractive woman interviewer when   sexual
the interview took place on a swaying suspension bridge at 230 feet above a
turbulent river, than when the interview was conducted on a solid wooden
bridge only 10 feet above a calm portion of the river. In the latter study, the
researchers concluded that the respondents mistakenly appraised their
feelings of _____ arousal.   fear

35. Positive emotions appear to motivate people to engage in behaviors that
will maintain their positive state and _____ motivation. In one study   intrinsic
relevant to the latter idea, after having received a small bag of candy which is
presumed to have made them feel happy, people tended to prefer the choice
of an unpaid task of solving an interesting _____ over a paid but   puzzle
boring number task.

E. Self-Quiz

For each of the following items, circle the letter which precedes the correct alternative.

1. The term "motivation" refers to process that _____ psychological and physical behaviors oriented toward a goal.
   a. initiate
   b. direct
   c. maintain
   d. all of the above
   e. none of the above

2. Instinctive behavior patterns are
   a. innate
   b. highly rigid
   c. complex
   d. unlearned
   e. all of the above

3. Which of the following is not a characteristic of drive reduction theory?
   a. drive is a temporary state of tension
   b. drives result in needs
   c. need reduction results in homeostasis
   d. homeostasis is a steady internal state

4. _____ is (are) at the top of the hierarchy of needs proposed by humanistic psychologist Abraham Maslow.
   a. Physiological needs
   b. Safety and security needs
   c. Belonging needs
   d. Self-actualization

5. Sensation-seekers are people who are high in _____ motivation
   a. hierarchical
   b. self-actualization
   c. stimulus
   d. response

6. Behaviors in which we engage for their own sake are referred to as _____ motivated.
   a. intrinsically
   b. extrinsically
   c. forensically
   d. incentively

7. _____ is the hormone used by the body to convert food into glucose, a form of stored energy used by body cells.
    a. Pitosin
    b. Indocin
    c. Insulin
    d. Formalin

8. The _____ hypothalamus is apparently quite crucially involved in sending signals to the body to "stop eating."
    a. frontal lobe of the
    b. parietal lobe of the
    c. occipital lobe
    d. lateral
    e. ventromedial

9. Ethologist Konrad Lorenz believed that aggression is
    a. an innate instinct
    b. learned by imitation
    c. acquired through competitive interaction with other members of one's species
    d. intrinsically-motivated
    e. none of the above

10. From the drive reduction perspective, aggression arises from the need to rid oneself of
    a. low self-esteem
    b. inadequate self-actualization
    c. archetypal motives and emotions inherited throughout the course of our evolution
    d. frustration
    e. all of the above

11. In the study cited in your text, police officers who watched a video of an officer interacting with a suspect, were more likely to perceive the suspect as threatening the officer when they watched that video
    a. when they were intoxicated with alcohol
    b. in a room in which the temperature was very high
    c. immediately after having been reprimanded for failing to follow department procedure
    d. immediately after having been told that their candidacy for promotion had been denied
    e. all of the above

12. Which of the following is not one of the four phases of the sexual response cycle as described by Masters and Johnson?
    a. excitement
    b. plateau
    c. orgasm
    d. guilt
    e. resolution

In what respects did the results of the NSHSL research indicate the importance of social and interpersonal context in sexual behavior?

    D. Achievement
       1. Individualistic Needs
          a. Personal Desire To Dominate, Control, Gain Mastery Over, And Surpass Others
          b. Search For Personal Characteristics Associated With Achievement Motivation
          c. Setting Of Challenging But Realistic Versus Unrealistic Goals
          d. Three Competing Factors Influencing Goal Choice
             (1) Need To Achieve
             (2) Expectations For Success
             (3) Fear Of Failure
          e. Achievement Motivation And Individualistic Versus Collectivistic Cultural Value Orientations And Experience

How has goal-setting been found to differ for people who are high as compared to those who are low in their achievement motivation?

       2. Collectivistic Needs
          a. Research From Individualistic Perspective Emphasizes Personal Rather Than Interpersonal Goals
          b. Achievement Motivation And Collectivistic Orientation
             (1) Goals That Meet With Social Approval
             (2) Disapproval Of Individual Success that Takes One Above The Group
             (3) Value Achievement Goals Emphasizing Group Harmony, Personal Loyalty, Humility, Interdependence
          c. Individualistic vs. Collectivistic Reasons For Pursuing Same Goals

Drawing from the material covered in Chapter 11, explain how research based exclusively on an individualistic cultural value orientation can produce a narrowly biased view of achievement motivation?

II. Emotion

As noted in your text, emotion is a coordinated package of what three component processes? Which of these components triggers or enhances the emotion, and which one refers to the nonverbal signals by which the emotion is communicated?

    A. Experiencing Emotion
       1. Primary and Secondary Emotions
          a. Primary Emotions
             (1) Like Primary Colors
             (2) The Fundamental Or Basic Emotions
             (3) Joy, Surprise, Disgust, Anger, Fear, Shame, Sadness

13. The _____ perspective hypothesizes that people will use condoms if their attitudes, feelings, and peer influences motivate an intention to use condoms.
    a. reasoned action
    b. social-cognition
    c. gestalt
    d. personal heuristic
    e. psychodynamic

14. Research noted in your text has indicated that achievement-motivated people tend to set _____ goals for themselves.
    a. easily-achieved
    b. unrealistically high
    c. challenging but realistic
    d. parent-referenced
    e. peer group-referenced

15. As noted in your text, which of the following kinds of goal emphases tends to be more characteristic of collectivistic than individualistic cultural value orientations?
    a. personal loyalty
    b. humility
    c. interdependence
    d. all of the above
    e. personal success

16. Which of the following is not one of the primary emotions?
    a. surprise
    b. disappointment
    c. disgust
    d. anger
    e. shame

17. According to the opponent-process theory, which of the following emotions would be most likely to follow the experience of joy upon winning a competition of some sort?
    a. surprise
    b. disappointment
    c. shame
    d. anger
    e. fear

18. In the study described in your text, a careful observer could have detected the emotionality experienced by respondents who were asked to try to hide their feelings while watching films which were designed to induce strong emotions, by noticing that the respondents
    a. grimaced slightly from time to time
    b. clenched their jaw from time to time
    c. blinked more than normal
    d. swallowed more than normal

19. We tend to perform best on unfamiliar tasks when arousal is
    a. low
    b. moderate
    c. moderately high
    d. very high

20. In support of the _____ hypothesis, respondents who were smiling because they held a pencil in their teeth, found a series of cartoons more humorous than did those who were not smiling because they held a pencil in their lips.
    a. psychodynamic
    b. stimulus motivation
    c. behavior social learning theory
    d. facial feedback
    e. Brawley-Richardson

For each of the following items, circle "T" if the statement is True, and "F" if the statement is False.

21. T F   From the individualistic perspective, the self is viewed as motivated by internal processes such as personal thoughts and feelings.

22. T F   In general, replacing intrinsic with extrinsic motivation results in a reduction in genuine interest in the activity.

23. T F   When an individual's body weight drops below the set point, metabolism speeds up.

24. T F   In contradiction to the social learning theory hypothesis, children who watched a televised episode of the Mighty Morphin Power Rangers subsequently showed no greater incidence of aggressive behaviors than did children who had not seen the program.

25. T F   According to Masters and Johnson's perspective, sexual behavior is due to an unlearned drive to reproduce the species.

26. T F   In the United States, most of the research on achievement motivation has originated from an individualistic perspective.

27. T F   As an emotion and the need for action energy fades away, it is the parasympathetic division of the autonomic nervous system that calms the body down.

28. T F   Lying <u>does</u> <u>not</u> produce a unique pattern of autonomic arousal which is detectable reliably in polygraphic interrogation.

29. T F   According to the James-Lange theory, people infer their emotions by noticing their bodily changes.

30. T F   In support of the Schacter-Singer two factor theory of emotion, men reported feeling significantly more sexual attraction to a female interviewer when the interview took place in a safe than in an anxiety-arousing situation.

F. Teaching-To-Learn Exercise

1. *Let Me Teach You This.*

Write in the space provided below, the five facts, ideas, etc., from this chapter that you'd most like to teach to your own student(s) if you were a teacher. Then, really do try to communicate these facts or ideas to someone in your life; or, pretend to teach this content to a hypothetical or "make-believe" student or class.

2. *Now Answer My Questions.*

Write in the space provided below, the five facts, ideas, etc., from this chapter that you'd most like to teach to your own student(s) if you were a teacher. Then, really do try to communicate these facts or ideas to someone in your life; or, pretend to teach this content to a hypothetical or "make-believe" student or class.

G. Bringing Psychology To Life Exercise

I. There is probably no formal model which has been more widely-cited in attempts to understand human motivation and personal development than Maslow's "hierarchy of needs" theory. In contrast to the work of Freud and countless other psychologists who focused on mental illness or psychologically dysfunctional people afflicted with various sorts of psychopathology, Maslow's approach was oriented to studies of psychologically healthy people whose achievements he saw as representative of the very highest level of human functioning.

312

Answer Key To Self-Quiz

1. d
2. e
3. b
4. d
5. c
6. a
7. c
8. e
9. a
10. d
11. b
12. d
13. a
14. c
15. e
16. b
17. b
18. c
19. a
20. d
21. T
22. T
23. F
24. F
25. F
26. T
27. F
28. T
29. T
30. F

CHAPTER 12

Personality & Testing

A. Learning Objectives

After your reading and careful, effective study of Chapter 12, you should:

1. Be able to define the concept of "personality" in terms of its emphasis on stable, internal inclinations underlying patterns of behavior.

2. Know the following with regard to the major alternative perspectives on the psychology of personality:
    a. What the primary approaches to understanding personality try to explain;
    b. With regard to the trait approach,
        (1) What is the focus of attention or objective of this approach;
        (2) What are the "Big Five" personality variables that have been revealed by trait-oriented research; and
        (3) The factors which influence the stability of a personality trait.
    c. With regard to the psychodynamic perspectives,
        (1) What is the fundamental premise of these perspectives;
        (2) How the psychodynamic schools of thought distinguish among the various levels of consciousness;
        (3) The idea of unconscious motivation as it is conceptualized from the standpoint of the psychodynamic perspective;
        (4) Some fundamentals of Freud's psychoanalytic theory, focusing on
            (a) Freud's conceptualization of the id, ego, and superego as the three conflicting aspects of personality; and
            (b) Freud's conceptualization of the psychosexual stages of personality development.
        (5) Some fundamentals of Jung's theory, focusing on
            (a) His introduction of the concepts of personal and collective unconscious; and
            (b) The way Jung conceptualized of individual differences in personality in terms of differences in the integration of opposing "archetypes," introversion-extroversion, and "persona" and inner person.
        (6) Some fundamentals of Karen Horney's theory, focusing on
            (a) The way in which Horney viewed anxiety as the basis for individual differences in personality; and
            (b) The three basic personality types in terms of which Horney conceptualized of differences in personality due to differences in the way in which basic anxiety is expressed.
        (7) The central role of inferiority feelings in Adler's theory.
        (8) In overall evaluation,

      (a) How the strengths of the psychodynamic perspectives may be viewed from the standpoint of their contribution of useful concepts to the field of psychology; and

      (b) How the "testability" of its concepts constitutes what is seen as a considerable weakness of the psychodynamic approach.

d. How the emphasis on environment distinguishes the learning perspectives on personality;

    (1) The fundamental differences among the behaviorist and social learning approaches; and

    (2) In overall evaluation, what are the major strengths and contributions as well as the major weaknesses and limitations of these learning perspectives.

e. The fundamentals of the social cognition perspectives, with special attention to,

    (1) The emphasis on "personality types" in these approaches;

    (2) How Belief Systems Theory studies of individual differences in beliefs and degrees of abstract, differentiated, integrated thinking have led to identification of four basic personality types;

    (3) The defining attitudinal characteristics of the authoritarian personality, as expressed in their stylistic mode of thought and behavior; and

    (4) In overall evaluation, the strengths and usefulness of the social cognition perspectives as evidenced in supporting research, and the weaknesses or limitations in the range or scope of personality characteristics to which they contribute understanding.

f. Some fundamentals of the behavior genetics perspective, including,

    (1) The search for the heritability of personality traits;

    (2) The three primary methods used by behavior geneticists; and

    (3) The unique characteristic distinguishing the behavior genetics approach from other approaches to the study of personality, and thus its major strength or usefulness.

g. Some fundamentals of the humanistic perspectives on personality, including:

    (1) What the humanistic psychologists see as the major flaw in psychodynamic views;

    (2) How the humanistic emphasis on the idea that we can choose to be the kind of people we want to be, stands in direct counterpoint to the psychodynamic views;

    (3) The basic premise of Maslow's theory, with its emphasis on self-actualization as the driving force of personality; and

    (4) The basic premise of Carl Rogers' theory, with its emphasis on the importance of "unconditional positive regard" for the individual's ability to embrace his/her "existential freedom" and fulfill his/her human potential; and

    (5) The difficulty involved in empirical testing of humanistic ideas as a major weakness in such approaches.

h. How culture, race, gender, and power issues become relevant to the social scientific study of personality.

i. How the same data may be interpreted in ways that lead to distinctly different descriptive inferences with regard to personality.

3. Know the following with regard to the methods of personality assessment used by psychologists:

    a. The essential premise and objective of projective tests, and the personality perspective with which they are most congruent, as exemplified in the Rorschach Inkblot Test and the Thematic Apperception Test;

    b. What is involved in the administration of self-report tests, as exemplified by the MMPI;

    c. Some key considerations regarding the usefulness and limitations of the various assessment methods, with special attention to:

        (1) The ease of administration and scoring of self-report tests;

        (2) The lack of adequate frame of reference and basis for judging the accuracy of responses to self-report tests;

        (3) The relative advantage of direct observation over self-report; and

        (4) The relative advantages and disadvantages of structured interviews involving preplanned questions as compared with unstructured interviews.

B. Preview/Review Outline Of Key Terms And Concepts

Before you read the corresponding chapter in your text, read over the following outline. It is designed to give you an overview of information presented in the chapter, and how the various elements of that information are related to each other. After reading through the whole chapter and/or before course exams, you may use this outline as a quick review guide. In your reviews, mask off one line of the outline at a time, and try to recite from your memory of the chapter, the information that you expect to appear on the next line or so.

In going over this outline as a preview before reading and studying the chapter, the questions posed in bold print will help to keep you focused on the learning objectives here, and keep you actively involved in the process of achieving those objectives. When using this section as a review, try to answer the questions. Refer back to the chapter in the text for a more detailed feedback check on your mastery of the material, and/or to strengthen your knowledge and understanding wherever you feel the need to do so.

I. The Concept of Personality: Who We Are

How do psychologists define "personality?"

How is a Western, individualistic cultural value orientation reflected in the traditional definition of personality and explanations of behavior by psychologists?

What was the astrological "theory" of personality?

How did somatotype theory attempt to predict and explain personality?

II. Alternative Perspectives on Personality: Why We Are The Way We Are

What are the six primary perspectives on personality?

    A. The Trait Perspective: Describing Personalities

How are questionnaires used in the trait approach to the study of personality?

How did psychologist Raymond Cattell distinguish between what he called "source" and "surface" traits?

How is factor analysis used in the trait approach to the study of personality? How did Cattell propose to describe individual trait differences among people?

To what specific characteristics did the trait dimensions of "introversion-extroversion" and "stability-instability" refer in Eysenck's trait approach? Based on the intersection of the latter two dimensions, what were the four personality temperaments described from the standpoint of this approach?

        1. The "Big Five"
            a. Extroversion
            b. Conscientiousness
            c. Openness To Experience
            d. Emotional Stability
            e. Agreeableness
        2. The Consistency of Traits
            a. Gordon Allport's View
                (1) Cardinal Traits
                (2) Central Traits
                (3) Secondary Traits
            b. Walter Mischel's View:
                Personality As Probable Responses To Situation
            c. Trait Perspective
            d. Situationist Perspective
            e. Interactionist Perspective
            f. Trait Consistency, Definition, And Situations Studied

What do people's social roles and perceptions of situations have to do with personality trait attribution? How does the situational adaptiveness of people from collectivist backgrounds illustrate this point?

        3. The Usefulness and Limitations of the Trait Approach
            a. Defines Personality In Terms Of Everyday Concepts
            b. No Required Theoretical Assumptions
            c. Doesn't Explain Why Personality Traits Develop
    B. Psychodynamic Perspectives: Focusing on Childhood and the Unconscious

What are the major differences between the psychodynamic and trait perspectives, with regard to what it is that they attempt to explain and the extent to which they are supported by empirical evidence?

What is the primary assumption underlying the psychodynamic approach, with regard to just what it is that our personalities reflect?

In his tri-level conceptualization of consciousness, how did Freud characterize and distinguish among what he referred to as the "conscious," "preconscious," and "unconscious?"

Influenced as he was by the ideas of 19th century physicists, just what does the term "psychodynamics" refer to in Freud's theory of personality, and what did he define as the role of the "libido" in such processes?

1. Sigmund Freud's Psychoanalytic Theory Of Personality
    a. Early Experiences And Current Symptoms
    b. Focus On The Role Of The Unconscious And Internal Conflicts
    c. Intrapsychic Conflicts As Determinants Of Personality
        (1) Id
            (a) Biological Drives And Instincts
            (b) Pleasure Principle
        (2) Superego
            (a) Sense Of Morality And Social Constraints
            (b) Sense of Right And Wrong
        (3) Ego
            (a) Perception, Thinking, Learning
            (b) Self-Concept
            (c) Realistic Satisfaction Of Id's Desires
    d. Psychosexual Stages
        (1) Changes In Expression And Satisfaction Of Id Urges
        (2) Changing Imbalances Between Id, Ego, Superego
        (3) Erogenous Zones
        (4) Oral, Anal, Phallic, Latency, & Genital Stages
        (5) Resolution Of Conflicts And Personality
        (6) Gratification Produces Both Satisfaction And Anxiety
        (7) Fixated Development

From the standpoint of Freud's psychoanalytic theory:
(a) What is the role of the ego?
(b) How do the conflicts experienced at the various psychosexual stages affect personality development?

2. Carl Jung
    (a) Personal Unconscious
    (b) Collective Unconscious
    (c) Archetypes
        (1) Animus, Masculine
        (2) Anima, Feminine
        (3) Psychic Wholeness

(4) Introverted, Extroverted

(5) Inner Self, Persona

(6) Personality Differences From Opposing Archetypes And
Tendencies

*From the standpoint of Jung's theory, what does it take to be psychologically healthy and
achieve psychic wholeness? Give some specific examples.*

3. Karen Horney

(a) Personalities From Relationships With Parents

(b) Basic Anxiety From Dependence On Other People

(c) Unconscious Hostility

(d) Three Ways Of Dealing With Anxiety

(1) Moving Toward Others

(2) Moving Against Others

(3) Moving Away From Others

(e) Maladjusted Personality Types

(1) Compliant Type

(2) Aggressive Type

(3) Detached Type

*From the standpoint of Horney's theory: (a) What is the cause of people's basic anxiety and
unconscious hostility?; and (b) What is the relationship between each of the three ways in
which people tend to deal with their basic anxiety, and the three maladjusted personality types
defined in this theory?*

4. Alfred Adler

(a) Feelings Of Inferiority

(b) Ordinal Position (Birth Order)

(c) Inferiority Complex

*From the standpoint of Adler's theory: (a) What are some of the different ways in which people
try to deal with their inferiority complexes?; and (b) How is it that changes in one's
personality can continue to take place throughout life?*

5. The Usefulness and Limitations of Psychodynamic Theories

a. Freudian Contributions

(1) Childhood Experiences As Basis For Personality

(2) Unconscious Feelings And Motives

(3) Compromise Among Desires, Fears, And Reality

(4) Aggressive And Sexual Urges And Personality

b. Contributions Of Jung, Horney, And Adler

(1) Opposing Parts Of Personality

(2) Feelings Of Anxiety And Inferiority

c. Provide Many Hypothetical Constructs

d. Limitations

(1) Not Well-Supported By Empirical Evidence

          (2) View Humans As Victims Of Drives
          (3) Failure To Account For Healthy Personality
          (4) Overestimate Permanency Of Personality
          (5) Some Notions Are Sexist

What are some of the major contributions and weaknesses of the psychodynamic perspectives?

    C. Learning Perspectives: Emphasizing the Environment
        1. The Behaviorist Perspective
            a. Born Of The Work Of Watson And Skinner
            b. Personality As Accumulation Of Learned Behavior Patterns
            c. Focus On Directly Observed Behaviors
            d. Reinforcement History And Generalizations Of Behaviors

How might Sherlock Holmes' personality be analyzed and explained from the behaviorist perspective?

        2. The Social Learning Perspective
            a. Largely Developed By Walter Mischel
            b. Personality From Learning, Modeling, Cognitive Processes
            c. Reciprocal Determinism
                (1) Thinking, Perception, Feelings
                (2) Behavior
                (3) Environmental Factors
             d. Self-Efficacy
             e. Person's Knowledge, Culturally Based Behavior Patterns,
                Sense Of Self-Efficacy, Values, Interpretations Of Events

How do people high in self-efficacy differ from those who are low in this characteristic, in their sense of themselves?

        3. The Usefulness and Limitations of Learning Approaches
            a. Much Research Indicating That Personality Is Learned
            b. Hides Richness Underlying Personality
             c. Insufficient Attention To Situational Interpretations And Beliefs
            d. Ignores Genetic Influences
    D. Social Cognition Perspectives: Identifying Personality Types

What is a personality type?

        1. Belief Systems Theory
            a. Identifies Four Different Personality Types
            b. Types Differ In Beliefs And Abstract Thinking
            c. Type 1
                (1) Traditional Beliefs And Values
                (2) Least Differentiated And Least Abstract In Thinking

d. Type 2
  (1) Believe Established Authority Is Usually Wrong
  (2) Don't Make Distinctions In Their Thinking
e. Type 3
  (1) More Differentiated And Integrated In Thinking Patterns
  (2) Act For Social Approval Without Thinking Of Selves
f. Type 4
  (1) Personalities Most Differentiated And Integrated
  (2) Believe Behaviors Should Reflect What One Thinks
2. An Authoritarian Personality
  a. Characterized By Ethnocentrism
  b. Obey And Respect People Of Higher Status
  c. Hostile Toward Those Believed To Be Of Lower Social Position
  d. Don't Precisely Differentiate Concepts
  e. From Families Where Discipline Is Harsh And Arbitrary
3. Usefulness and Limitations of Social Cognition Personality Theories
  a. Considerable Empirical Support
  b. Focus On Values And Family Relationships
  c. Don't Account For Full Range Of Personality Characteristics

According to the social cognition point of view, how do children raised by parents with authoritarian personalities perceive their parents?

E. The Behavior Genetic Perspective: Focusing on Genes and Environment

How is personality described from the standpoint of the behavior genetic approach?

How might development of shyness be explained from the behavior genetic perspective?

What does "heritability" of traits mean from the standpoint of the behavior genetic approach?

1. Searching for Genetic Effects
  a. Animal Studies
  b. Adoption Studies
  c. Studies Of Identical Twins Reared Apart
2. Genes and Their Impact on Personality
  a. Most Psychological Characteristics Have Genetic Basis
  b. 20% To 50% Of Trait Variance Due To Genes

What are some of the psychological traits noted in your text as among those found to be genetically influenced?

3. The Usefulness and Limitations of the Behavior Genetic Approach
  a. Genes Affect Hormones, Proteins, And Aging
  b. Difficult To Distinguish Genetic From Environmental Effects
  c. Most Studies Have Concentrated On European Americans

What observation(s) might you invoke to support the argument that the influence of environment on personality is underestimated in the behavior genetic approach?

    F. Humanistic Perspectives: Choosing a Personality

In what sense did humanistic theories of personality develop as a reaction against both behaviorist and psychoanalytic theories?

What is the humanistic assumption concerning "existential freedom?"

        1. Abraham Maslow
            a. Self-Actualization As Driving Force In Personality Development
            b. More Basic Needs Must Be Met First
            c. Self-Actualization As A Process

From the standpoint of Maslow's theory, how may social conditions inhibit the development of human potential?

        2. Carl Rogers
            a. Denial Of Feelings To Gain Approval Of Others
            b. Conditional Positive Regard
            c. Unconditional Positive Regard

From the standpoint of Rogers' theory, how may a person's success in meeting other people's standards have a quality of emptiness to it?

Also from the standpoint of Rogers' theory, what positive effects on an individual's personality are seen as increasingly likely when that person is raised in a family atmosphere of unconditional positive regard?

        3. The Usefulness and Limitations of Humanistic Theories
            a. View Of People As Thinking Creatures Who Make Life Choices
            b. Behavior Options And Opportunities For Personal Growth
            c. Insufficient Attention To Role Of The Unconscious
            d. Cultural Bias In Conceptualization Of Self-Actualization
            e. Concepts Frequently Too Vague To Test Empirically

What is the cultural bias implicit in the humanistic conceptualization of "self-actualization?"

    G. Other Perspectives: Identifying Cultural, Racial, Gender, and Power Effects
        1. Cultural Perspectives on Personality
            a. De Toqueville's 19th Century Characterization Of Americans
            b. Asian Americans Less Assertive Than European Americans
            c. Latino/a Script of *Simpatia*
            d. *Machismo* And Personality Of Latino Americans
            e. African Americans And Individualist Culture
        2. Racial Perspectives on Personality

a. Social Reactions To A Person's Race
b. The "Black Personality" And Racism
c. African American Perspectives On Energy And Bodily Rhythms

Citing the rationale given in your text, why do some African Americans feel that identifying themselves as "Americans" suggests rejection of their own racial group?

3. Gender Perspectives on Personality
    a. Most Studies Find No Consistent Or Large Gender Differences
    b. Patterns Of Differences On Some Characteristics
        (1) Aggressiveness
        (2) Task Performance Versus Relating To Others
        (3) Domination Of Others
        (4) Ways Of Dealing With Stress
        (5) Conformity
    c. Findings From Cross-Cultural Studies
        (1) Biological Roots To Gender Differences
        (2) Culture May Distort And Override Biological Tendencies

How may the patterns of slight to moderate gender differences in personality outlined in 3b above be explained in terms of cultural influences?

4. Alternative Data Interpretations: Describing Personality Differences (Box 12.1)
    a. Same Research Results May Support Different Interpretations
    b. Labeling A Personality Dimension Affects How We Think Of It

Give two examples to illustrate how gender differences in personality may be described or interpreted in quite different ways.

5. Social Power Perspectives on Personality
    a. Uneven Distribution Of Resources And Power
        (1) Between Males And Females
        (2) Among European Americans And Minority Groups
    b. Meaning Of Personality Characteristics And Social Power: The Locus Of Control
        (1) External Locus Of Control
        (2) Internal Locus Of Control
    c. Social Power And Expectations For Success
    d. External Locus Of Control In Asian Americans

As noted in your text, in historical perspective, what kinds of personality traits have been reinforced in lower-power groups in American society?

According to the rationale outlined in your text, how might an internal locus of control orientation represent delusional thinking rather than a realistic understanding of the environment for a person who is among those who are physically or economically handicapped or socially discriminated against?

How might the differences between Asian and European Americans in their social assertiveness be explained in terms of locus of control orientation and/or socially acquired assessments of power?

III. Methods of Assessing Personality: Comparing People
      A. Projective Tests: Revealing the Unconscious

What kinds of stimuli are used in projective tests? Why?

          1. Rorschach Inkblot Test
              a. Symmetrical Stimuli
              b. Respondent Describes What S/he Perceives
          2. Telling a Tale in the TAT
              a. Illustrations As Stimuli
              b. Respondent Asked To Tell A Story Based On Illustration
          3. The Usefulness and Limitations of Projective Tests
              a. Quick Sense Of Client's Attitudes, Beliefs, Conflicts
              b. To Establish Rapport
              c. European American Responses Regarded As Standard
              d. Questionable Scientific Reliability And Validity

How may the cultural bias implicit in the traditional use of projective tests result in gross misinterpretations of the responses given to the stimuli of those tests by minority group members? What is the example of such misinterpretation noted in your text?

      B. Self-Report Tests: Consciously Describing Ourselves

What does the expression "objective personality tests" mean, and what does it not mean with regard to self-report tests?

          1. An Objective Test:
              Minnesota Multiphasic Personality Inventory (MMPI) As Example
              a. Most Widely Used Self-Report Personality Test
              b. Respondents Indicate Whether Statements Characterize Them
              c. Consists Of Ten Clinical Scales
          2. The Usefulness and Limitations of Questionnaires
              a. Many People Can Be Tested Simply
              b. Often Used In Research
              c. Useful For Matching Of Subjects On Personality Characteristics
              d. MMPI-2 Has Widened Representativeness Of Norm Sample
              e. Often Less Valid For Minorities

f. Insufficient Frame Of Reference For Response To Items

g. Difficulty To Know If Respondent Is Answering Accurately

What is the technique suggested in your text for getting around the problem of having to rely on the accuracy of self-reported data?

    C. Observations and Interviews
        1. Observers Work Together to Assure Reliability Of Their Reports
        2. Limitations Due To Angle Of Observation
        3. Time Frame Limitations Of Observations
        4. Observers' Unintentional Misinterpretations Of Behaviors
        5. Supplementation Of Observation With Interviews
            a. Allow For Comparisons Across Respondents
            b. Might Overlook Rich And Relevant Information
            c. Might Produce Irrelevant, Useless Information, Or Unexpected Insights

C. Self-Generated Questions: What's In This One For Me?

Most people come to the first course in psychology expecting to learn some things which will help them to better understand themselves, other people in their lives, and/or the nature of life in the world in which they live. Along these same lines, students of psychology often look forward to discovering things about human behavior and experience which may help them to improve their own life by developing their talents, technical skills, knowledge and abilities, and/or the quality or their relationships with other people. On the basis of such self-interest, which tends to provide a framework in terms of which new learning becomes personally meaningful and thus easier to remember, write down a few questions in the space below, about the subject matter covered in this chapter. After reading and studying the chapter, come back to see how any of what you've learned may be useful to you in finding answers to these questions.

D. Completion Items

The words in the margins of this exercise are the ones that correctly complete the sentence on the corresponding line. To get the most out of this exercise, you should try to avoid looking at these words in the margin until after you've filled in the corresponding blanks with the words you think best complete the sentences. So, begin the exercise by covering up all of the margin words with a piece of paper. Then, for each blank, write in the word which you think completes the sentence. Even if you're not sure as to the word, write in your best guess, preferably in pencil so you can erase and re-write any incorrect responses you may make here.

After writing in your "answer," slide the paper covering up the margin words down just far enough to see the word for the blank you just filled-in. For each blank that you fill-in correctly, put a check mark (√) after your answer. If the word you wrote in doesn't match the word corresponding to that blank, mark an (X) next to your response and go on to the next blank. It's probably a good idea to go back to the text and try to strengthen your learning related to topic coverage that corresponds in the textbook chapter to those blanks which you filled-in incorrectly, since those items signal a weak link in your concept mastery chain for this chapter.

1. Psychologists define personality as the relatively _____ combination of beliefs, attitudes, values, motives, temperament, and behavior patterns arising from underlying, internal inclinations that an individual exhibits in various situations. The majority of research on personality, as in other areas of psychology, has been characterized by an _____ cultural orientation.

      stable

      individualist

2. When psychologists using the trait approach study personality, their focus isn't just on finding _____ traits, readily evident observable personality characteristics. They also want to examine _____ traits, basic personality characteristics, such as assertiveness or a strong sense of humor. When a personality questionnaire is administered, psychologists sometimes use _____ analysis to find several responses that often appear as a group or cluster which is analyzed in an attempt to identify an underlying, shared characteristic. Cattell found 16 clusters of responses, or personality dimensions, which he regarded as _____ traits -- that is, characteristics which all people have to some degree. Using this same approach, the Eysencks described two dimensions, introversion-_____ and stability - _____.

      surface

      source

      factor

      source

      extroversion/
      instability

3. The so-called Big Five dimensions of personality, found across cultures and both sexes, are: (1) extroversion, (2) conscientiousness, (3) _____ to experience, (4) _____ stability, and (5) agreeableness.

      openness/
      emotional

4. As conceptualized by Gordon Allport, _____ traits are those one or two dominant traits that affect almost all aspects of an individual's personality and behaviors. _____ traits are a few dominant traits that are thought to summarize an individual's personality.

      cardinal

      Central

_____ traits are the many traits that are much more subject to change over a lifetime, less consistently demonstrated, and less important in defining a person.   Secondary

5. While psychologists taking the _____ perspective assume   trait
that people have stable, internal personality characteristics that cause them to
behave consistently across situations, those taking a _____   situationist
perspective have argued that people's behaviors vary in different situations.
According to the _____ perspective, people have relatively   interactionist
stable personality traits, but their behaviors depend on the situation at hand.
People from _____ backgrounds are especially likely to adapt   collectivist
their behavior to the situation.

6. The trait approach is useful because it defines personality in terms of
understandable everyday concepts, making it immediately _____   meaningful
to consumers of psychological information. A major limitation of the trait
approach is that it doesn't explain why people _____ their   develop
personality traits.

7. _____ theories of personality assume that our personalities   Psychodynamic
reflect our past experiences and thoughts, feelings, memories, and intrapsychic
-- internal, psychological _____ at various levels of consciousness.   conflicts
The first level, the _____, contains the feelings, thoughts, and   conscious
memories we are aware of having and can remember at the current moment.
The _____ contains memories we can recall if we think about them.   preconscious
The _____ holds very disturbing or socially unacceptable fantasies,   unconscious
thoughts, impulses, memories, and psychological conflicts that play a major
role in determining behaviors and personalities.

8. Freud believed that our personalities reflect _____, processes   psychodynamics
by which people deal with, transform, and express dynamic -- or actively changing --
psychological urges and tensions. He used the concept of _____   libido
to describe the psychosexual energy which fuels this transformation, and
therefore, personality development.

9. Freud claimed that personality characteristics -- and in addition many of his
patients' mysterious symptoms -- developed from intrapsychic _____   conflicts
or imbalance. According to Freud, the _____ -- the only part of   id
personality present at birth -- consists of biological drives and instincts, and is
ruled by the _____ principle. It is what Freud called the   pleasure
_____ which is our partially unconscious, internalized sense of   superego
morality and social constraints. Freud referred to the _____ as   ego
consisting of mental abilities that enable us to perceive, think about, and learn
from the environment, and which tries to satisfy the id's desire for pleasure and
the superego's strict demands, in a way that is _____ possible.   realistically

10. Freud described a series of what he called _____ stages,   psychosexual
which he viewed as defined by marked changes in the ways in which the id's
urges for pleasure are expressed and satisfied. In each of these stages,
the search for pleasure is presumably focused on a different _____   erogenous
zone. According to Freud, if children are praised too much, not given behavior
standards, or become frustrated with the task they face at a any given stage,
the may become _____ at that stage. That is, their development   fixated
becomes stuck at that point.

11. Carl Jung used the term _____ unconscious to refer to   personal
unconscious thoughts implanted by an individual's personal experiences. By
contrast, the memories, ideas, and ways of behaving that form the content of
what Jung called the _____ unconscious are shared by all people.   collective
Jung thought that shared human experiences are cognitively represented in the
collective unconscious as _____, shared mental images or ways   archetypes
of perceiving and responding to situations and images. Much of Jung's theory
of personality is based on his claim that we have _____ parts   opposing
to our personality. For example, he argued that everyone has both the
masculine archetype, the _____, and the feminine archetype,   animus
the anima. Jung argued that to be psychologically healthy and achieve
psychic wholeness, we must _____ opposing parts of our   integrate
personality. To achieve psychological wholeness, Jung also thought, we
must resolve the inconsistency between our inner self, who we truly are,
and our _____, the part of personality that we present to others.   persona

12. Karen Horney assumed that every child feels basically anxious
because of his/her _____ on other people. She theorized that   dependence
people's personalities reflect the way they have managed the conflict between their
feelings of anxiety and _____. Horney identified three ways people   hostility
try to deal with this anxiety: (1) by moving _____ others, such as   toward
becoming dependent on others or trying to receive love; (2) by moving
against others, such as becoming aggressive or striving to gain control; and
(3) by moving _____ from others, such as by withdrawing.   away
She also described three maladjusted personality types:
(1) people with a _____ type of personality move toward other   compliant
people; (2) people with an _____ type of personality move against   aggressive
people; and (3) the _____ type of personality in which the   detached
person becomes socially withdrawn.

13. According to Adler, the way to analyze personality is in terms
of the person's attempts to deal with his/her feelings of _____.   inferiority
Such feelings, he believed, arise from the fact that people are vulnerable and
_____ when they are young, and are also related to the person's   dependent
ordinal position, or _____ order in the family. When people can't   birth
shake their feelings of inferiority, Adler argued, they develop an inferiority
_____, which some people deal with by trying to improve   complex

333

themselves and society, while others hide their feelings of inferiority by
_____ to be strong, self-assured, and capable.

pretending

14. Freud's contributions to the psychology of personality include (1) calling attention to the role of _____ experiences in the development of personality; (2) the idea that _____ feelings and motives are connected to everyday feelings, thoughts and behaviors; (3) the idea that behavior sometimes represents a _____ among desires, fears, and reality; and (4) the idea that aggressive and _____ feelings have an underlying role in determining personality. In addition to their lack of empirical support, psychodynamic theories have been criticized for (1) viewing humans as victims of drives beyond their control, thus excusing them from _____ for their own behavior; (2) failing to account for the development of _____ personalities; and (3) overestimating the _____ of personality characteristics.

childhood
unconscious

compromise
sexual

responsibility
healthy
permanency

15. The behaviorist perspective on personality assumes that what other psychologists call a "personality" is more accurately considered simply an accumulation of _____ behavior patterns. Since behaviorists focus on directly _____ behaviors, they aren't interested in underlying, unobservable dispositions. Instead, behaviorists think that any consistency in behavior is the result of consistencies in a person's _____ history and generalizations of behavior.

learned
observable

reinforcement

16. From a social learning perspective, personality results from a combination of learning, including modeling, and _____ processes, such as expectations and interpretation. Bandura argued that behavior of personality should be understood in terms of reciprocal _____, which involves the interaction of three factors: (1) an individual's thinking, perceptions, and _____, (2) the individual's behavior, and (3) _____ factors. According to Bandura, your personality affects how you perceive yourself, as with the characteristic of self-_____, the expectation that you will succeed in what you try to do.

cognitive

determinism
feelings
environmental

efficacy

17. A great deal of research has shown that behaviors commonly associated with _____ characteristics are learned. The behaviorist perspective has been criticized for not paying enough attention to how people _____ situations and people's personal beliefs can affect their behavior. It also ignores _____ motives and genetic influences.

personality

interpret

unconscious

18. In social cognition theories of personality, an individual's personality is defined by his or her _____ processes and relationships with other people. One such theory is the belief systems

cognitive

334

theory, which identifies four personality types, characterized by different beliefs and differences in the degree to which people think in _____ ways, form precise, differentiated concepts, and integrate their concepts. From the standpoint of this theory, Type 4 personalities are the most differentiated and integrated in their _____ and believe that their behaviors should reflect what they think is appropriate behavior rather than simply what other people tell them is popular or correct.

abstract

thinking

19. The authoritarian personality is characterized by _____, a tendency to assume that only the perspective of one's own ethnic or cultural group is valid. They obey and somewhat respect people of higher status, but are _____ toward those whom they think have a lower social position than their own. Authoritarian people are likely to come from families in which _____ is harsh and seemingly arbitrary, and children are fearfully submissive to the demands of their _____, whom they simultaneously idealize, fear, and resent.

ethnocentrism

hostile

discipline

parents

20. The principal drawback of theories that focus on one personality syndrome has been that they don't account for the full _____ of personality characteristics.

range

21. Behavior geneticists try to find out how _____ a trait is -- how much of a group's variability in a trait is due to genes, and customarily use animal studies, adoption studies, and studies of _____ twins reared apart. Using such methods, it has been found that of the personality traits with a known genetic influence, usually 20% to _____ of the variance, or difference among people, is due to genes.

heritable

identical

50%

22. One shortcoming of the behavior genetic approach is that distinguishing between genetic and environmental effects is difficult, particularly because psychological characteristics are often the product of _____ genes. Another limitation of this perspective is that most behavior genetics research has been concentrated on _____ Americans and the environments in which they live, thus overlooking the complete range of human environments, and possibly _____ the influence of environment in general.

many

European

underestimating

23. Humanistic theories of personality regard people as basically good and naturally seeking to fulfill their _____. Such theories assume that people have _____ freedom, the freedom to choose their personality, how they interpret what goes on around them, what kind of persons they are, and how to behave. People are seen as being _____ for their actions rather than merely hapless products of biological instincts.

potential
existential

responsible

24. Abraham Maslow thought that the desire to achieve self-_____, actualization or fulfillment of one's potential, is the driving force in personality development, but before it can become a motivator, more basic _____, such as those needs for food and physical safety, must be met.

25. In attempting to explain why so many people don't become self-actualizing, Carl Rogers noted that people often choose to deny how they truly feel in order to receive the _____ of those who can bolster their self-esteem. approval Although that choice can be socially adaptive, it can also restrict the realization of the individual's _____. Rogers also argued that potential children often receive _____ positive regard, which means that conditional their parents give them love and approval only when they mimic their parents' attitudes and values and behave in particular, socially approved ways. Rogers believed that parents should show their children _____ positive unconditional regard, which is constant love for the child and acknowledgment of the child's feelings, even when expressing disapproval of the child's _____. behavior

26. A strength of humanistic perspectives is their view of people as thinking creatures who make _____ in their lives. But critics find the choices humanistic approaches overly _____ about people's ability to optimistic move beyond the effects of their past experiences to fulfill their potential. This perspective has also been criticized for cultural bias in its assumption that individual self-actualization rather than _____ actualization is the group premiere status to attain. In this regard, such views fail to explore how people from _____ cultures could self-actualize in a way consistent with collectivist their cultural values.

27. In the 19th century, French historian Alexis de Toqueville characterized Americans this way: They believe individuals should be free to behave as they wish unless their behavior hurts society as a _____; they are whole interested in _____ knowledge, but not in deep analysis; they practical restlessly pursue material prosperity; and they dread the shortness of life and the possibility they have not found the shortest route to _____. happiness Their _____ cultural values may help to explain why many Asian collectivist Americans are less socially assertive in particular situations than are European Americans.

28. Some psychologists have examined the "black personality," referring to similarities in the personalities of African Americans due to their experiences with _____. Rather than focus on traits, African American perspectives racism sometimes explain behavior as the result of _____ flows and energy bodily rhythms.

29. U. S. women are more likely than U. S. men to acknowledge feelings of anxiety and _____ over any harm caused by their aggressive guilt behavior. This difference can be accounted for in terms of cultural standards: U. S. culture considers _____ to be more acceptable in males aggression

than in females. Across _____, males are described as more   cultures
dominant, autonomous, and aggressive than females. Females are described
as more affiliative, deferential, and _____ than males. Such   nurturant
similarities across cultures suggest that, in addition to cultural influences,
there may be underlying _____ roots to gender differences   biological
in personality.

30. The same research results can be _____ in more than one   interpreted
way. For example, one interpretation might be that females have less
self-confidence and self-esteem than do males, whereas an alternative
interpretation of the same data might be that males are just more
_____ than are females. One interpretation of data might be that   conceited
females conform more than do males, while the alternative interpretation of those
data might be that males more often _____ other people's behavior   disregard
than do females. Cattell labeled the opposite of "affected by feelings" as
"emotionally stable," whereas an equally valid depiction is that the opposite of
"affected by feelings" is "emotionally _____."   dead

31. Research indicating race and gender differences in personality has
been slowly pushing psychology into an examination of resources and
_____ as factors influencing personality. The meaning of   power
personality characteristics can also depend on how much social power
a person has. For example, the value psychologists have placed on an
_____ locus of control may reflect a cultural and economic   internal
bias, insofar as the latter personality characteristic is consistent with
American values of independence and "pulling yourself up by your
bootstraps," but inconsistent with the _____ cultural   collectivist
perspective that what happens in your life isn't simply due to your
personal effort.

32. Many clinical psychologists -- particularly those with a psychodynamic
orientation -- use projective tests, which call upon a person to respond to
a set of _____ stimuli. The idea behind these tests is   ambiguous
that perception of such stimuli will reveal needs, attitudes, conflicts,
motives, and other _____ aspects of personality. One   unconscious
widely-used projective test is the Rorschach _____ test,   inkblot
in which the respondent is asked to describe what s/he perceives in each
of a series of symmetrical images. In the Thematic Apperception Test (TAT),
the respondent is asked to make up a _____ about   story
a number of illustrations.

33. Projective tests can help the clinician gain a sense of the client's
attitudes, beliefs, and conflicts, and to establish the kind of therapist-
client _____ required for effective therapy. One drawback   rapport
to these types of tests is that they presuppose European American
responses as the standard, so that the responses of minority group
members may be interpreted as signs of _____ or negative   abnormality

personality characteristics. Thus, for example, the color red is taken as symbolic of anger, violence, and passion to European Americans, whereas it symbolizes _____ in Chinese culture. prosperity
Another drawback is that both the Rorschach and the TAT have questionable scientific reliability and _____. validity

34. The most commonly used _____ to assess personality questionnaires
are self-report tests, which rely on people's conscious characterization of their own customary behaviors. Such tests are generally called "_____ objective
personality tests" because they can be scored objectively without special training, such as with an answer key or by machine; but this term does not mean that these tests are without _____. bias

35. The Minnesota Multiphasic Personality Inventory (MMPI), is the most widely-used self-report personality test, and consists of ten _____ scales, each one including groups of statements that, clinical
taken together, indicate the possibility of a different psychological disorder. The MMPI - 2 has widened the representativeness of the sample whose responses constitute its _____, so that everyone's responses norms
aren't compared with those of European Americans alone. One drawback to objective tests is that they may underestimate the extent to which personality characteristics change and vary across _____ and during cultures
different times in history.

36. One way to get around the problem of relying on people to report their own behaviors accurately, is to have researchers _____ observe
people and take notes on the behaviors of interest. One limitation of the latter method, however, is that we don't know whether the behaviors observed are typical of the observed person because observations usually occur in a limited _____ frame. Another potential pitfall is that time
observers can unintentionally misinterpret behaviors. To alleviate such drawbacks, observations are sometimes supplemented with _____. interviews
_____ interviews are those in which only preplanned questions Structured
are asked in a particular order. In _____ interviews, the researcher unstructured
lets the interviewee and whatever interesting topics arise determine what is discussed.

E. Self-Quiz

For each of the following items, circle the letter which precedes the correct alternative.

1. The essential idea of somatotype theory is that personality characteristics can be predicted from a person's
    a. sense of humor
    b. body type
    c. beliefs
    d. food preferences
    e. astrological sign

2. Cattell found 16 clusters of responses, or personality dimensions, which he regarded as _____ traits characteristic of all people to varying degrees.
    a. surface
    b. type
    c. archetypal
    d. source
    e. depth

3. British psychologists Hans and Sybil Eysenck identified the following as the basic dimension(s) of personality?
    a. compliance-negativity
    b. passivity-aggressiveness
    c. introversion-extroversion
    d. stability-instability
    e. both c and d

4. Which of the following is not among the so-called "Big Five" dimensions of personality
    a. extroversion
    b. conscientiousness
    c. aggression
    d. emotional stability
    e. agreeableness

5. Gordon Allport used the term "_____ traits" to refer to those one or two dominant traits that affect almost all aspects of an individual's personality and behavior.
    a. cardinal
    b. central
    c. primary
    d. master
    e. focal

6. From the standpoint of the psychodynamic approach to the study of personality, the
_____ is the largest level of consciousness.
    a. conscious
    b. preconscious
    c. foreconscious
    d. unconscious

7. According to Freud, the transformation , expression and release of psychological tensions, and therefore, personality development, is fueled by the
    a. ego
    b. superego
    c. libido
    d. individual's cardinal traits
    e. individual's central traits

8. According to Freud, the _____ is the part of personality which consists of biological drives and instincts.
    a. id
    b. ego
    c. superego
    d. collective unconscious
    e. archetypal unconscious

9. Jung thought that shared human experiences are cognitively represented as what he referred to as the
    a. id
    b. ego
    c. animus
    d. anima
    e. archetypes

10. Jung argued that to be psychologically healthy and achieve psychic wholeness, we must
    a. transform the anima into the animus
    b. integrate opposing parts of our personality
    c. resolve our identity as either that of the anima or animus
    d. resolve the conflict between our personal and collective unconscious

11. According to Karen Horney, people's personalities reflect the way they have managed the conflict between their
    a. anima and animus
    b. id and superego
    c. id and ego
    d. anxiety and hostility
    e. sexuality and fear of death

12. Which of the following is not one of the three basic coping styles identified in Karen Horney's approach to the study of personality?
   a. moving toward others
   b. moving above and beyond others
   c. moving against others
   d. moving away from others

13. Which of the following is not one of the three maladjusted personality types identified in Karen Horney's approach to the study of personality?
   a. compliant type
   b. dependent type
   c. aggressive type
   d. detached type

14. According to Adler, the way to analyze an individual's personality is in terms of how s/he tries to deal with his/her
   a. feelings of inferiority
   b. archetypal fear of failure
   c. sense of aloneness and alienation
   d. need for self-actualization
   e. sexuality and aggression

15. Which of the following is not among the lasting and useful contributions of the psychodynamic theories?
   a. identification of childhood experiences as a basis for personality
   b. the idea of unconscious feelings and motives
   c. revision of sexist concepts and assumptions of other theories
   d. acknowledgment that behavior sometimes represents a compromise between desires, fears, and reality
   e. attention to the role of aggressive and sexual urges in personality

16. Which of the following is not among the three interacting factors of reciprocal determinism, as defined in Bandura's approach to the study of personality?
   a. an individual's thinking, perceptions, and feelings
   b. the individual's behavior
   c. the individual's unconscious fears, motives, conflicts, and wishes
   d. environmental considerations

17. According to Belief Systems Theory, a tendency to do whatever will result in social approval without thinking for oneself is most characteristic of _____ personalities.
   a. Type 1
   b. Type 2
   c. Type 3
   d. Type 4

18. As noted in your book, the syndrome defined as _____ personality is characterized by ethnocentrism.
   a. avoidant
   b. introversive
   c. intropunitive
   d. authoritarian
   e. utopian

19. The assumption of "existential freedom" is defined in your text as characteristic of which of the following approaches to the study of personality?
   a. psychodynamic
   b. behavioristic
   c. social learning
   d. humanistic

20. As noted in your text, individualistic cultural bias is revealed in which of the following concepts of the humanistic approach to personality?
   a. self-actualization
   b. conditional positive regard
   c. unconditional positive regard
   d. the persona
   e. the animus

For each of the following items, circle "T" if the statement is True, and "F" if the statement is False.

21. T F   Individualist explanations of people's behavior tend to emphasize stable, internal behaviors rather than situational determinants.

22. T F   A fundamental limitation of the trait approach is that it doesn't explain why people develop their personality traits.

23. T F   According to Carl Jung, the memories, ideas, and ways of behaving that form the content of what he called the "collective unconscious" are shared by all people.

24. T F   According to Freud, women wish they had a penis.

25. T F   A common criticism of psychodynamic theories is that they underestimate the permanency of personality characteristics.

26. T F   Two of the criticisms of learning perspectives noted in your text concern the overemphasis in such approaches on how interpretation of situations and personal beliefs affect behavior.

27. T F   The tendency for Asian Americans to be more socially assertive than European Americans is most appropriately attributed to the individualistic values characteristic of Asian culture.

28. T F   Cross-cultural studies provide very strong evidence proving the biological basis for gender differences in personality.

29. T F   The value psychologists have placed on an internal locus of control is inconsistent with the collectivist perspective that what happens in your life isn't simply due to your personal effort.

30. T F   A major advantage of the projective personality tests is that interpretation of responses on such tests tends to be free of cultural biases.

F. Teaching-To-Learn Exercise

1. *Let Me Teach You This.*

Write in the space provided below, the five facts, ideas, etc., from this chapter that you'd most like to teach to your own student(s) if you were a teacher. Then, really do try to communicate these facts or ideas to someone in your life; or, pretend to teach this content to a hypothetical or "make-believe" student or class.

2. *Now Answer My Questions.*

Here, write one multiple-choice and one True-False question for each of the facts, ideas, etc., you covered in the "Let Me Teach You This" section of this exercise.

G. Bringing Psychology To Life Exercise

I. From the standpoint of the <u>trait</u> <u>perspective</u>, it is assumed that people have stable, internal personality dispositions that cause them to behave in much the same way regardless of the situation. In contrast, the <u>situationist</u> <u>perspective</u> presupposes that people's behaviors -- and apparent personality -- vary from situation to situation. For the purposes of this exercise, give a hypothetical example of people's behaviors in real life situations which would support each of these alternative approaches to the psychological study of personality.

A. <u>The</u> <u>Trait</u> <u>Perspective.</u> Your example here should illustrate how the same person tends to behave in much the same way, expressing the same underlying personality characteristic in two, quite different situations.

B. <u>The</u> <u>Situationist</u> <u>Perspective.</u> Your example here should illustrate how the same person tends to behave in ways that reflect quite different expressions of a given dimension of personality in two, different situations.

C. A compromise view, known as the interactionist perspective, holds that people have relatively stable personality traits, but that their behaviors still depend to some extent on the situation at hand. In the space below, explain why you find this interactionist view to be either more or less valid than either of the other two perspectives concerning the consistency and stability of personality.

II. From the standpoint of humanistic psychologist Carl Rogers' approach to the study of personality, conditional positive regard refers to parental expression of love and approval only when the child mimics the parent's attitudes and values, and behaves in socially approved ways. But, Rogers argued that in order to maximize the likelihood that the child will grow to become a psychologically healthy adult, parents must give them, unconditional positive regard -- that is, constant love for the child, even when expressing disapproval of a child's behavior. For the purposes of this exercise, give examples of both of these styles of parenting. Your case examples may or may not be based on real life experience.

A. Conditional Positive Regard.

B. Unconditional Positive Regard.

III. As developed by psychologist Julian Rotter, the concept of *locus of control* refers to differences among people in the extent to which they feel as though they have control over what happens to them in life. People with an internal locus of control believe that, for most part, that they have such control, whereas people with an external locus of control orientation believe that what happens to them is mostly due to fate or chance, and thus beyond their control.

A. Would you characterize yourself as mostly "internal" or "external" on this locus of control dimension of personality?

B. Without revealing anything of what you might regard as a personally sensitive nature, describe an event in your life where your thoughts, feelings, and/or behaviors fit your description of yourself as mostly "internal" or "external" on this locus of control characteristic of personality.

C. To what extent do you think your locus of control orientation as described here, reflects your cultural and socioeconomic background, or other aspects of your life experience? Explain briefly.

Answer Key To Self-Quiz

1.   b
2.   d
3.   e
4.   c
5.   a
6.   d
7.   c
8.   a
9.   e
10.   b
11.   d
12.   b
13.   b
14.   a
15.   c
16.   c
17.   c
18.   d
19.   d
20.   a
21.   T
22.   T
23.   T
24.   T
25.   F
26.   F
27.   F
28.   F
29.   T
30.   F

CHAPTER 13

Stress, Coping, & Health

A. Learning Objectives

After careful, effective study of Chapter 13, you should:

1. Know something about the general sources from which stress arises, as related to (a) the events that occur in our lives, (b) our appraisal of these events as challenging or threatening, and (c) our feelings about our own ability to deal with the stress-evoking circumstances.

2. Know something about the way in which stressors are classified by health psychologists, focusing on:
      a. The technical definitions used to distinguish among what are referred to as hassles, pressure, frustration, and conflict;
      b. The technical distinction among the three basic types of conflict identified by psychologists as approach-approach, approach-avoidance, and avoidance-avoidance conflicts; and
      c. The way in which health psychologists distinguish among short-lived as compared to chronic stressors, major stressors, cumulative major stressors, and cumulative hassles.

3. Develop a working familiarity with different perspectives on the nature of and response to stress, focusing on:
      a. The kinds of factors which help to explain why different people may respond quite differently to the same sorts of stressors;
      b. How the study of life change associated with stress helps to provide a basis for understanding the kinds of stress experienced by immigrants;
      c. How important a consideration is gender in attempts to understand stress, as the cultural realities of gender are associated with
          (1) Male-female differences in work-related stress due to physical danger and overwork; as well as
          (2) Male-female differences in the experience of stress due to inadequate income, power, fringe benefits, job security, and opportunities for career advancement.
      d. The importance of socioeconomic status as a factor affecting what kinds of stress adults in our society experience, and how they treat their children.
      e. The importance of racism as a stressor, and how it may take different forms in different groups.

4. Develop a working knowledge of the biology of stress, with special attention to the following considerations:
      a. The commonalty of the biological effects of stress across groups of people;

b. The short-term effects of stress, as evidenced in heart and breathing rate and the release of hormones that stimulate the conversion of fats to sugar, and what happens as the body's resources become depleted;

c. How the hormones released in response to stressors tend to affect the buildup of fat or cholesterol on blood vessel walls, and the blood pressure consequence of such changes;

d. Why the changes described in "c" above may cause circulatory disorders resulting in heart problems and/or strokes that can have seriously debilitating effects on the person;

e. How the long-term effects of stress may result in suppression of the immune system, thus debilitating the body's ability to identify and defend against all sorts of viruses and bacteria; and

f. The kinds of intervening variables that affect whether or not a person under stress will become ill.

5. Develop some technical perspectives on individual difference factors which may affect response to stress, including the following:

a. How and why the same event may be responded to by some people as a threat from which they retreat, and by others as a challenge which they regard as an opportunity for personal growth;

b. How one's perception of an event influences his/her stress response to it, and how such perception is influenced by the individual's beliefs as to how effectively s/he can cope with it; and

c. The relationships between the personality characteristics of optimism-pessimism, Type A personality, hardiness, sense of humor, agreeableness, openness, and extroversion, coping strategies, response to stressors, and health.

6. Know something about what psychologists refer to as the "coping methods" -- that is the ways in which people can lessen the negative effects of stressors, including:

a. How relaxation and exercise can help people deal with stress;

b. What constitutes "social support," and the factors influencing how helpful such support tends to be in coping with the stresses of life;

c. What distinguishes the approach, avoidance, problem-focused, and emotion-focused coping strategies; and

d. How one's personal experience as influenced by his/her own race, ethnicity, and gender can affect one's interpretation of events and coping strategies.

7. Know what constitutes an effective coping strategy; and

8. Know how the various "mechanisms of defense" operate to help protect us from at least some types of stress in our lives, and the personal-developmental disadvantage associated with such defenses.

B. Preview/Review Outline Of Key Terms And Concepts

Before you read the corresponding chapter in your text, read over the following outline. It is designed to give you an overview of information presented in the chapter, and how the various elements of that information are related to each other. After reading through the whole chapter and/or before course exams, you may use this outline as a quick review guide. In your reviews, mask off one line of the outline at a time, and try to recite from your memory of the chapter, the information that you expect to appear on the next line or so.

In going over this outline as a preview before reading and studying the chapter, the questions posed in bold print will help to keep you focused on the learning objectives here, and keep you actively involved in the process of achieving those objectives. When using this section as a review, try to answer the questions. Refer back to the chapter in the text for a more detailed feedback check on your mastery of the material, and/or to strengthen your knowledge and understanding wherever you feel the need to do so.

What do the verbal attacks described in the book Snaps have to do with the game developed by African Americans during the slavery period of American history? What kinds of skills did people learn from playing this game? What is the theory cited in your text regarding the origin of the term "the dozens" to refer to this game, and how may it have contributed to the development of effective coping mechanisms for the people who played it?

What is a stressor? What is stress? How does stress differ from eustress?

I. Types of Stressors: From Everyone's Everyday Hassles To Unusual Disasters
    A. Hassles
    B. Pressure
    C. Frustration

How does pressure differ from frustration?

    D. Conflict
        1. Approach-Approach
        2. Approach-Avoidance
        3. Avoidance-Avoidance

Can you give some everyday life examples of each of the three major types of conflict?

    E. Temporary vs. Chronic Stressors
    F. Major vs. Accumulated Stressors

II. Perspectives on Stressors: Different Stressors for Different People
    A. Multiple Life Changes
        1. The Social Readjustment Rating Scale (SRRS)
            a. Points Assigned For Various Life Changes
            b. Does Not Consider Stress Of People Close To Respondent

   c. Assumes Events Equally Stressful For All Respondents
   d. Lists Events Not Representative Across Different Experiential
    Backgrounds

What are some of the major shortcomings of the SRRS?

  B. Gender Perspectives
   1. Work-Related Stress From Physical Danger And Overwork
   2. Stressors Related to Lack Of Adequate Income, Fringe Benefits, Etc.
   3. Differences Attributable To Social Status And Roles

How might gender differences in the personal experience of sexual harassment and discrimination be explained in terms of gender differences in social roles? How might immediate stressors associated with sexism be viewed as socioeconomic in origin?

  C. Socioeconomic Perspectives
   1. Differences In Stressors Encountered As Related To Education And Social
    Class
   2. Socioeconomic Class Differences In Stressors And Response To Stress As
    Related To Depression And Health Problems
   3. Stress And Child-Rearing Practices Among The Poor

Related to the kinds of stress they experience and the way they cope with it, how can the child-rearing practices characteristic of poor people impact on the personality development of their children?

  D. Racial Perspectives
   1. Feeling Of Pressure To Adopt Middle Class Euro-American Attitudes
    a. Adopting Euro-American Ways And Distancing From One's Own
     Minority Group Members
     (1) African Americans Feeling Like an "Uncle Tom"
     (2) Frustration In Finding That Racism Limits Validity Of
      Mainstream U. S. Views And Values
    b. Ethnic Stereotyping And Cultural Racism

How may the assumption that one is a racist be a source of stress for someone?

III. Biological Reactions to Stressors: Similar Reactions Among Different People

What is the role of the adrenal glands in mobilizing the energy the body needs to respond to stress? What is the role of the liver in helping to mobilize the body's energy to respond to stress? How does the narrowing of blood vessels near the surface of the body help to prepare the body to cope with a stressful emergency?

  A. The GAS Response
   1. Alarm Stage
   2. Resistance Stage
   3. Exhaustion Stage

How can chronic stress produce bodily changes that make us vulnerable to illnesses?

      B. Hypertension, Heart Disease, and Stroke
           1. Chronic Stress And Chronic High Blood Pressure
               a. Buildup Of Fat or Cholesterol
               b. Effects On Heart
               c. Effects On Blood Vessels

What are the bodily effects of chronic stress that can result in a fatal stroke? Give examples of life style behaviors that can contribute to such processes and outcomes?

      C. The Immune System
           1. Work Conducted By Psychoneuroimmunologists
               a. Relationships Among Psychological Variables, Immune System, and Health
               b. Stress And The Immune System
           2. Functions of the Immune System
               a. Detects Foreign Substances
               b. Destroys Or Neutralizes Foreign Substances
           3. Effects of Chronic Stressors or a Series of Stressors
               a. Stress And Development Of Various Illnesses
               b. Study Of Stress Experience And Susceptibility To Colds

How does chronic stress or a series of stressors affect the body in such a way as to suppress the immune system? What is the ultimate effect of such suppression on health?

           4. Research on People Exposed To Frequent And Intense Hassles
      D. "Applying Psychology to Health Care" (Box 13.1)
           1. Research In The Field Of Health Psychology
           2. Identification Of Behaviors that Contribute To Illness And Death
           3. Investigating Why People Smoke
           4. Improving Health By Behavioral Interventions
               a. In Treatment Of Smoking Addiction
               b. Providing Information About Symptoms Of Illness And Other Threats To Health
               c. Teaching People How To Lessen Risk Of Developing Cancer
               d. Teaching People The Signs Of Heart Attack And How To Respond To Them

What have health psychologists found concerning why most people who smoke started to smoke in the first place, and what keeps them smoking after they start? How might such knowledge be used in efforts directed to reducing the incidence of smoking in our society?

IV. Individual Characteristics Affecting Stress: Different Responses Among Different People
      A. Interpretations of Stressors

What are some of the factors that influence how we perceive potential stressors? What is involved in primary as compared to secondary appraisals of a stimulus as a potential stressor?

    1. Alternative Perspectives on Stressors
        a. Seeing A Potential Stressor As Threatening, Presenting Manageable Difficulties, Or As Interesting Challenge
        b. Lack Of Alternative Views And Interpretation Of Stressors
        c. Study Of Response To Film Of Ritual Genital Surgery

What was the essential difference among the three soundtracks used with different groups of participants in the study referred to in "1c" above? How did the results of this study, in terms of the kind of stress experienced by the different groups, support the view that the stressfulness of a stimulus depends upon how it is interpreted?

    2. Can I Affect the Stressor?
        a. Research On Perceived Control Over A Stressor
        b. Limitations Of Correlational Research
        c. Experimental Study Of Participants' Response To Photographs Of People Who Had Died Violently

How did the researchers manipulate participants' control over the stress-inducing stimulus in the experiment referred to in 2c above? How was the stress response measured in this experiment? What do the results of this study suggest concerning the effects of sense of control over a stressor?

        d. Understanding of a Stressor and Sense of Control Over It

How do the results of the research on women with breast cancer who experienced relatively little stress associated with that condition, support the view that our beliefs can influence the way we perceive a stressor and the effects that stressor has on us?

  B. Personality

How are the personality traits of agreeableness, openness, and extroversion related to the way in which people cope with stress?

    1. Optimism
        a. Positive Interpretation Of Situations
            (1) In Primary Appraisals
            (2) In Secondary Appraisals
        b. Health And Longevity
        c. Longitudinal Studies Of Optimism-Pessimism And Health
    2. A Sense of Humor
        a. Experience Of Negative Events And Self-Reported Mood
        b. And Perception Of Stressful Events As Threat Or Challenge
    3. Type-A Personality's Anger
        a. Characteristics Of Type A Personality

b. Health Of Type A As Compared To Type B Individuals
   c. Anger As Key Characteristic Associated With Ill Health, Etc.
   d. Anger And Arousal Of Autonomic Nervous System
   e. Longitudinal Study of Anger And Cholesterol Levels
   f. Type A Hostility And The Parasympathetic Nervous System
   g. Expression Of Anger, Health And Longevity

How may the health-illness findings with regard to hostility be explained in terms of the effects of anger on the autonomic nervous system? What are the applied health implications of the research on stylistic differences in expression/non-expression of anger?

   4. Looking for Challenges
         a. Characteristics Of The Hardy Personality
         b. Hardiness, Stress Levels And Health Problems In Men
         c. Hardiness And Stress-Resisting Techniques

What are the characteristics of "the hardy personality," and what have researchers discovered about susceptibility to stress-related health problems among people with these characteristics?

V. Coping Methods: Similar Ways People Deal With Stress
   A. Relaxation and Exercise
      1. Relaxation, Meditation, And The Autonomic Nervous System
            a. Deep Breathing
            b. Oxygen And Calming
      2. Exercise
            a. And Release Of Endorphins
            b. Blood Pressure, Fat In Bloodstream, Heart Attack, And Stroke
            c. Play As A Stress-Reducer

What are the biological processes by which exercise may help to prevent heart attack and stroke?

   B. Social Support
      1. Emotional Support
      2. Material Help
      3. Cognitive Support
      4. Socializing
      5. Factors Influencing Whether Or Not Support Is Helpful
            a. Amount Of Support Offered
            b. Source Of The Support
            c. Timing Of Support

Give examples to illustrate how the amount, source, or timing of support may or may not be helpful in alleviating stress in someone's life?

C. Coping Strategies
    1. Approach and Avoidance Strategies
        a. Approach Strategies
            (1) Straight-Forward Confrontation
            (2) Often Requires Monitoring Stressful Situation
        b. Avoidance Strategies
            (1) Minimizing Or Escaping From Stressful Situation
            (2) Often Involves Blunting
                (a) Cognitive Redefinition Of Stressor
                (b) Self-Distraction
                (c) Not Attending To Stressor
        c. Advantages/Disadvantages Of Approach Strategies
            (1) Attention To Opportunities To Be Rid Of Stressor
            (2) Increased Stress When Problem Cannot Be Changed
        d. Advantages/Disadvantages Of Avoidance Strategies
            (1) Helpful In Dealing With Chronic, Unavoidable Stressors
            (2) Allows For Dealing With Stressor At Gradual Pace
            (3) Can Mean Just Wishful Thinking Or Denial
            (4) Can Delay Resolving A Problem
            (5) Can Be Manifested In Unhealthy Ways
        e. Using Both Approach And Avoidance Strategies

How is the simultaneous use of both approach and avoidance strategies illustrated by the way some African-American families cope with environmental threats to their children's socioeconomic advancement?

    2. Problem-Focused and Emotion-Focused Strategies
        a. Problem-Focused Strategies
            (1) Taking Action To Change A Stressor
            (2) Instrumental Coping As An Approach Strategy
        b. Emotion-Focused Coping
            (1) Decreases Stress By Managing One's Emotions
            (2) Palliative Coping

What are some of the ways in which emotional reactions to a stressor can be managed?

D. Racial Perspectives
    1. Racial Differences In Experience And Interpretation Of Situations
    2. Situational Interpretation And Coping Strategy

How does the case study illustration of the African American woman rape victim who refused to identify her rapist illustrate the way racial-experiential history and perspectives can influence both the interpretation of and response to stressful events?

E. Ethnic and Socioeconomic Perspectives
    1. Body Weight And Appearance As Potential Stressors For Women
        a. More Stressful For Euro-American Women

           (1) Beauty Regarded As Specific, Unchanging Body Type

           (2) Negative Self-Comparison To Narrow Ideal

      b. Less Stressful For African-American Women

           (1) Beauty Regarded As Making Best Of What One Has

           (2) Developing Personal Best Presentation Style

  2. Use Of Social Activities To Cope With Stressors By Latino/a- As Compared to Euro-Americans

  3. Socioeconomic Class And Social Support

  4. Differences In Socialization And Ways Of Coping With Stress

F. Gender Perspectives

  1. U. S. Male-Female Differences In Coping By Seeking Social Support

  2. Males' Use Of Distracting Activities For Stress Reduction

  3. Use Of Emotion-Focused Coping Strategies By Females

  4. Reasons For Gender Differences

      a. Reinforcement

      b. Differences In Reward For Problem-Focused Assertiveness

      c. Attitudes Toward Help-Seeking As Weakness In Males

           (1) Comfort-Seeking, Independence, And Competence

           (2) Approach vs. Avoidance Strategies In Medical Care

How do men and women in the United States tend to differ with regard to their use of approach rather than avoidance strategies in dealing with their own health care problems? How can this gender difference be explained in terms of differences in the socialization of males and females in our society, and how such differences affect the way men and women differ in their perceptions of personal illness?

G. Defensive Coping Strategies

Against what do the distortion processes of the so-called "defense mechanisms" defend or protect? So, what is it that we may learn by examining our own defense mechanisms?

  1. Regression

      a. Reverting To Immature Forms Of Behavior

      b. Crying

  2. Denial

      a. Refusal To Acknowledge Certain Things

      b. Ignoring The Occurrence Of Threats To One's Self-Esteem

  3. Displacement

      a. Expressing Feelings Toward Substitute Target

      b. Females More Likely To Self-Blame

      c. Males More Likely To Cope By Behaving Antisocially

How may the expression of hostility toward a family member with whom one has a well-established loving relationship, reflect the defense mechanism of displacement?

4. Identification
    a. Adopting Behavior Of People One Sees As Powerful
    b. People With Authoritarian Personalities
5. Projection
    a. Misidentifying Sources Of Feelings
    b. Attributing One's Own Feelings Or Faults To Others
6. Rationalization
    a. Reasoning To Protect One's Own Self-Esteem
    b. Explanations To Avoid Self-Blame
7. Reaction Formation

In what way may reaction formation be the unconscious root of the behaviors of a persistently boastful, arrogant, often offensively overbearing know-it-all?

8. Sublimation
    a. Constructive Expression Of Otherwise Unacceptable Impulses
    b. Releasing Sexual Impulses In Dance

In the long run of our lives, how may the defense mechanisms interfere with our personal development?

C. Self-Generated Questions: What's In This One For Me?

Most people come to the first course in psychology expecting to learn some things which will help them to better understand themselves, other people in their lives, and/or the nature of life in the world in which they live. Along these same lines, students of psychology often look forward to discovering things about human behavior and experience which may help them to improve their own life by developing their talents, technical skills, knowledge and abilities, and/or the quality or their relationships with other people. On the basis of such self-interest, which tends to provide a framework in terms of which new learning becomes personally meaningful and thus easier to remember, write down a few questions in the space below, about the subject matter covered in this chapter. After reading and studying the chapter, come back to see how any of what you've learned may be useful to you in finding answers to these questions.

D. Completion Items

The words in the margins of this exercise are the ones that correctly complete the sentence on the corresponding line. To get the most out of this exercise, you should try to avoid looking at these words in the margin until after you've filled in the corresponding blanks with the words you think best complete the sentences. So, begin the exercise by covering up all of the margin words with a piece of paper. Then, for each blank, write in the word which you think completes the sentence. Even if you're not sure as to the word, write in your best guess, preferably in pencil so you can erase and re-write any incorrect responses you may make here.

After writing in your "answer," slide the paper covering up the margin words down just far enough to see the word for the blank you just filled-in. For each blank that you fill-in correctly, put a check mark (√) after your answer. If the word you wrote in doesn't match the word corresponding to that blank, mark an (X) next to your response and go on to the next blank. It's probably a good idea to go back to the text and try to strengthen your learning related to topic coverage that corresponds in the textbook chapter to those blanks which you filled-in incorrectly, since those items signal a weak link in your concept mastery chain for this chapter.

1. One theory as to the origin of the verbal attack game known as "the
_____," described in the book *Snaps,* is that African Americans   dozens
used it to toughen and emotionally defend themselves against the onslaughts
to their dignity by slave-owners. The game developed as a method for coping
with _____, demanding events, behaviors, or situations that put   stressors
a strain on the individual. The term _____, is used to refer to the   eustress
kind of stress that makes a person feel good or challenged rather than
threatened, as in competitive _____.   sports

2. _____ are the minor, day-to-day difficulties that cause stress.   Hassles
When a person feels that his or her behaviors must change or improve in
quality to meet standards, that person feels _____. The inability   pressure
to reach goals results in _____.   frustration

3. _____ arises when desires, goals, demands, opportunities,   Conflict
 needs, or behaviors compete with each other. Approach-_____   approach
conflict occurs when a person must choose between only one of two options,
both of which he likes. In an approach-_____, conflict, a person is   avoidance
both attracted to and repelled by the same stimulus. _____-   Avoidance
avoidance conflict occurs when a person has to choose one of two options,
both of which s/he finds to be unattractive, undesirable, or somehow unpleasant.

4. Stressors can be distinguished in terms of whether they are temporary or
_____, and whether they are due to one major source of stress or   chronic
the result of an _____ of stressors.   accumulation

5. In the Social Readjustment Rating Scale, one of the most widely used
measures of stressors, points are assigned to experiences of the various
kinds of _____ in life that all people are presumed to find stressful   changes
This scale fails to take into consideration that the way in which a person

perceives and _____ with an event can affect the degree   copes
to which that event is experienced as stressful. Neither does it list events that
are representative of the kinds of stressors experienced by people of
different _____, ethnic, and racial background.   socioeconomic

6. In the United States, men are more likely than women to experience work-
related stress from _____ danger and overwork. Women are more   physical
likely than men to have stressors related to a lack of adequate _____.   income
One reason that women face the stressors of _____ harassment and   sexual
discrimination more than men do may be that women's relative lack of power or job
security makes complaining difficult. Many of the immediate stressors associated
with sexism are _____, such as when females are paid less than males   socioeconomic
for the same work.

7. Many of the stressors encountered by poor people are _____,   chronic
such as being stuck in low-paying jobs and lacking job security. Stressors and
difficulties in dealing with them seem to contribute to depression and increased
risk of _____ problems among the poor. Poor parents, whatever   health
their ethnicity, tend to _____ their children more and give them   punish
less approval than other parents of the same ethnic group. These parenting
styles can create low self-esteem and stress for the children, who are thus
_____ by their inability to win expressions of approval from their   frustrated
parents.

8. Members of minorities sometimes feel _____ to become like   pressure
middle class Euro-Americans in their attitudes. Some minority individuals may
become _____ when they find that a mainstream U. S. view --   frustrated
such as the idea that by working hard, anyone can succeed, is less true for them
than for others because of racism. Another potential source of stress for
members of minority groups is from being subjected to ethnic stereotyping
and cultural _____, the belief that one culture, associated with a   racism
particular race, is inferior to another.

9. When we are under stress, _____ is needed to respond to it.   energy
The _____ glands, near the kidneys, release hormones that stimulate   adrenal
the conversion of fats into sugar. Extra sugar is sent from the liver to the muscles
so that we can respond physically by running away or _____.   fighting

10. The General _____ Syndrome or GAS, for short, characterizes   Adaptation
the body's general reaction to any kind of stress. In the first stage of this reaction,
the _____ stage, the autonomic nervous system is activated as the   alarm
body detects and tries to respond to stress. During the second stage, that of
_____, the body calls upon its reserve resources to combat the   resistance
stress. If the stress persists, the body reaches the _____ stage   exhaustion
because it can no longer sustain its resistance. Chronic stress uses up and
overwhelms the body's reserve resources, making us vulnerable to

_____.   illness

11. Chronic stress can lead to chronic high blood pressure, called
_____, because hormones that are released when we are under
stress increase the buildup of fat or _____, a substance in fat,
on blood vessel walls. When blood vessel walls are so blocked by fat deposits
that oxygen-carrying blood cannot reach the brain, the result can be a
fatal _____.

hypertension
cholesterol

stroke

12. Stress interferes with the body's ability to fight diseases by weakening
our _____ system, which has two primary functions: (a) it
detects foreign substances, such as bacteria or _____; and
(b) it destroys or neutralizes them, thus defending us against
_____. When we are dealing with a chronic stressor or a series
of stressors, the adrenal glands release hormones that suppress the
_____, which are the blood cells that fight invading bacteria,
viruses, and cancer. People exposed to frequent and intense
_____, such as dealing with annoying coworkers, often show
signs of poor health, such as flu, headaches, and backaches. Intense
_____, big changes in one's life, lack of sleep, and deeply-
felt grief are among the other stressors associated with a weakening of the
immune system.

immune
viruses

diseases

lymphocytes

hassles

pressure

13. Most smokers start in _____, often because they observed
parents and friends smoking, were reinforced for smoking, or were caught up
in a personal fable. Health psychologists have found that providing people
with information about symptoms of illness and other threats to their health
helps them to develop the schemata they need to _____
symptoms in a knowledgeable way and recognize the need for prompt
health care.

adolescence

interpret

14. How we _____ a stressor has a big influence on how much
stress the stressor triggers and its indirect effect on our health. When we
evaluate and interpret any stimulus, we make _____
appraisals of it, whereby we judge whether it is potentially harmful. We
then make _____ appraisals, evaluating our ability to deal
with the stressor.

interpret

primary

secondary

15. Several studies have demonstrated that the way in which one
_____ an event can affect its stressfulness. In one such
study, the stress experienced by people who watched a film of a ritual
surgical operation on the genitals of male, Australian, aboriginal
adolescents was found to differ significantly depending upon which of
three _____ accompanied the showing of the film.

interprets

soundtracks

16. Research in the United States has indicated that when people think
that they have _____ over a stressor, they tend to feel less
stress from it. Experimental studies, such as the one in which participants

control

361

were shown color photographs of people who had died violently, suggest that a sense of control has physical effects, at least on the _____ autonomic nervous system.   The perception that one _____ a stressor understands seems to foster a sense of control over it.   Thus, for example, women with breast cancer who experienced relatively little stress were found to be people who had constructed _____ that they knew why they developed beliefs cancer, and that they had gained an increased appreciation for life due to the illness.

17. Three of the so-called "Big Five" personality traits -- agreeableness, openness, and _____ -- predict how people cope with stress. extroversion People with those traits seek support from other people, keep an _____ outlook, and explore new solutions to their problems -- optimistic and they tend to have less stress than others.

18. _____ tend to interpret situations positively: Their primary Optimists appraisals are that stressors are not as threatening as pessimists think, and their secondary appraisals emphasize their _____ to deal with ability stressors. _____ studies, in combination with research on how Longitudinal interpreting stressors affects stress, suggest that optimistic orientations contribute to good health.

19. In a study of people who had experienced many negative events in the last year, those with a strong sense of _____ had less stress -- defined humor as fewer negative moods such as anger, confusion, depression, fatigue, and tension than did those with low scores on a measure of this personality dimension.

20. People with the Type _____ personality have a high desire to A achieve; are generally extremely competitive, aggressive, impatient, and angry. They are also more likely to have cardiovascular disease, headaches, stomachaches, and hypertension than are people with a Type _____ B personality, who are more easy going. Researchers have found that of the cluster of Type A characteristics, _____ is the key characteristic associated anger with poor health, heart disease, role conflicts, job stressors, and conflicts with other people. One reason for the latter finding is that the kind of chronic autonomic nervous system arousal associated with this personality trait tends to disrupt the metabolism of _____, speed the development of fats cholesterol and other cellular material in the walls of arteries, thus increasing blood _____ and susceptibility to heart attacks. Some researchers pressure think that chronically hostile men with Type A personalities have _____ nervous systems that are overly responsive in stressful sympathetic situations and parasympathetic nervous systems that don't calm them down quickly or efficiently. But how people deal with their anger may be an important consideration in this context. Thus, in one study, although women who were judged to be high in hostility were found to be more likely to be dead 18 years after the initial assessment of their hostility, those most likely to have died were those who seemed to have the most _____ anger. unexpressed

21. People with _____ personalities have a strong commitment   hardy
to work, values, and goals; enjoy change as a challenge and not as a threat;
feel as though they have _____ over their lives and the amount   control
of stress they encounter, and tend to be less susceptible to
_____ - related health problems than are other people.   stress

22. Relaxation and meditation tend to settle down the _____   sympathetic
branch of the autonomic nervous system activated during times of stress and
anger. Since exercise triggers the release of _____, the   endorphins
tranquilizing chemicals produced by the body, people can also reduce their
stress level and achieve a relaxed state by exercising. Exercise also decreases
the chances that one will develop dangerous high _____ pressure.   blood

23. _____ support refers to the help people receive from others in   Social
dealing with a stressor. It may take the form of emotional support, as when someone
listens to our problems and expresses concern. It may also be material help, such as
needed money, or _____ support, such as advice, information, and   cognitive
alternative ways to interpret a problem. Too much support can actually undermine
one's self-confidence and self-esteem and prevent them from developing their
own _____ skills.   coping

24. We use an _____ strategy to cope when we confront a problem   approach
in a straight-forward manner by gathering and then analyzing information, and then
take active steps to deal with that problem. We use an _____   avoidance
strategy to cope when we try to minimize or escape from stressful situations;
such strategies are helpful in dealing with _____ or unavoidable   chronic
stressors, but can be disadvantageous when they take the form of wishful
thinking, _____ the existence of a stressor, or giving up on goals.   denying

25. _____-focused or instrumental coping involves taking action to   Problem
change a stressor. Emotion-focused or _____ coping, involves   palliative
managing our emotional reaction to a stressor, and may be achieved by using
relaxation techniques, self-control, resigning ourselves to problem situations,
or redefining a problem as being _____ rather than intimidating.   challenging

26. Since people from different racial groups have different experiences, they
sometimes _____ situations differently and thus adopt different   interpret
strategies for coping with them. Body weight and appearance are potential
stressors for both African- and Euro-American females. But Euro-American
females are likely to find these aspects of life more stressful than African-
Americans, because Euro-American females tend to think of beauty as a
_____, unchanging body type that fits only a relatively narrow   specific
view of beauty, whereas African-American females tend to think of beauty in
terms of making the _____ of what an individual has.   best
Psychologists have found that people from lower socioeconomic groups
tend to have _____ social support than do people from higher   less
classes.

27. Females in the United States are more likely than males to cope by seeking _____ support, frequently by talking intimately about their emotional   social distress. Females tend to be more likely than males to use emotion-focused strategies and less likely to use _____- focused ones. One   problem explanation for such differences is that for large segments of U. S. society, help-seeking is viewed as a sign of _____ and more acceptable in   weakness females than in males. Related to the foregoing observation is the finding that when it comes to medical care, women in the United States take more of an approach strategy while men take more of an _____ strategy,   avoidance apparently because men are more likely to perceive illness as weakness and admitting weakness is opposed to the male gender _____   role expectation whereby men are expected to be strong and independent.

28. The purpose of the _____ mechanisms is to distort or   defense hide from consciousness any thoughts that threaten our self-concept and cause anxiety. _____ is the mechanism that involves reverting   Regression to behaviors characterizing a less mature stage of development. _____ is the refusal to acknowledge, even to oneself, any   Denial thoughts, feelings or personality characteristics that threaten one's self-esteem. _____ involves expressing feelings toward a safer, substitute   Displacement target other than the true target of those feelings. _____   Identification involves adopting the behavior of people whom one sees as powerful in order to protect oneself from stressful feelings of vulnerability. The mechanism of _____ involves attributing one's own unacceptable feelings or   projection faults to others. Another of these mechanisms is the one known as _____, whereby we come up with reasons which are not completely   rationalization accurate, but plausible enough to protect our self-concept from the reality of our own unacceptable or otherwise anxiety-arousing thoughts, feelings, or behaviors. _____ formation involves expression of feelings   Reaction or behaviors which are the exaggerated opposite of the underlying, anxiety-arousing ones. And _____ is the defense whereby an   sublimation otherwise self-concept threatening or anxiety-arousing impulse is expressed in some socially valued and constructive way.

E. Self-Quiz

For each of the following items, circle the letter which precedes the correct alternative.

1. As noted in your text, by "playing the dozens," African Americans learned all of the following except
    a. how to identify homosexuals
    b. how to hide emotional vulnerability
    c. how to think quickly under pressure
    d. how to control their anger

2. A student who has applied to and been accepted to <u>both</u> of the only two medical schools to which she has applied, both of which she regards as equally ideal for her own goals and life circumstances, is confronted with
    a. an approach-approach conflict
    b. an avoidance-avoidance conflict
    c. an approach-avoidance conflict
    d. no conflict at all

3. The Social Readjustment Rating Scale is designed to measure stress in terms of the _____ a person experiences in his/her life.
    a. conflicts
    b. anger
    c. failures
    d. changes
    e. illnesses

4. Which of the following <u>is</u> <u>not</u> one of the three stages of the general adaptation syndrome?
    a. alarm
    b. cognitive appraisal
    c. resistance
    d. exhaustion

5. The term "hypertension" refers to chronic
    a. frustration-induced emotional pressure in a person's life
    b. negative changes in a person's life
    c. anxiety
    d. high blood pressure

6. In one study cited in your text, volunteers who reported at the beginning of the study that they _____, were more likely to become infected and develop colds from an experimentally induced exposure to nose drops containing viruses that cause colds.
    a. held deep resentment and hostility for one or more members of their own immediate family
    b. really hated school and were only going to college to get a good job
    c. felt overwhelmed by stress
    d. had some sort of eating disorder
    e. had some sort of sleep disorder

7. The addictive characteristics of nicotine are explained in your text in terms of
    a. reinforcement
    b. cognitive theory
    c. unconscious motivation
    d. the general adaptation syndrome
    e. learned helplessness

8. In one study cited in your text, biological signs of stress among a group of participants who viewed a film of a ritual surgical operation on the genitals of male, Australian, aboriginal adolescents, were found to vary depending upon
    a. whether the participant/viewers of the film were male or female
    b. the content of the soundtrack accompanying the film
    c. the prior stress experiences of the participant/viewers of the film
    d. whether or not the male viewers of the film had been circumcised as infants
    e. the age of the participant/viewers of the film

9. The results of the experiment in which subjects were shown a series of color photographs of people who had died violently, supported the hypothesis that at least autonomic nervous system response to stress is affected by the stressed individual's
    a. other recent stress experiences
    b. prior experience in coping with similar stressors
    c. primary appraisal of the stressor
    d. secondary appraisal of the stressor
    e. sense of control over the stressor

10. Results of a study cited in your text indicated that women with breast cancer who experienced relatively little stress had
    a. more prior experience in coping with illness in their own lives and in the lives of friends
    and family members
    b. made more realistic primary appraisals of their disease
    c. made more realistic secondary appraisals of their disease
    d. constructed beliefs that they knew why they developed cancer

11. Which of the following is not among the "big three" personality traits which predict how people cope with stress?
    a. agreeableness
    b. openness
    c. depression
    d. extroversion

12. In one study cited in your text, it was found that people with _____ tended to think of stressful events less as a threat and more as a challenge than did other people
    a. an introverted personality style
    b. Type-A personality
    c. a strong sense of humor
    d. high scores on the Social Readjustment Rating Scale

13. Researchers have found that of the cluster of Type A personality characteristics, _____ is the one most closely associated with poor health, heart disease, role conflicts, job stressors, and conflicts with other people.
    a. the high desire to achieve
    b. extreme competitiveness
    c. restless impatience
    d. anger

14. Which of the following is not one of the ways in which the coping strategy of "blunting" is achieved?
    a. gathering and analyzing information about a problem
    b. cognitively redefining a stressor so that it doesn't seem stressful
    c. distracting ourselves with other activities or thoughts
    d. choosing not to pay attention to the stressor

15. Which of the following is not true of avoidance coping strategies?
    a. often involve the use of blunting
    b. focus on opportunities to be rid of the stressor
    c. helpful in dealing with chronic or unavoidable stressors
    d. give people the chance to acknowledge and deal with a stressor at a gradual pace

16. Problem-focused coping is also referred to as
    a. emotion-focused coping
    b. palliative coping
    c. instrumental coping
    d. one of the major avoidance coping strategies

17. Research cited in your text has indicated that Latino/a-Americans are more likely than Euro-Americans to cope with stressors by engaging in
    a. avoidance coping strategies
    b. instrumental coping
    c. social activities
    d. problem-focused coping

18. Which of the following is not among the reasons cited in your text to explain the findings with regard to gender differences in coping strategies?
    a. females are reinforced for using emotion-focused coping strategies
    b. females are less likely than males to be rewarded for problem-focused assertiveness
    c. help-seeking is viewed as a sign of weakness in large segments of U. S. society
    d. differences between men and women in brain organization and biochemistry

19. _____ is the defense mechanism wherein the person reverts to behaviors characteristic of a less mature stage of development.
  a. Regression
  b. Denial
  c. Displacement
  d. Identification
  e. Sublimation

20. _____ is the defense mechanism wherein one's own unacceptable feelings or faults are attributed to others.
  a. Regression
  b. Denial
  c. Displacement
  d. Projection
  e. Sublimation

For each of the following items, circle "T" if the statement is True, and "F" if the statement is False.

21. T F   When a person must choose between two unattractive options, s/he is experiencing an approach-avoidance conflict.

22. T F   In the higher, or upper socioeconomic classes, parents tend to punish their children more and give them less approval than do parents of the same ethnic group in lower socioeconomic classes.

23. T F   Cultural racism is the belief that one culture, associated with a particular race, is inferior to another.

24. T F   When we are dealing with a chronic stressor or a series of stressors, the adrenal glands release hormones that increase the production and release of lymphocytes to fight invading bacteria in our bodies.

25. T F   Primary appraisal of a stimulus involves a judgment as to our own ability to deal effectively with a stressor.

26. T F   Longitudinal studies have failed to support the hypothesis that optimistic people are more likely to be healthy than are pessimists.

27. T F   Research has indicated that the primary reason why people with a hardy personality experience low levels of stress, is that such people exercise more than other people do.

28. T F   As noted in your text, body weight and appearance are likely to be more important sources of stress in the lives of African-American than Euro-American females, because African-American females tend to think in terms of a specific body type that characterizes a narrow view of what a "beautiful" woman should look like.

29. T F   In the United States, females tend to be more likely than males to use emotion-focused coping strategies and less likely to use problem-focused ones.

30. T F   The defense mechanism of reaction formation applies to explaining why the person who unconsciously feels stupid acts like a know-it-all.

F. Teaching-To-Learn Exercise

1. *Let Me Teach You This.*

Write in the space provided below, the five facts, ideas, etc., from this chapter that you'd most like to teach to your own student(s) if you were a teacher. Then, really do try to communicate these facts or ideas to someone in your life; or, pretend to teach this content to a hypothetical or "make-believe" student or class.

2. *Now Answer My Questions.*

Here, write one multiple-choice and one True-False question for each of the facts, ideas, etc., you covered in the "Let Me Teach You This" section of this exercise.

G. Bringing Psychology To Life Exercise

From the standpoint of what is alternatively referred to as the *holistic, organismic, body-mind, mind-body,* or *systems approach* to health psychology, it is assumed that states of mind can affect our bodily processes and vice versa. In other words, a kind of reciprocity is acknowledged with regard to the relationship between these two aspects of ourselves as living entities. More specifically, it is assumed from this point of view, that psychological processes of thought, feeling, and/or behavior can affect biological conditions of the body, and that the reverse is also true.

Insofar as stress has been identified as a potentially powerful dimension of "mind" as related to bodily processes, studies of psychological stress have important implications for understanding the realities of health and illness in our lives. Sources of stress, which are known technically as *stressors*, are generally classified by health psychologists in terms of the four broad categories of (a) *hassles*, (b) *pressure*, (c) *frustration*, and (d) *conflict*. The term *coping* is used to refer to the way(s) in which we try to deal with stressors so as to minimize their disruptive effects on our lives.

Based on your own life experience or that of someone else's life, the task in this exercise is to (a) identify a source of stress from each of the four major stress categories described above and in the corresponding chapter of your text; (b) tell how the person confronted with this stressor tried (or is still trying) to cope with it, and (c) describe briefly how effectively this coping strategy seems to have worked or is working for that person. In your comments regarding the coping mechanism you see as most descriptive in each case, indicate whether it appears to be more of an *approach* or an *avoidance* strategy, and whether it appears to be *problem-focused* or *emotion-focused*, and the reasons why you see the strategy involved as such.

IMPORTANT NOTE: In writing your responses to in this exercise, **please be careful not to** reveal any confidences of a personally private or sensitive nature to you. Also, if you refer to an actual person other than yourself as the subject individual for any of the elements of this exercise, please disguise that person's identity thoroughly. The objective here, as with all of the other *Bringing Psychology To Life* exercises, is to give you an opportunity to learn about technical concepts in the field of psychology and understand the way they apply to real life experience. For these purposes, the fabrication of fictitious experiences and individuals, or reference to the lives of celebrities or fictitious characters portrayed in the media (e.g., a TV soap opera) is also perfectly acceptable at your discretion. Please note also that you may use the same person or different people as the subjects for each of the four stress categories.

A. **Hassles.** The term "hassles" refers to the minor difficulties of everyday life.

1. Describe a hassle experience in the life of a subject person of your choice.

2. How did the subject person try (or is s/he still trying) to cope with the hassle?

3. How effectively did this coping strategy seem to work for the subject person, or how well is it working if the hassle is one which s/he continues to confront? Explain.

B. **PRESSURE.** The term "pressure" refers to the kind of stress induced by feeling as though we must change or improve the quality of our behaviors to live up to our real or even imagined beliefs as to the standards of what other people in our life expect us to achieve or do.

1. What experience in your own or someone else's life comes to mind in this regard?

2. How did the subject person try to cope (or is s/he still trying to cope) with this pressure?

3. How effectively did this coping strategy seem to work (or is it working) for the subject person? Explain.

C. **FRUSTRATION.** "Frustration" refers to the unpleasant feeling we experience when our progress toward achieving some goal in our life is somehow blocked or thwarted. In other words, frustration occurs when there's something that we believe or feel that we want or need, and for some reason or other, that want or need isn't getting fulfilled.

1. Describe a frustrating experience in the life experience of a subject person of your choice.

2. How did the subject person try (or is s/he still trying) to cope with this frustration?

3. How effectively did this coping strategy seem to work for the subject person, or how well is it working if the frustration continues in the individual's life? Explain.

D. **CONFLICT**. "Conflict" situations are those in.. which we have to make a difficult decision about adopting only one of two or more competing and thus incompatible, alternative courses of action or goals.

1. Describe a conflict in your own life or in someone else's life. In doing so, tell why it is most accurately described as an (a) <u>approach-approach</u> conflict, involving a choice between two alternatives or goals that the person considers to be about equally desirable or attractive, (b) <u>avoidance-avoidance</u> conflict, involving a choice between alternatives which the person sees as about equally undesirable, or (c) an <u>approach-avoidance</u> conflict, involving a choice as to whether to take or leave a single stimulus or situation that has both desirable and undesirable features associated with it. Refer back to the corresponding chapter as necessary, to be sure that you understand these ideas before writing your response here.

2. How did the subject person try (or is s/he still trying) to cope with this conflict?

3. How effectively did this coping strategy seem to work (or is it working) for the subject person in attempting to deal with the conflict? Explain.

Answer Key To Self-Quiz

1. a
2. a
3. d
4. b
5. d
6. c
7. a
8. b
9. e
10. d
11. c
12. c
13. d
14. a
15. b
16. c
17. c
18. d
19. a
20. d
21. F
22. F
23. T
24. F
25. F
26. F
27. F
28. F
29. T
30. T

CHAPTER 14

Psychological Disorders

A. Learning Objectives

After careful, effective study of Chapter 14, you should:

1. Have a working knowledge of abnormality, as follows:
    a. The different ways in which abnormality can be defined;
    b. How abnormal behavior can be classified into categories of psychological disorders;
    c. How the DSM IV provides definitions of psychological disorders, and the cultural limitations on applicability of these definitions;
    d. The different explanations for abnormal behavior and psychological disorders offered by each of the following perspectives:
        (1) The biological perspective;
        (2) The learning perspective;
        (3) The cognitive perspective;
        (4) The psychodynamic perspective;
        (5) The biopsychosocial perspective; and
        (6) The spiritual perspective.

2. Develop a working familiarity with the so-called "anxiety disorders," as follows:
    a. The various types of conditions which are defined as anxiety disorders, what they have in common, and how they differ;
    b. The different perspectives in terms of which explanations for anxiety disorders have been proposed; and
    c. Differences in the frequency with which anxiety disorders occur among different groups of people, and how such differences may be explained.

3. Develop a working familiarity with what it is that the "mood disorders" have in common, as well as:
    a. The distinguishing characteristics of each of the following specific types of mood disorders:
        (1) The depressive disorders;
        (2) Some alternative perspectives on what causes people to commit suicide;
        (3) Dysthymia;
        (4) Seasonal affective disorder;
        (5) Bipolar disorder; and
        (6) Cyclothymia;
    b. Some of the major perspectives and observations which have been invoked in attempts to understand and treat the mood disorders, as follows:
        (1) From the biological perspective, consideration of how dopamine and serontonin action, abnormalities in neurological feedback

in the coordination of neurotransmitters, and genetic factors are
involved in the development of mood disorders;

    (2) From the psychological perspective, consideration of how
a person's reinforcement experience, self-defeating beliefs,
and/or psychological conflicts may contribute to the development
of mood disorders; and

    (3) From the biopsychosocial perspective, a combination of factors
are considered with regard to the development of such disorders.

  c. Differences among groups in the incidence of mood disorders, looking at:

    (1) Cultural differences in panic disorders; and

    (2) Attempts to explain gender differences in major depression
in terms of diagnostic considerations, stress, and coping
styles.

4. Know some of the fundamentals of schizophrenia, focusing on:

  a. The symptoms which define this condition;

  b. How differences in its onset are related to future course of the disease;

  c. The research indicating that schizophrenia involves different clusters of signs
and symptoms, and what such findings suggest about the structure and
causes of this disease;

  d. How factors such as genetics, dopamine sensitivity, enlarged brain ventricles, prenatal
stress and viral infection have been considered in attempts to understand
schizophrenia from the biological perspective;

  e. How the interaction between genetic vulnerability and exposure to stress
has been considered in attempts to understand this disease from the
biopsychosocial perspective; and

  f. The common features of schizophrenia as it is evidenced throughout the world; and

  g. The factors which make it difficult to identify schizophrenia in different cultures.

5. With regard to the so-called "body focused disorders,"

  a. Know the distinguishing symptoms of the eating disorders known as "anorexia
nervosa" and "bulimia nervosa;"

  b. Know what the authors or your textbook describe as some guidelines on how to help a
friend whom you believe to be suffering from a psychological disorder;

  c. Know the ideas emphasized in the following hypotheses proposed to understand
eating disorders:

    (1) genetics,

    (2) neurotransmitter imbalance,

    (3) beliefs about being thin,

    (4) displaced id impulses, and

    (5) biopsychosocial consideration of factors such as body type, family
relations, and body image.

  d. Know something about how ethnic and gender perspectives are relevant to
understanding eating disorders, especially with regard to,

    (1) the incidence of eating disorders among women of various
ethnic and socioeconomic backgrounds;

(2) how attitudes toward their own racial features may be a factor
in the development of eating disorders among ethnic minority women.
e. Know about the so-called "somatoform disorders," including
(1) The distinguishing symptomology characteristic of hypochondriasis
and conversion disorder;
(2) Some of the major perspectives in terms of which the development
of such disorders is explained by psychologists; and
(3) The importance of cultural context to understanding such disorders.
6. With regard to the so-called "dissociative disorders,"
a. Know the distinguishing symptomological characteristics of these disorders
in general;
b. Know the distinguishing symptomological characteristics of psychogenic
amnesia and psychogenic fugue in particular; and
c. Know how psychologists have considered that dissociative disorders may be the result
of psychotherapy or the individual's reaction to traumatic thoughts and feelings.

7. With regard to the personality disorders,
a. Know the distinguishing symptomoligical characteristics of these disorders in general;
b. Know the three different categories of personality disorder described in DSM IV; and
c. Know the distinguishing characteristics of antisocial personality disorder, and how that
disorder is understood from the standpoint of both the biological and
psychological perspectives.

B. Preview/Review Outline Of Key Terms And Concepts

Before you read the corresponding chapter in your text, read over the following outline. It is designed to give you an overview of information presented in the chapter, and how the various elements of that information are related to each other. After reading through the whole chapter and/or before course exams, you may use this outline as a quick review guide. In your reviews, mask off one line of the outline at a time, and try to recite from your memory of the chapter, the information that you expect to appear on the next line or so.

In going over this outline as a preview before reading and studying the chapter, the questions posed in bold print will help to keep you focused on the learning objectives here, and keep you actively involved in the process of achieving those objectives. When using this section as a review, try to answer the questions. Refer back to the chapter in the text for a more detailed feedback check on your mastery of the material, and/or to strengthen your knowledge and understanding wherever you feel the need to do so.

I. Abnormality
   A. Definitions of Abnormality

What is the significance of the fact that there are different definitions of "abnormality?"

      1. Rare Behaviors
         a. Statistical Approach

        b. Some Rare Behaviors Not Generally Considered Abnormal
        c. Limited By Sample On Which Statistics Are Based
    2. Socially Disagreeable Behaviors
        a. Based On Social Norms
        b. Group Variation In What Is Considered Acceptable Or Desirable
    3. Maladaptive Behaviors
        a. Result In Social Or Biological Harm To Oneself
        b. Careful Consideration Of Circumstances
    4. Distressing Behaviors
        a. Emphasizes Individual's Perceptions Of Pain
        b. Personal Pain Perceptions Influenced By Social Context

Give an example to illustrate how a person whose behavior would not be considered abnormal from the standpoint of either the statistical, social normative, or biological maladaptiveness criteria, might still feel considerable personal distress? Give another example to illustrate how a person might feel no personal distress, while engaging in behaviors that violate social norms and are enormously maladaptive for his/her own well-being?

    5. Behaviors that Injure
        a. Deliberate Attempts To Kill Or Mutilate Self Or Others
        b. Definition Typically Used For Psychiatric Hospitalization
B. Classifying Psychological Disorders

Why is it that abnormal behavior does not always indicate a psychological disorder?

    1. DSM IV: The Book of Psychological Disorders
        a. Standardized Criteria For Identifying Psychological Disorders
        b. Published By American Psychiatric Association
        c. Identifies Over 300 Psychological Disorders
        d. Common Language For Use By Mental Health Professionals
        e. For Each Disorder, Describes Pattern Of Symptoms And Signs
        f. Does Not Provide Theoretical Explanations
    2. The Limitations of DSM IV
        a. Descriptive, Checklist, Medical Model Approach
        b. Risks Ignoring Differences In Causes Underlying
            Psychological Disorders
        c. Psychological Disorder Labels, Discrimination And Prejudice

What could be the unfortunate consequence of attributing a particular psychological disorder to the wrong underlying cause?

How did Rosenhan's classic study in which seven normal adults got themselves admitted to a psychiatric hospital, illustrate the potential influence of a psychiatric label on perceptions of the individuals so-labeled?

    3. Using DSM IV With Different Cultural Groups
        a. Apparent Depression In Buddhist And Shi'ite Muslim Cultures

380

       b. No Word For Depression In Some Cultures

       c. Functional Equivalence In Physical vs. Psychological Disorders

       d. Culture Bound Syndromes

Give an example or two illustrating why it is important to consider the signs and symptoms associated with a psychological disorder relative to the cultural context in which they occur.

   C. Perspectives on Psychological Disorders

What is the practical implication of the particular perspective in terms of which a psychological disorder is considered, as far as the individual who is so diagnosed is concerned?

     1. The Biological Perspective
       a. Genetic And Physiological Links To Psychological Disorders
       b. Often Difficult To Determine What Causes What
     2. The Psychological Perspective
       a. Learning Theory Perspective
       b. Cognitive Perspective
       c. Psychodynamic Perspective

What is the biopsychosocial perspective on psychological disorders?

     3. The Spiritual Perspective
       a. Emphasizes The Supernatural
       b. In Aboriginal American Culture
         (1) View Of Abnormal Behavior Rooted In Idea Of "Soul"
         (2) Soul And Living In Harmony
         (3) Disruption Of Harmony And Soul Wound Or Loss

II. Anxiety Disorders

Give an example or two to illustrate the fact that people experience anxiety as a necessary and normal part of adapting to the environment?

   A. Disorders Featuring Anxiety
     1. Panic Disorder
       a. Sudden Episodes Of Intense Apprehension
       b. Hypervigilance After Having Several Such Experiences
     2. Phobia
       a. Irrational And Intense Fear
       b. Social Phobia
       c. Agoraphobia
       d. Simple Phobias
     3. Obsessive-Compulsive Disorder
       a. Obsession: Intrusive, Repeated, And Anxiety-Producing Irrational Thoughts
       b. Compulsions: Purposeful Repetitive Behaviors

      c. Obsessions Most Commonly Focus On Fears Of Contamination
         Or Sinfulness
   4. Posttraumatic Stress Disorder
      a. Anxiety Disorder Resulting From Specific Trauma
      b. Re-experiencing A Traumatic Event Involving Threat Of Bodily Harm
      c. Denial Or Avoidance Of Stimuli Associated With The Traumatic Event

What is psychic numbing, and how may it be helpful in the short run but disadvantageous in the long run to the individual?

   5. Generalized Anxiety Disorder
      a. Constant, Excessive Anxiety
      b. Feel Helpless About Handling Vague Troubles
      c. Inability To Relax
      d. Physical Symptoms Of Anxiety
B. Understanding Anxiety Disorders

What are the most common of all psychological disorders?

   1. The Biological Perspective
      a. Brain Conditions And Anxiety Disorders
      b. Hypersensitivity To Neurochemicals That Put Sympathetic Nervous
         System On Alert, Phobias And Panic Disorder
      c. Genetics And Anxiety Disorders
      d. Traumatic Stress And Hypersensitivity To Norepinephrine
   2. The Psychological Perspective
      a. Learning Perspective
      b. Cognitive Perspective
      c. Psychodynamic Perspective: Anxiety Disorders
        Reflective Of Maladaptive Defense Mechanisms
        (1) Generalized Anxiety Disorder And Reaction Formation
        (2) Obsessive-Compulsive Disorder And Undoing
        (3) Phobias As Symbolic Representations Of Unconscious
          Conflicts

From the standpoint of the learning perspective, what are the various mechanisms by which a phobia might be learned? Illustrate such mechanisms by referring specifically to a learned fear of flying.

From the standpoint of the psychodynamic perspective, how might the defense mechanism of reaction formation be indicated in a mother's anxiety about her children being kidnapped?

   3. Group Differences in Anxiety Disorders
      a. Culture and Panic Disorders
        (1) Similarities Among Different Groups
        (2) Cultural-Contextual Considerations
          (a) Kayak-Angst In Greenland

(b) Koro In Asia
    b. Gender and Anxiety Disorders
        (1) Greater Incidence Among Men Than Women
        (2) Gender Differences In Posttraumatic Stress Disorder
            (a) Denial And Avoidance Responses To Trauma
            (b) Emotional And Socioeconomic Hardships

What observations might you invoke to argue against the proposition that more women than men suffer from anxiety disorders because women are "mentally weaker" than men?

III. Mood Disorders

What is a mood? When does a mood become a "mood disorder?" What are the two ways in which extreme moods cause distress?

    A. Depressive Disorders
        1. Major Depression
            a. Depressed Mood
            b. Anhedonia
            c. Suicide
            d. Mental And Physical Sluggishness
            e. Dysthymia
            f. Seasonal Affective Disorder

What is the environmental variable that is considered the central factor affecting the mood fluctuations observed in what is referred to as "seasonal affective disorder?"

    B. Alternative Perspectives on Suicide (Box 14.1)
        1. In Young Adults
        2. Religious And Cultural Prescriptions And Oppositions
    C. Bipolar Disorders
        1. Bipolar Disorder Also Known As Manic-Depression
            a. Mania Is The "Up" Mood
                (1) Elevated Mood, Exaggerated Interest In Life
                (2) Much Energy
                (3) Thinking Sometimes Becomes Psychotic
            b. Cyclothymia As Milder Form Of Bipolar Disorder

    D. Understanding Mood Disorders
        1. The Biological Perspective
            a. Bipolar Disorder In Diverse Countries
            b. Genetic Predisposition Toward Mood Disorders
            c. Decreased Dopamine Action Associated With Anhedonia
            d. Decreased Serotonin Action Associated With Depressed Mood
            e. Abnormalities In Brain Feedback Systems Coordinating
                Neurotransmitters That Affect Mood

What is the unresolved logical question or issue concerning the relationship between brain abnormalities and depression?

       2. The Learning Perspective
          a. Depression And Positive Reinforcement
          b. Behavior That Elicits Punishment Instead of Positive Reinforcement
       3. The Cognitive Perspective
          a. Irrational, Self-Defeating Beliefs, Low Self-Esteem And Depression
          b. Learned Helplessness

Describe the way in which a progressive cycle of self-defeating beliefs and depression might occur, resulting in a steady "downward spiral" of deterioration in a person's life?

       4. The Psychodynamic Perspective
          a. Emphasizes Psychological Conflicts Caused By Loss
          b. Identification As Defense Mechanism To Hold Onto Lost Person
       5. The Biopsychosocial Perspective
          a. Biological Predisposition Expressed After Stress Experience
          b. Coping Style, Personality, And Social Environment
    E. Gender and Major Depression

How comparable is the incidence of depression among males and females as children? How comparable is the incidence of bipolar disorder among men and women? How comparable is the incidence of major depression among men and women?

       1. Differences in Detection
          a. Gender And Responses On Scale Measures Of Depression
          b. Scale Limitations Cannot Explain Gender Differences
       2. Differences in Hormones
          a. Hormonal Fluctuation Associated With Menstruation
          b. Depression Among Menopausal Age Men And Women

What has been found regarding the effects of medical treatments that alter hormones in menopausal women? What do such findings suggest about the validity of the argument that gender differences in depression are due to hormonal factors?

       3. Cognitive Differences
          a. View That Women Have More Negative Beliefs Than Men
          b. Women Encounter More Social And Psychological Stressors
          c. Powerlessness And Learned Helplessness
       4. A Combination of Differences

What are the coping styles which seem to be more characteristic of women than men, which might account for the increased risk of depression among women than men?

IV. Schizophrenia

What are the general characteristics of the disorder known as "schizophrenia?" What does it mean to say that schizophrenia is the psychological disorder most frequently characterized by "psychosis?"

    A. Symptoms of Schizophrenia

How does the technical meaning of the term schizophrenia differ from what many people assume the term means? What is the split which is actually referred to by the term "schizo?"

        1. Disturbed Thinking
            a. Word Salad
            b. Neologisms
            c. Delusions
                (1) Of Grandeur
                (2) Of Persecution
                (3) Of Reference
        2. Disturbed Perceptions

What is a hallucination?

        3. Disturbed Emotions and Actions
            a. "Split" Between Emotions And Social Reality
            b. Emotions Can Appear Disconnected From Experience
    B. Understanding Schizophrenia

What are the symptom patterns that distinguish catatonic, paranoid, and hebephrenic schizophrenics?

Give examples from each of the following types of symptoms of schizophrenia: (a) Factor I, or Negative Symptoms, (b) Factor II, or Disorganized Symptoms, and (c) Factor III or Positive Symptoms.

From the standpoint of understanding the condition, what is the clinical significance of the finding that changes in symptoms of one of the foregoing factors is not correlated with changes in either of the other factors?

With abnormalities of which part of the brain are symptoms within each of the three foregoing categories apparently most closely associated?

        1. The Biological Perspective
            a. The Dopamine Hypothesis
                (1) Dopamine Receptors In Schizophrenics
                (2) Improvement Of Symptoms After Age 50
                (3) High Dopamine Sensitivity In Other Disorders
            b. Enlarged Brain Ventricles In Some Schizophrenics
                (1) Brain Tissue Loss Around Limbic System
                (2) Brain Tissue Loss Around Frontal Cortex

      c. No Structural Brain Abnormalities In Some Schizophrenics

      d. Does Brain Tissue Loss Occur Before Or After Schizophrenia

      e. Genetic Factors In Development Of Schizophrenia

      f. Prenatal Factors In Development Of Schizophrenia

          (1) Fetal Stress And Brain Development

          (2) Second Trimester Of Gestation During Winter Months

How do the research findings with regard to the incidence of schizophrenia among identical as compared to fraternal twins tend to support the view that genetic factors contribute to the development of this condition?

How is the finding that a disproportionate number of people with symptoms of schizophrenia were in the second trimester of gestation during winter months interpreted as supporting the biological perspective on development of schizophrenia?

  2. The Biopsychosocial Perspective

      a. Biological Vulnerability And Stressful Psychosocial Conditions

      b. Schizophrenia More Common Among Lower Income People

      c. Improvement Of Condition And Critical, Hostile Parents

  3. Cultural Perspectives

      a. Common Features Of Schizophrenia Through World

      b. Importance Of Sociocultural Context In Judgment Of Behaviors

How does the condition known as <u>amok</u> illustrate the need for caution in judging the meaning and appropriateness of a behavior relative to the sociocultural context within which it occurs?

      c. Cultural Differences In Response To People With Schizophrenia

          (1) Differences In Supportive vs. Critical And Rejecting

              Responses

          (2) Family Response

              (a) In Developing vs. Developed Countries

              (b) Close Extended Family Relationships Helpful

What are the two ways in which close extended family relationships are thought to be helpful to people who have schizophrenia?

V. Body Focused Disorders

  A. Eating Disorders

What are some of the general characteristics of people with eating disorders?

  1. Anorexia Nervosa

      a. Intense Dread Of Becoming Fat

      b. Sense Of Control And Pride For Overcoming Hunger And Losing

         Weight

      c. Low Body Fat Upsets Hormonal Cycles

         (1) Causes Amenorrhea

          (2) Permanent Bone Calcium Loss

          (3) Premature Death Due To Heart Attack

  2. Box 14.2, Applications: How to Help a Friend in Distress

      a. Understand Basic Signs And Symptoms Of Disorders

      b. Pick An Appropriate Time To Talk About Problem

      c. Focus On Specific Behaviors

      d. Ask Friend To Talk About Feelings

      e. Avoid Being Judgmental

      f. Give Advice Only If Asked

      g. Avoid Spying

      h. Ask How You Can Help

      i. Offer To Accompany Friend To Counseling Visit

      j. Discuss Biopsychosocial Nature Of Disorders

      k. Know Your Limitations

  3. Bulimia Nervosa

      a. Alternate Between Starving And Stuffing

      b. Bingeing And Purging

  4. Understanding Eating Disorders

      a. Biological Perspective

          (1) Eating Disorders And Depression

          (2) Neurotransmitter Imbalances

      b. Cognitive Perspective

          (1) Cultural Ideals Of Female Thinness

          (2) Belief That Willpower Can And Should Be Used To Control The Body

How is dieting involved in the cyclical pattern of eating disorders?

      c. Psychodynamic Perspective

From the standpoint of the psychodynamic perspective, what is it that causes eating disorders?

      d. Research Findings Supporting Biopsychosocial Perspective

          (1) Biological Predisposition Toward High Body Fat

          (2) Psychological Disorder

          (3) Poor Family Relations

  5. Ethnic and Gender Perspectives on Eating Disorders

      a. Much Higher Incidence Of Eating Disorders Among Females

      b. Eating Disorders Rare Outside Of The Western World

      c. Occur Among U. S. Women From All Socioeconomic And Ethnic Backgrounds

As indicated by research cited in your text, what is it that fuels attempts at weight control when ethnic minority women identify with mainstream Euro-American culture rather than their own traditional culture?

  B. Somatoform Disorders

What is the distinguishing characteristic of the kinds of physical symptoms that occur in people who are diagnosed as having somatoform disorders?

    1. Hypochondriasis
        a. Nagging Feeling Of Being Sick
        b. Worry Motivates Repeated Medical Consultation
    2. Conversion Reactions
        a. Sudden Loss Of Function In A Body Part
        b. Condition Most Commonly Triggered By Stressful Conflict
    3. Understanding Somatoform Disorders
        a. Biological Perspective
            (1) Brain Dysfunction
            (2) Excess Dopamine Activity
        b. Learning Theory Perspective

How might the person who shows a somatoform disorder receive positive reinforcement for the symptom behaviors?

        c. Cognitive Perspective
            (1) Tendency To Think About And Exaggerate Symptoms
            (2) Beliefs About Emotional Expression
        d. Psychodynamic Perspective
            (1) Symptoms As Defense Mechanisms
            (2) Dissociation And Symbolizing Of Painful Emotions
    4. Cultural Perspectives on Somatoform Disorders
        a. Expression And Rate Of Occurrence Differs Across Cultures
        b. Occur Less Often In U. S. Than In Other Cultures

What argument might you offer as a less condescending, culturally sensitive interpretation than the traditional view that people with somatoform disorders are unaware of their own psychological experience? Can you given an example to support this alternative argument?

VI. Dissociative Disorders

How do the disssociatives disorder differ from the kind of dissociation that sometimes occurs during "normal" activities?

    A. Types of Dissociative Disorders

What is "depersonalization?"

    1. Psychogenic Amnesia and Psychogenic Fugue
        a. Psychogenic Amnesia
            (1) Memory Loss Of Personal Information
            (2) Caused By Trauma
        b. Psychogenic Fugue

     (1) Dissociation From One's Own Identity

     (2) Amnesia For Travel From Usual Surroundings

   2. Dissociative Identity Disorder

    a. Also Known As Multiple Personality Disorder

    b. At Least Two Distinct Personalities

    c. Different Personalities Called "Alters

    d. Alters Dominant At Separate Times

 B. Understanding Dissociative Disorders

   1. Learning Perspective

    a. Learning To Dissociate By Observing Others

    b. Use Of Dissociation To Escape From Trauma

   2. Learned Through Psychotherapy Experiences

Describe a hypothetical scenario in which a psychotherapist creates alters in his/her client by asking suggestive questions.

   3. Psychodynamic Perspective

    a. Disorder As Reflecting Coping Defense Of Repression

    b. Threatening Thoughts Or Feelings Pushed Into Unconscious

    c. Alters As Response To Experience Of Child Abuse

VII. Personality Disorders

What are the general characteristics of personality disorders? Why are personality disorders categorized separately from the other psychological disorders?

How do people with personality disorders tend to explain the trouble they have in their work and relationships with other people?

What are the general characteristics of paranoid personality disorder?

 A. Antisocial Personality Disorder

   1. Also Known As Manipulative Or Psychopathic Personality

   2. Consistent Violation Of Rights Of Others Without Feeling Guilt

   3. Con Artists

   4. Irresponsibly Impulsive

   5. Seek Immediate Gratification

   6. Deceive And Use Others To Satisfy Selfish Desires

   7. Associated With Antisocial Behaviors In Childhood

What are some of the antisocial behaviors of childhood associated with the development of antisocial personality disorder? About what percent of children who show a pattern of antisocial behavior later develop antisocial personality disorder?

 B. Understanding Antisocial Personality Disorder

   1. Biological Perspective

    a. Neurological Dysfunction May Play A Role

b. Biological Deficit Limiting Responsiveness To Pain
    (1) Less Sensitivity To Feeling Fear And Arousal
    (2) Do Not Fear Punishment And Don't Learn From It
2. Psychological Perspective
    a. Role Of Reinforcement Experiences
    b. Rewards For Antisocial Behavior
3. Cognitive Perspective

Give an example of the kind of irrational belief that might play a role in the development of antisocial personality disorder?

4. Psychodynamic Perspective
    a. No Normal Superego, No Established Sense Of Morality
    b. No Capacity For Enduring Attachments
    c. Inability To Understand Another's Feelings
    d. Exceptional Motivation To Satisfy Personal Needs

From the standpoint of the psychodynamic view, what is the early-developmental experience that causes antisocial personality disorder?

C. Self-Generated Questions: What's In This One For Me?

Most people come to the first course in psychology expecting to learn some things which will help them to better understand themselves, other people in their lives, and/or the nature of life in the world in which they live. Along these same lines, students of psychology often look forward to discovering things about human behavior and experience which may help them to improve their own life by developing their talents, technical skills, knowledge and abilities, and/or the quality or their relationships with other people. On the basis of such self-interest, which tends to provide a framework in terms of which new learning becomes personally meaningful and thus easier to remember, write down a few questions in the space below, about the subject matter covered in this chapter. After reading and studying the chapter, come back to see how any of what you've learned may be useful to you in finding answers to these questions.

D. Completion Items

The words in the margins of this exercise are the ones that correctly complete the sentence on the corresponding line. To get the most out of this exercise, you should try to avoid looking at these words in the margin until after you've filled in the corresponding blanks with the words you think best complete the sentences. So, begin the exercise by covering up all of the margin words with a piece of paper. Then, for each blank, write in the word which you think completes the sentence. Even if you're not sure as to the word, write in your best guess, preferably in pencil so you can erase and re-write any incorrect responses you may make here.

After writing in your "answer," slide the paper covering up the margin words down just far enough to see the word for the blank you just filled-in. For each blank that you fill-in correctly, put a check mark (√) after your answer. If the word you wrote in doesn't match the word corresponding to that blank, mark an (X) next to your response and go on to the next blank. It's probably a good idea to go back to the text and try to strengthen your learning related to topic coverage that corresponds in the textbook chapter to those blanks which you filled-in incorrectly, since those items signal a weak link in your concept mastery chain for this chapter.

1. A statistical approach defines abnormal behaviors as those that occur
_____. However, many behaviors are statistically rare, but not   infrequently
generally considered to be abnormal. The statistical definition of abnormality is
also limited by the _____ of individuals used as the basis for   sample
relevant statistical estimates.

2. Social _____, the standards for acceptable behaviors within   norms
a particular social group, provide a second way of defining abnormality.

3. Another way to define abnormality is in terms of the extent to which
behaviors are _____ -- that is, because they result in social or   maladaptive
biological harm to oneself.

4. A fourth definition of abnormality emphasizes an individual's perception of
physical or emotional _____. However, many people feel   pain
_____ distress while engaging in behaviors that violate social   no
norms and are also biologically harmful to themselves.

5. Deliberately trying to _____ or mutilate oneself or others is   kill
a fifth way of defining abnormality. This definition is the one typically used for
placing people in _____ hospitals.   psychiatric

6. A psychological disorder is a pattern of behavioral or psychological
dysfunction that causes _____, abnormal behavior, or an   distress
important loss of freedom. For each psychological disorder, DSM IV
describes a characteristic pattern of: (1) _____, defined as   symptoms
subjective thoughts or feelings, and (2) _____, or observable   signs
behaviors that occur together. The DSM IV does not provide a
_____ explanation for each psychological disorder, although   theoretical
it does provide empirical information.

7. One of the greatest criticisms of DSM IV is that its "checklist" or
_____ model approach, does not make sense for psychological   medical
disorders. This approach also runs the risk of ignoring the different underlying

_____ of psychological disorders. A classic study in which normal people got themselves admitted to a psychiatric hospital by lying about hearing _____, showed how the label of a psychological disorder can affect the way people are perceived and treated.

causes

voices

8. DSM IV cautions against its misuse with people of various cultural backgrounds because it was developed largely using research studies of _____- Americans. So, for example, although a pattern of negative emotion exists in all cultures, _____ as a psychological disorder does not. One reason why psychological disorders do not always "translate" to all cultures is that psychological disorders sometimes lack _____ equivalence across cultures. Culture _____ syndromes are psychological disorders that occur only in certain cultures. Mali-mali, a syndrome that occurs in the _____, is characterized by a person repeatedly shouting obscenities after being startled.

Euro

depression

functional

bound

Phillipines

9. A significant limitation to the biological perspective is that it is often difficult to determine whether biological abnormalities are the _____ or result of a psychological disorder.

cause

10. _____ theorists believe that psychological disorders are not the result of an underlying disorder, but the disorder itself. From the standpoint of the _____ perspective, psychological disorders are viewed as the result of maladaptive thoughts. The _____ perspective views psychological disorders as the result of unconscious conflicts, feelings, impulses, and the defense mechanisms involved with them. The biopsychosocial perspective views abnormal behavior as the result of an _____ between biological, psychological, and social factors. The _____ perspective on abnormal behavior emphasizes the supernatural.

Learning

cognitive

psychodynamic

interaction

spiritual

11. A _____ attack is a sudden episode of intense apprehension usually accompanied by physical symptoms, such as heart pounding. People with panic _____ have repeated panic attacks that cause distress and interfere with their lives.

panic

disorder

12. People with _____ have an irrational and intense fear of a person, place, or situation that causes significant distress and maladaptive avoidance of the feared stimulus. People with _____ phobia avoid all contact with people because of an irrational fear of being humiliated in social situations. People with _____ avoid public places.

phobia

social

agoraphobia

13. _____ are intrusive, repeated, and anxiety-producing irrational thoughts. Some people attempt to deal with their obsessions by engaging in _____, purposeful repetitive behaviors that they cannot resist acting out. Together, obsessions and compulsions comprise an _____ disorder known as obsessive-compulsive

Obsessions

compulsions

anxiety

disorder.

14. Unlike the other anxiety disorders, posttraumatic stress disorder (PTSD) results from a specific traumatic event or events that involve the threat of _____ or serious physical injury to oneself of others. In extreme cases, people with a denial or avoidance PTSD pattern experience psychic _____, a form of dissociation in which they feel as though the event never happened or was not genuinely traumatic.

death

numbing

15. People with _____ anxiety disorder live in a distressing state of constant, excessive anxiety. In addition, they tend to feel _____ about handling their vague troubles.

generalized

helpless

16. Preliminary evidence suggests that people with obsessive-compulsive disorder have abnormalities in the _____ ganglia and cerebral cortex. People who experience a phobia or panic disorder are hypersensitive to the neurochemicals that put the _____ nervous system on alert. In response to the inescapable stress of a trauma, the brain areas that receive _____ become hypersensitive.

basal

sympathetic

norepinephrine

17. From a learning perspective, people learn phobias and anxiety through imitation, observation, or _____. The cognitive perspective on anxiety disorders suggests that one's perceptions and _____ of events fuel anxiety.

reinforcement

interpretations

18. From a _____ perspective, anxiety disorders reflect maladaptive defense mechanisms against anxiety. Generalized anxiety disorder, for instance, reflects the use of _____ formation, obsessive-compulsive disorder involves the defense mechanism of _____, and phobias can involve the defense mechanism of _____, whereby a person avoids becoming aware of inner impulses by placing them onto another person or an external object.

psychodynamic

reaction

undoing
projection

19. In Greenland and Alaska, were most men hunt seals in the ocean for a livelihood, panic attacks take a culturally meaningful form known as _____-angst. In Asia, where many people are acutely sensitive to social rejection, panic attacks known as koro focus on a paralyzing fear that one's _____ are shrinking into the body and will eventually cause death.

kayak

genitals

20. Women tend to respond to trauma with _____ and avoidance, strategies that facilitate the development of PTSD. Women often face more emotional and _____ hardships than men after a trauma.

denial

socioeconomic

21. In cases of severe depression, the loss of interest in life activities is accompanied by _____, an inability to feel any joy. A milder

anhedonia

393

form of major depression that does not involve physical symptoms or interfere with general function, is known as _____. Seasonal affective disorder, or SAD, occurs more often in regions of the world that have exceptionally _____ daylight hours.

dysthymia

short

22. Young adults tend to commit suicide _____. Experiencing many stressful life events, suffering from a mood disorder, and coping ineffectively because of certain personality traits, such as aggressiveness, impulsivity, and low _____ tolerance, and having access to a gun at home increase a young adult's likelihood of committing suicide. Young adults who cope by abusing _____ and behaving in ways that result in social isolation are at particular risk for suicide. Suicide also occurs because of religious and _____ prescriptions under specified circumstances.

impulsively

frustration

drugs

cultural

23. _____ disorder, also known as manic-depression, is characterized by alternations between extreme "up" and extreme "down" moods, both of which interfere with general functioning. The "up" mood, _____, is characterized by elevated mood and an exaggerated interest in life activities. In this mood, thinking sometimes become so confused that it is _____, or seriously out of touch with reality. A milder form of this disorder characterized by mood swings that are not as severe as those in bipolar disorder, is known as _____.

Bipolar

mania

psychotic

cyclothymia

24. Decreased _____ action is associated with anhedonia, and decreased _____ is associated with depressed mood. Among people with depression the brain _____ systems that coordinate neuro-transmitters that affect mood may not work properly. Whether brain abnormalities cause or _____ from depression remains under study.

dopamine
scrotonin
feedback

result

25. The learning perspective suggests that people become depressed when they receive little positive _____. Also, individuals may behave in ways that elicit _____ from other people in their lives.

reinforcement
punishment

26. The cognitive perspective suggests that irrational, self-defeating _____ lead to lowered self-esteem and depression.

beliefs

27. The psychodynamic perspective emphasizes psychological _____ caused by the loss of a loved one, a cherished goal, or a valued self-perception. To hold onto the lost person emotionally, the grief stricken person might use the defense mechanism of _____, whereby behavior mannerisms of the person lost are adopted.

conflicts

identification

28. The biopsychological perspective proposes that some people have a biological predisposition for depression that expresses itself after they encounter a _____.

stressor

29. As children, boys and girls suffer _____ from depression.   equally
As adults, men and women suffer equally from _____ disorder.   bipolar
But roughly twice the number of women than men experience
_____ depression.   major

30. Some researchers have suggested that major depression goes
undetected in many men because of inadequacies in the _____   scales
used to identify the symptoms of depression.

31. An increase in rates of depression among _____ women   menopausal
is matched by a similar increase among men in their age group. Furthermore,
treatments that alter _____ in menopausal women help to improve   hormones
physical symptoms of menopause, not feelings of depression.

32. Another view proposes that women have more negative _____   beliefs
that trigger depression, perhaps because they experience more social and
psychological _____, such as sexism, employment and economic   stressors
disadvantage, and conflicting social roles, that can lead to a sense of powerlessness
and learned _____ resulting in depression.   helplessness

33. Schizophrenia is the psychological disorder most often characterized by
_____, a mental condition involving loss of contact with reality to the   psychosis
extent that all areas of one's life are affected. The term schizophrenia means
"split _____." It does not refer to a division in personalities, but   mind
to the tendency for a person's _____ of reality to be split off from   perception
reality.

34. In schizophrenia, thoughts crowd into the person's consciousness without
any rhyme or reason, and result in a word _____, a jumble of words   salad
that make no sense. One type of disturbed thinking observed in schizophrenia
involves delusions, which are firmly held but false _____ that have   beliefs
no basis in reality. Common delusions include delusions of _____,   grandeur
false beliefs about one's power or importance, and delusions of
_____, false beliefs that others seek to do one harm, or delusions of   persecution
_____, the false belief that one is the topic of conversation. People   reference
with schizophrenia also often have _____, false perceptions that   hallucinations
are not based on sensory stimuli.

35. People with schizophrenia are also "split off" from their emotions and the
social _____ around them. So, for example, they might suddenly   reality
giggle while discussing the death of a _____ one.   loved

36. People with _____ schizophrenia are motionless for hours,   catatonic
and unresponsive to the environment, those with _____   paranoid
schizophrenia appear nervous and suspicious, while those with
_____ schizophrenia giggle inappropriately.   hebephrenic

37. The Factor I symptoms of schizophrenia, known as _____   negative
symptoms, include a loss of ordinary functions, such as loss of fluency in thought
and speech, lack of emotion, anhedonia, lack of volition, and reduced
attention span. Factor II symptoms, known as _____ symptoms,   disorganized
include disorganized thought and speech and inappropriate affect. Factor III
symptoms, known as _____ symptoms, consist of disturbed   positive
perceptions, delusions, and hallucinations. Negative symptoms are associated
with the _____ cortex and do not improve in the long run.   prefrontal
Positive symptoms are associated with abnormalities in the _____.   hippocampus

38. People with schizophrenia have twice as many _____   dopamine
receptors as people without schizophrenia. But high sensitivity to this
neurohormone is also associated with other psychological disorders, such
as _____, and some symptoms of schizophrenia are associated   mania
with _____ levels of it. Researchers have also found that some   low
people with schizophrenia have enlarged _____, the fluid-filled   ventricles
areas of the brain; the latter condition is associated with brain tissue loss,
especially around the _____ region, the area of the brain that   limbic
regulates emotions and memory, and around the _____ cortex,   frontal
the brain area that affects attention and problem-solving. But some people with
schizophrenia have no structural _____ abnormalities, and the   brain
question of whether the tissue loss occurs before or _____ a person   after
experiences schizophrenia remains under investigation. Studies of twins
suggest a _____ link to schizophrenia. Between _____
genetic/fraternal twins, a twin has a 10 to 14 percent chance of having schizophrenia
if the other member has it. But between identical twins, the probability
increases to about _____ percent if the other member has it.   50
Studies indicate that a disproportionate number of people with schizophrenia
were in the second trimester of gestation during winter months when pregnant
mothers tend to catch viral _____.   influenza

39. The biopsychosocial perspective proposes that people with biological
vulnerability toward schizophrenia will develop the disorder under
_____ psychosocial conditions.   stressful

40. In general, people with schizophrenia who live in developing countries
show _____ levels of functioning than do those in developed   higher
nations. The close extended _____ relationships in many   family
developing cultures are thought to be helpful to people with
schizophrenia.

41. People with the eating disorder _____ nervosa have an   anorexia
intense dread of becoming fat, perceive themselves as fat even though
they weigh at least 15 percent below their normal body weight, and do
whatever they can to minimize their calorie intake. Their lack of body fat
upsets normal hormonal cycles and causes _____ in women,   amenorrhea
an absence of menses.

42. Approaching a friend who might need help with a psychological disorder
requires tact, knowledge, patience, and _____. The   understanding
following are a few considerations relevant to your attempts to help such
a person. Choose a _____ place to talk to your friend. Focus   private
on specific _____ and why they worry you. Give your friend   behaviors
_____ only if s/he asks for it.   advice

43. People with _____ nervosa alternate between starving   bulimia
and stuffing themselves. To cope with their feelings of shame, guilt,
depression, and stomach pain after a binge, they often _____   purge
the food on which they binged by vomiting, use enemas, laxatives, diuretics,
and/or exercise.

44. Low levels of _____, a neurotransmitter that regulates eating   serotonin
and moods, are correlated with both depression and with the lack of control in
bulimia nervosa. The _____ perspective suggests that cultural   cognitive
ideals of thinness combined with the belief that one can and should use
willpower to control the body contribute to eating disorders. The psychodynamic
perspective of eating disorders views the attempts to control one's body as the
result of _____ conflicts or disturbed interpersonal relationships.

45. The vast majority of people with an eating disorder are _____.   female
Eating disorders are still rare outside the _____ world. Research has western
indicated that when ethnic minority women identify with mainstream Euro-American
culture, their attempts at weight control are often fueled less by fears of being fat than
by dislike for their own _____ features.   racial

46. _____ disorders feature physical symptoms that have no   Somatoform
apparent medical cause. People with _____ have a nagging   hypochondriasis
feeling that they are sick. _____ disorder is characterized   Conversion
by the sudden loss of function in a body part for no apparent medical reason.

47. Brain dysfunction such as excess _____ activity, might be   dopamine
involved in somatoform disorders, as could positive _____ for   reinforcement
the behavior associated with it. From the cognitive perspective, conditions
such as a _____ reaction might result when people believe that   conversion
they cannot voice their feelings when they experience stress.

48. Somatoform disorders occur _____ often in the United States   less
as compared with other countries. In some cultures, people may know they have
negative moods and unacceptable feelings, but choose to express themselves
metaphorically through _____ symptoms rather than directly stating physical
their feelings.

49. _____ refers to the type of dissociative disorder in which   Depersonalization
one's body feels as though it is not human or as though it has a mind of its own.

397

Psychogenic _____ is an episode of memory loss of personal   amnesia
information due to psychological trauma. Psychogenic _____, a   fugue
state of dissociation from one's own identity, involves travel away from one's
usual surroundings and psychogenic amnesia for the experience. Dissociative
identity disorder, also known as _____ personality disorder, involves multiple
a splitting of a personality into at least two distinct personalities that are dominant
at different times. The different personalities, called _____,   alters
suddenly take independent control of the original personality.

50. From the standpoint of a psychodynamic perspective, dissociative
disorders involve _____, a coping defense that pushes   repression
threatening or upsetting thoughts or feelings into the unconscious
without one being aware of it. The observation that most people with
dissociative identity disorder suffered severe abuse during childhood
has led to the view that alters provide an emotional _____ and   escape
unconscious expression of feelings associated with the abuse.

51. People with antisocial personality disorder, also known as manipulative
or _____ personality disorder, show a willingness to consistently   psychopathic
violate the rights of others without feeling guilt. Apparently, people with this
disorder have a biological deficit that limits their responsiveness to
_____, making them less sensitive to feeling fear and arousal   pain
than other people. From a learning perspective, rewards for antisocial behavior,
such as excitement and a sense of "beating the system," can _____   reinforce
the behaviors associated with this disorder. From a _____   cognitive
perspective, this disorder is explained in terms of the development of
irrational beliefs, such as the idea that in order to avoid being controlled by others,
one must obtain and hold _____ over them. According to the   power
psychodynamic view, people with this disorder are exceptionally motivated to
satisfy their own _____.   needs

E. Self-Quiz

For each of the following items, circle the letter which precedes the correct alternative.

1. Which, if any, of the following approaches to the definition of "abnormality" is superior to
the others?
    a. statistical approach
    b. approach based on consideration of social norms
    c. approach based on consideration of maladaptiveness of behaviors
    d. approach emphasizing individual's physical and/or emotional distress
    e. none of the above is necessarily superior to any of the others

2. The descriptive, checklist approach of the DSM IV is also known as the _____ model approach.
   - a. medical
   - b. statistical
   - c. normative
   - d. learning
   - e. cognitive

3. Mali-mali is an example of a(n) _____ syndrome.
   - a. psychotic
   - b. bipolar disorder
   - c. dissociative disorder
   - d. culture bound
   - e. body dysmorphic

4. A(n) _____ is a purposeful repetitive behavior that a person cannot resist acting out.
   - a. obsession
   - b. compulsion
   - c. dissociative condition
   - d. hyperplasia
   - e. dysplasia

5. Which of the following is not among the types of traumatic events which qualify as potential causes of posttraumatic stress disorder?
   - a. rape
   - b. physical abuse by a spouse
   - c. flunking out of school
   - d. combat experience during a war
   - e. a life-threatening experience in a natural disaster such as a flood

6. From the standpoint of the psychodynamic perspective, which of the following defense mechanisms is the one which seems to be most directly involved in obsessive-compulsive disorder?
   - a. reaction formation
   - b. sublimation
   - c. displacement
   - d. undoing
   - e. projection

7. As noted in your text, severe cases of which of the following are accompanied by anhedonia?
   - a. obsessive-compulsive disorder
   - b. dissociative disorders
   - c. major depression
   - d. PTSD
   - e. psychogenic amnesia

8. The rate for completed suicides is _____ for men than women.
    a. twice as high
    b. three times higher
    c. four times higher
    d. ten times

9. _____ are firmly held beliefs that have no basis in reality.
    a. Delusions
    b. Hallucinations
    c. Fugue states
    d. Anhedonic perceptions
    e. Sanctifarious perceptions

10. Which of the following is not among the Factor I or "positive" symptoms of schizophrenia?
    a. disturbed perceptions
    b. hallucinations
    c. lack of emotion and volition
    d. delusions

11. Which of the following types of symptoms of schizophrenia typically do not improve in the long run?
    a. Factor I or negative symptoms
    b. Factor II or disorganized symptoms
    c. Factor III or positive symptoms
    d. Factor IV or synthetic symptoms

12. Between identical twins, a twin has about a _____ percent chance of having schizophrenia if the other member has it, as compared to about a 10 to 14 percent chance between fraternal twins.
    a. 10-14 (i.e., the same)
    b. 25
    c. 50
    d. 75

13. According to your text, which of the following is least likely to account for the tendency for people with schizophrenia who live in developing countries to show higher levels of functioning than those in developed nations?
    a. a more caring attitude toward family members with schizophrenia in developing countries associated with their collectivistic orientation
    b. access to superior medical treatment
    c. more frequent daily contact with kin and fictive kin in developing countries
    d. sharing of the burden of taking care of the person with schizophrenia among relatives in the developing countries

14. Which of the following was not among the factors characteristic of those members of a group of 116 teenage girls who were found to develop an eating disorder when followed over an eight year period?
    a. a biological predisposition toward higher than average levels of body fat
    b. a psychological disorder at the start of the study
    c. poor body image
    d. poor family relations
    e. high serotonin levels

15. Somatoform disorders feature _____ that have no medical cause.
    a. physical symptoms
    b. memory losses
    c. dissociative thinking
    d. visual perceptual dysfunctions
    e. states of learned helplessness

16. Which of the following is not among the dissociative disorders?
    a. depersonalization
    b. psychogenic amnesia
    c. psychogenic fugue
    d. conversion disorder

17. _____ is the condition wherein the individual feels as though his/her body is not human or has a mind of its own.
    a. Hypochondriasis
    b. Depersonalization
    c. Psychogenic amnesia
    d. Conversion disorder
    e. Dissociative identity disorder

18. From a psychodynamic perspective, dissociative disorders are seen as resulting from the pushing of threatening or upsetting thoughts or feelings into the unconscious by the coping defense of
    a. sublimation
    b. projection
    c. rationalization
    d. undoing
    e. repression

19. As noted in your text, it has been observed that most people with dissociative identity disorder have suffered severe
    a. head injury
    b. childhood abuse
    c. somatoform disorders also
    d. psychotic episodes from time to time
    e. all of the above

20. Which of the following is not among the three broad categories into which the different personality disorders are organized in DSM IV?
   a. paranoid personality disorder
   b. borderline or antisocial personality disorder
   c. dissociative disorder
   d. obsessive/compulsive personality disorder

For each of the following items, circle "T" if the statement is True and "F" if the statement is false.

21. T F   The DSM IV provides a theoretical explanation for each psychological disorder listed in it.

22. T F   Depression as a psychological disorder exists in all cultures.

23. T F   In American Aboriginal culture, the concept of abnormal behavior is rooted in the idea that disruption of harmony within oneself and the outside world causes a soul wound or soul loss in a person.

24. T F   Across cultures, more women than men suffer generalized anxiety disorder, panic disorder, and phobias.

25. T F   Decreased serotonin action is associated with depressed mood.

26. T F   Scientists have observed that symptoms of schizophrenia tend to increase in their severity after the age of 50.

27. T F   Studies indicate that a disproportionate number of people with symptoms of schizophrenia were in the second trimester of gestation during summer months.

28. T F   Somatoform disorders occur less often in the United States compared with other countries.

29. T F   People who are rigidly anxious and agreeable with social demands have borderline or antisocial personality disorder.

30. T F   Cutting school, lying, vandalizing property, and fighting are characteristic of childhood antisocial behaviors associated with antisocial personality disorder.

Answer Key To Self-Quiz

1. e
2. a
3. d
4. b
5. c
6. e
7. c
8. c
9. a
10. c
11. a
12. c
13. b
14. e
15. a
16. d
17. b
18. e
19. b
20. c
21. F
22. F
23. T
24. T
25. T
26. F
27. F
28. T
29. T
30. T

CHAPTER 15

Therapy

A. Learning Objectives

Your careful, effective study of Chapter 15, should lead you to develop a working familiarity with:

1. The procedures used as approaches to the treatment of psychological distress in different cultures, especially with regard to the fundamental differences between:
   a. The religio-magical approach whereby supernatural powers, rituals, herbs, or prayer are used by the healer in attempts to restore harmony for the person treated;
   b. The empirical-scientific approach, based on scientific theories and research into the nature of psychological distress and its treatment; and
   c. How Morita therapy, as practiced in Japan, exemplifies a form of treatment reflecting cultural values which are apparently integrally relevant to its effectiveness.

2. The biomedical approaches to treating psychological distress, focusing on:
   a. The general assumptions and objective of such approaches, especially as they focus on neurochemical imbalances associated with psychological disorders;
   b. Electroconvulsive therapy, the types of disorders it is designed to treat, and the risks/benefits associated with its application;
   c. The procedure known as lobotomy and other forms of psychosurgery;
   d. The psychotropic medications, including antipsychotic, antidepressant, antimanic, and antianxiety medications, their effectiveness and limitations.

3. The psychodynamic approaches, psychoanalysis and psychodynamic therapies, with their:
   a. Focus on bringing unconscious conflicts and feelings into consciousness, and
   b. Use of techniques such as free association, dream analysis, and analysis of the psychoanalyst-client relationship to help the client become aware of his/her repressed feelings.

4. The following aspects of the humanistic approaches:
   a. Their general orientation toward helping people to actualize their potential to become the best that they can be;
   b. Their use of treatments aimed at countering barriers to personal growth;
   c. Client-centered therapy with its emphasis on empathy and positive regard;
   d. Gestalt therapy with its emphasis on confrontation, experimentation, and the two-chair technique; and
   e. The cultural values implicit in the various humanistic approaches.

5. The activity-oriented approaches, with their orientations toward the learning of new behaviors and ideas, as in:
    a. The behavioral therapies, with their assumption that psychological distress is the result of learning experiences, and use of techniques based on principles of learning such as reinforcement and punishment; and
    b. Cognitive therapies, especially rational-emotive and cognitive-behavioral therapy, with their assumption that psychological distress results from maladaptive, irrational thoughts which need to be replaced with more adaptive, rational ones.

6. Some general evaluative considerations with regard to psychotherapy, such as:
    a. The difficulty involved in making evaluative judgments about the effectiveness of psychotherapy;
    b. How many therapy sessions it takes for improvement in the person's condition to occur;
    c. What has been found in surveys of consumers' satisfaction with the therapeutic experience;
    d. Whether or not people who receive treatment are better off than people who do not receive treatment;
    e. How the therapeutic alliance between client and therapist may be critical to the effectiveness of any form of psychotherapy; and
    f. The importance of cultural, racial, and gender differences between client and therapist in the formation of the therapeutic alliance.

B. Preview/Review Outline Of Key Terms And Concepts

Before you read the corresponding chapter in your text, read over the following outline. It is designed to give you an overview of information presented in the chapter, and how the various elements of that information are related to each other. After reading through the whole chapter and/or before course exams, you may use this outline as a quick review guide. In your reviews, mask off one line of the outline at a time, and try to recite from your memory of the chapter, the information that you expect to appear on the next line or so.

In going over this outline as a preview before reading and studying the chapter, the questions posed in bold print will help to keep you focused on the learning objectives here, and keep you actively involved in the process of achieving those objectives. When using this section as a review, try to answer the questions. Refer back to the chapter in the text for a more detailed feedback check on your mastery of the material, and/or to strengthen your knowledge and understanding wherever you feel the need to do so.

I. Cultural Perspectives on Treating Psychological Disorders

What was the advice offered by her Latino therapist, which led the severely depressed widow named Alma to reveal feelings and experiences concerning her dead husband which she had not related to her previous therapist? Why had Alma not revealed these feelings and experiences to her previous therapist? What did the Latino therapist recommend that Alma do

to try to lay her husband to final rest, and what did this suggestion have to do with <u>espiritus intranquilos?</u>

How are the terms "patient" and "client" used in the corresponding chapter in your text?

What is the function of "healers" as that term is used in the corresponding chapter in your textbook? What is the fundamental orientation to healing as practiced by: (a) religious healers, (b) medical doctors, and (c) psychotherapists?

    A. Alternative Perspectives: Morita Therapy (Box 15.1)
        1. Form Of Psychological Intervention Used In Japan
        2. Social Productivity As Desired Outcome Of Therapy
        3. Involves Three Steps
            a. Phase l: Total Bed Rest
            b. Phase II: Client Allowed To Participate In Light Manual Labor
            c. Phase III: Client Allowed To Handle Harder Physical Work

In Morita therapy, what is the fundamental assumption about the meaning of life? How is the latter assumption reflected in implementation of such therapy?

    B. Healing Based on Spirits
        1. Religio-Magical Approach
            a. Supernatural Agents As Cause Of Abnormal Behavior
            b. Vulnerability Due To Disharmony With the Spirit World
            c. Use Of Rituals, Herbs, Prayer
            d. Removal Of Evil Spirit And Suffering As Goal
            e. Ceremonies Used To Teach Cultural Traditions
        2. Ndembu African Cultural Perspective
            a. Psychological Distress As Religious Problem
            b. Prayer, Medicine, Ceremonial Dances
    C. Healing Based on Science
        1. Empirical Scientific Approach: Three Main Perspectives
            a. Biological
            b. Psychological
            c. Psychotherapy

What are the distinguishing characteristics of each of the main empirical scientific perspectives on the healing of psychological disorders?

        2. Licensed Psychotherapists
            a. Therapist Is Compassionate Yet Detached
            b. Therapist Has Specialized Training
            c. Legally Committed To Ethical Behavior
            d. Three Different Academic Training Backgrounds
                (1) Licensed Psychologists
                (2) Psychiatrists
                (3) Social Workers

What is meant by the objective of "detachment" regarding the professional relationship between a licensed psychotherapist and his/her clients? What is meant by "empathy" with regard to a licensed psychotherapist's way of relating to his/her clients?

3. Impact Of Managed Care Organizations

How has the growth of managed care organizations impacted on the practice of psychotherapy?

4. Flexible Views On Healing Of Psychological Disorders

II. Biomedical Approaches
    A. Electroconvulsive Therapy
        1. Shock Therapy
        2. Used Primarily For Severe Depression
        3. Successes Balanced By Losses
        4. Today Considered Safe And Effective For Narrow Range Of Patients
            a. Approximately 50% Of Patients Show Some Improvement
            b. Associated With Changes in GABA, Norepinephrine, Serotonin, And Dopamine

What is done to reduce the risks of shock therapy in modern applications of this procedure?

    B. Psychosurgerey
        1. Brain Surgery Designed To Alter Emotions Or Behaviors With No Known Medical Cause
        2. Lobotomy
            a. Widely Used During Mid-1950's
            b. Risks Quite Serious
            c. No Longer Performed
    C. Medications

The psychotropic medications offer an effective and much less risky treatment option to what alternative class of medical procedures in the treatment of psychological disorders?

What beneficial effects tend to be associated with the use of the psychotropic medications? What limitations are there on the therapeutic effectiveness of such treatment?

What is a placebo effect?

        1. Antipsychotic Medications
            a. Typical Antipsychotics
                (1) Lessen The Positive Symptoms Of Schizophrenia, Hallucinations And Delusions
                (2) Apparently Block Action Of Dopamine
                (3) Have Little Effect On Negative Symptoms
            b. Atypical Antipsychotics

  (1) Lessen Both Positive And Negative Symptoms

  (2) Enhance Serotonin, Thereby Inhibiting Dopamine

 2. Antidepressants

  a. Improve Symptoms Associated With Depression

  b. Classified Into three Categories

   (1) Selective Serotonin Reuptake Inhibitors, e.g., Prozac

   (2) Monamine Oxidase (MAO) Inhibitors

   (3) Tricyclic Antidepressants

  c. All Increase Norepinephrine Or Serotonin Activity

 3. Antimanic Medications/Lithium Carbonate

  a. Enhanced Release Of Serotonin And Norepinephrine

  b. In Treatment Of Bipolar Disorder

 3. Antianxiety Medications/Benzodiazepines

  a. Widely Used To Treat Anxiety Disorders

  b. Not Effective Treatment For All Anxiety Disorders

   (1) Posttraumatic Stress Disorder

    (a) Tricyclics

    (b) MAO Inhibitors

   (2) Obsessive-Compulsive Disorder

    (a) Tricyclics

    (b) Selective Serotonin Reuptake Inhibitors

  c. Regular Use

   (1) Dependence And Withdrawal Symptoms

   (2) Rebound Anxiety

III. Psychodynamic Approaches: Resolving Unconscious Conflicts

In psychodynamically oriented therapy: (a) What is the significance of "insight"? (b) What are the three components of unconscious conflicts?; and (c) How are the client's behaviors viewed?

 A. Psychoanalysis

  1. The Original Therapy Developed By Sigmund Freud

  2. Designed To Bring Unconscious Memories Into Consciousness

  3. Techniques Used To Reach Feelings Repressed By Defenses

   a. Free Association

   b. Dream Analysis

   c. Transference Relationship

    (1) Psychoanalyst's Interpretations

    (2) Resistance

  4. Catharsis

  5. Neutral Role Of Psychoanalyst

 B. Psychodynamic Psychotherapies

  1. Short-Term Focus

  2. Psychotherapist Takes Relatively Active Role

  3. Catharsis Viewed As Providing Corrective Emotional Experience

IV. Humanistic Approaches: Reducing the Barriers to Growth

From the humanistic perspective, what is it that causes emotional distress and maladaptive behavior? Accordingly, how is the latter assumption reflected in the primary goal of humanistically-oriented psychotherapy?

    A. Client-Centered Psychotherapy
        1. Based On Carl Rogers' Theory Of Personality
        2. Consistency Between Behaviors And Self-Concept
        3. Unconditional Positive Regard And Empathy
        4. Active Listening
    B. Gestalt Psychotherapy
        1. Fritz Perls' Directive Humanistic Approach
        2. Focus On Awareness Of Immediate Experience And Taking Responsibility For Experience
        3. Directive Techniques
            a. Confrontation When Words Contradict Behaviors
            b. Two Chair Technique

From the Gestalt psychotherapy perspective, how is the technique of free association regarded, and what is the function served by a client's physical and verbal experimentation?

    C. Cultural Perspectives on Humanistic Therapy
        1. Therapist's Assumptions About Development And Mental Health
            a. Therapist's Communication Of Values To Client
            b. Therapist's Values And Therapeutic Objectives
        2. Individualism As Euro-American Value
            a. Self-Awareness
            b. Self-Fulfillment
            c. Self-Discovery
        3. Collectivist Value Orientation And Therapy
            a. Family And Social Group Over Self
            b. Personal Needs As Fundamentally Selfish

How might humanistically-oriented therapy cause a client with a collectivist cultural value orientation to feel even more rather than less at odds with her or himself?

V. Active Approaches: Consciously Changing Behaviors and Ideas
    A. Behavioral Therapy

From the standpoint of the behavioral perspective on therapy: (a) How important are unconscious motivation and self actualization?; (b) What are "target behaviors?"; and (c) What are "trigger situations"?

        1. Reinforcement
            a. Principles Of Operant Conditioning
            b. Therapy Focuses On Changing Reinforcement Pattern

2. Punishment
　　　　　a. Aversion Therapy
　　　　　b. Treatment of Alcoholism With Antabuse
　B. Cognitive Therapies

What is the fundamental assumption underlying the cognitive psychotherapies? From a cognitive therapy perspective, how might "overgeneralization" and/or "polarization" in thinking lead to emotional distress or undesirable behavior? What is the goal of "cognitive restructuring" in cognitive therapy?

　　　　1. Rational-Emotive Therapy (RET)
　　　　　　a. Developed By Albert Ellis
　　　　　　b. Identifying ABC's Of A Client's Thoughts
　　　　　　　　(1) "A" Represents Activating Or Triggering Event
　　　　　　　　(2) "B" Refers To Client's Beliefs
　　　　　　　　(3) "C" Refers To Consequences Of Client's Beliefs
　　　　2. Cognitive-Behavioral Therapy
　　　　　　a. Developed By Aaron Beck
　　　　　　b. Uses Evidence Collected By Client
　　　　　　c. Observation Of Automatic Thoughts Following A Loss
　　　　　　　　(1) Diary Of Automatic Thoughts
　　　　　　　　(2) Examination Of Associated Emotions And Behaviors
　　　　　　　　(3) Focus On Assumptions Underlying Automatic Thoughts
　　　　　　d. And Alteration Of Brain Functioning
　　　　　　　　(1) Obsessive-Compulsive Disorder
　　　　　　　　(2) Brain Structures Involved In Fear Response
　　　　　　　　(3) Caudate Nucleus

What is the function of the caudate nucleus in the brain, and how was that structure found to change in people with obsessive-compulsive disorder who were given cognitive-behavioral therapy?

VI. Evaluating Psychotherapy
　A. The Overall Effectiveness of Psychotherapy

What does research indicate with regard to the improvement shown by people who do as compared to those who do not receive psychotherapeutic treatment for their psychological problems?

　B. Applications: How Many Sessions of Psychotherapy Make A Difference (Box 15.2)
　　　1. No Apparent One-To-One Relationship With Number Of Sessions
　　　2. Client Goes Through Five-Stages In Psychotherapeutic Process
　　　　　a. Ignores And Lives With Problems
　　　　　b. Becomes Aware Of Problems
　　　　　c. Establishes An Alliance With Therapist
　　　　　d. Experiences New Insights, Feelings, And Behaviors
　　　　　e. Practices And Consolidates Learning, Internalizes Changes

3. Clients With Clear-Cut Problems Require Fewer Sessions
4. Nature Of Client's Problems Can Affect Number Of Sessions

About what percent of all psychotherapy clients report significant improvement after only two months of treatment (i.e., 8 sessions)? About what percent of all psychotherapy client's report significant improvement after six months of treatment?

C. Consumer Satisfaction with Psychotherapy

In general, what did the results of the <u>Consumers Reports'</u> survey indicate about consumers' satisfaction with the effectiveness of their own psychotherapeutic experiences? How has the design of that survey research been criticized?

D. Therapeutic Alliance: The Key Element in Psychotherapy

What are some of the characteristics of a "good alliance" as established by successful psychotherapists? What do such therapists "give" their clients through such an alliance?

    1. Cultural Perspectives on the Therapeutic Alliance
        a. When Client And Therapist Are Of Different Backgrounds
        b. Case Of Chinese American Woman And Her Male Euro-American Therapist
        c. Case Of Aboriginal American Man
        d. Client's Perception Of Therapist's Empathy
        e. Case Of Ethiopian Immigrant Client
            (1) Client Fails To Return For Second Appointment
            (2) Therapist Calls Client's Home
    2. Racial Perspectives on the Therapeutic Alliance
        a. When Client But Not Therapist Is Member Of Racial Minority
        b. Cultural Mistrust
        c. Some Racial Minority Clients Hide Painful Racial Experiences

What can a therapist do to try to reduce a client's cultural mistrust and facilitate the therapeutic alliance?

    3. Gender Perspectives on the Therapeutic Alliance
        a. Clients Of Both Sexes Tend To Request Female Therapists
        b. Therapist Gender Preference And Power Differences

What has not been adequately ensured in the studies comparing the relative effectiveness of male and female therapists?

C. Self-Generated Questions: What's In This One For Me?

Most people come to the first course in psychology expecting to learn some things which will help them to better understand themselves, other people in their lives, and/or the nature of life in the world in which they live. Along these same lines, students of psychology often look forward to discovering things about human behavior and experience which may help them to improve their own life by developing their talents, technical skills, knowledge and abilities, and/or the quality or their relationships with other people. On the basis of such self-interest, which tends to provide a framework in terms of which new learning becomes personally meaningful and thus easier to remember, write down a few questions in the space below, about the subject matter covered in this chapter. After reading and studying the chapter, come back to see how any of what you've learned may be useful to you in finding answers to these questions.

D. Completion Items

The words in the margins of this exercise are the ones that correctly complete the sentence on the corresponding line. To get the most out of this exercise, you should try to avoid looking at these words in the margin until after you've filled in the corresponding blanks with the words you think best complete the sentences. So, begin the exercise by covering up all of the margin words with a piece of paper. Then, for each blank, write in the word which you think completes the sentence. Even if you're not sure as to the word, write in your best guess, preferably in pencil so you can erase and re-write any incorrect responses you may make here.

After writing in your "answer," slide the paper covering up the margin words down just far enough to see the word for the blank you just filled-in. For each blank that you fill-in correctly, put a check mark (√) after your answer. If the word you wrote in doesn't match the word corresponding to that blank, mark an (X) next to your response and go on to the next blank. It's probably a good idea to go back to the text and try to strengthen your learning related to topic coverage that corresponds in the textbook chapter to those blanks which you filled-in incorrectly, since those items signal a weak link in your concept mastery chain for this chapter.

1. The therapy process in the case of the severely depressed, 67-year old widow
Alma, hit a turning point when the conversation turned to death of loved ones and
the Latino belief in restless _____, *espiritus intranquilos.* In order to spirits
go on with their lives, the living need to _____ from the deceased.   detach
Her therapist suggested that she _____ to God to lay her husband   pray
to a final rest. In the context of this chapter, the term "patient" is used to refer
to someone who is receiving _____ treatment; the term client is   biomedical
used to refer to someone who is receiving psychotherapy. Religious healers
attempt to treat abnormal behavior or emotional distress through
_____ means.   supernatural

419

2. Morita therapy, aimed at the treatment of self-conscious, socially ineffective people, perfectionistic obsessions, and anxiety is
used successfully in _____, but is largely unknown in the U. S.   Japan
This form of treatment assumes that meaning in life comes from
_____, not from one's emotional experience. The objective of   work
this approach is not to remove the client's _____, but rather to   symptoms
teach the client to continue with his/her normal behaviors in spite of them.

3. Healers with a religio-_____ approach view supernatural agents,   magical
such as spirits, as the cause of abnormal behavior and emotional distress. People
are thought to make themselves vulnerable to attack by living in _____   disharmony
with the spirit world. In Korea a *mudang* chases away evil spirits, and a *piris*
in the _____ cultural tradition uses religious verses to treat emotional   Islamic
distress.

4. Two main perspectives, the _____ and psychological, comprise   biological
the empirical-scientific approach to therapy. Another principal form of such treatment
for psychological disorders is _____, wherein conversation is used to
psychotherapy reduce, remove, or alter a person's troubling emotions, attitudes,
behaviors, or thoughts.

5. Licensed psychotherapists receive training to develop _____,   empathy
the ability to emotionally and intellectually put oneself into someone else's
unique experience. Unlike friends or other healers, licensed psychotherapists
are _____ bound to follow certain ethical guidelines in their   legally
relationship with a client. Among the various types of professional specialists
formally trained to conduct psychotherapy, only _____ are licensed   psychiatrists
to provide biomedical treatments because they have medical training. Managed
care organizations are increasingly involved in setting treatment standards for
therapy and making treatment decisions based on _____-effectiveness.   cost

6. Electroconvulsive therapy (ECT), also known as _____ therapy,   shock
is a biomedical treatment in which brief electrical pulses are sent to the brain. Today
this form of treatment is reserved for patients experiencing suicidal or psychotic
_____ that has not responded to any other treatments. In an effort   depression
to reduce the risks associated with ECT, the patient is strapped to a bed, lower
intensity levels of _____ current are applied and fewer sessions are   electrical
used than was the case in the1950's. This form of treatment is believed to be
associated with changes in GABA, norepinephrine, serotonin,
and dopamine, _____ that play a role in depression.   neurotransmitters

7. _____ is a type of psychosurgery which involved cutting the   Lobotomy
neurons that connect the frontal lobe to the rest of the brain. Psychosurgery is
used only as a last resort and involves precisely targeted brain structures rather
than the entire _____ lobe.   frontal

8. Psychotropic medications reduce the signs and symptoms of psychological disorders without _____ them. Unlike other mind altering drugs, psychotropic medications have little positive effect on people without psychological _____. Also, medications can have a _____ effect, an improvement that results from the patient's expectation of change rather than a pill's actual chemical action.

curing

disorders

placebo

9. _____ antipsychotics lessen hallucinations and delusions, the positive symptoms of schizophrenia. They appear to do so by blocking the action of _____ in the brain. Atypical antipsychotics have shown promise for lessening both the positive and negative effects of schizophrenia, and have their effect by enhancing _____, which in turn inhibits the action of dopamine in the brain.

Typical

dopamine

serotonin

10. Antidepressant medications can be classified into three categories according to their pharmacological action: (1) _____ serotonin inhibitors, such as Prozac, (2) monoaminoxidase (MAO) inhibitors, and (3) _____ antidepressants. All the antidepressants increase norepinephrine or serotonin activity by blocking _____.

selective

tricyclic

reuptake

11. _____ carbonate is a medication which rapidly lessens the symptoms of mania, prevents future episodes, and lessens the mood swings of people with bipolar disorder. Once they stop taking the medication, however, the manic symptoms _____ within weeks.

Lithium

return

12. Benzodiazepines are a class of psychotropic medications most widely used to treat _____ disorders, but they are not useful in treating posttraumatic stress disorder (PTSD) or obsessive-compulsive disorder. Tricyclics and selective _____ reuptake inhibitors reduce some symptoms of obsessive-compulsive disorder. Patients who become physically dependent on benzodiazepines, and suddenly stop their medication, experience _____ anxiety, anxiety that is more intense than the original anxiety.

anxiety

serotonin

rebound

13. The psychodynamic approaches to psychotherapy, so named because they aim for clients to gain _____ into their problems, assume that psychological disorders, such as depression, result from _____ conflicts, usually arising from childhood experiences. These conflicts are thought to involve three components: (1) unacceptable impulses and feelings, (2) anxiety that the unacceptable impulses and feelings will enter conscious awareness, and (3) unconscious _____ behaviors designed to deal with the anxiety and unacceptable impulses and feelings. In their search for the impulses and conflicts that underlie human suffering, psychodynamic therapists view behaviors as _____ communications of unconscious activity.

insight
unconscious

defensive

symbolic

14. Psychoanalysis, the original psychodynamic therapy developed by Sigmund Freud, assumes that psychological defenses help people to _____ traumatic memories or unacceptable impulses. In the psychoanalytic technique

repress

known as free _____, a client simply says whatever comes to mind   association
without thinking about its logical or social acceptability. Another psychoanalytic
technique involves analyzing the symbolic meaning of the client's dreams, as a
way of discovering what is hidden in his/her _____ mind. It is also   unconscious
assumed that the client's unconscious feelings and impulses can reveal
themselves in the _____ relationship, whereby the client will   transference
transfer onto the psychoanalyst the emotional reactions that s/he associates with
personally significant people in his/her life, such as parents and/or lovers.
Sometimes, clients show _____ to the psychoanalysts'   resistance
interpretations. Psychoanalysts believe that change follows insight only if a
client intellectually and emotionally _____ its truth.   understands
Psychoanalytic clients are assumed to achieve full insight during moments of
_____, emotional release as one becomes aware of emotions,   catharsis
thoughts, or memories for the first time. People in Psychoanalysis tend to change
only after repeated insights over _____ of treatment.   years

15. Psychodynamic psychotherapies are short-term forms of psychoanalysis,
aimed at _____ conflicts rather than at whatever conflicts a client   specific
presents over years of treatment. Psychodynamic therapists view catharsis as
providing a _____ emotional experience, re-living an unresolved   corrective
conflict with a new outcome.

16. Unlike the psychodynamic therapies, humanistic approaches assume that
people are _____, constructive, positive beings who desire to   rational
mature and become autonomous. Humanistically-oriented therapies are
designed to counter the barriers which interfere with the individual's personal
_____ or actualization, and are thus the cause of his/her emotional   growth
distress and maladaptive behaviors.

17. Carl Rogers concluded that people become fully-_____   functioning
when they have a sense of consistency between their behaviors and their
self-concept. Rogers' _____-centered therapy aims to develop   client
or restore such consistency by focusing on the client and providing
unconditional positive regard and empathy, using the technique known
as _____ listening, in which the therapist restates the client's   active
feelings in a manner that reflects empathy. This approach assumes that once
the client experiences feelings that previously remained hidden, s/he will
begin to take _____ for them and move toward personal self-   responsibility
acceptance.

18. Gestalt therapy aims to relieve psychological distress by helping clients
to unify their _____ emotional, physical, and cognitive experience,   immediate
and to take responsibility for their experiences. This approach assumes that
awareness automatically restores the individual's potential for growth, and uses
_____ techniques designed to push clients into fully   directive
experiencing their immediate thoughts and feelings. The two
_____ technique is one such method used to facilitate the client's   chair

422

awareness.

19. One value that often differs between Euro-American psychotherapists and clients of other cultures pertains to _____, which tends to be associated with emphases on self-awareness, self-fulfillment, and self-discovery. In contrast, from the standpoint of a collectivistic cultural value orientation, personal needs may be viewed as fundamentally _____. Rather than to focus on self-actualizing, a client from a collectivistic orientation might prefer to learn how to overcome self interests in order to live in _____ with others.

individualism

selfish

harmony

20. Behavioral therapy, one of the most common applications of _____ theories, is typically a brief, problem-focused psychotherapy designed to reduce specific, unwanted behaviors. Unlike the psychodynamic approach, the behavioral approach is not concerned with the unconscious, and unlike the _____ approach, it has little use for concepts such as actualization. After finding out the specifics about the _____ behavior, that is, the one the client wants to change, a behavioral therapist will examine the different _____ situations that stimulate the unwanted behaviors.

learning

humanistic

target
trigger

21. Behavioral psychotherapists aim to alter a client's undesired behaviors by using the principles of operant _____, in order to change the behaviors by modifying the reinforcement patterns that sustain them.

conditioning

22. Another behavioral technique is _____ therapy, which involves the use of punishment, whereby the aim is to associate the target behavior with negative consequences. The latter technique is exemplified by use of the drug known as _____ in the treatment of alcoholism.

aversion

antabuse

23. Cognitive psychotherapies are based on the assumption that people actively _____ a view of the world through their thoughts. From the standpoint of the cognitive approach, cognitive biases are believed to lead to maladaptive _____, that in turn lead to emotional distress and/or undesirable behavior(s). Cognitive therapists use the technique of cognitive _____, a systematic method of replacing maladaptive thoughts with adaptive ones.

construct

thoughts

restructuring

24. In the cognitive approach known as _____-emotive psychotherapy, as developed by Albert Ellis, the therapist works to help a client learn how to change his/her emotions by changing his/her thoughts. The first step in this process involves identifying the ABC's of a client's thoughts: the A represents the _____ or triggering event, the B refers to the client's beliefs that follow the event, and the C refers to the _____ of the client's beliefs.

rational

activating

consequences

25. Cognitive-_____ psychotherapy, as developed by

behavioral

Aaron Beck, differs from rational-emotive therapy in that it uses evidence collected by the client rather than logic argued by the therapist, as the basis for cognitive restructuring. Beck found that the slide into depression which occurs in many people following a loss, such as the loss of a loved one, is associated with _____ thoughts, that is, repetitive,   automatic
unintentional, conscious thoughts that become habitual, and lead to a negative _____ of the self, the world around oneself, and one's   schema
future.

26. In people with obsessive-compulsive disorder, the brain structures involved with the _____ response function less independently   fear
than they should. Also, the caudate nucleus, a brain structure that sends off _____ signals, is overactive. In people with this disorder who   alarm
showed improvement following treatment with _____-
     cognitive
behavioral therapy, the caudate nucleus became less overactive, and the brain structures functioned more _____ than they had before treatment.   independently

27. In general, people with psychological problems who receive psychotherapeutic treatment show _____ improvement   greater
than do those who receive none. The outcome of psychotherapy does not appear to have a one-to-one relationship with the _____   number
of sessions that a client receives.

28. Psychotherapy involves a five-stage process:
(1) the client initially _____ and lives with problems and feelings of   ignores
distress, (2) the client becomes aware of problems and feelings, (3) the client and therapist establish an _____ and set goals for the therapy,   alliance
(4) the client experiences new insights, feelings, and behaviors through the therapy experience, and (5) the client practices and consolidates what has been learned and _____ the changes. This process helps to explain   internalizes
why clients who have clear-cut problems and who are ready to change require _____ sessions than do clients whose problems are more complex   fewer
and who are less ready to change. Accordingly, clients who receive _____ treatment usually obtain the most benefit from a moderate   behavioral
number of sessions, between 8 and 14; these clients most likely have clearly identified problems and treatment _____. In comparison, clients   goals
in _____ psychotherapies often do not experience positive gains   psychodynamic
until after 12 sessions. Half of all psychotherapy clients report significant improvement after only _____ months of treatment (8 sessions).   two

29. Although often reducing symptoms and improving a person's ability to function, psychotherapy does not _____ a psychological disorder.   cure

30. In one large national survey of 22,000 randomly selected subscribers of *Consumer Reports,* researchers found that almost _____ of   one third
respondents had sought help for emotional problems in the previous three

years, and that the vast majority of them felt that psychotherapy had helped to ease their problems, improved their functioning, gave them a sense of mastery, and enhanced their personal _____.   growth

31. The therapeutic _____, the "let's work together" bond   alliance
between therapist and client, is a key ingredient in successful psychological treatments of all kinds.

32. When a therapist and client are of different cultural backgrounds, establishing the _____ alliance can be complicated. In the case of the never   therapeutic
married, 28 year-old Chinese American woman, her male Euro-American therapist mistook her _____ as a sign of her emotional immaturity   virginity
based on his own cultural norms, whereas the woman regarded it as a sign of her own _____ based on her Chinese upbringing.   virtue

33. Cultural differences can also reduce a client's perception of the therapist's empathy, as illustrated by the case involving a Euro-American therapist who _____ the home of an Ethiopian immigrant client who failed   called
to return for a second appointment. In the latter case, from his own cultural perspective, the client regarded   the therapist's action as a violation of his (i.e., the client's) _____ boundary.   marital

34. Experiences with discrimination have led some racial minority group members to feel a cultural mistrust, mistrust of people -- including therapists -- who are identifiable as members of a population that has been known to be
_____.   racist

35. Psychotherapy clients of both sexes tend to request _____   female
therapists because they feel more comfortable with them. In addition, some psychologists feel that female clients can best establish a therapeutic alliance with a female therapist because there is less of a chance that the gender-linked _____ difference between men and women will interfere with the   power
client's progress. Studies comparing the relative effectiveness of male and female therapists have almost all been correlational, and do not ensure that the therapists in the research sample did not differ in level of experience and _____   skill
as well as in gender.

E. Self-Quiz

For each of the following items, circle the letter which precedes the correct alternative.

1. Morita therapy, which is used successfully in Japan but is largely unknown in the U.S., is aimed primarily at the treatment of
    a. generalized anxiety disorders
    b. obsessive-compulsive personality disorders
    c. antisocial personality disorder
    d. self-conscious, socially ineffective individuals
    e. paranoid personality disorder

2. Electroconvulsive therapy (ECT) is used primarily in the treatment of
    a. anxiety
    b. depression
    c. obsessive-compulsive disorders
    d. schizophrenia
    e. antisocial personality disorder

3. Which of the following is not among the four major kinds of psychotropic medication?
    a. antiobsessive-compulsive agents
    b. antipsychotic medication
    c. antidepressants
    d. antimanic agents
    e. antianxiety agents

4. Typical antipsychotic medications
    a. have no known side effects
    b. have little effect on positive symptoms of schizophrenia
    c. apparently have their effect by leading to increased dopamine levels in the brain
    d. lessen hallucinations and delusions

5. Which of the following is not among the three pharmacological action categories of antidepressant medications?
    a. selective serotonin reuptake inhibitors
    b. monoamine oxidase (MAO) inhibitors
    c. dopamine action accelerators
    d. tricyclic antidepressants

6. Lithium carbonate rapidly reduces the symptoms of
    a. obsessive-compulsive disorder
    b. schizophrenia
    c. phobias
    d. bipolar disorder
    e. generalized anxiety disorders

7. Benzodiazepines are a class of psychotropic medications most widely used to treat
   a. obsessive-compulsive disorder
   b. schizophrenia
   c. mania
   d. anxiety disorders
   e. depression

8. Which of the principal approaches to psychotherapy emphasizes the importance of insight?
   a. psychodynamic approaches
   b. humanistic approaches
   c. behavioral approaches
   d. cognitive approaches

9. Which of the following approaches to psychotherapy is designed to treat abnormal behavior by bringing unconscious memories into consciousness?
   a. cognitive therapy
   b. humanistically-oriented therapy
   c. rational-emotive psychotherapy
   d. traditional psychoanalysis
   e. Gestalt therapy

10. Which of the following is not true of the psychodynamic psychotherapies in comparison to traditional psychoanalysis?
   a. they are short-term forms of psychoanalysis
   b. they involve more free association and dream analysis
   c. they focus on specific conflicts
   d. the therapist takes a relatively active role in directing the client's attention
   e. they view catharsis as providing a corrective emotional experience

11. From the standpoint of Gestalt therapy, _____ automatically restores an individual's capacity for growth.
   a. unconditional positive regard
   b. negative transference
   c. active listening
   d. awareness of immediate experience
   e. the cathartic experience

12. Which of the following is most likely to be congruent with the therapeutic objectives of a client who values collectivism over individualism?
   a. overcoming his/her own selfishness
   b. self-awareness
   c. self-fulfillment
   d. self-discovery
   e. self-actualization

13. Prescription of the drug antabuse exemplifies a(n) _____ approach to the treatment of _____.
   a. psychodynamic/anxiety
   b. humanistic/depression
   c. aversion therapy/alcoholism
   d. cognitive/bipolar disorder
   e. psychoanalytic/antisocial personality disorder

14. Rational-emotive psychotherapy involves teaching clients how to change their emotions by changing their
   a. behaviors
   b. thoughts
   c. transference orientation
   d. collective unconscious
   e. all of the above

15. The caudate nucleus was found to become less overactive in people who showed improvement following cognitive behavioral therapy aimed at the treatment of their _____ disorder.
   a. antisocial personality
   b. generalized anxiety
   c. bipolar
   d. obsessive-compulsive personality
   e. paranoid personality

16. Research has shown that the vast majority of people who have obtained psychotherapeutic services felt that psychotherapy
   a. helped to ease their problems
   b. improved their functioning
   c. gave them a sense of mastery
   d. enhanced their personal growth
   e. all of the above

17. In the example of how therapist-client differences in cultural background may complicate the establishment of a therapeutic alliance, the Euro-American male therapist regarded his 28 year-old Chinese female client's virginity as a sign of her
   a. interpersonal insecurity
   b. emotional independence
   c. emotional immaturity
   d. generalized anxiety
   e. antisocial personality

18. For fear of being misunderstood or mistreated, clients with a high level of cultural mistrust are unlikely to talk honestly with their therapists about
   a. racial issues
   b. the humiliation of discrimination and prejudice
   c. anger at racism
   d. all of the above
   e. none of the above; clients tend to talk quite openly about such matters

19. Effective reduction of a client's cultural mistrust tends to be achieved effectively when the therapist
   a. talks directly with the client about race
   b. carefully attends to the client's therapy expectations
   c. reflects on his/her own beliefs and feelings about racial issues
   d. all of the above
   e. none of the above

20. Which of the following is not one of the five stages identified as characteristic of the process of psychotherapy?
   a. client ignores and lives with problems and feelings of distress
   b. client becomes aware of problems
   c. client represses the new awareness of problems
   d. client experiences new insights through the therapy experience
   e. client practices and internalizes changes brought about by the therapy

For each of the following items, circle "T" if the statement is True, and "F" if the statement is False.

21. T F   Throughout the corresponding chapter in your text, the term "client" is used to refer to an individual in therapy, regardless of whether the person is receiving biomedical treatment or psychotherapy.

22. T F   From the standpoint of Morita therapy, meaning in life comes from work.

23. T F   From a Ndembu African cultural perspective, psychological distress is strictly a medical problem requiring re-establishment of harmony among bodily fluids.

24. T F   Lobotomy is no longer used as a form of treatment for psychological disorders.

25. T F   Psychotropic medications, such as antidepressants, tend to have positive or beneficial effects, even if taken by people without a psychological disorder.

26. T F   All the antidepressants increase norepinephrine or serotonin activity by blocking reuptake.

27. T F   In their search for the impulses and conflicts that underlie human suffering, behavioral therapists view behaviors as symbolic communications of unconscious activity.

28. T F   To increase the client's chances of experiencing catharsis, psychoanalysts take a very neutral role in the therapist-client relationship.

29. T F   Cognitive restructuring is a systematic method of replacing maladaptive thoughts with adaptive ones.

30. T F   Psychotherapy clients of both sexes tend to request female therapists.

F. Teaching-To-Learn Exercise

1. *Let Me Teach You This.*

Write in the space provided below, the five facts, ideas, etc., from this chapter that you'd most like to teach to your own student(s) if you were a teacher. Then, really do try to communicate these facts or ideas to someone in your life; or, pretend to teach this content to a hypothetical or "make-believe" student or class.

2. *Now Answer My Questions.*

Write in the space provided below, the five facts, ideas, etc., from this chapter that you'd most like to teach to your own student(s) if you were a teacher. Then, really do try to communicate these facts or ideas to someone in your life; or, pretend to teach this content to a hypothetical or "make-believe" student or class.

G. Bringing Psychology To Life Exercise

In the corresponding chapter in your textbook, you read about a number of different approaches to the treatment of psychological disorders. The purpose of this exercise is to encourage you to respond to selected aspects of this material in a personally active way.

1. With regard to Morita therapy:

     a. What is the primary value which you see as explicitly or implicitly underlying this method?

     b. Generally speaking, how practical and/or effective do you feel Morita therapy would be for people living in "mainstream" American society? Explain briefly.

     c. Are there identifiable subgroups within American society for whom you believe Morita therapy might be particularly effective? Explain briefly.

2. Considerable attention is devoted in the corresponding chapter in your textbook, to personal values, acquired within cultural and subcultural contexts, as they may impact on the effectiveness of any approach to   psychotherapy. In this regard, what do you think a psychotherapist should know about your values on each of the following dimensions, as they have evolved within the cultural and subcultural contexts in which you developed and currently live, before s/he could help you with some kind of psychological problem? In other words, briefly stated, what do you think your therapist should know about the "value place" of each of the following in your life? (Note. Again, as with all such exercises here, if your answers to these questions are to be

431

submitted to your instructor as part of a course assignment, please do not divulge any information which you feel to be so private and personal that you choose not to disclose it.)

    a. <u>The</u> <u>Family.</u>

    b. <u>Religion.</u>

    c. <u>Education.</u>

    d. <u>Money</u> <u>And</u> <u>What</u> <u>You</u> <u>Can</u> <u>Buy</u> <u>With</u> <u>It.</u>

e. Close Relationships With People Outside Of The Family.

f. The Image Of Yourself That You Want To Communicate To People.

3. Ultimately, each of us is responsible for our own life. However, not unlike what may happen in availing oneself of other kinds of professional services, the inclination is often to abandon that responsibility all-too-completely to the helping person when seeking help from a clinical practitioner. In this regard, imagine that you are being treated by a professional therapist for some sort of psychological problem. What question(s) would you most want that person to answer for you in each of the following circumstances?

a. You have just completed your first session with the therapist.

b. The therapist has prescribed a drug for you to take as part of your treatment.

c. You've been in treatment for many weeks, and still don't feel that there's been any noticeable improvement in the condition or problem which is the objective of treatment.

Answer Key To Self-Quiz

1.   d
2.   b
3.   a
4.   d
5.   c
6.   d
7.   d
8.   a
9.   d
10.   b
11.   d
12.   a
13.   c
14.   b
15.   d
16.   e
17.   c
18.   d
19.   d
20.   c
21.   F
22.   T
23.   F
24.   T
25.   F
26.   T
27.   F
28.   T
29.   T
30.   T

CHAPTER 16

Social Psychology

A. Learning Objectives

After your reading and careful, effective study of Chapter 16, you should:

1. Have a working knowledge of the way in which interpersonal relationships reflect underlying cognitive processes as follows:
    a. The concept of attitude as it is used in the study of social psychology, and the various components of attitudes;
        (1) What kinds of attitudes tend to predict our behaviors, and why attitudes may fail to predict our behaviors.;
        (2) The learning principles in terms of which social psychologists conceptualize the way attitudes are formed;
        (3) What persuasion is, and the ways in which it can cause us to change our attitudes, with special attention to:
            (a) The characteristics of a persuasive communicator;
            (b) The characteristics of a persuasive message;
            (c) How a listener's mood, knowledge, and thinking can affect his/her persuasibility; and
            (d) Cognitive dissonance, how it may be relevant to changes in attitudes or behaviors, and how its relevance to such matters may be limited by cultural factors;
    b. The processes involved in the way in which we form impressions of others and they form impressions of us, focusing on:
        (1) The two kinds of attributions involved in our attempts to explain or make sense out of the behaviors of others;
        (2) How our impressions of others may reflect our own selective perceptions and personal perspectives;
        (3) How some attributional tendencies, such as the fundamental attribution error and temporal extension, may reflect and be influenced by cultural value orientation;
        (4) How certain attributional tendencies such as egocentric biases and and a belief in a "just world," may serve a kind of "self-protective" function;
        (5) How our own, implicit theories of personality may operate to influence the impressions we form of others, by "plugging the gaps" of information we may have about people or situations;
        (6) How our judgments of people tend to develop out of the process by which we categorize them;
        (7) How category-driven impressions may be unrealistically oversimplified, reflecting ignorance of, or failure to acknowledge individual differences among members of any given group;
        (8) How the development of stereotypes and prejudices may be

explained in terms of the way people are socialized, competition among people for limited resources (such as jobs), and/or rationalization of social and economic inequalities; and

(9) How the persistence of stereotypes and prejudices may be explained by our selective perception and memory of information that supports the stereotypes, and a failure to change our thinking when confronted with information that contradicts our stereotypes and/or prejudices.

2. Have a working knowledge of the social psychology of people's attraction to one another, as follows:

a. How our liking of others is affected by factors such as how close they live to us, their similarity to us in temperament, communication style, attitudes, and values, as well as their physical attractiveness;

b. What social psychologists have learned about the perception of and response to a person's physical attractiveness, including:

(1) The personal characteristics which tend to be regarded as attractive such as sex-associated body shapes, physical symmetry, and facial configuration;

(2) Cultural factors involved in the perception of human physical attractiveness; and

(3) Differences between men and women in their concern with physical attractiveness as compared with the socioeconomic security of potential mates, and how such differences may be explained in terms of either innate dispositions or learning;

c. The social psychology of love, focusing on:

(1) The distinguishing characteristics of what social scientists refer to as "passionate" and "companionate" forms of love; and

(2) The way Sternberg's triangular theory provides a model for understanding the types of love that result from different combinations of passionate love, intimacy, and commitment.

3. Have a working knowledge of the psychology of social influence, with regard to:

a. Altruistic behaviors, focusing on:

(1) Consideration of genetic components of such behaviors;

(2) The factors which seem to be associated with the occurrence of such behaviors, including the clear need for someone to help, feelings of empathy on the part of the person who helps, helpfulness as a personality characteristic, confidence in one's ability to help, and the number of bystanders available to help;

(3) Research findings with regard to gender differences in altruistic behaviors, and how the indications of such differences may be interpreted as a methodological artifact of congruence-incongruence with male and female gender roles in the helping situations represented in such research; and

(4) How a person's state of mind can influence his/her acting out of helping behaviors.

b. Conformity, with special attention to:
- (1) Situational factors associated with the inclination to "go along with" the group; and
- (2) The relevance of social roles or social position to conformity;

c. Obedience to authority, especially in cases with regard to the factors associated with an individual's likelihood of obeying demands from an authority figure to do harm to others; and

d. How an individual's likelihood of compliance to a request to do something, even when no reward or punishment is involved, can be manipulated by the so-called "foot-in-the-door" and "door-in-the-face" approaches.

4. Develop a working familiarity with the following fundamentals of the social psychology of group processes:
- a. The enhancement of effort expenditure by an individual in what is called "social facilitation" and the factors associated with that phenomenon;
- b. Some alternative explanations for reduced effort by an individual in a group in what is called "social loafing;
- c. The way decisions are made in a group, focusing on:
  - (1) What "polarization" is, how it occurs, and how it leads to a tendency for group decisions to be more extreme than decisions made by individuals;
  - (2) The particular type of polarization known as "groupthink," and how it can lead to irresponsible decisions when individuals sacrifice their own independence in a situation of false consensus;
  - (3) What it takes for numerical minorities to sway a majority in group decision making;
  - (4) The relevance of cultural value orientation in the consideration of group processes.

B. Preview/Review Outline Of Key Terms And Concepts

Before you read the corresponding chapter in your text, read over the following outline. It is designed to give you an overview of information presented in the chapter, and how the various elements of that information are related to each other. After reading through the whole chapter and/or before course exams, you may use this outline as a quick review guide. In your reviews, mask off one line of the outline at a time, and try to recite from your memory of the chapter, the information that you expect to appear on the next line or so.

In going over this outline as a preview before reading and studying the chapter, the questions posed in bold print will help to keep you focused on the learning objectives here, and keep you actively involved in the process of achieving those objectives. When using this section as a review, try to answer the questions. Refer back to the chapter in the text for a more detailed feedback check on your mastery of the material, and/or to strengthen your knowledge and understanding wherever you feel the need to do so.

What was the verdict of the Simi Valley jury in the case against the white Los Angeles police officers whose beating of black motorist Rodney King was videotaped by a bystander? How

were individual differences in their social behavior displayed by African Americans in Los Angeles following that enormously controversial verdict?

I. Social Cognition: Attitudes, Impressions, and Attributions

What is the term used by social psychologists to refer to the cognitive processes underlying social behavior?

    A. Attitudes

What are the three components of an "attitude" as the latter term is used in the study of social psychology?

       1. Attitudes and Behaviors
          a. Attitudes And Prediction Of Behavior
          b. Attitudes That Do And Do Not Predict Behavior
       2. Attitude Formation
          a. And Unconditioned Responses
          b. Generalization To Other Stimuli
       3. Attitude Change Following Persuasion
          a. Deliberate Attempts To Influence Attitudes Or Behaviors
          b. Direct And Indirect Persuasion
          c. The Elements Of Successful Persuasion

What are the three general categories of factors which, in combination, tend to determine the effectiveness or success of attempts at persuasion? How does a listener's or an audience's (a) liking of a speaker, and (b) perceptions of his/her honesty and expertise tend to affect that speaker's persuasiveness?

            (1) Numerous Logical And Strong Arguments
            (2) Two-Sided Rather than One-Sided Message
            (3) Targeting Of Issues That Listeners Care About
            (4) Appealing To An Audience's Emotions
            (5) Direct Points Ending With Clear Conclusion
         d. Importance Of Listener Characteristics
            (1) Messages And Listener's Self-Concept
            (2) Relevance Of Listener's Mood
         e. How To Avoid Being Persuaded: Some Common Persuasive Strategies (Box 16.1)
            (1) Pre-giving
            (2) Aversive Stimulation
            (3) Debt
            (4) Positive Self-Feeling
            (5) Negative Self-Feeling
            (6) Altercasting
            (7) Negative Altercasting

Try to think of an example of each of the seven common persuasive strategies that you've encountered in your own "real life" experience?

4. Attitude Change Following a Change in Behavior
   a. Festinger's Concept of Cognitive Dissonance
   b. Limited Cultural Relevance of Cognitive Dissonance
      (1) Assumed Need For Consistency Between Attitude And Action
      (2) As Applied To Individualist vs. Collectivist Cultures
      (3) Heine & Lehman's Study
         (a) Canadian And Japanese Respondents
         (b) Market Research Paradigm
         (c) Paying Respondents With Their 5th & 6th Ranked CD Choices
         (d) Dissonance Response In Re-Ratings Shown By Canadians, But Not Japanese Respondents

How do the results of Heine & Lehman's study indicate the cultural-contextual limitations of Festinger's theory of cognitive dissonance?

B. Forming Impressions of People

What do social psychologists mean by the term "attribution"? What is a "dispositional attribution"? In what sense do our attributions tend to be "automatic"?

Why do different people tend to interpret behavior differently?

What is the fundamental attribution error? As noted in your text, what is there about American culture that may enhance the inclination toward fundamental attribution error?

What is temporal extension, and what does it have to do with the impressions we form of people? What is "egocentric bias" and how have you seen it operate in at least one situation in your own life?

How might you explain the tendency for weaker inclinations toward fundamental attribution error in collectivist as compared to individualist cultures?

1. Forming Impressions that Protect Ourselves
   a. Defensive Elements In Our Schema
   b. The Just World Hypothesis
      (1) Decreased Sense Of Vulnerability To Bad Events
      (2) And Incorrect Attributions

How might the just world hypothesis affect the perception of a rape victim by people who hear about the rape? How might the just world hypothesis affect the rape victim's own attributions concerning the rape s/he experienced? Erroneous as the latter attribution may be, how might it provide a kind of comfort to the rape victim?

2. Personal Theories about Personality
   a. Implicit Personality Theory
   b. Filling Gaps In Our Information About Others
   c. And Interpretation Of Ambiguous Behaviors
   d. Influence On Our Perceptions Is Largely Unconscious
3. Judging People by the Category They Fit in
   a. Categorization
   b. Transference
   c. Functional Inference
   d. Halo Effect

Give at least one example of how functional inferences and halo effects may lead to false impressions of people?

4. Stereotypic Overgeneralizations
   a. Categorizing People In Terms Of Ethnicity, Gender, Etc.
   b. Simplified Perceptions Of People
   c. Perceptions Of In-Group Members As Unique, Out-Group Members As Similar
   d. Factors Contributing To Stereotype Formation
      (1) Ignorance
      (2) Socialization
      (3) Competition Over Limited Resources
      (4) Rationalization Of Inequalities

What is xenophobia and what is the explanation offered in your text for why less educated, working class Euro-Americans tend to be more prejudiced than Euro-Americans of higher socioeconomic classes?

5. The Persistence of Prejudice and Stereotypes
   a. Regarding People Who Don't Fit Stereotype As Unusual
   b. Confirmation Bias
      (1) Selective Noticing, Interpreting, And Remembering
      (2) Men With Sexist Stereotypes
   c. Dispositional Attributions Of Confirmatory Behaviors
   d. Situational Attributions Of Contradictory Behaviors
   e. Perception Of People Affects Our Behavior Toward Them
   f. Subtle Effects Of Stereotypes: Steele & Aronson's Research
      a. Intellectually Challenging Test Administered To African- and Euro-American Students
      b. Fill-In-The-Blank Test Before Difficult Test
      c. Experimental Condition And Accessibility Of Stereotypes

Under what experimental circumstances did the African- and Euro-American student participants in the Steele & Aronson study perform equally well on an intellectually challenging test? Under what experimental circumstances did the African-American participants do worse on this test than the Euro-American students? How do the results of the aspect of this research involving the fill-in-the-blank test help to explain the observed performance difference between the two groups of participants?

II. Social Relations: Interpersonal Attraction and Love

"Interpersonal attraction" is a technical term which refers to what familiar aspect of everyday life in our relationships with other people?

    A. Liking Others
        1. Liking People Who are Nearby
            a. Geographic Proximity
            b. Mere Exposure Effect
            c. Endogamy
            d. Alternative Perspectives On Intermarriage (Box 16.2)
                (1) Historically, Intense Social Disapproval As Barrier
                (2) "Outsider" Seen As Threat
                (3) Intermarriage As Reducing Pool Of Eligible Mates
                (4) Parental Opposition
                (5) Condemnation Has Shaped Popular Speculations
                    (a) "Jungle Fever"
                    (b) "Yellow Fever"
                (6) Scholarly Attribution Of Ulterior Motives
                (7) Compatibility And Shared Interests, Values, Ideas

What do you regard as the most reasonable of the traditional cultural oppositions to intermarriage? What do you regard as the most unreasonable or even outrageous views concerning intermarriage?

        2. Liking People Who are Similar to Ourselves
            a. Similarity Positively Correlated With Attraction
            b. Similarity In Personal Characteristics
            c. Factors Underlying Similarity-Attraction Correlation
                (1) Familiarity Associated With Ease And Comfort
                (2) Intrinsic Rewards
                    (a) Positive Reinforcement
                    (b) Extrinsic Reinforcement
             d. Little Evidence That Opposites Attract

What kind of extrinsic reinforcement might accrue to attraction toward people who are similar to ourselves?

        3. Liking People Who are Physically Attractive
            a. Beauty In The Eye Of The Beholder

b. Some Physical Features Seen As Attractive Across Cultures And Ethnic Groups
    (1) And Attribution Of Health And Reproductive Ability
    (2) International Presence Of Euro-American Beauty Ideals
c. Physical Attractiveness Unimportant Between Close Friends

What are some of the physical features which are seen as attractive across cultures and ethnic groups?

4. Gender Perspectives on Interpersonal Attraction
    a. Women Attract With Beauty, Men With Socioeconomic Security
        (1) Men Care More About Physical Attractiveness
        (2) Women Care More About Socioeconomic Status
    b. Socialization Perspective
        (1) Repeated Exposure To Parental, Peer, Media Influence
        (2) Social Exchange Theory
    c. Biological Perspective: Attraction And Survival Of Offspring
        (1) For Women, Economic Support
        (2) For Men, Reproductive Capability

How does the social exchange theory apply to attempts to explain how people attract their mates?

From the standpoint of the biological perspective, what explanation is offered for the established findings with regard to differences between men and women in the extent to which they apparently regard physical attractiveness as compared with socioeconomic status as an important factor in mate selection?

B. Loving Another
  1. Passionate Love
    a. Thoughts, Feelings, Physiological Arousal, Longing, Desire
    b. Can Motivate Behaviors Uncharacteristic Of Individual
    c. Involves More Than Sexual Lust
    d. Tends To Diminish Over Time
  2. Companionate Love
    a. Feelings Of Affection And Caring
        (1) People's Lives Deeply Connected
        (2) Grows From Mutual Sharing Of Personal Thoughts
    b. Companionate Without Passionate Love
  3. The Triangular Theory of Love
    a. Identifies Three Components Of Love
        (1) Passion
        (2) Intimacy
        (3) Commitment
    b. Different Patterns Of Love
        (1) Intimacy Alone
        (2) Passion Alone

        (3) Commitment Alone

        (4) Romantic Love

        (5) Companionate Love

        (6) Fatuous Love

        (7) Balanced Love

From the standpoint of Sternberg's triangular theory, what is "consummate love"?

III. Social Influence: Helping, Conforming, Obeying, and Complying

What are social norms and how do they tend to influence the way people relate to each other?

  A. Altruism: Helping Others

    1. Prosocial Behavior

    2. Genetic Predisposition View

    3. Factors Identified In Social Psychological Research

      a. Perception Of Clear Need For Help

      b. Feeling Of Empathy For Persons In Need Of Help

      c. Helpfulness As Personality Characteristic

      d. Sense Of Interdependence With Others

      e. Feeling Of Competence To Help

      f. Number Of Bystanders

        (1) Diffusion Of Responsibility

        (2) Bystander Effect

    2. A Critical Analysis of Gender Perspectives on Helping

      a. Males Found To Help More Than Females In Research Studies

      b. Operational Definitions Of Helping Biased

      c. Short-Term, Potentially Dangerous Encounters With A Stranger

        (1) More Congruent With U. S. Male Gender Role

        (2) Emotional Nurturance And U. S. Female Gender Role

      d. Gender Differences In Long-Term Relationships

      e. Gender Differences And Traditional Sex-Typing

      f. When Situation Doesn't Involve Traditionally Male Behavior

    3. A Biased Frame of Mind

      a. Study At Princeton Theological Seminary

      b. Students Sent To Record Their Sermons At Nearby Building

      c. Students Encountered Man Needing Help

      d. Differences In Helping Behavior And Students' Frame Of Mind

What was the experimental ruse used to manipulate students' frame of mind in the Princeton Theological Seminary experiment? How did the results of this experiment support the view that helping behavior may depend on the prospective helper's frame of mind?

  B. Conforming to Group Norms and Social Roles

    1. Going Along with the Group

      a. Solomon Asch's Classic Experiments

      b. Subjects Required To Judge Length Of Lines

445

      c. Judgments Of One Third Of Subjects Affected By Flawed Norm
   2. Research Using Experimental Set-Ups Other Than Asch's
      a. Group Size And Apparent Expertise Of Group Members
      b. Small To Moderate Gender Differences
         (1) Females More Likely To Conform
         (2) U. S. Gender Roles And Conformity
   2. Basing Behaviors on Social Position
      a. Zimbardo's "Jail" Simulation Study
         (1) Volunteers Randomly Assigned Role Of Guard, Prisoner
         (2) Experiment Stopped After Six Days
         (3) Many "Guards" Became Tyrannical
      b. Assigned Roles And Conformity In Everyday Life
         (1) Nonconformity To Traditional Gender Roles
         (2) Role Of Audience Assigned To Racial Minorities

How might assignment of members of racial minority groups to the role of audience rather than participant in a group's activities affect the way such people are perceived?

  C. Obeying Authority
   1. Obeying Orders to Harm
      a. Why Do People, As Did Nazis, Obey Orders To Harm Others?
      b. Milgram's Classic Study
         (1) Real Subjects Assigned Role Of Teacher
         (2) Role Of Learner Played By Experimental Confederate
         (3) Subject Told To Shock Learner For Incorrect Responses
         (4) Most Subjects "Shocked" Learner To Maximum Levels

What made the subjects' shock delivery behavior appear so cruel and insensitive to the pain and possible injury they were inflicting upon the individual they were instructed to believe was a "learner" in the Milgram experiment? What was there about the subjects in this experiment that made these results so disturbing to psychologists?

   2. When and Why People Obey
      a. Cross-Cultural Research Using Milgram's Method
      b. Obedience To Orders To Harm Given By Authority Figures
         In A Variety Of Cultures
      c. Factors Affecting Obedience Across Cultures And Gender
         (1) Subjects Removed From Process Of Harming
         (2) Experimenter And Subjects In Physical Proximity
         (3) Order-Giver Perceived As Having High Status
         (4) Others Involved In Administering Shocks
         (5) No Social Support For Disobeying Orders
         (6) Refusal Of One Person Can Have Ripple Effect
         (7) Nothing Victim Said Affects Obedience To Orders
         (8) Personality, Likelihood And Perception Of Obedience

What particular personality dimension has been found to be associated with individual differences in both the likelihood of obeying an authority figure, and the perception of obedient people's responsibility for carrying out orders to harm people?

      D. Complying with Requests

Generally speaking, what kinds of expectations do we tend to have regarding strangers' compliance with our requests? Can you give a concrete example or two of such expectations?

           1. The Foot-in-the-Door Approach
              a. Large Request Followed By Smaller One
              b. Classic Example Of Research
                  (1) Subjects Requested To Put Up Large, Ugly Lawn Sign
                  (2) Compliance Greater After Compliance For Small Sign
                  (3) Results Explained In Terms Of Cognitive Accessibility

Apart from an availability heuristic explanation, how might the results of the foot-in-door study be explained in terms of the subjects' feeling of involvement with the person making the request?

           2. The Door-in-the-Face Approach
              a. Outrageous Request Followed By Smaller, Sincere One
              b. Researchers Ask People At Mall To Hand Out Flyers
              c. Based On Principle Of Give-And-Take

How may the effectiveness of the door-in-the-face method be explained in terms of people's everyday life expectations with regard to compromise and reciprocity in interpersonal negotiations?

IV. Group Processes: Individual Effort and Group Decisions

      A. Social Facilitation: Working Hard in the Presence of Others
           1. Increase Of Individual Effort In Presence Of Others
              a. As Observed In Bicyclists
              b. As Observed In Children Winding Fishing Reels
           2. In Everyday Life
              a. Juvenile Criminal Behavior
              b. Making Remarks Against Racism
           3. Presence Of Others And Diminished Individual Performance
           4. Contradictory Findings Explained In Terms Of Arousal

Using the arousal rationale, under what circumstances should the presence of an audience either facilitate or interfere with an individual's performance?

      B. Social Loafing: Slacking Off on a Group Effort
           1. Working Less Than Usual When Individual Contributions Unnoticed
           2. As Self Protection From Other Loafers

3. Deindividuation: Diffusion Of Responsibility Combined With Arousal
C. Decision Making as a Group
  1. Making Extreme Decisions as a Group
    a. Group Polarization
    b. Risky Shift
    c. Cautious Shift
    d. Processes Contributing To Polarization
      (1) Hearing One's Own Arguments Repeated
      (2) Learning Additional Arguments For One's Position
      (3) Shifting Opinion In Direction Of Consensus
  2. Making Decisions Based on False Consensus: Groupthink
    a. A Specific Type Of Polarization In A Cohesive Group
    b. Helps Preserve Self-Esteem And Morale
    c. Offers Members A False Sense Of Security

What are some of the "symptoms" of groupthink? As a leader or even a member of a cohesive group given responsibility for making a decision, what might you do to help prevent groupthink?

  3. Numerical Minorities Influencing Group Decisions
    a. One Person's Refusal Gives Others Courage To Disobey
    b. Importance Of Making A Strong Argument

How can a numerical minority convey strength to the rest of the group?

  4. Cross-Cultural Perspectives on Influencing Group Decisions
    a. Collectivist Cultures Tend To Prize Group Harmony, Consensus
      (1) Avoidance Of Disruption Of Group
      (2) Movement Of Majority Toward Minority Opinion (Japan)
    b. Influence Attempted Through Means Other Than Influence
      In Collectivist Cultures

How might minority members in a Japanese group gain influence without repeating a dissenting view?

C. Self-Generated Questions: What's In This One For Me?

Most people come to the first course in psychology expecting to learn some things which will help them to better understand themselves, other people in their lives, and/or the nature of life in the world in which they live. Along these same lines, students of psychology often look forward to discovering things about human behavior and experience which may help them to improve their own life by developing their talents, technical skills, knowledge and abilities, and/or the quality or their relationships with other people. On the basis of such self-interest, which tends to provide a framework in terms of which new learning becomes personally meaningful and thus easier to remember, write down a few questions in the space below, about the subject matter covered in this chapter. After reading and studying the chapter, come back to see how any of what you've learned may be useful to you in finding answers to these questions.

D. Completion Items

The words in the margins of this exercise are the ones that correctly complete the sentence on the corresponding line. To get the most out of this exercise, you should try to avoid looking at these words in the margin until after you've filled in the corresponding blanks with the words you think best complete the sentences. So, begin the exercise by covering up all of the margin words with a piece of paper. Then, for each blank, write in the word which you think completes the sentence. Even if you're not sure as to the word, write in your best guess, preferably in pencil so you can erase and re-write any incorrect responses you may make here.

After writing in your "answer," slide the paper covering up the margin words down just far enough to see the word for the blank you just filled-in. For each blank that you fill-in correctly, put a check mark (√) after your answer. If the word you wrote in doesn't match the word corresponding to that blank, mark an (X) next to your response and go on to the next blank. It's probably a good idea to go back to the text and try to strengthen your learning related to topic coverage that corresponds in the textbook chapter to those blanks which you filled-in incorrectly, since those items signal a weak link in your concept mastery chain for this chapter.

1. After seeing a _____ of several white Los Angeles policemen   videotape
beating black motorist Rodney King in 1991, a Simi Valley, California jury decided
that the police were not guilty of using excessive force. In the aftermath of this
verdict, violence, arson, and _____ spread throughout Los Angeles.   looting

2. Social psychology is the study of how we think about and _____   relate
to others, and how our behaviors, feelings, and thoughts are influenced by others.
The cognitive processes underlying social behavior are referred to as
_____ cognition.   social

3. An attitude is a _____ predisposition to act toward or react to   learned
people or situations in positive or negative ways. Attitudes include enduring
thoughts, _____, and behavioral tendencies that guide us as we   feelings
interact with people and situations. Attitudes that can predict behavior tend to be
cognitively _____, long-standing attitudes that we feel are correct,   accessible
have acquired from personal experience, and have thought through carefully.

4. Some attitudes develop as unconditioned responses to unconditioned stimuli. Once established, an attitude can then _____ to other stimuli, and operant conditioning can help to reinforce it. As one observes others, _____ learning can then solidify an attitude.

generalize

social

5. _____ persuasion involves a listener's deliberate analysis of evidence for and against an idea. Attitude change can also occur indirectly, without conscious, effortful thinking about the evidence related to an attitude, when the person receiving the persuasive message uses mental shortcuts, or _____, to decide whether to change his/her attitude. A speaker who seems honest and knowledgeable about the topic about which s/he communicates is more likely to be persuasive than others because listeners feel that the message is _____.

Direct

heuristics

credible

6. Persuasive messages typically have the following characteristics. Persuasive messages present numerous _____ and strong arguments. Persuasive messages present two-sided arguments. Two-sided arguments tell the listener that the speaker is aware of both sides of an issue and is not _____ in his/her views. Persuasive messages target issues that listeners care about, and appeal to an audience's _____, perhaps even by provoking moderate levels of fear. Persuasive messages make direct points and end with a clear _____ rather than with indirect or implied arguments.

logical

biased

emotions

conclusion

7. Attitudes that are related to one's self-_____ are less likely to be influenced by persuasion than are other attitudes. A good mood can also affect our persuasibility. Being happy tends to increase our persuasibility because it decreases our efforts to _____ systematically about the arguments of a persuasive message. When people feel good, they selectively attend to the arguments of a message that _____ their good mood, do not notice the points that might spoil it.

concept

think

reinforce

8. In order to avoid being persuaded, it can be helpful to be aware of the following persuasive strategies. In _____, the persuader gives a reward before making a persuasive appeal. With aversive stimulation, the persuader continuously _____ you until you agree. In another common persuasive strategy, the persuader reminds you of old debts you owe to him/her. With the strategy of _____ self-feeling, the persuader suggests that you will feel better about yourself if you agree. With altercasting, the persuader suggests that a person with "_____" qualities would agree, or negative altercasting, implies that only someone with bad qualities would disagree.

pre-giving

punishes

positive

good

9. Cognitive _____ is the idea that people feel uncomfortable tension when their behaviors are inconsistent with their attitudes. Because this concept assumes a person's need for _____ between attitude and behavior, it might have limited relevance across cultures. This need is relevant in individualist cultures wherein people receive a great deal

dissonance

consistency

of self-esteem from having a stable set of personal _____ and   traits
attitudes. But collectivists tend to have a more _____ sense of   interdependent
self which leads them to behave in ways that fulfill situational demands and
social obligations, even if the behavior goes against their _____   personal
attitudes. In at least one study relevant to this issue, in which Canadian and
Japanese subjects were asked to rate and rank the desirability of popular CDs,
the results indicated that the Japanese subjects did not experience the kind
of cognitive dissonance that requires relief when they behave in ways that
_____ from their attitude.   differ

10. Social _____ or impression formation is the process of forming   perception
impressions of people or social situations. When we form impressions, we try to
explain behaviors or events by making _____, identifying   attributions
characteristics of people of situations. When we try to explain behavior in terms
of someone's personality, desires, or needs, we are making _____   dispositional
attributions. In contrast, when we explain behavior in terms of circumstances, we
are making _____ attributions. We interpret behavior differently   situational
because we each perceive and construct interpretations _____, in   selectively
ways that reflect our own values, perspectives, attitudes, defenses, etc.

11. Social psychologists use the term _____ attribution error to refer   fundamental
to the tendency to account for other people's behavior in terms of what we assume
to be their stable personality characteristics rather than the
_____ they face. In individualist cultures, the tendency to assume   situations
that the way a person behaves on limited occasions indicates a personality
characteristic of that individual is known is known as _____   temporal
extension. The tendency to overestimate the degree to which others feel, think,
and behave as does oneself, is known as _____ bias. Instead of   egocentric
making dispositional attributions, people in _____ cultures often   collectivist
make situational attributions because they see themselves as behaving in ways that
promote harmonious social relationships.

12. The _____ world hypothesis is a belief that bad events   just
happen to bad people and good events and situations happen to good people.
This belief tends to operate defensively to decrease an individual's feeling of
_____ to bad events happening to him/herself.   vulnerability

13. When we form impressions of people, we often rely on a particular schema,
known as our _____ personality theory, which is based on our own   implicit
defenses, personal experiences, and culture, consisting of our ideas about what
_____ generally occur in which people.   traits

14. One manifestation of categorization in our perceptions of people is
_____, the usually unconscious attribution of characteristics to
        transference
someone we meet because that person reminds us of someone else with
those characteristics. A specific form of such attribution is _____   functional

451

inference, drawing conclusions about people's personality based on their physical characteristics. The _____ effect, is the simplifying assumption that a person who has one positive characteristic has other such characteristics as well.

halo

15. When one assumes that everyone in a particular social group shares certain characteristics, that categorization of members of the social group becomes a _____. The major factors contributing to the formation of stereotypes include, _____ of differences within groups, socialization, competition over limited resources, and rationalization of inequalities among people. _____ is a mistrust or hatred of foreigners. The tendency to selectively notice, interpret and remember information which confirms our existing beliefs, known as the confirmation _____, is a major factor contributing to the persistence of stereotypes and prejudices. When people learn that a person has behaved in ways consistent with their expectations, they tend to make _____ attributions. But when the person has behaved in a way inconsistent with their expectations, there is a tendency to use _____ attributions. Together, the results of the studies by Steele and Aronson suggest that concepts associated with stereotypes about African Americans become accessible to African American students faced with a test that has been identified as a test of _____.

stereotype
ignorance

Xenophobia

bias

dispositional
situational

ability

16. One factor which helps to account for the importance of geographic _____ in interpersonal attraction, that is, the tendency for people to be friends with and marry those who live near them, is the mere _____ effect, by which a stimulus becomes familiar after we encounter it repeatedly. Another explanation for the proximity effect is related to _____, the practice of marrying within one's own group.

proximity

exposure

endogamy

17. Historically, intense social _____ was a primary barrier to intermarriage. Racial intermarriage was illegal throughout the United States for decades, and it was not until _____ that the United States Supreme Court ruled as unconstitutional the legal ban against it. Some people feel that inclusion of an "outsider" through marriage _____ their customs and views on life. Some people oppose intermarriage because they think it reduces the pool of eligible _____ within their own group. Many parents oppose intermarriage out of concern that the couple will face social _____ and discrimination. The notion of "jungle fever" perpetuates the myth that Euro-American women seek out and prefer African American men because African American men are _____ over-endowed. Similarly, the idea of "yellow fever, " or "_____ syndrome," suggests that men of various races marry Asian or Asian American women to have an exotic, man-pleasing wife. Most intermarriages occur between people of similar _____ backgrounds.

disapproval

1967

threatens

mates

stigma

sexually
shogun

socioeconomic

18. Several factors underlie the tendency for similarity in _____

personal

452

characteristics, such as temperament, communication style, attitudes, and values, to be associated with feelings of _____. To begin with, people who seem similar to ourselves appear familiar, and familiarity can increase our sense of ease and _____ around a person. Also, people tend to experience _____ rewards when they are with people who are similar to themselves. That is, they positively _____ each other's attitudes, values, and behaviors. In addition, people sometimes receive extrinsic reinforcement for their association with people similar to themselves, with that reinforcement derived from social _____. Contrary to popular belief, their is little evidence that _____ types of people tend to attract each other.

attraction

comfort
intrinsic
reinforce

approval
opposite

19. Most people find a _____ figure attractive on a female but not on a male. Bodies with _____ features, such as similarly sized and shaped eyes, eyebrows, breasts, and hands, are considered more attractive than bodies with asymmetrical features. People may innately find these particular features to be attractive because they serve as rough indicators of health and _____ ability. An alternative explanation for cross-cultural similarities in standards of beauty is that they result from the international presence of _____ beauty ideals.

curvy
symmetrical

reproductive

Euro-American

20. Across different ages, races, and cultures, women tend to attract mates with their _____, and men, with their socioeconomic security. This is partly because men care more about a mate's _____ attractiveness than her personal qualities, while women care more about a man's socioeconomic status. Social _____ theory tells us that people seek relationships in exchange order to achieve valued goods, such as social status or economic security. From the biological perspective, people are attracted to a mate who is likely to increase the chances of _____ for their offspring.

beauty
physical

survival

21. People experiencing _____ love are absorbed in thoughts about a loved one, feel intensely attracted to that person, and do whatever they can to show their feelings. This kind of love tends to dwindle over time because the fantasies and _____ that fuel it tend to diminish.

passionate

arousal

22. _____ love involves feelings of affection and caring between people whose lives are deeply connected, and features intimacy and commitment prominently.

Companionate

23. The three components of love according to Sternberg's triangular theory are:
(a) _____, which consists of feelings of sexual and physical attraction; intimacy, which involves the kind of emotional bonding that occurs in companionate love; and _____, which includes both short- and long-term obligations to the relationship. From this point of view, _____ love, the kind that grows and endures, results from a balanced combination of the three basic components of love.

passion

commitment
consummate

24. Social _____ are the standards of accepted and expected behavior established by groups.

norms

25. Altruism, which is helpful, unselfish behavior, is a often described as _____ as opposed to antisocial behavior. Other than genetic predisposition, research has shown that persons who are most likely to help: (a) perceive a clear _____ for help; (b) feel empathy for the persons needing help; (c) have personalities characterized by a desire to be helpful; (d) see their relationship with other people as one of interdependence; (e) feel _____ to help; and (f) are the lone bystander to an emergency rather than part of a _____ of bystanders. When other people are present, individuals tend to experience a diffusion of _____ and assume that someone else will get or provide help, resulting in what is known as the _____ effect.

prosocial

need

competent
group

responsibility
bystander

26. The majority of studies of gender differences in _____ behavior have found that males help more often than females. Critical analyses of this apparent gender difference, has focused on the fact that the kinds of helping behaviors studied have generally been more consistent with the U. S. male gender _____, namely, situations requiring a short-term, potentially dangerous encounter with a _____, such as a hitchhiker or a person with a flat tire. Research has shown that when the needed help doesn't involve such _____, gender differences in altruistic behavior are reduced or even disappear.

altruistic

role
stranger

risks

27. The importance of a person's frame of _____ as a factor affecting the willingness to help is illustrated by the results of a study with Princeton Theological Seminary students on their way to record their sermons. Those students who encountered a man in need of help were more likely to help him when they were not in a _____.

mind

hurry

28. In Solomon Asch's classic experiments on _____, subjects were given the task of identifying out loud which of three lines matched the length of a fourth line while among a group of others assigned the same task. Although most of the real subjects gave non-conformist answers, one third of them conformed to a flawed norm established by _____ of the experimenter who identified the wrong line as the matching line.

conformity

confederates

29. In Zimbardo's famous "_____" simulation study, college student volunteers were randomly assigned to the play the roles of prisoners and guards. Many of the guards became _____, degrading prisoners and unnecessarily forcing them to deal with social isolation or to do push-ups, reflecting the way these individuals _____ the social roles they were assigned to play.

jail

tyrannical

interpreted

30. In Milgram's study of _____, two people, one a confederate

obedience

454

in the experiment, were told they were going to be in a learning study. The real
subject was cast in the role of "_____" and the confederate in the   teacher
role of "learner." The subject was instructed to deliver what he was lead to believe
were increasingly intense levels of _____ electric shock to the   painful
learner, by means of a panel of switches that supposedly but not actually controlled
such stimulation, each time the learner gave an _____ response.   incorrect
Despite the learner's pleading that he couldn't stand the pain as the shock levels
increased, and protesting that he had a _____ condition and then   heart
making no noise and giving no answers after 350 volts, 62.3% of the subjects
continued to deliver shocks, including the _____ 450 volts.   maximum

31. Milgram and others have found that across cultures and gender, participants
are more likely to obey the orders of an _____ figure to hurt others   authority
when: (a) the subjects are _____ from the process of harming;   removed
(b) the experimenter and subjects are physically _____ to each other;   close
(c) the person giving the orders is perceived as having high _____;   status
(d) other people are also involved in administering the shocks; and (e) there is
no social _____ for disobeying orders. On the positive side, the   support
_____ of one person to obey can have a ripple effect encouraging   refusal
others to disobey. On the negative side, nothing the victims said or did affected
the likelihood that the participants would obey the experimenter's

_____ .   orders

32. _____ means doing as one is requested by someone who   Compliance
offers no reward for performing the action nor threatens any punishment for not
performing the behavior. The _____-in-the-door approach is based   foot
on the finding that people are likely to comply with a large but reasonable request
if they have first complied with a smaller one. One explanation of this technique is
that compliance with a small request increases the cognitive _____   accessibility
of the related attitude. The _____-in-the-face approach involves   door
making an outrageous request that is certain to result in a rejection, followed by a
smaller, sincere request.   The latter technique is based on the principle of give-and-
take that characterizes _____ between people with equal power.   negotiations
People who want to avoid being perceived as unfriendly feel they must
_____ if the other person has made compromises.   reciprocate

33. The increase of individual effort that results from the presence of others is
known as social _____ . In some circumstances, however, the   facilitation
presence of others is associated with diminished, rather than enhanced
_____ performance. Psychologists have attempted to resolve these   individual
two apparently contradictory tendencies in terms of the role of _____   arousal
in human performance. People become aroused in the presence of others, partly
because they become aware of being _____ according to the   evaluated
social norms for their behavior. Arousal tends to increase the performance of
well-learned behaviors, but it tends to decrease the performance of new or
_____ behaviors.   unfamiliar

455

34. The phenomenon of social _____ refers to the tendency for individuals to slack off when working in a group, when their individual contributions to a group effort go unnoticed. The latter phenomenon may be explained, in part, by the idea of _____ of responsibility, which may combine with arousal to result in _____, an individual's sense of having no personal identity and no individual responsibility.

loafing

diffusion

deindividuation

35. Group decisions are often characterized by group _____, a tendency for the group to reach a decision that is more extreme than the decisions of its individual members. A shift toward group decisions that are riskier than individuals might make alone is called a _____ shift. A shift toward a decision less risky than one might make alone is called a _____ shift.

polarization

risky

cautious

36. _____ is a specific type of polarization in which a cohesive group puts consensus ahead of careful, realistic analysis of available information. When the latter phenomenon occurs, members mistakenly equate _____ with being right, and limit their discussion to only a few options. They do not ask for outside advice or fully consider information that _____ the point of view which is apparently the one on which the group members agree. This way of thinking helps members to preserve their self-esteem and morale and offers a false sense of _____.

Groupthink

consensus

challenges

security

37. Members of a group who are in the numerical _____ with regard to their opinion(s), can enhance their influence in the group by making strong arguments and giving the impression of having some kind of strength, such as power, status, or _____.

minority

expertise

38. In a collectivist culture such as Japan, a majority tends to move its opinion toward the minority if the difference between them is _____. Also, members of the group whose opinion is in the minority in a Japanese group would gain influence by acting as though they had high social _____. The latter objective is accomplished by speaking first and taking a high status seat during a meeting, and not by _____ a dissenting view.

small

status

repeating

E. Self-Quiz

For each of the following items, circle the letter which precedes the correct alternative.

1. Effectiveness of persuasion depends on the
    a. merit of the argument
    b. characteristics of the message
    c. characteristics of the speaker
    d. characteristics of the listener
    e. all of the above

2. Which of the following is not true of persuasive messages?
   a. they present numerous arguments
   b. they appeal to an audience's emotions
   c. they present arguments that are implied rather than direct, so that listeners can draw their own conclusions
   d. they target issues listeners care about
   e. all of the above

3. Attitudes related to which one of the following aspects of a person's life are least likely to be influenced by persuasion?
   a. his/her self concept
   b. his/her social class
   c. his/her political ideology
   d. his/her religion
   e. his/her aesthetic judgments

4. Which of the following is not one of the persuasive strategies noted in your text as among those to know about in order to be able to evaluate persuasive messages rationally?
   a. aversive stimulation
   b. pre-giving
   c. pre-taking
   d. positive self-feeling
   e. negative self-feeling

5. Relevant to cultural limitations concerning the validity of Festinger's theory of cognitive dissonance, collectivists' sense of self-esteem does not depend on the establishment of a set of personal traits and attitudes that are
   a. influenced by classical conditioning
   b. influenced by operant conditioning
   c. acquired by observation and modeling
   d. consistent across situations
   e. measurable

6. Dispositional attributions involve explanations of a person's behavior based on all but which one of the following?
   a. the person's needs
   b. the person's desires
   c. the person's personality
   d. the situation in which the behavior occurs

7. The tendency to regard behaviors observed in limited situations as reflecting a constant personality characteristic of the person whose behavior is observed, is known technically as
   a. clinical historicity
   b. temporal extension
   c. cognitive dissonance reduction
   d. fundamental attribution error
   e. attributional altercasting

8. The egocentric bias leads to a tendency to
    a. underestimate the uniqueness of individuals
    b. overestimate the uniqueness of individuals
    c. selectively overemphasize the importance of situational factors in attributions
    d. underestimate the value of one's own cultural group
    e. have a low sense of self-esteem

9. Our impressions of other people are often guided by our own, _____ personality theory, so-named because most of us never formally articulate its assumptions to anyone, even ourselves.
    a. just world
    b. archetypal
    c. existentialistic
    d. implicit
    e. explicit

10. _____ inference is that form of transference which involves drawing conclusions about a person's personality just on the basis of his/her physical characteristics.
    a. Transactional
    b. Implicit
    c. Explicit
    d. Structural
    e. Functional

11. Which of the following is not among the factors noted in your text as contributory to the formation of stereotypes?
    a. ignorance
    b. socialization
    c. state dependency
    d. competition over resources
    e. rationalization of inequalities

12. The term xenophobia refers to a
    a. particular type of halo effect
    b. kind of anxiety about one's own unconscious homosexual tendencies
    c. fear of abandonment
    d. hatred of foreigners
    e. anxiety about the sexual infidelity of one's mate

13. Confirmation biases contribute to the persistence of stereotypes and prejudices through selectivity in the _____ of information relevant to one's beliefs.
  a. noticing
  b. interpreting
  c. remembering
  d. all of the above
  e. none of the above

14. Research cited in your text indicated that African Americans performed worse than did Euro-Americans on an intellectually challenging test when both groups of participants were told that
  a. the test was being used to test the hypothesis that racial minorities are served ineffectively in the American system of education
  b. scores on the test would be averaged and compared across racial groups
  c. the test was a measure of intellectual ability
  d. only those participants with extremely high scores would be invited back to participate in subsequent aspects of the study
  e. those participants with the highest scores on the test would be eligible for substantial scholarship awards

15. Which of the following is not among the three factors noted in your text as having been identified through social psychological research as consistently associated with interpersonal attraction?
  a. cognitive consistency
  b. geographic proximity
  c. similarity
  d. physical attractiveness

16. The mere exposure effect refers to the tendency to perceive a stimulus as _____ after encountering it repeatedly.
  a. endogamous
  b. exogamous
  c. boring
  d. familiar
  e. distasteful

17. The ban which made interracial marriage against the law in sixteen states was declared unconstitutional by the U. S. Supreme Court in
  a. 1857
  b. 1907
  c. 1947
  d. 1967
  e. 1987

18. Which of the following is not among the features characteristic of female faces which are judged to be exceptionally attractive across different cultural and racial groups?
   a. similarly sized and shaped eyes
   b. high cheek bones
   c. a think jaw
   d. smaller, narrow set eyes
   e. a small nose

19. Social psychological research has indicated that the tendency for women to attract mates with their beauty and men with the security of their socioeconomic position, holds across different
   a. ages
   b. races
   c. cultures
   d. all of the above
   e. none of the above

20. From the standpoint of Sternberg's triangular theory of love, _____ love results from a combination of passion, intimacy, and commitment.
   a. fatuous
   b. consummate
   c. romantic
   d. companionate

21. The bystander effect results from
   a. a diffusion of responsibility
   b. cognitive dissonance
   c. insufficient social support
   d. groupthink
   e. dispositional attributions

22. The results of the study of Princeton Theological Seminary students indicated that a person's _____ is an important factor affecting the likelihood that s/he will behave altruistically.
   a. cultural value orientation
   b. moral value orientation
   c. gender
   d. attitude toward the type of intervention required
   e. frame of mind

23. The results of Zimbardo's "jail" simulation study indicated the powerful influence of _____ on people's behavior.
   a. social role playing
   b. cultural value orientation
   c. moral value orientation
   d. educational background
   e. primacy and recency effects

24. In Milgram's classic study on obedience to authority, _____ of the subjects continued to deliver what they were led to believe were powerful electric shocks to a "learner," right up to the maximum level of 450 volts, even after the individual had protested that he had a heart condition and made no noise after the 350 volt shock was administered.
> a. about 20%
> b. about one third
> c. about 60%
> d. over 80%
> e. all

For each of the following items, circle "T" if the statement is True, and "F" if the statement is False.

25. T F   Persuasive messages tend to present only the side of an argument the communicator wants the listener(s) to adopt.

26. T F   In negative altercasting, the persuader implies that only a person with "bad" qualities would disagree.

27. T F   The fundamental attribution error refers to a focus on situational factors and a failure to consider the role of personality in attempts to explain people's behavior.

28. T F   The tendency toward fundamental attribution error is stronger in collectivist than individualist cultures.

29. T F   The halo effect illustrates an inclination toward simplification in the perception of people.

30. T F   Stereotyping leads to an underestimation of within group variability.

31. T F   When people learn that a person has behaved in a way consistent with their expectations, they tend to make situational attributions.

32. T F   There is a considerable body of social psychological research to support the idea that opposite types of people tend to be attracted to each other.

33. T F   Passionate love involves nothing more than sexual lust.

34. T F   The majority of studies of gender differences in altruistic behavior have found that males help more often than females.

35. T F   The door-in-the-face approach to persuasion is based on the finding that people are likely to comply with a large but reasonable request if they have first complied with a smaller one.

36. T F   Social facilitation refers to an increase in individual effort due to the presence of others.

F. Teaching-To-Learn Exercise

1. *Let Me Teach You This.*

Write in the space provided below, the five facts, ideas, etc., from this chapter that you'd most like to teach to your own student(s) if you were a teacher. Then, really do try to communicate these facts or ideas to someone in your life; or, pretend to teach this content to a hypothetical or "make-believe" student or class.

2. *Now Answer My Questions.*

Here, write one multiple-choice and one True-False question for each of the facts, ideas, etc., you covered in the "Let Me Teach You This" section of this exercise.

G. Bringing Psychology To Life Exercise

1. In addressing the problem of "how to avoid being persuaded," seven common persuasive strategies are outlined in Box 16.1 of the corresponding chapter in your text. Give an example of how each of these seven strategies, as given below, might be used by someone, in a morally irresponsible way, to persuade his/her lover not to practice safe sex with him/her.

     a. Pre-giving.

b. Aversive Stimulation.

c. Debt.

d. Positive Self-Feeling.

e. Negative Self-Feeling.

f. Altercasting.

g. Negative Altercasting.

2. *Stereotypes* are rather rigid, and not necessarily rational beliefs about what certain groups of people are "really like." *Prejudice* involves the kinds of beliefs, feelings, and behaviors associated with negative or unfavorable stereotypes. *Discrimination* occurs when negative prejudices motivate behaviors whereby individual members of the target group (or people who are assumed to be members of that group) are somehow disadvantaged or mistreated, simply because they are seen as members of that target group.

For the purposes of this exercise, describe the most memorable example from your own experience, of how you or someone you know was discriminated against in a way that you feel reflects prejudice of some sort. **As with all such case study anecdotes, please disguise the identify of the people involved.** In your narrative, tell:

A. What was the target group toward whom the prejudicial attitudes were held?

B. What were some of the negative stereotypes involved concerning the group toward whom the prejudicial attitudes were held?

C What led up to the incident?

D. What was the discriminatory treatment involved?

E. Was anyone hurt by this incident, either physically or emotionally? Explain.

F. What was the aftermath or result of this incident in terms of how it affected the subsequent thoughts, feelings, and/or actions of the people involved?

G. How might this incident have been avoided entirely?

H. If you had to choose just one word to characterize this whole incident, what would that word be?

3. The term *altruistic behavior* is used to refer to conduct in which people engage in order to benefit one or more other people, without any apparent external reward such as money or recognition for helping. For the purposes of this exercise, describe the most memorable incident of altruistic behavior in your own life experience.

A. Who were the people involved?

B. What led up to the incident?

C. What was the altruistic behavior?

D. Did the helping person(s) in this case risk any kind of personal loss by doing what s/he/they did? Explain.

E. What kind of personal benefit or advantage resulted from this altruistic action for the person(s) who was (were) helped?

F. What was the aftermath or result of this incident in terms of how it affected the subsequent thoughts, feelings, and/or actions of the people involved?

G. If you had to choose just one word to characterize this whole incident, what would that word be?

Answer Key To Self-Quiz

1. e
2. c
3. a
4. c
5. d
6. d
7. b
8. a
9. d
10. e
11. c
12. d
13. d
14. c
15. a
16. d
17. d
18. d
19. d
20. b
21. a
22. e
23. a
24. c
25. F
26. T
27. F
28. F
29. T
30. T
31. F
32. F
33. F
34. T
35. F
36. T

STATISTICS APPENDIX

A. Learning Objectives

After careful, effective study of this section, you should:

1. Have a working familiarity with the fundamentals of descriptive statistics, including:
    a. What it is that descriptive statistics allow the researcher to do with his/her data;
    b. The construction and use of bar graphs and frequency polygons;
    c. The three types of "averages" used in summarizing data, and how they differ in the kind of information they provide about a data set;
    d. The quantitative characteristics of the bell-shaped or "normal" distribution curve;
    e. The way in which differences among the scores in a distribution can be indexed by using the two measures of such "variance" known as the range and the standard deviation; and
    f. The concept of correlation, focusing on:
        (1) How a correlation coefficient provides a quantitative representation of both the direction and magnitude of the relationship between two variables;
        (2) The difference between positive and negative correlations;
        (3) How to estimate the percentage of variance in a distribution which is accounted for by a correlation;
        (4) What kind of information is not provided by correlational data; and
        (5) The kinds of questions or problems for which correlational studies are especially appropriate.

2. Know the following about inferential statistics:
    a. The general function served by inferential statistics;
    b. How the "statistical significance" of quantitative differences between and among variables is established, and how "chance" serves as the frame of reference in terms of which such differences are inferred;
    c. The level of probability arbitrarily adopted as indicative of a difference which is so large that it could not have occurred by chance alone, and the kind of research inference drawn when differences at or beyond this level of statistical significance are obtained; and
    d. The difference between the "statistical significance" and "importance" of a research finding.

B. Preview/Review Outline Of Key Terms And Concepts

Before you read the corresponding chapter in your text, read over the following outline. It is designed to give you an overview of information presented in the chapter, and how the various elements of that information are related to each other. After reading through the whole chapter and/or before course exams, you may use this outline as a quick review guide. In your reviews, mask off one line of the outline at a time, and try to recite from your memory of the chapter, the information that you expect to appear on the next line or so.

In going over this outline as a <u>preview</u> before reading and studying the chapter, the questions posed in bold print will help to keep you focused on the learning objectives here, and keep you actively involved in the process of achieving those objectives. When using this section as a <u>review,</u> try to answer the questions. Refer back to the chapter in the text for a more detailed feedback check on your mastery of the material, and/or to strengthen your knowledge and understanding wherever you feel the need to do so.

What is the general function served by statistics?

I. Descriptive Statistics: Summarizing Data

What do descriptive statistics allow a researcher to do with his/her data?

    A. Frequency Distributions

What is it that gets summarized in a frequency distribution? What gets represented visually in this summary?

        1. Bar Graphs (Histograms)
           a. Horizontal Axis (Independent Variable)
           b. Vertical Axis (Dependent Variable)
           c. Frequencies Within Distinct Categories, Or Qualitative Variables
        2. Frequency Polygons
           a. Line Graphs
           b. Representation Of Quantitative Or Continuous Variables
    B. Averages

To what does the term "central tendency" refer with regard to the descriptive statistical summary of data?

        1. The Mean ($\overline{X}$)
           a. Sum ($\sum$) Of Scores Divided By Number Of Scores
           b. Very Sensitive To Extreme Scores

Give an example of a situation wherein the use of the mean, because of its sensitivity to extreme scores, might produce a misleading impression of a data set?

        2. The Median
           a. Sometimes Preferred For Data With A Few Extreme Scores
           b. The Middle Score In A Distribution
        3. The Mode
           a. The Score That Occurs Most Frequently In A Distribution
           b. Easiest Measure Of Central Tendency To Calculate
    C. Bell-Shaped (Normal) Distributions
        a. Most Scores Cluster Around Mean
        b. Symmetrical

   c. Mean Mode And Median All The Same Number

Why are bell-shaped curves symmetrical? What is the relationship between distance of a score from the mean and its frequency in a normal distribution?

  D. Variance: How Much Scores Differ
    1. The Range
      a. Distance Between Lowest And Highest Scores
      b. A Very General Measure Of Variability
    2. The Standard Deviation (SD)
      a. Tells How Much Scores Vary From Mean
      b. Normal Distribution And Percentages Of Scores
        (1) 68.26% Within One SD Above And Below Mean
        (2) 99.74% Within Two SDs Above And Below Mean

Why is the standard deviation so much more sensitive a measure of the variance in a distribution than is the range?

  E. Correlations: Relationships Between Variables
    1. The Correlation Coefficient
      a. Ranges Between -1.00 and +1.00
      b. Positive Correlation
      c. Negative Correlation
      d. Scattergram
      e. Strength Of Relationship
      f. Finding Percentage Of Variance Accounted For By Correlation
      g. Correlation Does Not Show Causality
      h. Usefulness, Appropriateness Of Correlational Research

What is the difference between a positive and a negative correlation with regard to what a correlation coefficient indicates about the relationship between the variables measured? How is the direction (i.e., positive or negative) of a correlation indicated in the correlation coefficient? How is the strength of a correlation indicated in the correlation coefficient?

II. Inferential Statistics: A Basis for Drawing Conclusions
  A. Observed Differences And Chance
  B. Statistical Significance

What is the arbitrary level of probability adopted as the criterion for identifying statistically significant differences in psychological research? What does "statistical significance" mean with regard to: (a) the magnitude of differences observed, and (b) the inferences or conclusions drawn in a study?

C. Self-Generated Questions: What's In This One For Me?

Most people come to the first course in psychology expecting to learn some things which will help them to better understand themselves, other people in their lives, and/or the nature of life in the world in which they live. Along these same lines, students of psychology often look forward to discovering things about human behavior and experience which may help them to improve their own life by developing their talents, technical skills, knowledge and abilities, and/or the quality or their relationships with other people. On the basis of such self-interest, which tends to provide a framework in terms of which new learning becomes personally meaningful and thus easier to remember, write down a few questions in the space below, about the subject matter covered in this chapter. After reading and studying the chapter, come back to see how any of what you've learned may be useful to you in finding answers to these questions.

D. Completion Items

The words in the margins of this exercise are the ones that correctly complete the sentence on the corresponding line. To get the most out of this exercise, you should try to avoid looking at these words in the margin until after you've filled in the corresponding blanks with the words you think best complete the sentences. So, begin the exercise by covering up all of the margin words with a piece of paper. Then, for each blank, write in the word which you think completes the sentence. Even if you're not sure as to the word, write in your best guess, preferably in pencil so you can erase and re-write any incorrect responses you may make here.

After writing in your "answer," slide the paper covering up the margin words down just far enough to see the word for the blank you just filled-in. For each blank that you fill-in correctly, put a check mark (√) after your answer. If the word you wrote in doesn't match the word corresponding to that blank, mark an (X) next to your response and go on to the next blank. It's probably a good idea to go back to the text and try to strengthen your learning related to topic coverage that corresponds in the textbook chapter to those blanks which you filled-in incorrectly, since those items signal a weak link in your concept mastery chain for this chapter.

1. When psychologists conduct their research, they use statistics to mathematically summarize and analyze the _____ gathered in their studies.

    data

2. _____ statistics allow the researcher to mathematically organize, portray, and summarize data about participants in a study and relationships between and among the variables measured.

    Descriptive

3. A _____ distribution is a simple descriptive statistical technique which provides a summary of the number of times various behaviors occur or attitudes are reported.

      frequency

4. One way of providing a visual representation of a frequency distribution is by means of a bar graph or _____, wherein the various bars indicate the frequency of scores in each category considered. The _____ variable in a study is usually represented along the horizontal axis of the bar graph, and the dependent variable along the _____ axis. Any given _____ is represented on the graph in a way that simultaneously indicates its value on the vertical and horizontal axes. Bar graphs can be used to summarize the frequency of events or responses in distinct _____, such as stressful school-related experiences in the example given in the Statistics Appendix of your textbook, or _____ variables, characteristics of individuals or situations that differ in kind and cannot be measured quantitatively.

      histogram

      independent

      vertical/score

      categories

      qualitative

5. A frequency _____, which represents data as a line on a graph, is a particularly useful way of giving a visual summary of quantitative variables, which are also referred to as continuous variables.

      polygon

6. Statistical measures of _____ tendency, are averages which provide summaries of data in a single number. The _____ is that measure of central tendency which is calculated by adding all the scores and then dividing that sum, signified by the Greek letter _____, by the total number of scores. Another kind of statistical average is the _____, which is obtained by finding the middle score in a distribution when all of the scores are arranged from highest to lowest. The _____ is that score which occurs most often in a distribution.

      central

      mean

      Σ

      median

      mode

7. When scores representing behaviors or personality characteristics are plotted on a frequency polygon, the result is often a _____-shaped curve, in which most of the scores cluster around the mean; the farther away a score is from the mean, the _____ it occurs. Such a curve is symmetrical, with an _____ number of scores above and below the mean, and occurs so often that it is referred to as a _____ distribution.

      bell

      less

      equal

      normal

8. The _____ in a distribution refers to how much difference there is among the scores. The _____ is calculated by finding the difference between the highest and lowest scores in a distribution. The _____ deviation is that measure of variance that tells the degree to which scores are clustered around the mean, and takes into account all of the scores in a distribution and not just the two most _____ scores. The larger the standard deviation, the greater the _____ of scores from the mean.

      variance

      range

      standard

      extreme

      variability

9. A correlation coefficient is a number which indicates both the direction and
strength of relationship between two _____, and is indexed by   variables
numerical values ranging from -1.00 to +1.00. A plus sign before the correlation
coefficient indicates a _____ correlation, meaning that high scores   positive
on one variable tend to be associated with high scores on the other variable. A
_____ correlation, signified by a minus symbol before the correlation negative
coefficient, indicates a tendency for high scores on one variable to be associated
with low scores on the other one. The numerical amount or magnitude of the
correlation coefficient indicates the _____ of the relationship between   strength
the variables. When pairs of scores are collected, such as two tests on a each of a
number of different individuals, the stronger is the correlation the more reliably we can
_____ a person's score on either variable or measure from knowledge   predict
of the corresponding paired score on the other. We can find the percentage
of variance in a distribution which is accounted for by a correlation by
_____ the correlation coefficient.   squaring

10. Since correlations do not indicate the extent to which one variable may
or may not be _____ the other one, psychologists rely on the   causing
experimental method for evidence of causal relationships between the
variables in which they are interested. In experiments, researchers manipulate
or vary the _____ variable while holding constant other variables   independent
that could conceivably affect the dependent variable(s) -- i.e., the behaviors or
outcomes of interest in the study. Under these circumstances, changes in
the _____ variable are assumed to be due to the independent   dependent
variable. But correlational research designs are useful for investigating
problems where experimental manipulations would be either _____,   unethical
or impractical.

11. _____ statistics are mathematical methods used as a basis for   Inferential
drawing conclusions about data. In order to conclude logically that the difference
obtained between the average scores of the experimental and control groups
in an experiment was due to the experimental manipulation in the study, the
researchers must first establish that the observed score difference(s) was (were)
_____ due to chance. The numbers produced by the sometimes   not
complex mathematical methods of inferential statistics indicate the
_____ that such obtained differences are due to chance alone.   probability
When these mathematical procedures indicate that the obtained differences are
probably not due to chance, the differences are said to be statistically
_____. The _____ level of statistical   significant/minimum
significance that will be accepted by the scientific community is .05, which
means that the odds are _____ than five out of 100 that the   less
obtained difference is due to chance. Statistical significance, however,
does not mean that the findings are _____.   important

476

E. Self-Quiz

For each of the following items, circle the letter which precedes the correct alternative.

1. Bar graphs are also called
    a. availability heuristics
    b. frequency polygons
    c. histograms
    d. difference threshold diagrams
    e. all of the above

2. In a bar graph, the score values for the _____ variable are usually represented along the _____ axis, and the _____ variable is represented on the _____ axis.
    a. dependent/vertical/independent/horizontal
    b. dependent/horizontal/independent/vertical
    c. controlled/horizontal/independent/vertical
    d. controlled/vertical/dependent/horizontal

3. Which of the following is a qualitative variable?
    a. height
    b. weight
    c. sex
    d. body temperature
    e. sound intensity or loudness as measured in decibels

4. Line graphs are also known as
    a. histograms
    b. availability heuristics
    c. frequency polygons
    d. difference thresholds
    e. all of the above

5. The _____ is calculated by adding up all of the scores in a distribution and then dividing that sum by the total number of scores summed.
    a. mean
    b. mode
    c. median
    d. range
    e. standard deviation

6. When all of the scores in a distribution are arranged in order from highest to lowest, the middle score is the

    a. mean
    b. mode
    c. median
    d. range
    e. standard deviation

7. The _____ is that measure of central tendency which is most sensitive to extreme scores.

    a. mean
    b. mode
    c. median
    d. range
    e. standard deviation

8. In a normal distribution, the more extreme a score is,

    a. the closer it is to the mean
    b. the closer it is to the median
    c. the less often it occurs
    d. all of the above
    e. the more often it occurs

9. The standard deviation is a measure of

    a. central tendency
    b. experimental control for potentially confounding variables
    c. variability of scores around the mean
    d. correlation
    e. statistical significance

10. Correlation coefficients range from

    a. 0.0 to 1.00
    b. -1.00 to +1.00
    c. 0 to 100
    d. .05 to .001
    e. -.001 to +.001

11. Which of the following correlation coefficients would allow for the most reliable prediction of scores from one variable to another?

    a. -1.00
    b. -.50
    c. 0.0
    d. +.50

12. The percentage of variance in a distribution which is accounted for by a given correlation can be obtained by
    a. dividing the standard deviation by the mean
    b. dividing the correlation coefficient by the standard deviation
    c. multiplying the standard deviation by 100
    d. squaring the correlation coefficient
    e. squaring the standard deviation

13. The minimum level of statistical significance that will be accepted by the scientific community is
    a. .001
    b. .005
    c. .01
    d. .05
    e. .10

14. Which of the following is the strongest, or most impressive level of statistical significance for a research outcome?
    a. .05
    b. .01
    c. .005
    d. .001
    e. .95

15. When a research outcome is found to be statistically significant, this means that
    a. it has not been reported previously in the scientific literature
    b. its standard deviation is so large that it could not be attributable to chance
    c. it allows for reliable prediction of important outcomes
    d. the difference obtained is so large that it probably is not due to chance
    e. all of the above

For each of the following items, circle "T" if the statement is True, and "F" if the statement is False.

16. T F   A frequency distribution is a simple descriptive statistic.

17. T F   Line graphs are particularly useful for representing data on quantitative or continuous variables.

18. T F   The mode is the easiest measure of central tendency to calculate.

19. T F   In a normal distribution, the mean, median, and mode are all the same number.

20. T F   The standard deviation is obtained by subtracting the lowest score from the highest score in a distribution.

21. T F   A correlation shows that one variable causes another.

F. Teaching-To-Learn Exercise

1. *Let Me Teach You This.*

Write in the space provided below, the five facts, ideas, etc., from this chapter that you'd most like to teach to your own student(s) if you were a teacher. Then, really do try to communicate these facts or ideas to someone in your life; or, pretend to teach this content to a hypothetical or "make-believe" student or class.

2. *Now Answer My Questions.*

Here, write one multiple-choice and one True-False question for each of the facts, ideas, etc., you covered in the "Let Me Teach You This" section of this exercise.

G. Bringing Psychology To Life Exercise

Why Bother To Learn Anything About Statistics?

We can answer the question which is the prompt for this exercise in two ways. The first way has to do with the specific educational objectives of the course in which the Uba/Huang textbook has been adopted. Psychology is, after all, a science. As with any other science, the knowledge which accrues in the science of psychology is, ultimately, based on data gathered by a formal set of rules known as "the scientific method." These rules govern the conduct of inquiry regardless of whether the content of one's discipline involves the study of chemicals, metals, electricity, the cells and tissues of the body, or the way people think. Statistics are the mathematical tools which scientists use to summarize descriptively, to analyze and draw conclusions about the data they gather according to the rules of the scientific method. So, in a very real sense, a reasonable understanding of *psychology* as a science, requires at least a rudimentary familiarity with the statistical procedures in terms of which the research findings covered in the first course have been established as "scientifically worthy" of such representation.

But learning about statistics has educational importance well beyond the specific objectives of the particular course for which the Uba/Huang text and this study guide have been written. The fact of the matter is that life in contemporary society is becoming steadily more data- and science-oriented. In this fast-paced, "high-tech" world of the 21st century, whether or not we choose a career in the sciences, we are almost inevitably going to be confronted with the need to make all sorts of judgments and decisions in our personal lives. Just as inevitably, the validity of such judgments and decisions may be greatly facilitated or impaired, respectively, depending upon our knowledge or ignorance of statistics.

There is an almost endless range of personal decision situations where a knowledge of statistics can be extremely helpful. Public information may arouse the need for such decisions when we are confronted with reports of new findings as to the toxicity of certain foods, "quick-and-sure" weight loss drugs and/or diets, remedies and nostrums which promise to give us a blemish-free complexion or rid our skin of wrinkles, cures for baldness, methods for revitalizing our intimate relationships, and so on. But a knowledge of statistics may take on even greater meaning in circumstances where we have to decide on a course of action that will have rather immediate and profound consequences for our own life, and/or the life of a loved one -- e.g., medical diagnosis of a condition for which there are conflicting research data as to the safest and most effective of several alternative treatment approaches.

So, you don't have to be a scientist or aspire to a career in the sciences to benefit from an understanding of statistical concepts and principles. Indeed, such familiarity can be enormously useful to us in becoming informed consumers of information in modern society, and just a little less than totally at the mercy of those who are sophisticated in such knowledge, skills, and abilities. The purpose of this exercise is to give students an opportunity to take on the role of a researcher, in order to get some first-hand, "learn-by-doing" experience with a fundamental principle of scientific research and statistical reasoning.

Significance Testing And The Scientific Method

When experimental research data are collected and differences are observed between groups tested under different conditions (e.g., an experimental group to which an independent variable treatment such as a drug of some sort has been administered, vs. a control group to which no such treatment has been administered), the researcher must answer the following question before s/he draws any conclusions as to the effect(s) of whatever treatment variable(s) has (have) been tested: Is the difference observed statistically significant?

Briefly stated, according to the established rules of statistical inference, a difference is interpreted as statistically significant when it is unreasonable to attribute that difference to chance -- i.e., random variations in the measurement of whatever is the dependent variable, such as reaction time, physical strength, memory for a list of words, etc. The .05 level is generally accepted as the cutoff point for outcomes to be regarded as statistically significant. Thus, if a difference or effect is so extreme that it would be expected to occur no more than five times out of 100 by chance alone, that difference or effect is interpreted to be "statistically significant."

So, for example, let's say that a researcher is testing the effects of a new drug on memory, and finds that a group of people to whom the drug was administered showed a substantially higher level of recall for a learned task, in comparison to a group of people tested under the same conditions without prior administration of the drug. If the difference in recall between the two groups is so great that such a difference would be expected to occur <u>less than five times in every 100</u> if nothing other than chance were operating to influence these outcomes, the memory performance difference between the two groups would be accepted as "statistically significant." The researcher would then have established a scientific basis for concluding that the drug tested <u>does</u> help people to remember what they have learned.

On the other hand, if the memory difference between the drug and the no-drug groups was of a magnitude that would be expected to occur <u>five times or more in every 100</u> by chance alone, the conventional rules of statistical inference require that the observed difference be regarded as <u>not significant.</u> In the latter case, the experimental results would be seen as having failed to support the argument (or hypothesis) that the drug has any effect on memory.

A Do-It-Yourself Test Of ESP

In order to get a feel for the idea of using the laws of probability in scientific inference, conduct the following exercise to test the Extrasensory Perception (ESP) ability of a volunteer with whom you will work as "communication partners." For your stimulus materials here, you'll need five 3 x 5 cards, on each of which you have printed   one of the letters A, B, C, D, or E. These cards will be the message items for this exercise.

For the purposes of this exercise, you'll need the help of a volunteer whose task it will be to try to "receive" your telepathic communications. During the actual test session have your volunteer ESP partner sit with his/her back toward you to help minimize any nonverbal cues that you might unintentionally convey as you conduct your test trials.

<u>**Collecting The Data.**</u> Tell the person who has volunteered to participate in this exercise with you that you are conducting a mini-project dealing with extrasensory perception for your psychology class. Tell him/her also that it will be his/her task to try to receive telepathic messages that you will try to communicate to him/her as to letters of the alphabet written on 3 x 5 cards. Then, show him/her the 5 cards on each of which is printed either an A, B, C, D, or E. Make it clear to your volunteer participant in this exercise that s/he'll be sitting with his/her back to you, and that you'll try to convey to him/her which of the five cards you're looking at, one at a time, just by concentrating on the card at which you're looking. Once the volunteer understands the nature of the task and your "laboratory" set up, you're ready to begin with the test trials.

Tell your partner in this exercise that you'll be concentrating on the cards, one at a time, for a period of approximately 10 seconds per card. Then tell him/her that you'll say "Now" to announce that you've begun to concentrate on the letter which appears on the particular card you've selected randomly from the deck of five cards, and that you'll ask "Which one is it, A, B,

C, D, or E?" after the ten second period during which you've tried to communicate the letter on that card to him/her by doing nothing other than to concentrate on it. Tell him/her also that after each such test, you're going to turn all five cards face down, shuffle them, and then randomly select the next card on which to concentrate. Finally, tell him/her that you'll do this 100 times.

After answering any questions your ESP test partner may have about the procedure, proceed to conduct 100 test trials just as described above. Keep a record of whether or not your partner in this exercise correctly identifies the card (i.e., letter) on which you were concentrating on each of the 100 test trials. Score each correct identification as a "hit," and each incorrect response as a "miss." Finally, get the total number of such "hits" and "misses" for the 100 test trials.

Analyzing And Interpreting The Data.

1. How many of each of the following occurred in the 100 trials?

Total Hits = _____   Total Misses = _____

2. In your judgment, do the data obtained here provide any credible scientific support for the inference that you and your ESP test partner in this exercise were actually communicating telepathically in any effective way? Explain your answer.

3. How many "hits" would you expect in the 100 trials here, by chance alone -- that is, if no ESP whatsoever were involved? (Hint: The probability of your partner guessing the card correctly on any given trial can be calculated by considering the number of alternatives from which s/he had to choose on any given trial.)

4. Take a guess at how you might establish the number of "hits" required before you could conclude logically that you had obtained a "statistically significant" departure from the number of "hits" to be expected by chance alone. Explain your answer briefly.

Answer Key To Self-Quiz

1.   c
2.   a
3.   c
4.   c
5.   a
6.   c
7.   a
8.   c
9.   c
10. b
11. a
12. d
13. d
14. d
15. d
16. T
17. T
18. T
19. T
20. F
21. F